Foundations of Retailing

Foundations of Retailing

J. Barry Mason

and

Morris L. Mayer

both of

Graduate School of Business
College of Commerce and Business Administration
The University of Alabama

1981

BUSINESS PUBLICATIONS, INC.   Dallas, Texas 75243
Irwin-Dorsey Limited   Georgetown, Ontario L7G 4B3

ISBN 0-256-02546-0
Library of Congress Catalog Card No. 80–68037

Printed in the United States of America

1 2 3 4 5 6 7 8 9 0 D 8 7 6 5 4 3 2 1

Preface

We wrote this book because we think retailing offers students some of the most exciting and diversified opportunities available in the marketplace of the 1980s. We wanted to communicate to our readers the spirit which we feel in the world of retail management. What a broad spectrum of career directions exists for the aspiring retailer! Let's examine just a sample for a moment.

What types of stores are "out there?" Large ones like JCPenney and small ones like your neighborhood drugstore. Fancy ones like Neiman-Marcus and "no frills" ones like the limited assortment, box stores selling nonperishable grocery items at a discount price. Intimate boutiques selling high fashion, trendy ready-to-wear to high-income customers. Large-sized, mass-merchandised Walmarts in small towns offering budget-priced ready-to-wear to price-conscious customers.

Where are retail stores found? Everywhere that there are people! The free enterprise spirit of our country leads entrepreneurs to seek profitable opportunities in the smallest rural areas and also to compete with thousands of others in major metropolitan areas like Chicago. You find "mom and pop" stores offering hardware in a small, strip shopping center; shoes for children in 60-store, community malls; and stationery and gifts in sophisticated regional malls with over 100 stores. The neighbors of the very small stores may be Macy's, Bloomingdale's, or Saks Fifth Avenue—the "anchor tenants."

Where is the "action" in retailing predicted to be during the 80s? The small, secondary markets look good to many strategic planners. The "outlying" regional malls in metropolitan areas will still be quite attractive investments. What about downtown (the central business district—CBD)? Evidences of exciting revitalization programs are well-known. For example: Boston's Faneuil Hall/Quincy Market development; Philadelphia's Gallery on Market Street; Chicago's State Street experiment in trying to bring that "great street" back to retailing prominence. Examples of inner-city investments which are not examples of revitalization but rather new investment opportunities are New York's Citicorp development, Miami's Omni, and Chicago's magnificent up-scale showcase, Water Tower Place on North Michigan Avenue. What names are part of the big retail action? There is Carter Hawley Hale and Federated in the department store field. You might think of Safeway, Jewel, and Kroger in food. What will be the "action" with the big three national general merchandise chains—Sears, Penneys, and Wards? A good question! Will Macy's outdistance Bloomingdale's for the New York mystique award for the 80s? Watch Casual Corner and The Limited in fashions, B. Dalton in books, the "concept" shoe boutiques such as Fanfare, deli departments in superstores, franchising in services and fast food (e.g., Century 21 in real estate and McDonalds in fast food) and more; much more!

What does all this diversity mean to you, the student? Obviously, many choices for different types of careers—choices in types of retailing, locations, size, and degree of dynamics. Many types of skills are needed. Perhaps the quickest way to get into management is via the training program of a retailing company. Also, perhaps the easiest way to go into business for yourself is to get into the retail business. (But a warning—it's more difficult than you think.) Retail organizations need people to manage all of the functions which must exist to serve the customer. This book is directly concerned with this aspect of the opportunities available for career-oriented people.

Approach of the text

The approach we use in this book is "how to" within a management context. We face up to all questions which will be asked by a person who is interested in going into the retail business as either an owner or a manager of an enterprise or as an employee who is uncertain of future directions. The answers to the questions we raise are stated from a pragmatic, how-to, small-business point of view. But we have not sacrificed the conceptual and analytical soundness necessary in a book of this type. The approach we have taken assumes no prior knowledge from any courses in business; thus, the material is presented in simple, straightforward language. With our assumption of "no prerequisites needed" we have defined all terms carefully. We also provide many real-life examples to illustrate the points to be clarified by such efforts.

The book has a strong career focus as we have implied. Such a focus will provide you the opportunity to learn more about the world of work, regardless of whether you ever find yourself in retailing.

The framework of the book is "The Student's Guide to Retailing." This frame is an overview which helps you see the entire course at a quick glance. You can also look at the guide as a tool which can be used to look at yourself and the real world. Even if you have only a tentative interest in retailing as a career, we believe the guide can be used to help in making career decisions.

The objectives of this text are to ask and answer questions relating to the following:

1. Things which you must know before making a decision (either careerwise or investmentwise) about retailing as a career.
2. Things which must be considered in planning over which there is no control by management (that is, the environments).

3. The ways a person can assure that the operation performed will be profitable.
4. How good a job has been done up to this point (as determined by accounting and control systems).
5. The specific question of whether retailing is a viable career (or investment) in the future for you.

We have written this book from the point of view of the student who is asking questions about retailing as a career and as a possible small-business venture. After studying the book you will know the opportunities, problems, challenges, and success potential of operating a retail business or working for someone else who does.

Organization of the text

The flow of the book is logical because each topic fits into a planned framework. Part I of the framework, "In the beginning . . ." discusses what retailing is like today. The first chapter quickly initiates you into the retailing fraternity! Chapter 2 asks and answers critical questions about the consumer followed by concepts of lifestyle merchandising, location decisions, and building design and layout. After these basic issues are considered, Part II admits that ". . . you are ready for the retail business . . . but" be aware of the environmental forces which affect your managerial decisions.

The framework continues into Part III which faces the problems of ". . . planning for profit." In this pragmatic, hands-on part you assume the role of the manager who is budgeting, pricing, receiving and marking, selling, and promoting.

"Have you done a good job? You must measure results. . . " which is addressed in Part IV's attention to control and accounting systems. Part V, finally, faces the critical question—". . . Now—is retailing for *you* . . . ?" Specific questions about careers and the future assist you to answer the question. Thus the framework has brought you full circle.

Some other things about the book

We have tried to make this book interesting and reflect the excitement of retailing. You will find some entertaining cartoons scattered throughout. Some of our good friends in the "field" have provided excellent photographs of things which are impossible to describe in words. You will find in many chapters "Study Aids" which give you some additional substance to enlighten the topic you're studying.

Let us give you a good key to approaching this book. Look carefully at the first page of each chapter. This information is valuable. It tells you what you will find in the chapter and spells out the specific objectives. If you can answer the questions raised on the first page, you're making real progress. It's a good "preview" and "review." Use the assistance well. Each chapter also includes a group of "discussion questions" which should make you think about what you've read. After reading each chapter, the discussion questions should "test your memory" and understanding of what the chapter is about. In certain chapters, practice problems are given so you can see if the skills which are explained in the book are really understood. Always work the problems. We have also included in each chapter *discussion motivators* in the form of mini-cases. These cases force you into a real situation and ask you to assume that you are involved in making a real decision or judging the actions of someone. These cases are fun and good learning experiences.

ACKNOWL-EDGMENTS

Many persons from both the business world and the world of academics have been valuable in assisting us throughout this experience.

Among our academic friends and colleagues at Alabama whom we want to extend warm thanks for their assistance are Wilma Greene and Bob Robicheaux. Without the valued assistance of Hazel Ezell, this book would not be in print. She has been a constant consultant throughout the long hours of writing and research. She has put together the outstanding teacher's guide which accompanies this book and has prepared the index. We give our colleague special thanks.

Our sincerest appreciation is extended to the following persons who graciously assisted in the preparation of the manuscript: Gemmy Sweet Allen, Mountain View College-Dallas; Dean Allmon, University of West Florida; Wilma Green, University of Alabama; and Robert L. Stephens, Kennesaw College.

The following business firms have been so very generous with their time and materials—our sincerest gratitude to: Aronov Realty, Macy's, National Cash Register, Parisian, The Jewel Companies, J. C. Penney Company, Inc., and The Doody Co.

J. Barry Mason
Morris L. Mayer

Contents

ship? Consider forming a corporation. How will you operate? What is a marketing system? Why are marketing systems growing? Types of distribution systems: *Corporate systems. Administered systems. Contractual systems.* Other types of retailing positions. Appendix: *Checklist for going into business.*

Management strategy decisions: *Geographic concentration. Market saturation.* Why are smaller communities so popular? What is trading area analysis? How do you choose a location within a community: *What are the features of shopping centers? What are shopping center strengths and weaknesses? What about a central business district location? Consider a stand alone location.* How do you measure a trading area? *Study your existing stores. License plate analysis. Check clearance. Credit records. Customer survey.* How much business can be done in the trading area? *Retail saturation.* How do you go about site evaluation? *Restrictions on locating in a shopping center. Rental agreements.* Should you build, lease, or buy?

Key ideas: *Atmosphere and image.* Store layout: *Allocation of total store space. Classification of merchandise into departments.* What are the types of layout arrangements? How do you allocate space? How do you locate selling departments? Where do you locate sales-supporting activities? How do you display within departments? Appendix: *Store planning: A critique.*

PART II

What is restraint of trade? *The Sherman Act. The Clayton Act. The Federal Trade Commission Act.* What are unfair methods of competition? What are trade regulation rules? What laws affect the retailing mix? *What are sales below cost? What about price discrimination? What are illegal promotion practices? What are illegal distribution practices?* What about product problems? How can you monitor potential legal problems?

Strategic surprises. What are the new consumer demographics? *Smaller households. Working wives. Growth of suburbs. Changing family relationships. Age mix changes. Sunbelt growth. Growth in smaller communities.* Today's consumer: *And what is the "age of me?"* What are the new consumer segments? *The growing shortage of time.* What about changes in the economy? *What are the effects of rising energy costs? What about inflation?* What are the changes in the competitive environments? *What about foreign competition?* Watch out for money problems. How can you avoid merchandise shortages? *How can you increase productivity?* What are your competitors doing? The environment and social issues.

How do you recruit, select, train, and evaluate employees? How do you recruit? *Sources of applicants. Recruiting.* How do you select employees? *Selection techniques. Selection tests.* How do you train employees? How do you evaluate employees? *Reasons for evaluation. Frequency of evaluation. Techniques of evaluation.* How do you handle employee pay and benefits? *Decide on methods of compensation. What about fringe benefits?* Problems in union-management relations: *Management's dealing with unions. Employee griev*ance procedure: *Procedures for discipline. A final word on unions.* What about motivation and job enrichment? *What is job enrichment? How do you motivate employees?*

The role of the computer and electronics in retailing: *Sales analysis. Inventory control. Sales forecasting. Managing credit.* Sources of data: *What is POS?* Item marking: *Universal product code (UPC). What is OCR-A?* What is universal vendor marketing (UVM)? What is an electronic funds transfer system (EFTS)? Think metric.

PART III

THE THINGS YOU MUST KNOW AND DO TO MAKE A PROFIT

Key terms. How can you look at stock balance? *Width (or breadth). Support (or depth). Dollars.* How do you plan your merchandise budget? *What factors affect your profits? How do you plan the width and support of assortments?* Expense budgeting.

How are retail firms organized for profitable operations? *Key functions of a retail store. Trends in organizing.* How can the merchandising function be organized? Role and responsibilities of the buyer: *What merchandise to buy. When to buy. How much to buy. What to charge. Where to buy and how to get the best price possible.* What are your merchandise resources? How do you make market contacts? Getting the best price from your vendors. Negotiations: *Cost (list) price. Discounts. Cash datings. Future datings.* Appendix: *Your wholesalers' services.*

What factors affect the prices you charge: *Type of goods. Type of store (store image). Profit wanted. Customer demand. Market structure. Suppliers' policies. Economic conditions. Governmental regulation.* What store policies affect prices you can charge? *"Level of prices" policy. One-price versus variable-price policy. Private brand policy. Psychological pricing. Trade-in allowance policy. Price-line policy. Single-price policy. Leader pricing policy.* Kinds of pricing adjustments made after your original pricing decision. The arithmetic of retail pricing: *Retail price. Markup. Planning required initial markup. Computations.* Appendix: *"A pricing checklist for small retailers."*

What physical handling functions must you perform? Does store size affect physical handling? *Centralization? Location?* Problems of receiving, equipment, layout, and operation: *Receiving procedures.* What must you know about checking? *Quantity. Quality.* What must you know about marking? *Bulk marking. Nonmarking. Remarking.* Controlling the receiving, checking, and marking activities. What about distributing?

Self-service or full service: The selling process: *What are the types of retail selling?* How can you help people to buy? *Prospecting. Approaching the customer. Determining customer needs and wants. Demonstrating and handling merchandise. Meeting objections and answering questions. Closing the sale. Follow-up.* How can you increase sales force productivity? *Better training and supervision. Improved departmental layout. More attention to self-selection. Faster sales processing.* What about sales training programs? *What should training include? What about training in sales techniques?* Managing retail sales personnel. How will you pay your retail salespeople?

What are your goals? What makes for good promotion plans? How do you set budgets? What are your media options? *How do you evaluate radio? How do you evaluate TV? What about newspapers? Should you use magazines? What about direct mail?* How can you look at the effectiveness of media? How do you measure the results of advertising? *What are the tests for sales response?* Guides to media planning. Essentials of a good advertisement: *Select a strategy. Developing the copy.* Should you use an agency? Special promotional events: *Special sales. Other special events. Trading stamps, coupons, tickets. Publicity.* Essentials of display. How displays affect behavior. The principles of display. Types of displays: *Window display. Interior displays.* Appendix: *Checklist for interior arrangement and display.*

What about retail credit? *Advantages and disadvantages of credit. What types of credit can you offer? What about a charge card?* Managing internal credit? *Use credit scoring. Don't violate Equal Credit Opportunity Act. Remember the Fair Debt Collection Practice Act.* What about shopping services? Services that make money for you. How about educational programs? Will you deliver? Will you offer extended shopping hours? How will you handle complaints? Are your services cost effective? Review your service offering.

PART IV

HAVE YOU DONE A GOOD JOB? YOU MUST MEASURE RESULTS.

PART V

NOW—IS RETAILING FOR YOU . . . ?

In the beginning . . .

When you were a youngster trying to write a theme for English you probably said at one time or another ". . . but I don't know where to begin my paper." "Just start at the beginning," was probably the response from your parent or teacher who wasn't as concerned as you would have liked. "That's really no help!" you probably thought.

In the initial planning stage of this book we felt very much like you did in the theme-writing situation. We asked each other the same question—where should we begin this text? Would you think we were trite if we told you we decided to begin at the beginning? And where is that? Do you begin with a history of the subject and take the reader back to ancient times? We could, you know, because when the first person exchanged something with a neighbor for something else, retail marketing took place. (They called it *barter,* but it was still "at the beginning" of retailing.) We agreed, however that tracing the history of retailing would be a dull way to begin.

When starting at the beginning, we could have given you some present-day examples of what retailing is all about. We might have described in some detail the Boston Faneuil Hall Marketplace which is the most exciting downtown shopping complex in our country. We could have told you that the original buildings were built in 1826 and the new developments, in the original buildings, opened between August 1976 and August 1978. After all, it's a good story and a *new* beginning. But that doesn't make much sense because it's hard to understand how it all happened without some background. Starting at *that* beginning would be like reading the last chapter of a "whodunit" before you read the first chapters!

So after all of our worry about the beginning, we came up with our notion of the *Guide to Retailing.* Just look at Figure I-1 and there it is—"In the beginning." (Box A in the top part is where we are starting.) There are "things" you must know as background before you can begin to understand retailing. That's not only true in *studying* retailing, but in *practicing* retailing (and anything else perhaps). So our guide is presented from *your* point of view as a student of retail marketing and as a student considering retailing as a career someday—as a managerial opportunity.

We see our guide as having dual purposes. The first obvious one is to serve as a guide for you to follow as you go through the book. And we have something else in mind. Suppose that you are trying to decide what you want to do after you have finished college. Think about retailing as a serious career possibility—as a way to achieve a management role rather quickly.

View this course in two ways: (1) Try to learn a lot about the subject and get a good grade. (2) Learn what it would take to open your own store (or at least what someone would have to do before the doors open) and what has to happen for you to make a profit. (Profit is simply the dollars left after all of the expenses have been paid.)

In other words, if you can look at Figure I-1 as a guide in getting through

FIGURE I–1
The student's guide to retailing

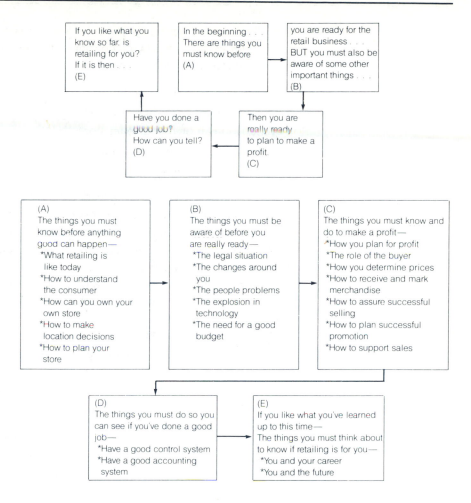

the book *and* as a guide to help you make a career decision, we have something pretty good going for you, don't we? The guides we suggest might also be useful to you in making other decisions.

Now back to box A—"In the beginning . . . There are things you must know before" (and follow the arrow to box B) "you are ready for the retail business . . . but you must also be aware of some other important things. . . ." From (B) the arrow takes you to (C) "Then you are really ready . . . to plan to make a profit."

Further, in anything you do, you always want to know, as the arrow from (C) to (D) indicates, "Have you done a good job? How can you tell?" Then in (E), "If you like what you know so far, *is* retailing for you? If it is, *then* . . ." start over and look at what you have learned in boxes (A) through (E).

Part I of the book is concerned with box A—point out things you need to know as the basics before getting specific in your study. The next five chapters then discuss still other things you must know, really think about before planning for profit (see boxes in the bottom section in our guide). Specifically after you study Part I you will know:

What retailing is like today.

How to understand the consumer.

How you can own your own store.

How to make location decisions.

How to plan your store.

The things you must know (except for what retailing is like today and how to understand today's consumer) are often "onetime decisions" in the life of a retail business. We don't want to mislead you, though. You should occasionally go back to the questions which we raised to make sure that the answers in the years after you open your store are about the same as when you asked them the first time. For example, a particular location may have been excellent for your store when you first choose it. But, after a few years, is that location as good as it was?

These questions are like taking a physical exam with your doctor. Things change that affect your health and you have to continue to let an expert look at you. So over time you become the expert and to "check the health" of your business every few years. (Just a reminder—you can check the "health" of your career at various stages too. If you're "in good health" keep on doing what you are doing. Get the point?)

The book contains four other major parts. Our guide shows them as boxes B, C, D, and E. We will briefly discuss each part (as we are doing here) at the right place in the text to show you where you are and why each part is important.

But let's begin! The first thing you need to know "in the beginning" is "what is retailing like today." Chapter 1 lets you know.

1

WHAT IS RETAILING LIKE TODAY?

This chapter will help you understand:

- The different kinds of stores.
- The types of locations for the stores.
- Different ways to look at retailing.
- How retailing is different.
- Exactly what retailing is.
- The meaning of the following terms:

Central business district (CBD)	String street location
	Solo location
Discount department stores	Parasite location
	Proprietorship
Hypermarkets	Partnership
Combination stores	Corporation
Catalog showroom	Retail structure
Warehouse retailer	Middleman
Variety stores	Channel of distribution
Specialty retailers	Retail marketing

The best way for you to understand retailing today is to "experience" it. Of all the subjects we might discuss, retailing is one of the easiest for you to experience because you have visited many stores in your lifetime.

Here's what we want you to do. Let's suppose that you are living in a city which is fairly large—say over 100,000 people. A city of that size is necessary for you to "experience" the diversity of retailing. And that is the purpose of this chapter—for you to get a good appreciation of what retailing is like—as we've said: this is the beginning. You can't understand what follows without a good foundation on which to build.

WHAT ARE THE DIFFERENT KINDS OF STORES?

In your city of 100,000 suppose you live about eight miles from "downtown"—out in the suburbs. (We call downtown the central business district—CBD. That is the part of your city which your parents thought of years ago when they wanted to go shopping; go to a good restaurant; or maybe go to a movie. You may not think that way today. We'll see!) Now assume that a friend from a very small town in another part of the country is visiting you and you want to "show off" your city to your visitor. Get in your gasoline-efficient car (fuel shortages are worrying everyone) and drive from your home in the suburbs to the downtown area. You will get a quick sandwich at your grandparents' condominium, a new development right on the edge (called fringe) of downtown. They've just moved there. They used to live even further out than you and your parents do.

Your parents chose the location in the suburbs some years ago because the ring road (a part of the Interstate Highway system which takes through traffic around the city and also serves as a commuter road) had just been completed. Even though they felt "in the country," the highway system make it possible to be in any part of the city in a few minutes—except, of course, during rush hours. Use Figure 1-1 to picture the imaginary trip with your friend from "home" in the suburbs (the northeastern corner of the figure) to the condominium near the CBD.

A short distance from home you pass a strip, neighborhood shopping center (1) which contains the following firms: drugstore, supermarket, cleaners, beauty–barber shop, branch of a local bank, and a freestanding (not connected to the main group of stores) gasoline service station (2). You stop for gas at the strip center, and your mother has asked you to stop at the cleaners to pick up a suit for your dad which he needs that evening. This neighborhood group of stores is a convenience for the people living nearby. In fact, centers of this type are called convenience centers just for this reason. The stores carry items which people buy often and routinely. Neighborhood customers do not wish to make long trips for such purchases. Many such centers exist in all large, urban areas like yours.

You now take the ring road to the main thoroughfare going downtown.

FIGURE 1-1

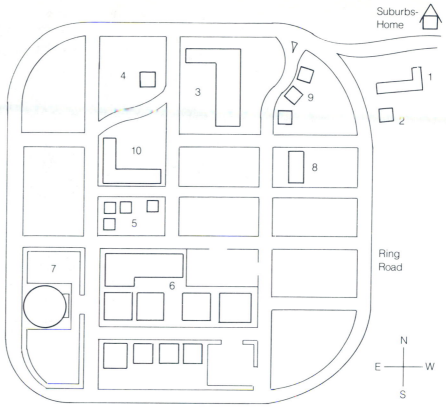

Legend:
1–Strip neighborhood shopping center.
2–Freestanding location
  (gasoline service station).
3–Regional shopping center.
4–Catalog showroom.
5–Neighborhood cluster.

6–Central business district.
7–Civic Center.
8–Solo (isolated) Kmart.
9–String street location.
10–Bedford Place condominium.

Since you have pride in the new University Mall (3) you explain to your friend that it is the largest shopping center in the state and that you have heard it is called a *regional* mall. You point out to your friend that there are four anchor (major) tenants—Sears, Penneys, and two local department stores in the mall. The four large stores and the 90 other smaller stores draw customers from a very large trading area—or region covering several counties—and you are so enthusiastic about the center that your friend wants to stop and take a look around; after all, someone from a small town does not see regional centers often. Also, the fact that he comes from a part of the country where ice-skating is unheard of interests him since you have told him that the central attraction in the mall is a year-round skating rink.

You look at the mall through the eyes of your friend and realize that it

Regional shopping center showing a department store anchor

Courtesy Aronov Realty, Montgomery, Alabama

is quite a place. You see a superdrugstore; a leisure living shop; a cheese shop; a variety store; many apparel and accessory stores and boutiques for men, women, and children; a wine store; a delicatessen; a fine jewelry store (called a guild jewelry store) and a credit jewelry store; a gift store; a craft shop; a book store; a music store; a TV sales and service store; several women's, children's, men's and family shoe stores; and a whole wing of eating establishments. (These different kinds of retail outlets are explained in Figure 1–2. But realize this is but one way you can look at the various types of stores.)

FIGURE 1–2
Different kinds of retail firms

Kinds of retail firms	Examples (no examples given if stores are usually locally owned)
Mass merchandisers:	
Discount department stores (budget department stores)	Kmart; Woolco; Bradlees; Walmart; Target
Jumbo food stores (superstores)	Most major chains have some 40,000-square foot stores; e.g., Kroger; Jewel; A&P; Safeway
Hypermarkets	European (and Canadian) development; up to 250,000 square feet; food and nonfood; BRA in Sweden; Wertkauf in Germany; Carrefour in France; Hypermarche in Canada
Superdrugstores	Greatly expanded drug lines; scrambled merchandising pattern (merchandise found in a store which is not traditional; e.g., food items and traffic appliances such as crock pots)
Combination stores and family centers	Two separate stores each with its own checkout—one handling food and the other general merchandise; all the convenience needs for a family
Leisure living stores	
Home improvement centers	
Special line supermarkets	Lionel City (toys); Pier 1 Imports (gifts)—Self-selection, supermarket techniques applied to other than food lines

FIGURE 1–2 *(continued)*

Kinds of retail firms	Examples (no examples given if stores are usually locally owned)
Retail catalog showrooms	Wilsons; feature self-service checkout; large gift and jewelry business; catalogs mailed to home and customers' shop stores
Warehouse retailers	
Food stores	Stripped down services; self-service; functions shifted to customer; Warehouse groceries
Furniture stores	Levitz
Department store retailers	
Local and regional traditional department store companies	Joske's; Foleys; Jordan Marsh; Lazarus; Rich's; Bloomingdales (carry traditional lines of apparel and home furnishings and furniture; often part of an ownership group: e.g., Federated Stores—a holding company for a group of stores as noted in the examples)
Vertically integrated corporations	Sears; Penneys; Wards (these firms are essentially national in operation and control the production and all levels of distribution in much of their lines; centralized control)
Departmentalized specialty stores	Neiman-Marcus; Lord & Taylor; Barney's—large stores which are not full line (usually specialize in apparel and accessories) but are departmentalized
Variety stores	Limited lines, characterized by the old Woolworth and Kresge stores; markets rapidly changing—more aggressive companies have changed retail marketing approaches; e.g., Kmart from Kresges
Specialty retailers	
Apparel and accessories stores or boutiques (men's, boys, women's), including shoe stores	The Limited; Casual Corner; J. Riggings; Chandler Shoes
Home furnishing stores (including appliances and TV and radio stores)	Sloane's (furniture); Radio Shack
Crafts, gifts, and related merchandise stores	John Simmons; Craft Shack; Hallmark stores
Beer, wine, cheese, and dairy stores and delicatessens	Hickory Farms; Swiss Colony
Automotive dealers	Oldsmobile; Plymouth
Tire, battery, and accessory stores	Western Auto
Drugstores (traditional lines)	Usually local or regionally owned
Convenience food stores and limited assortment food stores	These differ in that the limited assortment stores offer fewer than 1,000 grocery items and limited or no perishable products; convenience food stores offer the best-selling item in a full grocery line
Gasoline and related convenience merchandise stations	Service stations carry basic petroleum products and a very limited offering of items such as bread and milk

Your friend is impressed and in fact buys a new record from the music store and very thoughtfully gets a box of candy from the superdrugstore to take to your grandparents.

As you leave the regional mall and get back on the major street, you point out a catalog showroom across the highway from the mall (4). You indicate that your mother finds many household items there much cheaper than at other places in town. Your father (who is in the real estate business) says that this store is considered by mall tenants as a parasite (lives

Crowds inside a mall

Courtesy Aronov Realty, Montgomery, Alabama

Grand Court as a central focus in a regional retail development of the Taubman Company, Inc.

Courtesy Woodfield Mall, Schaumburg, Illinois

off the traffic generated by University Mall) but he thinks the showroom draws its own traffic. (See Figure 1–3 for the types of locations found in an urban area.) Your friend needs some luggage and wonders if the catalog showroom might be the place to look. You say that it's possible and while in town, a special trip can be made to the store. "Do they take major credit cards?" You say that you know they take Visa and Master Charge (Master Card) because you saw the emblems displayed outside once. Your dad says that they pay a lot less rent standing "solo" (no other stores around) than if they were in the mall across the street. That makes sense. The amount of rent which is paid is a result of how valuable a location is. Traffic makes a retail location valuable. A mall generates lots of traffic!

Next stop, Bedford Place condominium (10; see Figure 1–1 again). "What a great location." The area has been completely cleared of old, tenament-type apartments, old homes, and empty shops on the edge of the CBD. From the town-house-styled buildings, you can actually see the tall, downtown office buildings several blocks to the south. The entire block has been beautifully landscaped; a swimming pool and assembly hall area are included as is a fine restaurant. Everyone says it is the best in the city.

Also, you note that your grandparents do not have to go downtown *or* to the mall for convenience items. Right across the street from them is a small, neighborhood cluster of shops serving the area (5). Since the entire fringe of the downtown area is being revitalized and improved, this cluster is likely to expand, your father says. Since the neighborhood is appealing to high- and

FIGURE 1–3
Retail locations

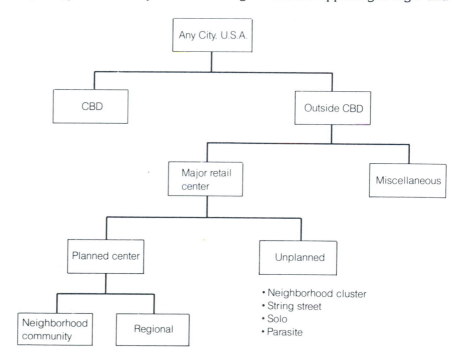

upper middle-income families, some of the most expensive specialty retailers are moving in. (See Figure 1–2 again for the types which might move in.)

After a pleasant lunch with your grandparents, they suggest that a walk through the "new" downtown would be fun. They walk every day and any excuse is used to get exercise. Luckily, the investment in downtown redevelopment has been successful and they have no fears of walking from their home to the center of the city.

Since both of the older people were born in the city, they have seen many changes and like to talk about them. They are quick to point out that the first home they had was in the very block that they are in now. Over the years, the "close in" residential areas became blighted. Owners of property did not keep it in good condition. The real decline took place after World War II when the rush to the suburbs took place. They remembered when the only shopping available was in the downtown area. Thus, they stayed near downtown until good roads were built and shopping facilities were developed to serve the suburban movement.

"I remember when the first shopping center was developed," your grandfather remarks. "It was a long, strip development with a Kresges on one end and a Safeway at the other. We built within a mile of that center and I don't think Grandmother went downtown more than once a year while the kids were growing up. Downtown was awful. No parking; terrible traffic; poor movement of traffic on inadequately planned streets; and a kind of 'mildew' seemed to be settling in. As new shopping centers opened and the local stores opened branches during the 50s and 60s, the downtown stores seemed to go to pot.

"But something interesting happened in the early 70s. The historical society discovered that some of the old downtown buildings held great interest. So many of the buildings which had been forgotten were bought up by smart investors and renovated. Downtown began to rediscover itself. Some smart developers put lots of money into a downtown mall and as you can see, we can walk through much of the area and see no cars; and there is lots of green space for sitting and relaxing.

"It's different; but the change is good. The stores have freshened up. There are still some empty spaces; but we all think a new day is dawning for the CBD. Condos like ours will be springing up in other areas near the center. Our traffic system is good now. The tram system taking people from the multilevel parking decks to the center of the downtown area has been successful. It takes cooperation . . . real estate developers; city government; property owners; and tenants, mainly retailers. Of course, you will see that the nature of downtown is changing. The civic center [7—right on the western fringe of the CBD] is a real attraction. Major banks, savings and loan associations, public utility offices, and other office buildings are perhaps as important as retailing to downtown today."

Is our "make-believe" city typical of others in the country? A trend? Only time will tell! We believe that our "make-believe" city and scenario are not unique. We have seen enough recently to believe that our example is typical of what's happening in many cities in the United States in the early 80s. We know that what happened after World War II *is* typical. The rebirth of the CBD will naturally occur, *if* it occurs, at different times and at different rates in varying cities.

Before walking back to the condo to pick up your car, your grandfather makes one more important point for you. He says that the real secret to downtown change and redevelopment is a good mass transit system. With the high cost and shortages of energy facing all of us, it may be that the most attractive shopping area in the city will again be downtown. He says that they don't worry because they can walk to all the places they need to go downtown and enjoy all the attractions of the area. You know, however, that living in such a convenient location is expensive; and your grandparents are among the lucky people who can afford such a lifestyle.

You decide to return to your home by going north to the ring road on another major north-south thoroughfare. This street is not unlike the one you came in on, but it is another experience. A *solo;* Kmart Plaza (8) (no other retail stores nearby) is passed; next an Automobile Row (9) before you get to the ring. These automobile dealers are in "string street" locations. In other words, retailers are strung out along a major thoroughfare because of the traffic on that street. You also see many fast-food stores like McDonalds, Kentucky Fried Chicken, and Burger King on the street. You see motels, service stations, and several large furniture stores in the string street locations.

So—this "experience" of yours has helped you begin to see what retailing is like today. You have been able to get an appreciation of the different kinds of stores which make up modern retailing (excluding nonstore retailing such as "Avon Calling"). You have also been introduced to the changing nature of retailing. You have begun!

For a fuller understanding of retailing, let's look at some other things which make retailing what it is today.

OTHER WAYS TO VIEW RETAILING

We need to continue our "experiencing" retailing exercise. Your friend has gone back home. Imagine it is summer, and you are working in your Dad's real estate office. Your father is heavily involved in commercial property and he has many retail clients.

He asks you to help him with a project he has been thinking about for some time. He would like you to look at his retail clients and identify them in as many ways as possible. He asks you first to think of the various ways; then break these down into subgroups; and finally assign his various customers to one or more of the classifications. His reason for wanting you to do this is to get a better understanding of his clients so that he can serve them better. You feel that it can also help you look at retailing as a possible career. (Chapter 20 discusses this in detail.) The more ways you look at something, the more you can evaluate its various components.

The types of retailing which you come up with (various classifications) include retailing operations based on:

1. Kind of merchandise carried.
2. Ownership.
3. Size of establishment.
4. Method of consumer contact.
5. Location.
6. Type of service rendered.
7. Legal form of organization.

Kind of merchandise carried

Your grouping on this basis is derived from the U.S. Census and includes the following:

Automotive dealers
    Passenger car, other automotive dealers
    Tire, battery, accessory dealers
Furniture, home furnishings, and equipment
    Furniture, home furnishings stores
    Household, appliance, TV, radio stores
Building materials and hardware
Apparel
    Men's and boys' wear
    Women's apparel, accessory stores
    Shoe stores
Drugstores
Eating and drinking places
Food stores
Gasoline service stations
General merchandise
    Department stores
    Variety stores
Liquor stores

You remember your trip through the city recently and you have little trouble placing all the stores which you saw that day and on your father's list in this category. (Note: Figure 1–2 includes many of the same types of stores. That classification, however, is based on the type of *retail marketing* rather than on *goods handled* as we are talking about here. We admit there is overlapping—just another way of looking at the same general thing.)

Ownership

To determine the ownership of a particular store is difficult unless you know something specific about the company you are trying to classify.

Your father says that most of his clients are *independent* operators. Independents operate a single unit and are typically family owned. They account for a vast majority of all retail establishments in the United States (94 percent) and over 55 percent of all retail sales. You cannot tell, however, if a firm is a single-unit operation unless you recognize the name or know that it is a *chain* or multiunit company (operating more than one unit). For example, you know that the Sears and Penney stores at the mall are units of major chains. You will have to check with your father about many of the clients since there is no way you can tell.

Other ownership possibilities becomes a part of your list as you think about it carefully. The following completes this category: (1) *manufacturer owned*—the Goodyear stores are examples; (2) *government owned*— military commissaries; (3) *consumer cooperatives*—faculty and students at a local university own their own store which carries food and general merchandise and is managed by a retailer who is hired; (4) *farmer owned*—roadside stands are examples; and (5) *public utility owned*—the electric power company owns its own retail space in which it sells appliances to the public.

Size of establishment

You have trouble here. Size can be measured by number of employees, physical square footage, and/or dollar sales volume. You can find out some of this information from your father's records, but you still do not know what *is* small, medium, or large. In questioning various people you find that there is no magic formula to go by. You also learn that when it is important for a store manager to place his operation into a certain size category, guidelines will be provided for assistance. For example, a trade association (e.g., Mensware Retailers) may group stores into certain sales volume sizes to share operating information with members. The retailers will be told to specify the size and the decision is made by the trade group. Stores under $500,000 annual sales might be classified as small.

Method of consumer contact

You come up with this classification quite easily, even though you had originally thought of "retailing" as being the same as "stores." Your subgroups are:

1. Regular store (e.g., Wards)
2. Mail order
   a. Catalog selling (Sears; Spiegel)
   b. Advertising in regular media (most all department stores in local communities)
   c. Membership club plans (Book-of-the-Month)

3. Household contact
   a. House-to-house canvasing (Avon, Fuller)
   b. Regular delivery route service (milk delivery)
   c. Party plan selling (Tupperware)

Location

After your trip from your home to the CBD recently, you have the location possibilities firmly in mind. (See Figure 1–3 for a reminder of what you would come up with.)

Type of service rendered

You think about the various stores you know and come up with a descriptive, service-rendered category: *full, limited,* and *self-service.* Your father's favorite menswear store offers a full variety of services—e.g., credit, delivery, alterations, and layaway. The mass-merchandise outlet (Kmart; Woolco) offers some limited services and those offered are usually at a cost to the customer. Of course, your mother's favorite supermarket is self-service. The new warehouse grocery stores even shift some of the normal services to the customer. Customers may mark prices on merchandise and bag their own groceries as well as carry them out to their cars.

Legal form of organization

The final way you can look at retailing is based on the legal form of the organization: *proprietorship, partnership,* or *corporation.* The proprietorship (often called *sole* proprietorship) is a business owned by *one* person while a partnership is a relationship based on a contract between two or more persons who share in ownership and profits of a retail business. A corporation is a legally chartered business wherein the owners (two or more) share based on their amount of ownership and specific agreements. You think that a small, independent, neighborhood drugstore giving full service is likely to be a proprietorship, but could certainly be a partnership and less likely a corporation. The major national large, chain, department store organizations (e.g., Penneys) are almost all corporations.

Recap

At this point we have "experienced" retailing in two ways. We know many ways that you can classify the vast variety of retail establishments and have indicated in the discussion thus far the changes which have and are taking place in the retail structure. (The *retail structure* includes all of the retail outlets through which goods move from the point of production to the final consumer—the retail customer.)

You may ask, "So what's important about knowing all about the retail structure and changes?" You are encouraged to ask "So what" about *every* topic discussed. There must be a reason for *every* subject in this book!

If you are aware of the vast range of different kinds of retail opportunities, you see many possible career choices. You see a highly competitive environment—a real challenge to creative entrepreneurs (risk takers who want to make a profit).

As you note changes which are taking place, you realize that retail marketing is dynamic—not static. What is a success today may not be tomorrow. Retailing is exciting. You see opportunities for the big and small.

We now want to see how retailing differs from other businesses and thus develop a usable definition of retailing which we can use throughout this book.

RETAILING IS DIFFERENT

Before we see how retailing is different, let's clarify certain key terms. Specifically:

Manufacturer—that organization which creates *form* utility. In other words a manufacturer is a business firm which satisfies some market need by physically changing raw materials into useful products. (A manufacturer of cotton fabric takes cotton yarn and weaves it into cloth.)

Middleman—a business person who is between the manufacturer and the ultimate consumer (that person who purchases a product for household use). This intermediary (businesses *between*) does the following things at various times: stores, sells, reships, extends credit, estimates market needs, promotes, and assembles. A middleman may be a wholesaler or a retailer.

Wholesaler—stands between the manufacturer and the retailer and performs some or all of the noted activities which the manufacturer believes can best be done by a specialist. This middleman, of course, also does things for the *retailer* (a specialist at distributing goods to the ultimate consumer) which can best be done at the wholesale level of the *channel.* (*Channel* refers to the *channel of distribution,* which is the path taken by the goods as they pass from manufacturer to ultimate consumer.)

Customer—in the context here, is the person who buys from the *retail store* (run by a retailer) and is the ultimate consumer who actually consumes a good or service.

So, how is retailing different? In effect, retailing is the business function which serves the ultimate consumer (customer) directly. The manufacturer (normally) does not deal directly with the ultimate consumer; the wholesaler does not (normally) deal directly with the ultimate consumer. (*Normally* suggests that under certain circumstances the ultimate consumer *may* have certain opportunities to deal directly with manufacturers and/or wholesalers, but such relationships are unusual.)

The fact that retailing deals directly with the ultimate consumer presents certain specific challenges for the retailer to understand this consumer—a complex individual (see Chapter 2).

The retail *store* (the physical establishment within which the business of retailing is carried out) is open to the public. The manufacturers' and wholesalers' places of business are *not* open to the public. This "openness" brings into importance the marketing activities of promotion and selling (see Chapters 16 and 17). The customer normally must be *in* the store so that selling may be effective.

Thus, the day-to-day contact with the ultimate consumer makes retailing different from other business activities. The differences present challenges and opportunities for you. Many types of skills are called for; all levels of education are needed; there is indeed something for everyone in the broad field of retailing. The significance of these facts become apparent as you go through this text.

JUST WHAT IS RETAILING—FROM YOUR POINT OF VIEW?

You cannot understand retailing without an appreciation of what marketing is. We have spoken several times about *retail marketing*—so it is essential to get agreement on what marketing is. As many definitions of marketing exist as there are authors who write on the subject. Let us make it simple and say that a manager who is also a marketer believes that a business can operate profitably only if it serves its customers better than its competitors do. The key lies in understanding just what it is that the customer wants and satisfying that want profitably. Retail marketing then applies this way of thinking to the retail establishment. The differences in the retailing structure offer the clever retail marketer many opportunities. The way that the retailer makes an impact on the consumer is by being better at certain operations. These operations (or activities) are called the "retailing mix." Our list of these mix components include:

1. Where to locate (Chapter 5).
2. What kinds of people are hired (Chapter 9).
3. What are the merchandising strategies (Chapters 11, 12).
4. What pricing decisions are made (Chapter 13).
5. What sales supporting services are offered (Chapter 17).

SUMMARY

You are now introduced to the subject. We have begun. You know what retailing is like today; you know what retailing is; and you are ready to begin to be "retail marketers"—to understand the consumer—the basis of all retail successes.

DISCUSSION QUESTIONS

1. Why is retailing easy for you to "experience"?
2. Describe a *regional mall.* What kinds of stores are you likely to find there?
3. What are *mass merchandisers?* Explain several types and give some "real-life" examples.
4. What is a *warehouse retailer?*
5. Discuss the characteristics of department store retailers. What are some of the various types you can find?
6. How do specialty retailers differ from other types?

7. How do convenience stores differ from limited assortment stores?
8. What are the various locations which are available to you as locations for a store? Briefly explain each type of location.
9. Explain retail stores based on "kinds of merchandise handled (or carried)."
10. What are the various ways you might discuss retail companies based on "ownership"?

11. What are the several ways retailing companies contact the customer?

12. What are the various degrees of service which may be rendered by a retail store?

13. Explain the legal forms of retail organizations.

14. Why is it important to know all you can about the retail structure and changes?

15. Explain how "retailing is different."

16. What is *retail marketing* and why is it an important concept?

PROJECTS

1. In your local community, draw a map similar to the imaginary trip in Figure 1–1. Take a beginning point and locate all the various types of shopping areas. Classify each one by type of location; plot them all on the map you draw. Include only major streets on which major retail opportunities exist.

2. Select either (or both) the downtown (CBD) or a shopping center (preferably a regional one) in your local community. Walk the area; list every tenant; describe each type of store in as many ways as you can. Make any necessary assumptions to do this job.

3. Take a careful look at the CBD in your town. Describe what is happening in the core and in the fringe. What do you think will happen in the near and distant future to that part of the city? Give your reasons.

Minicase 1–1   Kathy Franklin graduated some years ago from a retailing program at her state university. She married immediately after graduation. Her husband had been in the army and was just beginning his college education. He had the GI Bill, but expenses were high and Kathy had to work; Bill had to have part-time work too. Kathy got a job at the university in the payroll department—not what she had prepared herself for, but she figured no good job was immediately available in retailing and she really wanted her own store! The university was in their hometown so Kathy and Bill decided to save as much money as possible during the next few years. Bill's part-time job was at a local department store and he liked the business too. During his senior year, Kathy, with a generous loan from her father, opened a small (1,000 square feet) arts and crafts shop. She had always been good at all the needlework crafts and she went to several good stores in larger cities and studied their merchandise lines, brands, and displays. Within six months she opened in a small strip center on a main thoroughfare leading toward a middle- to high-income residential area. The strip was not in a good retail location; she shared the space with an insurance agency, pest control branch office, and a real estate office. You could hardly see the store from the heavily traveled street. And yet Kathy was doing well. From the outset, she had a following for her knitting classes and macrame instructions. She advertised in the local newspaper and on the radio station which she felt reached the best potential customers. Bill was about to graduate. The business interested him, but was there enough in the small shop to keep him interested and to make it financially attractive? They both thought not. Just as Bill was beginning job interviews, a shopping center developer announced that leasing was available in a new regional mall to be constructed five miles from Kathy's shop. Kathy's father said since he was already seeing a return on their investment, he would help her again. Assume you are Kathy and Bill. The rent in the regional mall will be five times more than in the small strip. The mall will include four department stores and 104 smaller shops. What should she and Bill do?

Minicase 1-2   Tom Redder has an idea for a new fast-food chain to be known as U-Grill-It. The chain will introduce a new concept in the steak line. Customers will select a cut of meat from an open freezer, pay for it, grill the meat themselves on a long grill at one end of the dining area, and take it to their table. Other foods to go with the steaks, such as baked potatoes, salads, and drinks, will also be available on a serve-yourself basis. Tom believes that this method will allow him to offer a price substantially below those being offered by the present steak chains.

Evaluate the possibility of success for such a business in your community. How much below the price of existing steak businesses do you believe Tom's price would have to be in order to attract significant business away from them?

Do you believe that price will be the only appeal of Tom's new procedure? What are some other attractions it may offer?

2

WHAT ARE THE KEYS TO UNDERSTANDING THE CONSUMER?

This chapter will help you understand:

- The consumer as a shopper.
- Where consumers buy, what they buy, how they buy, and when they buy.
- The meaning and importance of segmentation to you as a retailer.
- How you can segment retail markets.
- Consumerism and how to deal with it.
- The meaning of the following terms:

Out shopper	Market segmentation
Store image	Life cycle
Open code dating	Lifestyle
Unit pricing	Consumerism
Private brands	Voluntary action groups
Coupons	Generics
Nonstore shopping	

TYPES OF CONSUMER DECISIONS

We all need to understand more about consumers. But how can this be done? A start is by *not* viewing consumers as mechanical beings. Keep in mind the following points:

1. Consumers are problem solvers. You need to help them to solve buying problems.
2. Consumers try to lower the risk in buying goods by seeking information.
3. Consumers shop for many reasons other than to buy. Pay close attention to these other reasons for shopping.
4. Store choice for shopping depends on many things, such as location, image, hours, and price.
5. Many factors such as atmosphere and courtesy of salesclerks affect the in-store behavior of consumers.

A CONSUMER DECISION PROCESS MODEL

The consumer decision process differs widely depending on the product to be bought. Most decisions are simple, such as buying a loaf of bread, since they have been made many times before. Other decisions, however, may be very involved as when buying high-priced and infrequently bought goods such as jewelry or a car.

The consumer decision-making model can be viewed as four types of activities in the process of purchasing, as shown in Figure 2–1. These four steps are (1) problem recognition, (2) information search and evaluation, (3) purchasing processes, and (4) postpurchase behavior.

Problem recognition

The consumer must first realize that a problem exists. A problem exists when there is a difference between what the consumer desires and what he/she actually has. Sometimes consumers may simply be out of an item

FIGURE 2–1
Consumer decision process model

Source: David L. Loudon and Albert J. Della Bitta, *Consumer Behavior: Concepts and Applications* (New York: McGraw-Hill Book Company, 1979, p. 451.

such as a loaf of bread. Other things which may trigger problem recognition are a lack of satisfaction with an existing product, getting a raise or having one's mate go to work which means more money is now available, or perhaps a change in dress styles.

Information search and evaluation

Once the problem is recognized, the consumer starts seeking and evaluating information. Information is simply knowledge. The search may be either physical or mental. Mental search will mean drawing on past experience for information. The consumer may also need up-to-date information about products, prices, stores, or terms of sale. Physical search may then be required.

Purchasing processes

Choosing a store may be a part of the search process. Choosing a store may depend on signing, prices, merchandise available, and customer service. Also, layout, displays, and other information as noted above may be quite useful.

Postpurchase behavior

Consumer decisions continue even after the product is purchased. Decisions to be made may include how to pay for the item and the purchase of other products or services such as a warranty or delivery. The level of consumer satisfaction may also influence whether a person will recommend the product to a friend, complain to the store, or simply not return to the store again. Awareness of these decisions can help the retailer get "plus" business.

Above all, this portion of the chapter focuses on the "where," "what," "how," and "when" of consumer shopping behavior. You need to (1) have the right goods, (2) at the right place, (3) at the right time, and (4) at the right price and quality to match consumer decisions on where to buy, what to buy, how to buy, and when to buy. These processes are shown in Figure 2–2.

Where means the choice of a downtown location or a shopping center, the store at which to shop, and in-store behavior. The *what* question looks at price-quality relationships, whether consumers purchase store brands or no-

FIGURE 2-2

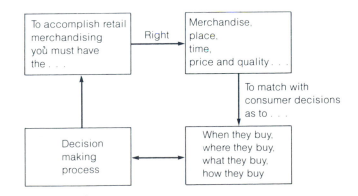

tional brands, and how consumers evaluate new products. Similarly, *how* answers such questions as store or nonstore shopping and the distance consumers travel to purchase. The *when* looks at consumer decisions on such matters as time of day, day of week, and single or multiple trips in shopping. Let's look at each of these decisions.

WHERE DO CONSUMERS SHOP?

Downtown

Clearly, some people shop downtown, others in the suburbs and others in another city—out-shoppers. Why? Each city is unique, but we can draw some conclusions. Often consumers shop downtown because of better delivery service there and city buses may be available. Also some people work downtown and it is thus easier to shop there.

Shopping centers

Shopping centers are often chosen because (1) it is easier to take children, (2) it may be the best place to meet friends, (3) less walking may be required, (4) it may be safer, (5) better store hours are likely, (6) a wider selection of goods may be available, and (7) the climate is controlled.

Out-shopping

Out-shoppers may go out of town to shop because (1) the selection may be better, (2) they may want to get out of town for a visit, including perhaps a good meal, (3) they may work out of town and do their shopping after work, and (4) store hours, store personnel, and services such as repair may be better in the other community.

The importance of image

We still need to think about how shoppers choose a specific store. Here, the image of an outlet is important. Table 2-1 is a summary of many studies on image.

Image is how consumers view a store overall. Such things as (1) item assortment, (2) service, (3) layout, (4) convenience, (5) promotions, and (6) store atmosphere help shape shopper images and the stores at which

TABLE 2-1
Key attributes of store image emerging from academic research

Attribute	Frequency of occurrence (percent)
Merchandise selection, assortment	63
Salesclerk service	63
Pricing	53
Merchandise quality	50
Locational convenience	47
Service, general	37
Styling, fashion	33
Advertising	33

Source: J. Barry Mason and William O. Bearden, "Consumer Images of Retail Institutions," in Arch Woodside et al., *Foundations of Marketing Channels* (Austin, Texas: Lone Star Publishers, 1978), p. 161.

consumers will shop. You need to be aware of how consumers view your store so the negative things can be changed.

Less research has been done on shopping center image than store image. However, the things most consumers look for in choosing a shopping center include: (1) the range of goods offered, (2) services available, (3) store hours, (4) visual appearance of the center, (5) price levels of the goods, (6) ease of movement, and (7) parking.

WHAT DO CONSUMERS BUY?

Price and brand

Price and brand are two major things which affect purchases by consumers. Price is important because it is a measure of worth and quality. Brand is a similar key. Other factors which help consumers decide what to buy include: open code (freshness) dating, shelf displays, unit pricing, and coupons.

Price.   As you would guess, consumers ordinarily can't tell you the exact price of a product. But, they are usually right within well-defined ranges. The higher income consumer is usually less price-conscious than the lower income consumer for the same product. Also, the more of a shopper's income spent on an item the greater price awareness is likely to be. Also, price is not as important to the nondiscount shopper as to the discount shopper.

Consumers have ranges of acceptable prices for products. Prices outside their range result in no sale. Within a range of choices, consumers are likely to pick the middle-priced item.

Brands.   Some consumers purchase only well-known national brands. This helps them avoid a bad purchase. But many consumers are now buying *nonbranded* items (or *generics*), such as paper products, hard goods, drugs, and liquors. They can save up to 30–40 percent on the price of these products. They rely on the reputation of the store in buying the items. Some stores, such as A&P, sell their own brands. These are known as *private brands.*

Open code dating

Open code dating means that the consumer can tell the date after which a product should not be used. Food shoppers need this information. The strongest users are young consumers with higher income, higher levels of education, and who live in the suburbs.

Shelf displays

Management tends to give the most shelf space to products with the best profit margins. But profits tend to drop if you shift store displays and layout too often. Finally, point-of-sale materials, even simple signs, can increase item sales by as much as 100 percent. End-of-isle and special displays can have even larger effects.

Unit pricing

Unit pricing states price in such terms as price per pound or ounce. Shoppers use this information as a guide to best buys. Here again, the younger, higher income consumers are more likely to use the data. Brand switching often occurs when prices are stated on a per unit basis.

Coupons

Coupons can be used to draw new customers to a store. They can also be used to offset the negative features of a store—for example, by drawing customers to a poor location. Nine out of ten persons redeem coupons at one time or another during a year. The users are big spenders.

HOW DO CONSUMERS SHOP?

How consumers select products and services and the distance they will travel to shop affects merchandising decisions. Some shoppers buy many items by catalog, telephone, or from door-to-door salespersons. These shoppers are usually higher risk takers.

Nonstore shopping

Catalog and telephone shopping are based on convenience. Nonstore shoppers also see less risk than other consumers in buying by mail or telephone. These shoppers are also likely to have higher incomes and education. Buying convenience, ease of credit, and good product guarantees help promote nonstore shopping. The high costs of gas and less free time are also encouraging nonstore shoppers.

The costs of shopping

Consumers try to minimize the costs of shopping. *The costs of shopping are money, time, and energy. Money costs* are the cost of goods purchased and the cost of travel. *Time costs* include the time spent getting to and from the store(s), time spent in getting to and from the car, and time spent in paying for goods. *Energy costs* include carrying packages and problems such as traffic jams, parking, and waiting in line.

The importance of the above costs vary by consumer and type of goods bought. For some goods such as groceries, the time saved by buying at the nearest store is more important than the money saved by shopping at several stores.

Location

The smart retailer tries to help the consumer make as many purchases as possible on a single trip. Shopping center locations are important in this regard. Other retailers locate close to competitors to try and get consumers to visit several stores before buying.

Time spent shopping

Overall, less time is spent today in shopping than in the past. The reasons include: (1) advertising which makes information more easily available, (2) the higher cost of gas, and (3) less time for shopping by women now working outside the home. Many shoppers do not visit more than two stores even in buying items such as a TV set.

In choosing a location, try to be located (1) close to as many shoppers as possible, and (2) close to competing outlets to make comparison shopping easier.

Distance to travel

How far are consumers willing to travel? Most shoppers at corner food stores live within a half mile of the store. Shoppers usually will travel ten minutes or so in shopping for higher priced items. Typically, 75 percent of the persons at a large shopping center live within 15 minutes of the center. However, when a shopper wants to buy a special brand or type of item he or she may travel a long way to shop.

WHEN DO CONSUMERS BUY?

Sunday and 24-hour-a-day store openings are attractive to many shoppers. Sunday is often the only time some families can shop together. Also, working wives are more likely to shop in the evenings and on Sunday.

Many retailers don't like Sunday openings or 24-hour openings. They feel they drive up costs without helping profits. But, consumer desires for these hours and competitive pressures are making them more common.

Certain times of the year are also very good ones for retailers. For example, some retailers make one third of their annual sales in November and December. Spring dresses sell well just prior to Easter. Picnic supplies sell best in the summer and ski equipment during the winter.

WHAT IS SEGMENTATION?

By now you know that consumers differ in desires, demands, and tastes in their shopping behavior. Try to develop marketing plans which recognize these differences. *Segmentation* in this process means selecting the group(s) of consumers who are the best market for your outlet. These groups of individuals will be more alike in their behavior as consumers than the population as a whole.

This portion of the chapter helps you to understand: (1) the meaning of segmentation, (2) how to segment, and (3) how segmentation affects decisions on price, promotion, location, and goods sold.

Segmentation helps you to: (1) pick out the best markets to serve and (2) figure out how to appeal to the markets. These two steps then help you to:

a. Select the right merchandise.
b. Price it in the right way.
c. Develop hard-hitting promotions.
d. Choose the right location.

But what do you look for in segmenting markets? First, remember that you want consumer groups which are as alike as possible. Second, study the backgrounds and behavior of the people that you can best appeal to.

You can view consumers in terms of: (1) an aggregation (all alike), (2) each being different, or (3) in groups (segments).

Aggregation. Many retailers try to reach as many people as possible by viewing them as all alike. They have one marketing plan. This approach is the least expensive since you have one approach to the entire market.

A policy of aggregation creates great competition for the largest market segments. Promotion efforts are on the basis of mass advertising and a universal theme of low prices. Warehouse grocery outlets follow such a policy as do catalog discount firms.

Uniqueness. Here you offer customized products made for each customer. An example would be a tailor who custom fits clothes before making them. Here your salespeople need to know a great deal about the product. Also, you must (1) handle more specialized product lines, (2) offer more personal service, and (3) offer more product depth. Price is not very important here and the market is thin.

Firms in this category include those specializing in maternity wear or high fashion women's wear. The high-priced, New York-based Lady Madonna chain is an example of such a firm. Also, bookshops catering only to mystery lovers reflect uniqueness. Such shops include Murder Ink (New York), and Who Dunit (Philadelphia). A final example is Ted E. Bear and Company in the Pier 39 shopping area of San Francisco. This shop sells nothing but teddy bears from 1½ inches and 50 cents to 8 feet high and $2,500.

Segmentation. Most retailers follow this approach and try to reach broad groups of people. Sears and Penneys try to do this. They know that they can't serve the very low-income people or the highest income people but try to reach the middle class. Thus, in their thinking they divide the total market into several groups which are alike in important ways, such as the price-conscious shopper for appliances, and the do-it-yourself home repair hobbyist.

But what decisions must you make in segmenting?

1. Decide on who you want to sell to and whether the group is large enough to make it profitable.
2. Decide how to reach the people you select.
3. Decide on the right combination of merchandise, price, and promotion plans.
4. Select the right location.

SEGMENTING MARKETS

You can think of its customers in many ways. These include demographic, subcultural, or lifestyle differences and life cycle. Let's briefly look at some of these ways of segmenting shoppers.

Demographic differences

Age. Our population is not growing very fast. But, major changes are occurring in the age makeup. Three age-groups are growing rapidly. The *first group* consists of children under five. The *second group* are persons 20–34 years of age. This group increased by 14 percent from 1975 to 1980 compared to 2.4 percent for the total population. The *third* includes persons 65 or more years of age. Data on these groups are shown in Figure 2–3.

Most retailers use age in segmenting markets. For example, 82 percent of Wendy's hamburger business comes from customers over 25. In contrast, McDonald's generates 35 percent of its revenues from youngsters under 19.

FIGURE 2–3
35-to-44 age-group to explode in the 80s

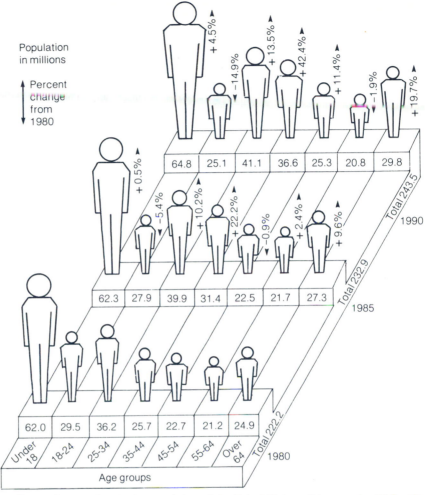

Population in millions

Percent change from 1980

	Under 18	18-24	25-34	35-44	45-54	55-64	Over 64	Total
1990	64.8	25.1	41.1	36.6	25.3	20.8	29.8	243.5
% change	+0.5%	-14.9%	+13.5%	+42.4%	+11.4%	-1.9%	+19.7%	
1985	62.3	27.9	39.9	31.4	22.5	21.7	27.3	232.9
% change	-5.4%	+10.2%	+22.2%	-0.9%	+2.4%	+9.6%		
1980	62.0	29.5	36.2	25.7	22.7	21.2	24.9	222.2

Age groups

During the next decade the population of the United States will increase by 21.3 million people (9.6 percent) according to informed projections. The most dynamic upswing will be among the well-educated, affluent 35-to-44s, who can be expected to be a receptive market for a wide range of the goods offered by supermarkets. Two groups will actually shrink in number during the 80s: 18-to-24s, whose 4.4 million drop will soften demand for youth-oriented products; and 55-to-64s, who will drop in the second half of the decade after a marginal gain between now and 1985.

Source: Fabian Linden, "Who Will Buy? A Preview of Tomorrow's Customers," *Progressive Grocer* (August 1979), p. 87: chart by Nigel Holmes.

Similarly, Steak and Ale says that their customers are "basically between 24 and 45," college educated and middle income or better.[1]

Each age-group has special needs. One way of looking at age differences is in terms of the *life cycle* of shoppers, as shown in Table 2–2. Buying patterns differ depending on one's stage in the life cycle.

Household makeup. Today 50 percent of all wives are working compared to 25 percent in 1950. Two-income households are more likely to buy

TABLE 2-2
An overview of
the life cycle

Bachelor stage: Young single people not living at home
    Few financial burdens
    Fashion opinion leaders
    Recreation oriented
    Buy: Basic kitchen equipment, basic furniture, cars, equipment for the mating game, vacations

Newly married couples: Young, no children
    Better off financially than they will be in near future
    Highest purchase rate and highest average purchase of durables
    Buy: Cars, refrigerators, stoves, sensible and durable furniture, vacations

Full nest I: Youngest child under six
    Home purchasing at peak
    Liquid assets low
    Dissatisfied with financial position and amount of money saved
    Interest in new products
    Like advertised products
    Buy: Washers, dryers, TV, baby food, chest rubs and cough medicine, vitamins, dolls,
        wagons, sleds, skates

Full nest II: Youngest child six or over
    Financial position better
    Some wives work
    Less influenced by advertising
    Purchase larger sized packages, multiple-unit deals
    Buy: Many foods, cleaning materials, bicycles, music lessons, pianos

Full nest III: Older married couples with dependent children
    Financial position still better
    More wives work
    Some children get jobs
    Hard to influence with advertising
    High-average purchase of durables
    Buy: New, more tasteful furniture, auto travel, nonnecessary appliances, boats, dental services,
        magazines

Empty nest I: Older married couples, no children living with them, head in labor force
    Home ownership at peak
    Most satisfied with financial position and money saved
    Interested in travel, recreation, self-education
    Make gifts and contributions
    Not interested in new products
    Buy: Vacation, luxuries, home improvements

Empty nest II: Older married couples, no children living at home, head retired
    Drastic cut in income
    Keep home
    Buy: Medical appliances, medical care, products which aid health, sleep, and digestion

Solitary survivor in labor force:
    Income still good but likely to sell home

Solitary survivor retired:
    Same medical and product needs as the other retired groups; drastic cut in income
    Special need for attention, affection, and security

    Source: Robert Haas and Leonard Berry, "Systems Selling of Retail Services," in Leonard Berry and L. A. Capaldini ed. *Marketing for the Bank Executive* © 1974 by Litton Educational Publishing, Inc. Reprinted by permission of Van Nostrand Reinhold Company.

such items as microwave ovens, instant foods, apartment cleaning services, and other products which provide convenience to busy people.

Subcultural differences

Blacks and Spanish-speaking Americans are the fastest growing portions of our population. They also tend to live in a few areas and are thus easy to reach. More than 23 million blacks live in the United States. In nine cities— Atlanta, Baltimore, Birmingham, Detroit, New Orleans, Newark, Richmond, St. Louis, and Washington, D.C.—they number over 40 percent of the total population.

Over 19 million Spanish-speaking Americans, including illegal aliens, live in the United States. The Spanish-speaking market in New York City alone is over $3 billion. Miami is another huge Spanish marketplace. Other ethnic groups also exist but their numbers are small and/or they have largely been absorbed into the population.

Blacks and Spanish-speaking Americans, however, often represent growing segments to which you can appeal. For example, you may have to use the Spanish language in seeking to serve the Spanish Americans. Minorities are also often highly brand and store loyal.[2]

Blacks tend to favor basic ingredients for food over convenience foods. Pork sales are higher among blacks, as are southern green vegetables.[3] Blacks also spend more of their food dollar on meat, poultry, and grain products and less on milk products, vegetables, and fruit than do whites. Differences continue to exist when the households are grouped by place of residence, income, and quality of diet.[4]

Income and education. Education affects buying behavior. Highly educated persons are best candidates for books and classical music. Some items cannot be purchased without a minimum level of income, for example, a new luxury automobile. Also, middle-income consumers are the heaviest shoppers. For example, Korvettes, a large discount department store, defines its market as households with incomes of $15,000–$30,000.[5]

Sex. Even today wives are more likely to purchase food, paper goods, household cleaners, and vacuum cleaners while husbands are most likely to purchase autos. Wives also often "scout" for men's clothing. The men then choose from among the items selected for them.

One of the hottest trends in merchandising today among males is for the "better young man." Saks Fifth Avenue calls its young men's shop the "Early On." Other recent trends include the growth of so-called career shops for women. Examples include Charles A. Stevens Company, Executive Place (Chicago), Filenes Corporate Image (Boston), and W. Robertson's Career Shop (Los Angeles). Also, one of the more successful new retailing franchises is the Winning Woman, parallel in concept to The Foot Locker and The Athlete's Foot for men.

Segmenting the apparel market on the basis of size and lifestyle

Courtesy Aronov Realty, Montgomery, Alabama

Lifestyle differences

One of the most useful ways for segmenting markets is to look at differences in people's lifestyles. *Lifestyle analysis* looks at how consumers spend their time, what interests them, and how they view themselves.

Lifestyle analysis means that customers can more easily be thought of in such terms as *swinger, bargain hunter, hobbyist,* or *fashion conscious* than in such terms as age or income.

The ways of segmenting consumers by lifestyle are shown in Table 2–3. You may need to conduct a consumer survey to find out the lifestyles of the people you want to serve. Lifestyle merchandising is covered in more detail in Chapter 3.

Summary

Why worry about segmenting markets? Simply because you can't be all things to all people. You need to pick out a few groups to serve. Normally, follow a strategy which says that consumers are neither all alike nor all different.

WHAT ABOUT THE UPTIGHT CONSUMER?

A study of the consumer would not be complete without talking about the consumer view of retailing. *Consumerism* is a collective expression of dissatisfaction with the business system. Consumers have been unhappy in recent years about the cost of energy, poor service in retail firms, poor product warranties, and other similar problems for which they blame business.

It's too simple to say the customer is always right. Some consumers don't pay their bills, shoplift, switch price tags, and so forth. But the retailer also sometimes uses bad credit information, messes up a customer's account, sells

"Just remember if it weren't for dissatisfied customers like me you'd be out of a job."

Reprinted by permission The Wall Street Journal

bad merchandise, and has poor salespeople. No one can blame the consumer for being unhappy when this occurs.

Too often management fails to ask consumers what is bothering them. But you should ask, since complaints are a signal that all is not well in the business.

TABLE 2–3
Lifestyle dimensions

Activities	Opinions
Work	Themselves
Hobbies	Social issues
Social events	Politics
Vacation	Business
Entertainment	Economics
Club membership	Education
Community	Products
Shopping	Future
Sports	Culture
Interests	Demographics
Family	Age
Home	Education
Job	Income
Community	Occupation
Recreation	Family size
Fashion	Dwelling
Media	Geography
Achievements	City size
	Stage in life cycle

Source: Reprinted from Joseph T. Plummer, "The Concept and Application of Life Style Segmentation," *Journal of Marketing,* vol. 38 (January 1974), p. 34. Published by the American Marketing Association.

How do consumers view business?

Figure 2–4 shows that business rates weakest in communicating with consumers, being interested in customers, providing value for money, and honesty in what they say about products. As shown in Table 2–4, large department stores and retail food chains rate in the top ten in the quality of job they perform. However, auto dealers and appliance repair services were at the bottom of the list.

Where do consumers go for satisfaction?

Consumers are more likely to start with the retailer when they are unhappy, as shown in Figure 2–5. But consumers too often have problems in getting satisfaction. Still, satisfaction with the response of retailers was higher than for manufacturers or government agencies. You need a way to hear from these persons. A "hot line" is one such way. Be courteous in responding. Gather all needed information. Take appropriate action as it is called for. If no action is justified, be calm but firm when responding. Finally, follow up if necessary.

Dissatisfied consumers are likely to be younger, better educated, have higher incomes, and be more politically active. These kinds of persons are usually the best customers.

What's being done about problems?

Retailer responses. Freshness dates now appear on many products. Nutritional labeling is being practiced. Unit pricing is another aid to the consumer.

Some stores provide (1) in-store consumer consultants, (2) consumer

FIGURE 2-4

What's good—and bad—about American business	
Business is strongest in-	Business is weakest in-
Developing new products	Communicating with customers
Providing products and services that meet people's needs	Being interested in customers
Hiring members of minority groups	Communicating with employes
Paying good wages	Providing value for money
Communicating with stockholders	Controlling pollution
Improving the standard of living	Dealing with shortages
Producing safe products	Helping solve social problems
Providing steady work	Being honest in what is said about products
Maintaining strong competition	Conserving natural resources

Source: Reprinted from *U.S. News and World Report,* Copyright 1978
U.S. News and World Report, Inc., February 20, 1978, p. 16.

TABLE 2-4

How 31 Industries Rate With Customers

Those taking part in the *USN&WR* survey were asked to score major U.S. industries and services on their job performance. On the rating scale, 1 is "poor," 7 "excellent." The results—

On the Overall Job They Do

		Average Rating
1.	Airlines	5.47
2.	Aluminum companies	5.02
3.	Banks	4.93
4.	Savings and loan associations	4.91
5.	Large department stores	4.77
6.	Retail food chains	4.72
7.	Forestry companies	4.71
8.	Wine producers	4.57
9.	Appliance manufacturers	4.56
10.	Tire manufacturers	4.55
11.	Telephone companies (tie)	4.50
11.	Food manufacturers (tie)	4.50
13.	Plastics companies	4.40
14.	Prescription drug manufacturers	4.35
15.	Liquor distillers	4.33
16.	Electric utilities (tie)	4.31
16.	Life insurance companies (tie)	4.31
16.	Steel manufacturers (tie)	4.31
19.	Building materials companies	4.20
20.	Chemical companies	4.14
21.	Gas utilities	4.08
22.	Gasoline service stations	3.94
23.	Property/casualty insurance companies	3.87
24.	Nonprescription drug manufacturers	3.83
25.	Oil and gasoline companies	3.72
26.	Automobile manufacturers	3.66
27.	Medical/hospitalization insurance companies	3.53
28.	Railroads	3.51
29.	Automobile dealers	3.44
30.	Appliance repair services	3.42
31.	Automobile insurance companies	3.35

Source: Reprinted from *U.S. News and World Report*, Copyright 1978, U.S. News and World Report, Inc., February 20, 1978, p. 17.

advisory panels, (3) consumer affairs forums, (4) buyer booklets, (5) employee training on consumer rights, and (6) signs, sales notices, and applications in Spanish for Spanish-speaking areas. The need for more information and how to provide it are shown in Study Aid 2–1 and Figure 2–6.

FIGURE 2-5

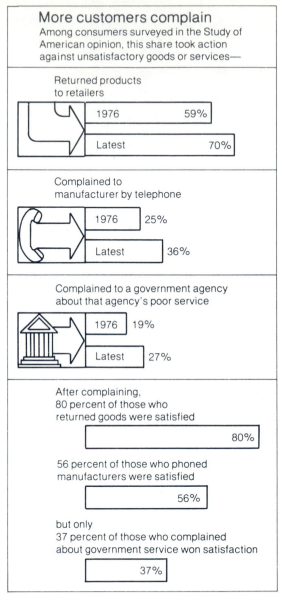

Source: Reprinted from *U.S. News and World Report*, Copyright 1978, U.S. News and World Report, Inc., February 20, 1978, p. 18.

Action groups

More and more action groups are also emerging to help consumers. The following is a partial list of agencies which you can contact if you have product complaints:

Air travel: Civil Aeronautics Board, Office of Consumer Affairs, Washington, DC 20428.

STUDY AID 2-1

TODAY'S CONSUMERS
...and how to reach them

ARE COMMITTED TO CONVENIENCE AND SIMPLIFICATION
List important items in large type; mention convenience features you offer, such as hours, parking, delivery, etc.

ARE SKEPTICAL OF ADVERTISING CLAIMS
Make your claims factual and specific

WANT MORE PROTECTION AND SECURITY
Convey reliability — of your business and the products and services you provide

ARE CONCERNED ABOUT HIGH AND RISING PRICES
Indicate quality and value. List other features not included in price, such as free estimates, delivery service, and credit cards you honor

FEEL MORE SECURE WITH BRANDS THEY KNOW
Specify all major brands you handle — those your potential customers will be looking for

ARE MORE SELECTIVE IN THEIR BUYING HABITS
Supply complete information about all the products or services they can obtain from you with one trip or call

ARE BECOMING DO-IT-YOURSELFERS
Indicate that you have full supplies, rent tools, are qualified to advise or perform labor

ARE HEALTH AND SAFETY CONSCIOUS
Note health, nutritional, safety or security information that appeals to their interests

ARE CONCERNED ABOUT WASTE
If your product or service saves energy, resources or money, say so. But add supportive information

ARE CONCERNED ABOUT PRODUCT QUALITY
Information such as major brands, manufacturer guarantees, years in business and completeness of service help eliminate fears about quality

ARE CONCERNED ABOUT SERVICE AND REPAIRS
Reassure with explicit policy copy. List any special training and all brands you are qualified to service

KNOW HOW AND WHERE TO COMPLAIN . . . AND THEY DO
Avoid potential problems with initial communication that is informative, factual and specific

They Want More Meaningful Information

Source: L. M. Berry & Company, *There's a New Breed of Consumer in the Marketplace* (Dayton, Ohio: L. M. Berry & Company, 1979), p. 3.

Appliances: (air conditioner, dehumidifier, dishwasher, garbage disposer, washer, dryer, range, or other nonportable appliance):   Major Appliance Consumer Action Panel (MACAP), 20 N. Wacker Drive, Chicago, Il 60606.

Automobiles: Department of Transportation, National Highway Traffic Safety Administration, Washington, DC 20590, 800–424–9393, or Automobile Consumer Action Panel (AUTO CAP), 200 K Street, N.W., Washington, DC 20006.

Carpet and rugs: Carpet and Rug Institute, Box 1568, Dalton, GA 30720.

Dry cleaning: International Fabricare Institute, Textile Approval Division, Empire State Building, 350 Fifth Avenue, New York, NY 10001.

FIGURE 2–6

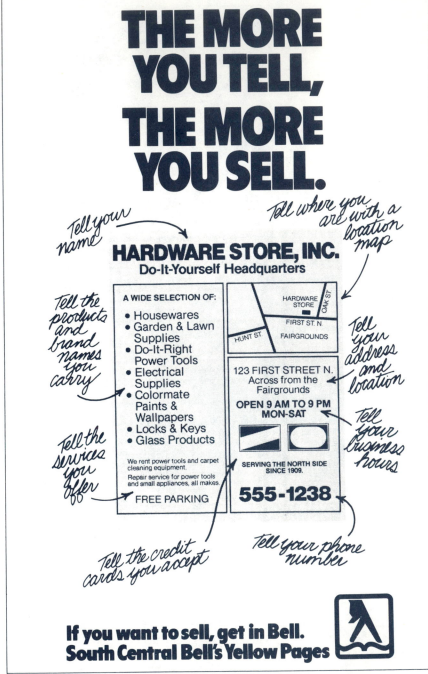

Source: *The Tuscaloosa News*, Friday, May 4, 1979, p. 5.

Food and cosmetics: Food and Drug Administration, Office of Consumer Inquiries, PA-10, 5600 Fishers Lane, Rockville, MD 20852.

Furniture: Furniture Industry Consumer Action Panel (FICAP), Box 951, High Point, NC 27261.

Hazards of any kind: U.S. Consumer Product Safety Commission, Washington, DC 20207. Toll free 800-638-8326.

Insurance: Federal Trade Commission, Pennsylvania Avenue and 6th Street, N.W., Washington, DC 20580.

Magazine subscriptions: Magazine Publishers Association, 575 Lexington Avenue, New York, NY 10022.

Mail orders: The Consumer Advocate, U.S. Postal Service, Washington, DC 20260; Direct Selling Association, 1730 M Street, N.W. Washington DC 20036.

Moving: Interstate Commerce Commission, Constitution Avenue and 12th Street, N.W., Washington, DC 20423.

Packages that are deceptive: Federal Trade Commission, Pennsylvania Avenue and 6th Street N.W. Washington, DC 20580.

Photographic equipment and film: Consumer Affairs Department, Photo Marketing Association, 603 Lansing Avenue, Jackson, MI 49202.

Household insulation: Director, Bureau of Consumer Protection, Federal Trade Commission, Washington, DC 202-523-3727.

But as a consumer you also need to act properly. The so-called Ten Commandments for Consumers as shown below make this point.

TEN COMMANDMENTS FOR CONSUMERS

☐ Thou shall not lie, shoplift, pass bad checks, or default on payments.

☐ Thou shall be courteous in all dealings.

☐ Thou shall look for value and be a wise shopper.

☐ Thou shall not be a price tag switcher.

☐ Thou shall have respect for the merchandise you handle.

☐ Thou shall use good judgment and not yield to advertising and commercial pressure.

☐ Thou shall not yield to the lure of excessive credit.

☐ Thou shall take time to write letters of complaint to disreputable and irresponsible companies and businessmen.

☐ Thou shall return faulty or unsatisfactory merchandise rather than keeping it.

☐ Thou shall keep thyself up to date on changes in laws that affect consumers.

Source: Alabama Office of Consumer Protection, *Newsletter,* February 1978.

Better Business Bureaus

Better Business Bureaus can serve a useful purpose in handling consumer problems at the local level. Complaints about false advertising and mislabeling of items are often taken to Better Business Bureaus. The bureau in each community is supported by dues from member firms. Membership is voluntary.

The purpose of the Better Business Bureau is to allow local firms to police themselves and thus keep unethical merchants from taking advantage of consumers. They cannot require an offending firm to stop illegal or unethical practices. However, they may bring great pressure on them to do so. Also, they can report the behavior to an appropriate government agency for action.

Some smaller communities do not have a Better Business Bureau. The function of the bureaus is then carried out by local chambers of commerce which usually exist even in the smallest community.

A philosophy of action for the retailers

Retailers need to be more alert to the new attitudes and demands of consumers and to practice better customer relations. The demands of consumers normally are not realistic. Consumers simply want more and better information and employee honesty in dealing with them.

You may need to do research from time to time to learn how customers feel about your store and its products. Take a positive approach in dealing with customers. Clearly, retailers do not want to make money by selling products which hurt or kill people or drive them away. Some retailers, however, sometimes act as if that is what they want to do. Customer hostility then occurs. Consumers simply want better labels, honesty in advertising, and full information on credit terms. Such information makes it easier for them in their role as buyers.

One problem though is how far the retailer can go in meeting the demands of consumers while still having to compete with other stores who may not be so responsive to consumers. Many trade-offs exist in serving consumers.

SUMMARY

You need to constantly seek information from the consumer in order to make the right merchandising decisions.

Keep three things in mind. *First,* have the right merchandise, at the right place, time, price, and quality to match with consumer decisions as to where to buy, what to buy, how to buy, and when to buy to be a retailing success.

Second, recognize that all consumers are not alike. But the hard part is deciding *(a)* which consumers you want to serve, *(b)* what common features they have, and *(c)* how to reach them.

Third, remember that not all consumers are satisfied consumers.

We will leave you with one final thought: If you take your eye off the consumer for even a moment, you are likely to be in trouble as a retailer.

NOTES

1. ''Wendy's Hones-in on Young Adults,'' *Business Week,* July 7, 1977, p. 60.
2. Judy Greenwald, ''Uptapped Latin Market Outlined in New York Seminar,''

Supermarket News, May 2, 1977, p. 5; "It's Your Turn in the Sun," *Time,* October 16, 1978, pp. 48–61; Jessica Sinha, "Ethnic Marketing: Is It Worth an Extra Effort?" *Product Marketing* (June 1977), pp. 29–34.

3. "Black Products: There Is a Difference," *Progressive Grocer* (June 1975), p. 9.

4. Constance Word, "Food Spending Patterns of Southern Black Households," *Family Economics Review* (Fall 1975), p. 9.

5. "New Marketing Strategy Positions Korvettes as 'Promotional' Chain, *The Marketing News,* March 21, 1980, p. 16.

DISCUSSION QUESTIONS

1. Many products which consumers purchase do not involve much search. Why is this so? Is it to your advantage to try to get consumers to search more?

2. What is the importance of image to the retailer? How does it affect the shopping behavior of consumers? Now, think of the two largest department stores in your community. How would you describe their images?

3. What does market segmentation mean to you? Apply it to retailing.

4. Discuss the requirements for good segmentation.

5. Discuss the ways by which markets can be segmented.

6. What are some of the steps which you can take to lessen the effects of consumer dissatisfaction?

7. Discuss activities which you know are being undertaken by consumer groups and businesses in your area to help stop consumer dissatisfaction.

8. What are some retailers doing to help consumers buy more effectively?

9. Why does lifestyle segmentation appeal to many retailers?

10. What is the use of the life cycle concept in segmenting markets?

PROJECTS

1. Visit a national supermarket in your community, a discount or warehouse grocery food outlet, and a 7-Eleven type of food store. Prepare a paper which points out the similarities and differences between the three types of stores. Write a brief statement which summarizes your thoughts about the image of each type of outlet. Describe the characteristics of the people whom you think are most likely to shop at each of the three outlets.

2. Briefly interview 10–15 of your fellow students. Find out the latest experience about which they were dissatisfied with a retail outlet. What action did they take, if any? What was the response of management to the situation if it was called to their attention? Will the situation cause the dissatisfied person not to shop at the outlet again? Write a short paper summarizing their experiences.

Minicase 2-1   Barry Walters recently took his lawn mower for repair to a national chain store in Any Town. He told the person at the service counter that the carburetor seemed to have trash in it which was blocking the fuel line. He asked the clerk to call him with an estimate of repair charges. Approximately two weeks later he was called and told that the lawn mower had been repaired and was ready for him to pick up. Barry went to the shop and was shocked to find that the bill was $38. In addition to repairing the carburetor, the shop personnel had sharpened the blade, changed the oil, replaced the spark plug and several other parts of the electrical system. Barry was really upset and asked the repair person why he hadn't called with an estimate. The man said, "Don't look at me. I only repair them. Nobody at the service desk told me to provide an estimate of the cost."

Barry then went to see the manager and told him, "Man, you run a real rip-off operation! I asked the person at the service desk to call me with an estimate of repair costs. Also, less than a month ago I changed the oil in the lawn mower, sharpened the blade, replaced the spark plug and other parts in the electrical system myself. Your people did the same thing to me last year when I brought the lawn mower in for repairs. It seems to me you go ahead and do some things automatically whether they need it or not. Let me tell you this. I'm not going to pay you $38. I'm also going to do everything in my power to tell all the people I know what a sorry place of business you have."

Analyze the situation. Look at it from Barry's point of view, the manager's point of view, the repair person's point of view, and from the viewpoint of the person at the service desk. What would you do? What could be done to prevent such things from occurring in the future?

Minicase 2-2   Robert Sharma has recently opened a specialty high-fi shop in Metro town. He carries the best name brands and full lines. He opened the shop with the thought that he would serve the needs of serious high-fi hobbyists such as himself. He also figured that he could make sales to such professionals as attorneys and medical doctors. After six months Bob realized that he was in real trouble. His sales were far too low. He talked to a friend at the local university who told him that the market was probably too thin in the city to support his type of operation. Bob then arranged to sell lower quality (and lower priced) high-fi equipment. But that wasn't successful either. He tried talking to a few young adults who told him they purchased such items from the leading department stores in the city. They told Bob they weren't interested in coming to his shop because the prices were too high. Now Bob really has a problem. He's read the retailing text which his professor friend left him and understands that he was trying to serve the wrong market segment. He is now trying to figure out the market segment he should serve and what it would take to serve the market. What did Bob do wrong in the first place? What did he then do to make his problem worse? Now, assume that Bob is starting all over. What would you advise him to do first?

3

WHAT IS LIFESTYLE MERCHANDISING?

The purposes of this chapter are:

- To explain the changes in our culture which affect the lifestyles of consumers.
- To explain the techniques of lifestyle analysis.
- To explain the benefits of lifestyle merchandising.
- To speculate on the future of lifestyle analysis.
- To acquaint you with how to include lifestyle merchandising in your retail strategy mix.
- To explain the meaning of the following terms:

Psychographics	Market positioning
Lifestyle	Market targeting
Activities, interests, and opinions	

Lifestyle will have a major effect on retailing throughout the 1980s. You'll see the ideas show up in advertising, display and presentation, merchandising, sales promotion, special events, and even on the sales floor. Lifestyle merchandising especially influences almost everything in the world of fashion.

The two key terms in this chapter are "lifestyle" and "psychographics." Lifestyle is a person's pattern of living as reflected in the way in which products are purchased and used. *Psychographics* consists of the ways for defining and measuring the lifestyles of consumers.

Selling products by lifestyle means showing consumers how a product or service fits their particular lifestyle. Many products quickly come to mind—Schlitz beer, Revlon's Charlie perfume, and Irish Spring soap, for example. What do these products say about the people who use them?

Why has lifestyle merchandising become so important? We live in an age in which great differences exist between persons in the same age-groups. This problem makes it hard to divide markets into groups based on age, income, and education alone. You need to know something about how people (1) spend their time, (2) their money, and (3) what they value (to go with the bare statistics), in order to serve them in the best way. Lifestyle characteristics give you a more true-to-life picture of your customer.

WHAT SHAPES OUR LIFESTYLES?

We pointed out in Chapter 1 that you need to understand economic forces, changes in technology, changes in government regulation and changes in the society about you to be a successful retailer. This chapter looks at changes in our culture to help you understand the lifestyles emerging today that will affect your merchandising plans.[1]

We are all a product of the society in which we live. We very early learn things such as honesty and the value of money which stay with us through life. These cultural influences plus economic and demographic patterns over time produce our lifestyles—the traits, activities, interests, and opinions which affect our general behavior. Each individual is a little different in the above terms but we can be grouped in such a way as to yield broad groups of individuals with similar characteristics. These broad groups are known as market segments.

Where do lifestyles come from?

Our lifestyles are rooted in our values. *Values* are simply beliefs or expectations about behavior, shared by a number of individuals.[2] We all learn our values from society. Some of these values do not change much over time. Others can change quite fast. The major forces shaping our values include (1) the influence of the family, (2) religious institutions, (3) schools, and (4) early lifetime experiences.

Clearly, cultural and economic and demographic realities are important lifetime experiences. These are the values that shape a person's existence. A study of lifestyles which come about as a result of these influences offers some

Super Shirts capitalize on lifestyles of specific groups

Courtesy Aronov Realty, Montgomery, Alabama

of the most important and interesting ways of understanding consumers and how to change things in your business to serve them better.

What do we know about changing cultural patterns?

One, we know that less time is now spent by parents with very young children. Thirty percent of preschool children are in day-care centers today, for example.

Jeans West understands lifestyle merchandising

Courtesy Aronov Realty, Montgomery, Alabama

Two, the divorce rate is climbing rapidly. As a result the value patterns of many of today's children are also changing rapidly. More children are raised without fathers in the home. All of this means that they learn values from many persons other than the family.

Three, people move more often than in the past. Thus, less influence comes today from persons such as grandparents, aunts, uncles, and so forth. Many of today's young people thus lack "roots."

Four, religion is declining in importance in many people's lives.

Five, schools are becoming more important in shaping values. More young people are staying in high school, and approximately half now go on to college. Young people are exposed to the large number of different values in our educational system.

Six, persons in each generation have different experiences. More than 70 percent of consumers today were not alive during the depression of the 1930s, for example. Many of them have little awareness of World War II. Our young people grew up in a time when credit was seen as good, jobs were plentiful, and they thought less about job security and loyalty to one's country than their parents. Yet, these young people grew up with the Vietnam War, an energy crisis, and a variety of other things which also affect how they view the world and how they handle their own lives.

Determining consumers' values

What have been the results of the forces shaping the values of today's consumers? Consider the following:

1. Instant gratification.
2. Credit explosion.
3. The new theology of pleasure.
4. Life simplification.
5. Sexual revolution.
6. Changing concepts of time and leisure.

Instant gratification. Many people won't wait very long for anything. They want goods and services available when they need them.

The credit explosion. People used to think of the use of credit as showing that a person did not know how to manage money. But young people don't think this way. They are not afraid to use credit; they look upon credit as a type of convenience, not as debt.

The new theology of pleasure. Many people today think that if something brings pleasure, then do it. We all know the saying, "If it feels good, do it." Freedom and comfort are what people are looking for today in everything from dress to automobiles and furniture.

Life simplification. More and more people today want to simplify their lives. This explains the popularity of such things as self-cleaning ovens, microwave ovens, and easy-to-clean products of all types. This move also is behind "instant" cake mixes, and such things as air conditioning and dish-washers.

Sexual revolution. The values many people hold about sex are changing quite rapidly. Sex is an important part of the creative strategies by many retailers today. Many products are sold by retailers by showing their appeal to the opposite sex.

Changing concepts of time and leisure. People have less time to shop than ever before. More women are working outside the home and are always in a hurry. Leisure activities are often job related.

Other results of the value shifts are as follows (some of these are discussed in Chapter 8, "The World around You—Economic and Social):

New work ethic.

Youth orientation.

Emphasis on physical appearance and youth.

Novelty, change, and escape.

Naturalism.

Personal creativity.

International orientation.

Return to edited past.

Institutional reliance.

Loss of confidence in institutions.

Conservation ethic.

Price-value orientation.

Consumerism.[3]

Think for a moment about what these value shifts means to you as a retailer.[4]

HOW DO YOU SEGMENT MARKETS BY LIFESTYLE?

Research looks at people's activities

Lifestyle segmentation research looks at the activities, interests, and opinions (AIOs) of persons. Specifically, you measure (1) how people spend their time, (2) what most interests or is important to them, and (3) their opinions and views about themselves and the world about them.[5]

The information used in forming lifestyle segments comes from consumer questionnaires. The questionnaires ask about the products which they purchase, their media habits, and their activities, interests, and opinions. An example of the results of a lifestyle questionnaire to look at differences among females by age is shown in Table 3–1.

Levels of agreement with the various statements are related to the use of a product and to demographic characteristics (age, income, and sex of the consumer). Similar consumers are then grouped together. Study Aid 3–1 shows five female and five male lifestyle segments which were found based

TABLE 3-1
Female interests and opinions (percent agreeing by age-group)

Statement	Sample total	Age-group				
		Under 25	25–34	35–44	45–54	55 and older
Optimism and happiness						
My greatest achievements are still ahead of me	64%	92%	84%	73%	52%	28%
I dread the future	23	20	18	17	24	30
I am much happier now than I ever was before	79	85	82	80	74	74
Modern-traditional ideas						
I have somewhat old-fashioned tastes and habits	86	78	84	87	88	89
There is too much emphasis on sex today	87	70	74	90	89	93
I like to think I am a bit of a swinger	26	43	34	26	19	15
A woman's place is in the home	46	39	39	44	49	60
The working world is no place for a woman	17	15	11	14	19	28
Young people have too many privileges	76	57	74	77	76	83
The United States would be better off if there were no hippies	55	32	37	46	54	82
My days seem to follow a definite routine—eating meals at the same time each day, etc.	67	59	62	61	67	75
Travel						
I would like to take a trip around the world	67	78	83	73	65	51
I would like to spend a year in London or Paris	34	38	40	34	34	25
I would feel lost if I were alone in a foreign country	68	66	66	64	68	76
I like to visit places that are totally different from my home	85	85	83	86	82	88
Mobile						
We will probably move at least once in the next five years	38	71	53	27	28	23
Our family has moved more often than most of our neighbors have	24	36	32	26	18	17
Anxious						
I have trouble getting to sleep	33	29	24	26	33	49
I wish I knew how to relax	52	51	49	49	51	59
Personal adornment and self						
Dressing well is an important part of my life	81	84	80	78	79	83

TABLE 3-1 *(continued)*

Statement	Sample total	Age-group				
		Under 25	25–34	35–44	45–54	55 and older
I like to feel attractive to members of the opposite sex	85%	93%	91%	77%	82%	72%
I want to look a little different from others	69	71	78	70	63	72
I often wear expensive cologne	28	19	24	28	27	33
I have more stylish clothes than most of my friends	30	31	34	27	29	27
View toward income, personal equity, and spending						
I will probably have more money to spend next year than I have now	45	71	70	58	53	30
Five years from now our family income will probably be a lot higher than it is now	65	87	85	75	61	26
Our family income is high enough to satisfy nearly all our important desires	74	59	66	78	78	80
No matter how fast our income goes up we never seem to get ahead	53	62	65	61	47	32
Investing in the stock market is too risky for most families	86	79	83	82	85	87
Our family is too heavily in debt today	27	36	33	37	23	11
I like to pay cash for everything I buy	77	83	79	74	71	77
I pretty much spend for today and let tomorrow bring what it will	22	33	21	22	25	18
Staying at home						
I would rather spend a quiet evening at home than go out to a party	65	50	66	64	68	78
I am a homebody	69	59	65	64	72	79
I stay home most evenings	83	81	95	80	83	83
Husband and children						
A wife's first obligation is to her husband, not her children	69	53	65	74	74	76
When children are ill in bed, parents should drop everything else to see to their comfort	74	61	71	73	80	83
Children are the most important thing in a marriage	52	42	44	49	56	64
When making important family decisions, consideration of the children should come first	54	69	58	44	48	56
A wife should have a great deal of information about her husband's work	82	83	84	75	88	85

TABLE 3-1 *(concluded)*

Statement	Sample total	Age-group				
		Under 25	25–34	35–44	45–54	55 and older
View toward durable goods						
Our home is furnished for comfort, not for style	90%	83%	88%	88%	94%	94%
If I must choose, I buy stylish rather than practical furniture	17	19	31	13	15	15
When buying appliances, I am more concerned with dependability than price	90	85	89	89	89	94
A subcompact car can meet my transportation needs	66	85	74	60	61	57
Housekeeping and cooking						
When I see a full ashtray or wastebasket, I want it emptied immediately	71	77	70	72	64	64
I am uncomfortable when the house is not completely clean	67	76	67	70	61	68
The kind of dirt you can't see is worse than the kind you can see	77	77	72	73	79	85
I am a good cook	91	93	92	88	90	91
I like to cook	87	91	88	84	85	87
I like to bake	40	43	43	42	39	38
Meal preparation should take as little time as possible	42	42	41	40	41	41
Grocery shopping						
Shopping is no fun anymore	54	49	43	58	55	51
Before going shopping, I sit down and prepare a complete shopping list	72	68	73	71	69	74
I try to stick to well-known brands	74	58	67	71	82	86
I find myself checking prices even on small items	90	89	93	92	89	86
I like to save and redeem savings stamps	75	72	70	70	75	83
I pay a lot more attention to food prices now than I ever did before	90	92	91	88	88	87
I am an impulse buyer	38	39	40	37	42	27
I shop a lot for specials	84	85	86	83	84	81
Health and nutrition						
I am very concerned about nutrition	87	87	89	87	82	89
I am concerned about how much salt I eat	56	52	55	56	50	66
I am careful what I eat in order to keep my weight under control	57	63	57	58	62	68
I try to avoid foods that are high in cholesterol	62	37	53	60	65	79
I try to avoid foods that have additives in them	56	45	52	57	53	62
I get more headaches than most people	28	30	31	28	27	22
I eat more than I should	70	68	70	75	73	69

Source: Needham, Harper & Steers Advertising, Inc., *Life Style Survey,* 1975.

STUDY AID 3-1

PSYCHOGRAPHIC PROFILES

The female segments

Thelma, the old-fashioned traditionalist (25 percent)

This lady has lived a "good" life—she has been a devoted wife, a doting mother, and a conscientious housewife. She has lived her life by these traditional values and she cherishes them to this day. She does not condone contemporary sexual activities or political liberalism, nor can she sympathize with the women's libbers. Even today, when most of her children have left home, her life is centered around the kitchen. Her one abiding interest outside the household is the church which she attends every week. She lacks higher education and hence has little appreciation for the arts or cultural activities. Her spare time is spent watching TV, which is her prime source of entertainment and information.

Mildred, the militant mother (20 percent)

Mildred married young and had children before she was quite ready to raise a family. Now she is unhappy. She is having trouble making ends meet on her blue-collar husband's income. She is frustrated and she vents her frustrations by rebelling against the system. She finds escape from her unhappy world in soap operas and movies. Television provides an ideal medium for her to live out her fantasies. She watches TV all through the day and into late night. She likes heavy rock and probably soul music, and she doesn't read much except escapist magazines such as *True Story*.

Candice, the chic suburbanite (20 percent)

Candice is an urbane woman. She is well educated and genteel. She is a prime mover in her community, active in club affairs and working on community projects. Socializing is an important part of her life. She is a doer, interested in sports and the outdoors, politics, and current affairs. Her life is hectic and lived at a fast clip. She is a voracious reader, and there are few magazines she doesn't read. However, TV does relatively poorly in competing for her attention—it is too inane for her.

Cathy, the contented housewife (18 percent)

Cathy epitomizes simplicity. Her life is untangled. She is married to a worker in the middle of the socioeconomic scale, and they, alone with their several preteen children, live in a small town. She is devoted to her family and faithfully serves as mother, housewife, and cook. There is a certain tranquillity in her life. She enjoys a relaxed pace and avoids anything that might disturb her equilibrium. She doesn't like news or news-type programs on TV but enjoys the wholesome family entertainment provided by Walt Disney, "The Waltons," and "Happy Days."

Eleanor, the elegant socialite (17 percent)

Eleanor is a woman with style. She lives in the city because that is where she wants to be. She likes the economic and social aspects of big city living and takes advantage of the city in terms of her career and leisure-time activities. She is a self-confident on-the-go woman, not a homebody. She is fashion-conscious and dresses well. She is a woman with panache. She is financially secure; as a result she is not a careful shopper. She shops for quality and style, not price. She is a cosmopolitan woman who has traveled abroad or wants to.

The male segments

Herman, the retiring homebody (26 percent)

Herman is past his prime and is not getting any younger. His attitudes and opinions on life, which are often in conflict with modern trends, have gelled. And he is resistant to change. He is old-fashioned and conservative. He was brought up on "motherhood and apple pie" and cherishes these values. Consequently he finds the attitudes of young people today disturbing. He realizes he cannot affect any change, and has withdrawn into a sheltered existence of his own within the confines of his home and its surroundings. Here he lives a measured life. He goes to church regularly, watches his diet, and lives frugally. He longs for the good old days and regrets that the world around him is changing.

Scott, the successful professional (21 percent)

Scott is a man who has everything going for him. He is well educated, cosmopolitan, the father of a young family, and is already established in his chosen profession. He lives a fast-paced active life and likes it. He is a man getting ahead in the world. He lives in or near an urban center and seems to like what a big city has to offer—culture, learning opportunities, and people. He also enjoys sports, the out-of-doors, and likes to keep physically fit. He is understandably happy with his life and comfortable in his lifestyle.

Fred, the frustrated factory worker (19 percent)

Fred is young. He married young and had a family. It is unlikely that he had any plans to get a college degree; if he did, he had to shelve them to find work to support his family. He now is a blue-collar worker having trouble making ends meet. He is discontented, and tends to feel that "they"—big business, government, and society—are somehow responsible for his state. He finds escape in movies and in fantasies of foreign lands and cabins by quiet lakes. He likes to appear attractive to women, has an active libido, and likes to think he is a bit of a swinger.

Dale, the devoted family man (17 percent)

Dale is a wholesome guy with a penchant for country living. He is a blue-collar worker, with a high school education. The father of a relatively large family, he prefers a traditional marriage, with his wife at home taking care of the kids. His home and neighborhood are central in his life. He is an easygoing guy who leads an uncomplicated life. Neither worry nor skepticism are a part of him. He is relaxed and has a casual approach to many things. He is a happy, trusting soul who takes things as they are.

Ben, the self-made businessman (17 percent)

Ben is the epitome of a self-made man. He was probably not born wealthy, nor had he the benefit of higher education, but through hard work and shrewd risk-taking he has built himself a decent life. He has seen the system work. He believes if you work hard and play by the rules you will get your share (and perhaps some more). Therefore, he cannot condone hippies and other fringe groups whom he sees as freeloaders. He embraces conservative ideology and is likely to be a champion of business interests. He is a traditionalist at home, and believes it is a woman's job to look after the home and to raise a family. He is gregarious and enjoys giving and attending parties. And he likes to drink.

Source: Reprinted from Sunil Mehrotra and William D. Wells, "Psychographics and Buyer Behavior: Theory and Recent Empirical Findings," in Arch G. Woodside, Jagdish N. Sheth, and Peter D. Bennett, eds., *Consumer and Industrial Buying Behavior* (New York: Elsevier North-Holland, 1977), pp. 54–55.

on responses from 3,300 persons. Study Aid 3–2 is a minicase of the use of lifestyle analysis in action by a major Chicago department store.

Two steps are involved in seeking to segment markets by lifestyle:

1. Decide on which lifestyle segments contain the largest number of profitable consumers you can serve.
2. Then use media habits and demographics in communicating with consumers.

Why worry about lifestyle merchandising?

The use of lifestyle analysis offers you: (1) a better opportunity to develop marketing strategies which speak to a lifelike view of your target customer, (2) the ability to look at your market in many additional ways and position your store so that it is at least partially shielded from direct price competition, (3) the opportunity to learn more about the shopping behavior of your customers, and (4) the chance to observe how consumer views are changing.

The "bottom line" however, is that you will be far better able to describe and understand the behavior of consumers. You should routinely think in terms of the activities, interests, needs, and values of the consumers you want to serve. Then gear your products, services, and promotion efforts directly to their needs. But, keep in mind that lifestyle analysis only adds to the demographic, geographic, and socioeconomic information you need in serving your market segments effectively. Lifestyle analysis is not a substitute for the use of these kinds of information. Rather, all information sources overlap somewhat in giving you a richer view of your customers and in helping you serve unrecognized consumer needs. Tougher competition will also force you to seek out market segments not now well served in order to give you an advantage over competition.

WITH LIFESTYLE MERCHANDISING, STORES MEET NEEDS OF THREE FASHION TYPES

With lifestyle merchandising, today's department stores are meeting the needs of three customer fashion types, according to Lois Patrich, vice president, sales, promotion, and advertising, Carson, Pirie, Scott & Co., Chicago.

"While demographic lines between these types may sometimes be blurred, each has a personal lifestyle quite divergent from the next," she said. "So, department stores buy differently for each, develop in-store presentations (an increasingly more important part of our business) differently for each, and advertise differently towards each in terms of creative concept and media.

"By far, the largest segment of these fashion types is (1) the conservative or traditional customer," Patrich said. "Demographically she is older, married, has less formal education, is less affluent and wears a larger dress size.

"She is less concerned with style and high fashion and prefers comfortable, straightforward, tailored clothes. She is apt to be price conscious and is certainly quality conscious; fit, comfort, and durability are important.

(2) "In contrast, the updated or contemporary type is far more fashion conscious," she said. "This woman enjoys evenings on the town, nightclubs, elegant restaurants, and discos. She believes in careers outside the home and is the most likely of the three to be working.

"She is well educated and affluent, aware of fashion, has a few avant-garde items but these do not dominate her wardrobe, and is very responsive to in-store displays.

(3) "Compared to the other two types, the third, the avant-garde fashion type, is most likely younger and single and spends more money than average on clothes," Patrich said. "However this is the smallest market segment.

"Price is not an important consideration in her purchasing decisions. The trendy, whippy, latest fashions and sex appeal are important. Ads and in-store visual presentations must have a young, up-to-the minute look," she said.

Since these types cut across price lines, stores may have, for example, contemporary budget departments. They also have their counterparts in the men's fashion and home furnishings areas.

Patrich also discussed special events that department stores are staging, such as (1) showcasing disco dancers and (2) exercise and (3) cooking classes. "Restaurants in department stores also have made great contributions in life-styling the store's environment.

"Serving a divergent market in retailing calls for a total coordination of every department," she said. "The pull must be in the same direction. Being all things to all people is not a successful policy.

"But, the way to go is to concentrate merchandise and promotional skills, advertising, visual presentation, and special events on markets identified as the most profitable to the store." Patrich said. "The key is that all departments are positioned toward common goals concomitant with the total store image."

Source: *Marketing News*, April 21, 1978, p. 12.

HOW DOES LIFESTYLE MERCHANDISING MAKE YOU A BETTER RETAILER?

These days you have to more than segment your markets. You have to be *on target*—by the right combination of quality, price and value—in order to get consumers to spend.[6] You have to aim your merchandise and its presentation at particular lifestyle audiences. Even through radio station programming you can now reach specific lifestyle target audiences.[7]

Kenneth for Kids, Macy's hair salon targeting in on an affluent segment and lifestyle

Courtesy Macys

Target marketing: Positioning

Positioning means placing yourself in a unique position relative to other retailers. Projecting this uniqueness into your market's mind involves the following ten aspects of positioning:

1. Merchandise diversity.
2. Size of store and range of customers served.
3. Fashion distinctiveness.
4. Competitiveness.
5. Convenience.
6. Service quality.
7. Innovativeness.
8. Lifestyle awareness.
9. Dependability.
10. Community identification.[8]

The above elements help you to emphasize what you want customers to recognize and remember about you. They also reflect what you have determined are the most important things which can give you a unique position in the market.

The store-within-a-store concept

Here merchandise is brought together from all areas of the stores for its lifestyle appeal. Lifestyle merchandising breaks down departmental barriers. This approach allows your salespeople to sell primarily to one lifestyle customer. In this way they can avoid having to deal with a broader range of customer requirements and interests as was necessary under the old departmental setup. Today you need to group merchandise the way customers want to buy it, not the way the store thinks it is easiest to sell—not putting dresses into departments labeled better, moderate, budget, and so forth.[9]

Effects on retail salespeople

More and more your retail salespeople will have to be able not only to identify with the items being sold but with the lifestyle of the customer buying the items. Even your branches will need to be better tailored to the lifestyles of the customers living in that particular area. Your salesperson selling tennis equipment should be an avid tennis player, for example.

The director of marketing

Even a new retailing executive position is being created. This new position is called director of marketing. The responsibilities include everything from target marketing to various lifestyle audiences to the creation of an overall "store image." This person directs the activities of the various managers and advises top corporate officers seeking the best performance possible from all areas of the store. They pay particular attention to visual merchandising. Much of their effort is directed at special events productions which are lifestyle oriented. Results of such special productions are measured in increased sales, customer traffic, goodwill, and free publicity.

Better promotion efforts

Lifestyle merchandising is changing the media mix used by many retailers. Lifestyle programming by various stations which offer sports, middle-of-the-road music, or all news programs appealing to the executive-professional are designed to appeal to a specific lifestyle and are now also a key to reaching your target audience.

Visual merchandising

The sight of attractively displayed merchandise and the way it relates to a consumer's lifestyle strongly increases the consumer's desire to buy. Lifestyle merchandising based upon this psychology is becoming a highly refined art. Promotional displays are likely to be strong, dramatic, and striking, yet must be understandable in getting the attention of consumers, and should be keyed to the same theme as merchandise ads.

Creating an artistic environment so essential in lifestyle merchandising requires a unique blending of lighting, background, and props. All visual merchandising themes should start with what the customer wants and should communicate important fashion information.

SUMMARY

Today, you need to know more about your consumers than simply their demographics or socioeconomic background. Successful merchandising today requires a richness in promotion, pricing, and other aspects of merchandising which statistics alone cannot give you.

Lifestyle analysis through the use of psychographics is one way to understand the consumers and how to offer merchandise which will appeal to their outlook on life. Successful store positioning through application of lifestyle segmentation creates a unique place in the mind of the consumer for you. This approach will put you ahead of the competition and allow you to compete in the market on some basis other than price.

NOTES

1. This material is based on Roger Blackwell and Wayne Talarzyk, "Adaptive Strategies in an Era of Changing Lifestyles—Part 1," *Partners Journal,* vol. 3, no. 2 (Spring 1977).
2. Roger Blackwell and Wayne Talarzyk, "Adaptive Strategies in an Era of Changing Lifestyles—Part 2," *Partners Journal* vol. 3, no. 3. (Fall 1977).
3. For further details, see Barry Berman and Joel Evans, "Lifestyles of the 1980s," *Retailing Management* (New York: Macmillan Co., 1979), pp. 541–46.
4. Berman and Evans, "Lifestyles of the 1980s," pp. 541–46.
5. David Loudon and Albert Della Bitta, *Consumer Behavior* (New York: McGraw Hill Book Company, 1979), p. 100.
6. "Positioning for Growth: Marketing Challenge," *Stores* (February 1979), p. 31.
7. "Lifestyle '78: Refining the Concept to Embrace Target Marketing," *Stores* (February 1978), p. 44.
8. "Market Positioning to Maintain Momentum," *Stores* (February 1979), p. 33.
9. "'New Woman's' Wardrobe to Be Varied, Voluminous: Moss," *The Marketing News,* April 8, 1977, p. 7.

DISCUSSION QUESTIONS

1. Define lifestyle and psychographics. What is the relationship of one to the other?
2. What is the role of consumer activities, interests, and opinions in lifestyle analysis?
3. What are some of the changes in society which are shaping American values today?
4. What have been the effects on consumer behavior of changing values in society?
5. What is the meaning of market positioning? How does positioning differ from segmentation?
6. How does lifestyle merchandising affect the way in which items are grouped in a firm?
7. Why has the position of director of marketing become more important in some firms today?
8. Why is it important for the backgrounds of your salespeople to match the lifestyles of the customers they are serving?

PROJECTS

1. Interview several of your female friends using the survey statements in Table 3–1. See where they fall in the lifestyle segments. What conclusions can you draw from this experience?

2. Do the same thing for males and females utilizing the psychographic profiles in Study Aid 3–1. Categorize your interviewees. What have you learned by this experience?

3. Visit several department and specialty outlets in your area. Describe examples of lifestyle merchandising which you discover in your visits. Try to relate the strategy to positioning which you believe the store managements are attempting.

Minicase 3–1   Utilize Study Aid 3–2 as the springboard for a discussion in class. This Study Aid will help you more than any case to really understand the importance of lifestyle merchandising in the real world.

4

WHAT ARE YOUR RETAIL BUSINESS POSSIBILITIES?

The purposes of this chapter are to explain:

- The advantages and risks of business ownership.
- The differences between a single proprietorship, a partnership, and a corporation.
- The meaning of a marketing system.
- Administered merchandising systems, wholesaler-sponsored cooperatives, retailer-sponsored cooperatives, and franchises as ways of creating your own business while getting help from others.
- The meaning of the following terms:

  Partnership   Contractual systems
  Single proprietorship   Wholesaler-sponsored cooperative
  Corporation   Retailer-sponsored cooperative
  Corporate systems   Franchise, franchisee, franchisor
  Administered systems

You may be thinking of going into business for yourself. If so, you can get started in several ways: (1) You can start your own business and operate completely alone; (2) you can work with other retailers or wholesalers as a group to have more power in buying goods; or (3) you can become a franchisee. The appendix at the end of this chapter provides a detailed "Checklist for Going into Business," which might be quite helpful for you.

THINK ABOUT WORKING IN A SMALL RETAIL FIRM FOR THE EXPERIENCE

Almost 2 million retail businesses exist in the United States. Two thirds of these firms have less than four employees. And, 90 percent are single-unit establishments.[1] Clearly most retail businesses are small by any definition. You may want to start your retail career with a small firm if you want to one day manage a family business.

But start with a small firm only for the experience unless you can buy into the business. Beginning in a small firm exposes you quickly to all sides of the business.

WHAT ABOUT BUSINESS OWNERSHIP?

Retailing offers more chances for ownership than other types of businesses. Read the newspaper on almost any day and you can find several retail businesses for sale. Also, most suppliers and bankers will be glad to help you start your own firm.

Small retailers often compete successfully with national firms. Retailing is local in nature. Most store trading areas are small and all outlets are viewed as part of the local community. You can do things that a national firm cannot do since they cannot vary their operations from town to town.

What about the risks of ownership?

Going-out-of-business signs are a part of every community. Few persons voluntarily go out of business. But don't be discouraged about starting your own business. The rewards can be large.

Failure by line of business. As shown in Table 4–1, sporting goods stores most often fail, followed by cameras and photographic supplies, men's wear, and infants' and children's wear. Businesses least likely to fail are women's accessories, automotive outlets, and food stores.

Early failure is likely. The first five years will be the toughest for you. Two thirds of all retail firms fail in their first five years.

What are the causes of failure? The reasons for failure are incompetence, unbalanced experience, lack of experience in the type of retailing in question, and a lack of managerial experience. Failure because of neglect, fraud, or disaster is unusual, as shown in Table 4–2.

HOW CAN YOU START YOUR OWN BUSINESS?

Let's assume for now that you have decided to start your own business. How do you get started? You can form a (1) single proprietorship, (2) partnership, or (3) corporation. The advantages and disadvantages of each are shown in Table 4–3.

TABLE 4–1
Retail lines ranked
by failure rate

Line of business	Failure rate per 10,000 operating concerns
Sporting goods	64
Cameras and photographic supplies	51
Menswear	47
Infants' and children's wear	43
Furniture and furnishings	42
Women's ready-to-wear	39
Books and stationery	33
Appliances, radio and TV	32
Shoes	31
Gifts	30
Dry goods and general merchandise	26
Auto parts and accessories	22
Toys and hobby crafts	22
Drugs	17
Eating and drinking places	17
Hardware	17
Jewelry	16
Lumber and building materials	16
Bakeries	13
Department stores	12
Groceries, meats, and produce	12
Automobiles	11
Women's accessories	7

Source: *The Business Failure Record, 1977*, Business Economics Department, Dun and Bradstreet, Inc. (New York, 1978), p. 6.

TABLE 4–2
Cause of retail failures

Underlying causes	Percent
Neglect	1.0%
Fraud	0.4
Lack of experience in the line	14.4
Lack of managerial experience	15.8
Unbalanced experience*	22.2
Incompetence	40.8
Disaster	0.5
Reason unknown	4.9
	100.0%
Number of failures	3,406
Average liabilities per failure	$141,679

* Experience not well rounded in sales, finance, purchasing, and production on the part of the individual in case of a proprietorship, or of two or more partners or officers constituting a management unit.

Source: *The Business Failure Record, 1977*, Business Economics Department, Dun and Bradstreet, Inc. (New York, 1978), p. 12.

TABLE 4-3
The advantages and disadvantages of each form of private ownership

Form of ownership		
Single proprietorship Advantages	**Partnership** Advantages	**Corporation** Advantages
1. Retention of all profits	1. Ease of formation	1. Limited financial liability
2. Ease of formation and dissolution	2. Complementary management skills	2. Specialized management skills
3. Ownership flexibility	3. Expanded financial capability	3. Expanded financial capability
		4. Economics of larger scale operation
Disadvantages	*Disadvantages*	*Disadvantages*
1. Unlimited financial liability	1. Unlimited financial liability	1. Difficult and costly ownership form to establish
2. Limits to financing	2. Interpersonal disagreements	2. Tax disadvantage
3. Management deficiencies	3. Lack of continuity	3. Legal restrictions
4. Lack of continuity	4. Complex dissolution	4. Alienation of some employees

Source: Louis Boone and David Kurtz, *Contemporary Business* (Hinsdale, Ill.: Dryden Press, 1979), p. 59.

Let's look at the single proprietorship

The *single proprietorship* is the most common form of ownership today. Small firms such as barber and beauty shops are often single proprietorships. Single proprietorship means that everything belongs to you as the owner.

Such a business is the easiest to create. Little paperwork is necessary. Few regulatory restrictions exist other than where inspection or licensing, for example, is needed. Likewise, the manager can go out of business very quickly and easily, perhaps simply by locking the door and hanging a sign in the window which says "closed."

Being the only owner has several advantages. For example: (1) You are your own boss. (2) You get to keep all the profits. (3) You can decide on the goods to be sold, store hours, and so forth. (4) Start-up costs are small, as are going-out-of-business costs.

But problems also exist. For example:

1. The risk of loss is yours alone.
2. You can be forced to pay your business debts out of your personal assets.
3. You have limited borrowing ability.
4. You may have trouble getting good people to work for you.
5. You probably will be able to offer fewer fringe benefits to your employees than larger employers.
6. No one will be legally able to run the business other than you.

What is a partnership?

A *partnership means that two or more persons jointly own a business.* Partnerships can take many different forms. For example, in a general partnership a person shares all of the responsibilities and benefits of the partnership, including profits and management authority. Other types of partners are more limited in their business. *Limited partners are persons whose input is limited to one area of the business.* For example, a lawyer may be a limited partner.

Silent partners likewise have limited liabilities with the firm. Often they do not want to be active in the management of the business but are willing to let their names be used as one of the partners. Sometimes these persons are well known in the community and the use of their names is worth a great deal to the firm. *Secret partners do not allow their names to be used.* They do not always have limited liabilities.

The above disadvantages make partnerships less popular than other forms of organization. Such problems become very complicated when a firm has several secret partners. Partnerships may cease to exist when any of the partners becomes incapable of continuing in the business for mental or psychological reasons. Likewise, the unlimited liability for the debts of the business and the fact that the actions of one partner are binding on all others makes matters difficult. Finally, if one partner is more wealthy than the others that partner may have to pay out a larger share of the loss than the other partners.

In summary, the articles for a partnership are very important. They need to spell out the roles of the partners, the ways for a person to get out of the business if the individual can't get along with the others, and what happens when one of the partners dies or becomes disabled.

Consider forming a corporation

A "corporation" is a separate legal entity apart from the owners. Thus, your liability is limited to the amount you have invested in the firm. Also you can more easily attract good management skills. Borrowing money may also be easier since stock can be sold. Also, large firms can often borrow money at lower rates than smaller ones.

But again some disadvantages exist. For example, earnings are taxed differently. First, corporate earnings are taxed. Then dividends to stockholders are also taxed.

Corporations may be either open or closed. Closed corporations are those owned by a few persons or perhaps a family. Persons outside the corporation cannot buy the stock on the open market. The stock value does not have a known market value and does not vary widely in price. *Open corporations* are those in which the stock of the firm can be purchased on the open market. Normally, only large retailers are open corporations.

A special form of corporation is the subchapter S corporation. Under this arrangement, a business can be classified as a corporation but taxed as a partnership. This special arrangement provides the advantages of limited liability and avoidance of the burden of double taxation for corporations. Vari-

Sears and Wards—examples of corporate distribution systems

Courtesy Aronov Realty, Montgomery, Alabama

ous conditions must be met, including a provision of ten or fewer stockholders who are not aliens and not more than 20 percent of the gross revenues from the business derived from interest, dividends, rents, or royalties or from the gain or sale of securities. Most small businesses readily meet these provisions.

Establishing a corporation is easy to do. Most states have laws which standardize the process. Normally at least three persons are needed to establish a corporation. They are issued a corporate charter which is a contract between the state and those persons which allows them to set up the corporation.

HOW WILL YOU OPERATE?

Deciding on the legal form of ownership is not enough. You still need to decide how you will operate. You can "go it alone" without any direct continuing involvement with any other firm. But you will have to deal with several suppliers in getting needed items. You probably also would have little influence with any one supplier because your volume would be small. The best route is probably some type of tie-in with other firms as a system for buying and selling goods.

WHAT IS A MARKETING SYSTEM?

Firms—usually retailers and a wholesaler or manufacturer—often band together as a system to compete with other firms. The group of firms can purchase in larger quantities, have better promotion plans, and better management talent available when needed, since the costs are shared by all members of the system—see Figure 4–1 for examples.

The idea of such systems is not new. Auto dealerships and gasoline service stations have operated this way for years. The recent growth is what is new. Why is it occurring?

WHY ARE MARKETING SYSTEMS GROWING?

More and more money is needed to start a new business. Thus, sales have to be higher to make a profit. High levels of sales are easier if the system helps provide high-quality advertising, good sales forecasts, and skill in buying the right goods at the right price.

Retailing is getting more complex. Data processing systems and other help in such things as store location and legal matters are needed. As a retailer operating alone you may not be able to afford these types of help.

TYPES OF DISTRIBUTION SYSTEMS
Corporate systems

Corporate systems occur when manufacturing, wholesaling, and retail outlets are under one ownership. Sears and Firestone are examples. They manufacture some of their goods, handle their own storage, and own retail outlets. You probably will not be part of such a system unless you are bought out after you have been in business for several years.

Administered systems

Administered systems occur when suppliers control their line of goods that you sell. The suppliers work to develop ways of helping you sell a high

FIGURE 4–1
Types of distribution systems

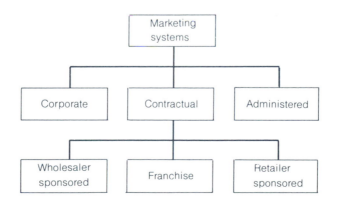

volume of their line(s). But final authority still rests with you. Their expertise is what will cause you to follow their ideas, not a legal contract. You and the supplier work together to reduce the cost of such things as advertising, transportation, and data processing, while increasing sales. Housewares and sporting goods suppliers often work this way with retailers.

Just what can a supplier offer you in this way that you would have trouble doing alone? They help (1) plan your sales and profit levels, (2) plan your inventory, (3) train your salespeople to sell their goods, (4) plan your advertising and sales promotion, and (5) and plan your merchandise displays.[2] Clearly this type of help is one good reason to consider becoming part of such a system for the lines of the supplier you will carry.

Contractual systems

Contractual arrangements are the most common type of systems today. Here retailers and a wholesaler or a manufacturer sign an agreement to work together in selling goods or services. Such systems may be either (1) a wholesaler-sponsored voluntary group, (2) a retailer-sponsored cooperative, or (3) a franchise.

Wholesaler-sponsored voluntary groups. *Here a wholesaler signs an agreement with many different retailers to help them in their sales efforts.* An example is Independent Grocers' Alliance in groceries. All the retailers make their purchases from the one wholesaler. The wholesaler in turn provides financial help in opening a store, help in location, provides planned advertising programs, and handles price marking, storage, and central data processing. Lower prices are also possible to the retailers because of volume discounts.

Wholesaler cooperatives are often very large. In the food field, they rival giants such as A&P or Safeway.

Retailer-sponsored cooperatives. *The retailer-sponsored cooperative is a voluntary association of retailers.* An example is Associated Grocers. The retailers working together have more market power in dealing with suppliers. In effect the retailers own and operate their own wholesale company. They are able to obtain prices and other assistance from suppliers which they would not get acting alone.

Franchising. *A franchise is an agreement whereby the owner of a unique way of doing business (the franchisor) allows you (the franchisee) to start a firm using the franchisor's way of doing business.* The agreement is a legal contract which states the rights of both parties. Under such an agreement, you pay the franchisor for the right to do business as part of the franchise system. For example, McDonald's "sells a 20-year license for about $200,000, picks the site, buys the land, builds the store, equips and rents it for 8.5 percent of gross annual revenues plus a 3 percent annual franchise fee.[3]

What are the types of franchises? Franchises exist in almost all business fields. The most common franchise is a *dealership*. This grants you the sole right to sell a product or service in a given area. *Mobile franchises* are similar to dealerships but business is done from a vehicle which moves about. Snap-On Tools Corporation is an example of this type of franchise.

You can also operate a *distributorship.* Here you would keep warehouse stocks for sale to other franchises. You take title to the goods and provide needed services to other customers. An example of this type of franchise is Bear Brand Automotive Equipment.

Ownership franchises are those in which the franchisor has an ownership interest in your operation—for example, the Travelodge system.

Service franchises are those in which you are licensed to offer a service under a trade name. Snelling & Snelling (personnel consultants) and H & R Block (tax preparation) are examples.

As a franchisee you can go into business with confidence even if you have no retailing experience. A good franchisor will teach you how to run a successful business in a matter of weeks. But you have to agree to follow completely the system as laid out.

What are the disadvantages for the franchisor? Franchisors:

1. Are limited in the amount of control that can be exercised over your business. You are really an independent business person who has a contractual agreement with the franchisor.
2. Often have trouble getting rid of weak franchisees.
3. May have a problem attracting qualified franchisees.
4. Often have trouble getting franchisees to perform at a high level.
5. Often have legal problems with franchisees.

What are key franchisor decisions?   A major decision is the type of income you will pay. Possibilities include:

1. An initial fee to allow you to start the franchise.
2. Royalties—either a monthly fee or a percentage of your sales.
3. Renting or leasing your building.
4. Selling or leasing special equipment to you.
5. Selling you finished goods for resale.
6. Selling supplies or raw materials to you.
7. Selling area distributorships to you.

What are the problems you may face?   (1) The terms of a franchise are designed for a long-term contract. Thus it is hard to get out of a franchise arrangement. (2) In order to be granted a franchise you have to give up much of your freedom as a business person. (3) The franchisor has more financial and management power than you and thus is likely to beat you in any conflict which may arise. (4) Some franchisors will have little interest in your problems. (5) The franchisor may own some retail outlets and compete with the ones you own. (6) You may suffer when other franchises go down in quality or when the parent company gets in trouble. (7) You may become overdependent on the franchisor and lose your drive to succeed.

What are the advantages to you?   Don't overlook the advantages of franchising: (1) franchising gives you a chance to be an independent business person. Research has shown that over half of the owner-managers in franchising would not be otherwise self-employed.[4] (2) The failure rate in franchising is lower than for other types of independent retailers. (3) You have access to financial and management talent which otherwise would not be the case.

OTHER TYPES OF RETAILING POSITIONS

We do not want you to think after reading this chapter that you have to go into business for yourself to be a success in retailing. You can have many other good jobs in retailing as discussed in Chapter 20, ''What about a Career in Retailing?'' The jobs range all the way from fashion buyer to accountant.

SUMMARY

More than 2 million small businesses exist in the United States today. Most of these businesses are retail firms with fewer than four employees. Still, most of us are familiar with such retailing giants as Sears, A&P, and Penneys.

Many of you will want to open your own business. Good opportunities for success exist, but the risk of failure is also high. You probably should get experience working for someone else before investing your own money.

You have the choice of forming your new business as a single proprietorship, a partnership, or as a corporation. The choice of how you do business is up to you. Also, you can operate as an independent or become part of a marketing system.

One of the safer ways to operate your own business is to become a franchisee. However, you lose a lot of control over the business which you would have if you were truly independent. Offsetting advantages include the availability of good management training programs to you, assistance in location, assistance in financing your business, and lower prices for goods. In general, retailing does require a lower capital investment in getting started than does any other type of business.

NOTES

1. Paul L. Pleiffer, *Retailing,* Small Business Bibliography No. 10 Washington, D.C.: U.S. Small Business Administration, 1975), p. 2.

2. Bert C. McCammon, Jr., ''Perspectives for Distribution Programming,'' in Louis Bucklin, ed., *Vertical Marketing Systems* (Glenview, Ill.: Scott, Foresman and Company, 1970), pp. 48–49.

3. ''Horatio Hamburger and the Golden Arches,'' *Business Week,* April 12, 1976, p. 14; see also, ''There's More to Fast Food Than Big Mac and Chicken,'' *Fortune* (March 1977), pp. 213–19.

4. Shelby D. Hunt, ''The Socioeconomic Consequences of the Franchise System of Distribution,'' *The Journal of Marketing,* vol. 36 (July 1972), p. 33.

DISCUSSION QUESTIONS

1. What are the three major types of marketing systems today?

2. Why should you think about working for someone else for a while before beginning your own business?

3. Why are the risks of business ownership so high today?

4. What are the major causes of business failure?

5. Discuss the three forms of business ownership and the strengths and weaknesses of each form.

6. What are the types of assistance which usually are available to you as part of an administered marketing system?

7. What is the difference between a wholesaler-sponsored voluntary and a retailer-sponsored voluntary?

8. What are the different types of franchises available to you?

PROJECTS

1. Visit a wholesale, retail, or consumer cooperative and find out why the cooperative was developed and the products it carries. Visit a manufacturer's outlet, a franchise operation, and a conventional retailer. Compare and contrast the operations of these three types of stores. Look at such things as product offerings, pricing policies, design and layout, and customer services offered.

2. Franchising is one of several types of marketing systems. In your local area select one franchise type (for example fast food) and interview several different franchisees. Compare the franchises on such bases as: training programs for franchisees, financing required, and fixtures and equipment provided.

Minicase 4–1 Several years ago Suzanne Kramer opened Accessories Unlimited, a shop dealing with shoes, handbags, belts, and other accessories. Since then she has expanded twice. She was very successful at selling but found buying and inventory control tedious and boring. Wampum, a national manufacturer of turquoise jewelry contacted her about becoming their exclusive outlet in the city. In return they agreed to perform financing, inventory control, and advertising functions for her. This arrangement worked well until a large department store chain built an outlet in the same city. It too carried Wampum's products. All of a sudden Suzanne was no longer pleased with the agreement. Why not? What problems are connected with agreements such as this between small, independent merchants and nationwide manufacturers which provide such a vast array of services?

Minicase 4–2 The Fashion Shop began as a high-fashion specialty store. After a period of time and as the manager, Jo Ann Thompson, acquired experience in the field and grew in confidence, she added more lines. Jo Ann also decided to expand selling space and leased the store next to the Fashion Shop. But soon afterward Jo Ann found that she could no longer control all of the operations herself. About this time she met another woman, Mrs. Merit, who had a noncompetitive specialty operation. Mrs. Merit suggested that Jo Ann let her do Jo Ann's buying and handle Jo Ann's credit operations, saying that this would free Jo Ann to spend most of her time with her customers. Jo Ann was excited about the suggestion and accepted it. After a while, however, Jo Ann began to feel that Mrs. Merit was running her business.

What should Jo Ann do?

APPENDIX	### Checklist for Going into Business*

You want to own and manage your own business? It's a good idea—provided you know what it takes and have what it takes.

Starting a business is risky at best. But your chances of making it go will be better if you understand the problems you'll meet and work out as many of them as you can before you start.

Here are some questions to help you think through what you need to know and do. Check each question if the answer is "yes." Where the answer is "no," you have some work to do.

BEFORE YOU START

How about you?

Are you the kind of person who can get a business started and make it go? (Before you answer this question, use Work Sheet 1.) _____

Think about *why* you want to own your own business. Do you want to badly enough to keep you working long hours without knowing how much money you'll end up with? _____

Have you worked in a business like the one you want to start? _____

Have you worked for someone else as a foreman or manager? _____

Have you had any business training in school? _____

Have you saved any money? _____

How about the money?

Do you know how much money you will need to get your business started? (Use Work Sheets 2 and 3 on pages 73 and 76 to figure this out.) _____

Have you counted up how much money of your own you can put into the business? _____

Do you know how much credit you can get from your suppliers—the people you will buy from? _____

Do you know where you can borrow the rest of the money you need to start your business? _____

Have you figured out what net income per year you expect to get from the business? Count your salary and your profit on the money you put into the business. _____

Can you live on less than this so that you can use some of it to help your business grow? _____

Have you talked to a banker about your plans? _____

* Source: U.S. Small Business Administration, *Checklist for Going into Business* Small Marketers Aid No. 71, (Washington, D.C.: U.S. Government Printing Office, September 1977).

How about a partner?   If you need a partner with money or know-how that you don't have, do you know someone who will fit—someone you can get along with?   _____

Do you know the good and bad points about going it alone, having a partner, and incorporating your business?   _____

Have you talked to a lawyer about it?   _____

How about your customers?   Do most businesses in your community seem to be doing well?   _____

Have you tried to find out whether stores like the one you want to open are doing well in your community and in the rest of the country?   _____

Do you know what kind of people will want to buy what you plan to sell?   _____

Do people like that live in the area where you want to open your store?   _____

Do they need a store like yours?   _____

If not, have you thought about opening a different kind of store or going to another neighborhood?   _____

GETTING STARTED

Your building   Have you found a good building for your store?   _____

Will you have enough room when your business gets bigger?   _____

Can you fix the building the way you want it without spending too much money?   _____

Can people get to it easily from parking spaces, bus stops, or their homes?   _____

Have you had a lawyer check the lease and zoning?   _____

Equipment and supplies   Do you know just what equipment and supplies you need and how much they will cost? (Work Sheet 3 and the lists you made for it should show this.)   _____

Can you save money by buying secondhand equipment?   _____

Your merchandise   Have you decided what things you will sell?   _____

Do you know how much or how many of each you will buy to open your store with?   _____

Have you found suppliers who will sell you what you need at a good price?   _____

Have you compared the prices and credit terms of different suppliers?   _____

Your records   Have you planned a system of records that will keep track of your income and expenses, what you owe other people, and what other people owe you?   _____

Have you worked out a way to keep track of your inventory so that you will always have enough on hand for your customers but not more than you can sell?   _____

Have you figured out how to keep your payroll records and take care of tax reports and payments?   _____

Do you know what financial statements you should prepare? _____

Do you know how to use these financial statements? _____

Do you know an accountant who will help you with your records and financial statements? _____

Your store and the law

Do you know what licenses and permits you need? _____

Do you know what business laws you have to obey? _____

Do you know a lawyer you can go to for advice and for help with legal papers? _____

Protecting your store

Have you made plans for protecting your store against thefts of all kinds—shoplifting, robbery, burglary, employee stealing? _____

Have you talked with an insurance agent about what kinds of insurance you need? _____

Buying a business someone else has started

Have you made a list of what you like and don't like about buying a business someone else has started? _____

Are you sure you know the real reason why the owner wants to sell his business? _____

Have you compared the cost of buying the business with the cost of starting a new business? _____

Is the stock up to date and in good condition? _____

Is the building in good condition? _____

Will the owner of the building transfer the lease to you? _____

Have you talked with other businessmen in the area to see what they think of the business? _____

Have you talked with the company's suppliers? _____

Have you talked with a lawyer about it? _____

MAKING IT GO

Advertising

Have you decided how you will advertise? (Newspapers—posters—handbills—radio—by mail?) _____

Do you know where to get help with your ads? _____

Have you watched what other stores do to get people to buy? _____

The prices you charge

Do you know how to figure what you should charge for each item you sell? _____

Do you know what other stores like yours charge? _____

Buying

Do you have a plan for finding out what your customers want? _____

Will your plan for keeping track of your inventory tell you when it is time to order more and how much to order? _____

Do you plan to buy most of your stock from a few suppliers rather than a little from many, so that those you buy from will want to help you succeed? _____

Selling

Have you decided whether you will have salesclerks or self-service? _____

Do you know how to get customers to buy? _____

Have you thought about why you like to buy from some salesmen while others turn you off? _____

Your employees

If you need to hire someone to help you, do you know where to look? _____

Do you know what kind of person you need? _____

Do you know how much to pay? _____

Do you have a plan for training your employees? _____

Credit for your customers

Have you decided whether to let your customers buy on credit? _____

Do you know the good and bad points about joining a creditcard plan? _____

Can you tell a deadbeat from a good credit customer? _____

A FEW EXTRA QUESTIONS

Have you figured out whether you could make more money working for someone else? _____

Does your family go along with your plan to start a business of your own? _____

Do you know where to find out about new ideas and new products? _____

Do you have a work plan for yourself and your employees? _____

Have you gone to the nearest Small Business Administration office for help with your plans? _____

If you have answered all these questions carefully, you've done some hard work and serious thinking. That's good. But you have probably found somethings you still need to know more about or do something about.

Do all you can for yourself, but don't hesitate to ask for help from people who can tell you what you need to know. Remember, running a business takes guts! You've got to be able to decide what you need and then go after it.

Good luck!

WORK SHEET 1

Under each question, check the answer that says what you feel or comes closest to it. Be honest with yourself.

Are you a self-starter?

☐ I do things on my own. Nobody has to tell me to get going.

☐ If someone gets me started, I keep going all right.

☐ Easy does it. I don't put myself out until I have to.

How do you feel about other people?
- ☐ I like people. I can get along with just about anybody.
- ☐ I have plenty of friends—I don't need anyone else.
- ☐ Most people irritate me.

Can you lead others?
- ☐ I can get most people to go along when I start something.
- ☐ I can give the orders if someone tells me what we should do.
- ☐ I let someone else get things moving. Then I go along if I feel like it.

Can you take responsibility?
- ☐ I like to take charge of things and see them through.
- ☐ I'll take over if I have to, but I'd rather let someone else be responsible.
- ☐ There's always some eager beaver around wanting to show how smart he is. I say let him.

How good an organizer are you?
- ☐ I like to have a plan before I start. I'm usually the one to get things lined up when the group wants to do something.
- ☐ I do all right unless things get too confused. Then I quit.
- ☐ You get all set and then something comes along and presents too many problems. So I just take things as they come.

How good a worker are you?
- ☐ I can keep going as long as I need to. I don't mind working hard for something I want.
- ☐ I'll work hard for a while, but when I've had enough, that's it.
- ☐ I can't see that hard work gets you anywhere.

Can you make decisions?
- ☐ I can make up my mind in a hurry if I have to. It usually turns out O.K., too.
- ☐ I can if I have plenty of time. If I have to make up my mind fast, I think later I should have decided the other way.
- ☐ I don't like to be the one who has to decide things.

Can people trust what you say?
- ☐ You bet they can. I don't say things I don't mean.
- ☐ I try to be on the level most of the time, but sometimes I just say what's easiest.
- ☐ Why bother if the other fellow doesn't know the difference?

Can you stick with it?
- ☐ If I make up my mind to do something, I don't let *anything* stop me.
- ☐ I usually finish what I start—if it goes well.
- ☐ If it doesn't go right away, I quit. Why beat your brains out?

How good is your health?

☐   I *never* run down!

☐   I have enough energy for most things I want to do.

☐   I run out of energy sooner than most of my friends seem to.

Now count the checks you made.

How many checks are there beside the *first* answer to each question?   _____

How many checks are there beside the *second* answer to each question?   _____

How many checks are there beside the *third* answer to each question?   _____

If most of your checks are beside the first answers, you probably have what it takes to run a business. If not, you're likely to have more trouble than you can handle by yourself. Better find a partner who is strong on the points you're weak on. If many checks are beside the third answer, not even a good partner will be able to shore you up.

Now go back and answer the first question.

WORK SHEET 2

ESTIMATED MONTHLY EXPENSES

Item	Your estimate of monthly expenses based on sales of $_____ per year Column 1	Your estimate of how much cash you need to start your business (See column 3.) Column 2	What to put in column 2 (These figures are typical for one kind of business. You will have to decide how many months to allow for in your business.) Column 3
Salary of owner-manager	$	$	2 times column 1
All other salaries and wages			3 times column 1
Rent			3 times column 1
Advertising			3 times column 1
Delivery expense			3 times column 1
Supplies			3 times column 1
Telephone and telegraph			3 times column 1
Other utilities			3 times column 1
Insurance			Payment required by insurance company
Taxes, including Social Security			4 times column 1
Interest			3 times column 1
Maintenance			3 times column 1

Item		Column 2	Notes
Legal and other professional fees			3 times column 1
Miscellaneous			3 times column 1
STARTING COSTS YOU ONLY HAVE TO PAY ONCE			Leave column 2 blank
Fixtures and equipment			Fill in worksheet 3 and put the total here
Decorating and remodeling			Talk it over with a contractor
Installation of fixtures and equipment			Talk to suppliers from who you buy these
Starting inventory			Suppliers will probably help you estimate this
Deposits with public utilities			Find out from utilities companies
Legal and other professional fees			Lawyer, accountant, and so on
Licenses and permits			Find out from city offices what you have to have
Advertising and promotion for opening			Estimate what you'll use
Accounts receivable			What you need to buy more stock until credit customers pay
Cash			For unexpected expenses or losses, special purchases, etc.
Other			Make a separate list and enter total
TOTAL ESTIMATED CASH YOU NEED TO START WITH	$		Add up all the numbers in column 2

WORK SHEET 3

LIST OF FURNITURE, FIXTURES, AND EQUIPMENT

Leave out or add items to suit your business. Use separate sheets to list exactly what you need for each of the items below.	If you plan to pay cash in full, enter the full amount below and in the last column.	If you are going to pay by installments, fill out the columns below. Enter in the last column your down payment plus at least one installment.			Estimate of the cash you need for furniture, fixtures, and equipment
		Price	Down payment	Amount of each installment	
	$	$	$	$	$
Counters	$	$	$	$	$
Storage shelves, cabinets					
Display stands, shelves, tables					
Cash register					
Safe					
Window display fixtures					
Special lighting					
Outside sign					
Delivery equipment if needed					
Total Furniture, Fixtures, and Equipment (Enter this figure also in Work Sheet 2 under "Starting Costs You Only Have to Pay Once".)					$

5

HOW DO YOU MAKE
LOCATION DECISIONS?

This chapter helps you to do the following things:

- Understand the strategies available to you in retail location decisions.
- Select a community in which to locate your store.
- Decide between a downtown, a shopping center, or a stand alone location.
- Choose a specific store site.
- Decide whether to build, lease, or buy a firm.
- Understand the following terms:

Market saturation   Central business district
Market penetration   Trading area analysis
Secondary markets   Market potential analysis
Neighborhood shopping centers   Site evaluation
Regional shopping centers   Rental agreements
Community shopping centers

Why worry about location? The location decision is so important because (1) opening a business costs a lot of money, (2) you are committed to the location for a long period of time, even with a lease, (3) competition is getting tougher and a good location is one way to beat the competition, and (4) problems such as inflation, high interest rates and tough zoning laws are making good locations harder to find.

Simply estimating possible sales is not enough in the location decision. You also have to pay attention to the types of customers who are candidates for your merchandise, prospects for future growth in the trading area, the life-styles of your customers, and the probable future competition.

MANAGEMENT STRATEGY DECISIONS

Above all, always think in terms of the best opportunities for growth of your outlet when deciding on a philosophy of location for your organization. Retail location decisions have both a strategy dimension and an operating dimension. Three primary strategic location possibilities seem best today: (1) geographic concentration, (2) market saturation, and (3) emphasis on smaller towns and communities.[1] These strategic decisions are important even in opening your first outlet because they indicate the path to the greatest amount of growth for your firm over the years.

After deciding on one of these three overall guiding routes to follow, several other more mechanical decisions need to be made, namely: (1) selection of the specific community in which you want to locate, (2) defining the trading area for your outlet, and (3) selecting the best site.

Let's look briefly at the strategy alternatives in location and then look at the simpler decisions to be made.

Geographic concentration

Advantages.   You may decide to stay in one region, say the Southeast, and become the strongest retailer in the region for your type of outlet. The *advantages* of such a decision include:

1. Lower costs of distribution because you can ship merchandise to all of your stores from one central warehouse.
2. Economies of scale in advertising.
3. Easier supervision of personnel.
4. The ability to better know the needs of your customers.
5. The company probably can build a better reputation in the area.

Increasingly, firms are limiting their investments to such areas as the Sun-belt which have a strong long-term growth potential, a sound base of industry, a pleasant climate, and often less energy problems than other regions of the nation.

Examples of geographic concentration abound.   Let's look at a few of them.

Handy Dan, a division of Daylin, "All new units will be located in existing market areas, expanding the company's clustering store concept which provides optimum utilization of advertising and merchandising resources while maximizing customer awareness and response."[2]

Montgomery Ward in announcing its five-year plans indicated that it planned to open 90 to 100 units, concentrating on major markets now served by the retailer where earnings can benefit most by enlarging market share.[3]

Scotty's, a chain of home improvement centers, expresses this view of location as follows: Why enter a new market when that will mean new advertising campaigns and in some cases higher distribution costs?[4]

Some firms in recent years have withdrawn from certain regions of the country in order to better concentrate on their strengths. For example, *Kroger* closed its midwestern stores so as to concentrate all of the stores in a 200-mile radius of Atlanta and "reduce transportation costs, provide quick management response to problems and dominate its market area."[5]

The same strategy was followed by the *Jack Eckerd Company* in closing its Denver stores. The Denver stores had problems with distribution, no name recognition, and undesirable locations. The company felt that it would get a better return on its money by staying in the more familiar Southeast region.[6]

Market saturation

This strategy is similar to regional dominance. But here dominance is limited to a metropolitan market. The *advantages* include: (1) economies in advertising, (2) simpler distribution problems, and (3) ease of employee supervision.

A single store, even of a national chain, in a large market area will have a tough time getting name recognition and drawing customers. Sometimes it may take five to ten stores to make an investment in a large city pay off. Firms such as Kmart are well known for building and opening several stores in a community at the same time to get needed market share.

WHY ARE SMALLER COMMUNITIES SO POPULAR?

Why are smaller communities so popular in location decisions today? Local regulations make it hard to build, and the cost of building in large cities is high. Competition is also tougher. The 300 largest areas are now served by at least one of the nations 11 largest merchants. Sears, Kmart, and Penneys alone can reach more than 70 percent of the population through their locations.[7]

In the face of these problems and the fierce competition, secondary markets, or communities of 50,000–200,000, are becoming very popular. These are often known as "midmarket" towns. Such areas are growing faster than the major cities. Why? The reasons for fast growth of such areas are because:

1. Tough national competition is less in these communities.
2. They often welcome a new business.
3. Quality of life is higher as viewed by many people.

4. Wage rates are less.
5. Union problems are easier to deal with.
6. The market is more similar overall than in large cities.

Even towns of 10,000 and under are experiencing a revival in retailing. Consider the following examples of small town location:

Walmart: the firm opens big discount stores in small towns where they then become the dominant retailer in their surrounding rural trade areas of 25,000–30,000 people each.[8]

Dollar General Stores (operators of 800 stores in 22 states and selling irregulars and closeouts): "Dollar General has its typical 4,000-square-foot store in a community of 10,000 population or less. . . ."[9]

Kuhns Big K follows a similar strategy of locating in smaller communities. Even *Kmart* is experimenting with smaller stores which it locates in communities of 10,000 or less persons.

Other possibilities exist in guiding location decisions. But the point is that management decides early on their location needs in relation to their merchandising philosophy. Such a decision quickly narrows the location decision and makes the rest of the job easier.

Now, let's turn to the choice of a community since we are assuming that guidelines as to the type of community in which to locate have been agreed on.

WHAT IS TRADING AREA ANALYSIS?

Trading area analysis means (1) deciding on where to locate your outlet, (2) finding out how far people will travel to shop at your store, and (3) finding out how much business you can do at the site you select. Trading area analysis begins with the evaluation of alternative communities which meet management guidelines for investment.

You need to consider such factors as: (1) size and composition of the population; (2) labor availability; (3) closeness to source of supply; (4) opportunities for a good promotional mix; (5) the type of jobs available in the community; (6) existing and probable future competition; (7) availability of store sites, and (8) local, state, and federal regulations.[10] These are highlighted in Table 5–1.

Population composition is often a key in choosing a community. For example, you need to study the number of people in the area, their education, their income, their ages, family composition, and probable future growth of the area.

Labor availability can be a problem. Management talent is most readily available in larger areas but is more expensive, as is clerical help. But in smaller communities, management talent may not be locally available and may not want to move to the area. Clerical labor is not likely to be a problem. Wage rates are also likely to be lower.

TABLE 5-1
Major factors to consider in evaluating a community

Population size and characteristics
Total size
Age distribution
Average educational level
Percent of residents owning homes
Total disposable income
Per capita disposable income
Occupation distribution
Trends

Availability of labor
Management
Management trainee $\qquad$ analysis of:
Clerical

    a. High school and college graduates
    b. Out-migration of graduates
    c. Average wages in the area versus average wages in the United States

Closeness to source of supply
Delivery costs
Time
Number of manufacturers and wholesalers
Availability and reliability

Promotion
Availability and frequency of media
Costs
Waste

Economic base
Dominant industry
Extent of diversification
Growth projections
Freedom from economic and seasonal
    fluctuations
Availability of credit and financial facilities

Competitive situation
Number and size of existing competitors
Evaluation of strengths and weaknesses for
    all competitors
Short-run and long-run outlook
Level of saturation

Availability of store location
Number and type of locations
Access to transportation
Owning versus leasing opportunities
Zoning restrictions
Costs

Regulations
Taxes
Licensing
Operations
Minimum wages
Zoning

    Source: Barry Berman and Joel R. Evans, *Retail Management: A Strategic Approach* (New York: Macmillan Co., 1979), p.202.

Distribution problems include how long will it take to get deliveries of merchandise to the store, the frequency of delivery service to the community, and the reliability of merchandise delivery.

The promotion issue centers around the availability of a variety of media such as newspapers, radio stations, and television coverage. Also, you need to make sure that good production facilities are available to help you develop your commercials.

The types of industries in the area are also important. Large manufacturing plants with highly skilled workers who are paid union wage rates provide a better market potential than small plants with unskilled labor and low wages. On the other hand, large unionized firms are more subject to strikes which can hurt retail sales.

Employment in service organizations such as hospitals and government offices provide more stable employment but lower wage rates. Seek a community with a variety of different types of employment. Also seek one with a history of growth and a community which is aggressive in seeking new industry. Be careful about locating in a community with a history of labor problems or which is losing population.

Pay attention to competition. Who are the firms you will likely compete with? Are any national firms located in the market? How long have they been in the market? What has been the turnover of the firms? Can the market support you without taking away business from competition?

Are decent sites available? Does the community already have several types of shopping centers with vacancies? If you usually locate downtown, does the downtown area look "alive?" Are there plans to revitalize downtown? Is land available at reasonable prices for purchasing a site if you are going to build a stand alone location?

Finally, do not overlook regulations. Is the land on which you want to build zoned properly? What are the chances of getting it rezoned? Will you have trouble getting a business license to operate and how much will it cost? Will you be able to open on Sundays if you want to do so? Can you use an existing building without violating any local regulations?

Now, suppose you have decided on a community.

HOW DO YOU CHOOSE A LOCATION WITHIN A COMMUNITY?

First, decide on whether you want to be located downtown, in a shopping center, or in a stand alone location. Even if you decide to go into a shopping center you can choose between a neighborhood center, a community center, or a regional center. Table 5–2 shows the strengths and weaknesses of a central business district location versus shopping center locations and the characteristics of each of these types of locations.

What are the features of shopping centers?

Each of the three shopping center types may be planned or unplanned. *Unplanned shopping centers* occur when stores are built over time and the

TABLE 5-2
Strengths and weaknesses of selected location alternatives

Type of location	Typical location characteristics	Location strengths	Location weaknesses
Central business district	Variations defy categorization. Almost every type of merchandise is sold and customers are drawn from the entire metropolitan area. Serves as a cultural and entertainment center as well as shopping area.	Drawing power of a flagship department store Mass transit connections Availability of urban redevelopment funds The city as a work/cultural center creates store traffic	Suburban shift Lack of parking Shopping hours Outmoded facilities Consumer fears regarding urban crime
Neighborhood shopping center	Typically a strip center with from 5 to 15 stores with around 50,000 square feet of area, with emphasis on convenience goods, and a trading area of about five minutes driving time.	Ease of shopping Customer reliance on convenience Relatively low costs	Applicable to only a few types of tenants Susceptible to newer centers in better locations
Community shopping center	Usually a strip of L-shaped center with 15 to 50 stores and 100,000 to 300,000 square feet of space. Both convenience and shopping goods are sold and the trading area extends to about ten minutes driving time.	Very low rent charges Ease of shopping	Many such centers are old and deteriorating Poor tenant mix High vacancy rate
Regional shopping center	New centers are almost exclusively malls with 50 to 250 stores and 400,000 to 2 million square feet of space. Predominately shopping and specialty goods are carried, and trading areas stretch to 30 minutes driving time and beyond.	Parking availability Large number of stores Attractive facilities	Excessive size of new centers High rental costs, from $6 to $15 per foot for specialty stores, $2 for anchor tenants

Source: Albert D. Bates, *Retailing and its environment* (New York: D. Van Nostrand 1979). © 1979 by Litton Educational Publishing Inc. Reprinted by permission of D. Van Nostrand Company.

center is not planned for the overall good of all tenants. Downtown shopping districts are also unplanned locations.

A *planned shopping center* is owned by a single organization which owns the buildings and leases them to different retailers. Planned shopping centers usually have one or more large anchor tenants (usually a large department store) and many smaller stores. The developers exercise control over (1) the types of establishments in the center, (2) architectural plans, and (3) parking and similar aspects of the center. They seek a *balanced tenancy*. This simply means that they want the types and number of stores in the center which can meet all of the shopping needs of the population in the trading area. They don't want six men's shoe stores and no drugstore, for example.

What are shopping center strengths and weaknesses?

The *strengths* of shopping centers, especially malls, are:

1. Balanced tenant mix.
2. Common store hours.
3. Centerwide promotions.
4. Controlled climate.
5. Few parking problems.
6. Longer store hours.
7. Pleasant environment for attracting shoppers.

Small shopping center stores can take advantage of the traffic drawing ability of large mass merchandisers. Often, people will shop in the small shops even though they came to the shopping center primarily to shop at the large mass merchandisers.

But shopping centers also have *weaknesses*. The primary problems center around what you as a merchant can and cannot do. Specifically, you probably will face restrictions on (1) what you can sell, (2) restrictions on store hours, (3) you may find that the policies of the center may be dictated by the large anchor tenant(s), and (4) your rent will be higher than in an isolated location.

What about a central business district location?

Central business district (downtown) locations offer several *advantages,* namely:

1. Rents will be lower than shopping centers in many cities.
2. Public transportation may be available to downtown.
3. The locations are usually close to large office complexes which employ many people.
4. You probably can remodel an older building for less than you can build.

But, downtown locations also present *problems.* Namely:

1. Parking is a problem.

2. The stores do not have common hours nor a planned and balanced mix of stores.
3. Safety is a problem—for example, in crossing streets.
4. Downtown stores are often not open at night.
5. Crime is often higher.
6. Traffic congestion is bad.
7. Downtown areas are often decaying and run down.

Consider a stand alone location

Finally, you may want to go into a freestanding location. Often discount houses such as Kmart follow the strategy of a stand alone location.

Stand alone locations on heavily traveled streets have several *advantages*, including:

1. The lack of close competition.
2. Lower rent.
3. More space for parking and expansion.
4. Greater flexibility in store hours and other methods of operation.

But, *disadvantages* also exist with this type of location. For example:

1. Stores in these locations often have difficulty attracting consumers because no comparison shopping is possible.
2. Advertising costs are often higher than if you were in a shopping center with other stores which would advertise together.
3. You probably will have to build a store rather than rent one.

The most successful stores in stand alone locations are those with a strong national reputation and a wide assortment of merchandise from which consumers can choose.

Let's assume for now that you have decided on the type of location. How do you go about choosing a site?

"Stand alone" location strategy

Courtesy The Jewel Companies, Inc.

HOW DO YOU MEASURE A TRADING AREA?

Techniques for measuring a trading area range from a simple "seat of the pants" approach to fancy mathematical models. Many retailers still think that they can simply drive by several sites and then decide how far customers will travel to reach the outlet.

Some stores watch what the "big boys" are doing and then follow them. For example, specialty outlets such as County Seat, Jeans & Things, and similar specialty apparel outlets look at the shopping centers where mass merchandisers such as Sears, Wards, or Penneys are locating and follow them into the same centers. They rightly figure that these outlets have done their homework and know they can draw customers from a long distance away.

The mass merchandisers often use high-powered mathematical models which are beyond the focus of this text. All of their models however usually include measures of time and distance in the formulas used.

You can also choose among a series of subjective but useful ways of measuring your trading area. Let's look at some of these ways and see how they can help you in your location decisions.

Study your existing stores

Retailers with existing stores have an advantage over a person seeking to open an outlet for the first time. The experienced retailers can use information which they have obtained about their existing stores in making decisions about a planned new store. If the new store is basically like the old one in terms of size, merchandise offered, and trading area characteristics, you can expect it to follow a pattern similar to that of the existing stores. But make sure that the stores are alike in all key respects.

License plate analysis

One of the more common methods for existing stores is that of automobile license plate analysis. You determine the address from public records of the vehicles in the parking lot of your stores or one similar to the one you plan to open. By plotting these locations on a map, you can get a feel for the general nature of the store trading area. This information can be used in planning for additional stores.

Check clearance

Check clearance data can also be used to determine where customers are coming from. You have to assume that the distribution of cash customers and charge customers is basically the same. The approach is most often used to determine the percentages of trade which is being attracted from surrounding areas.

Credit records

Credit records can also be analyzed as a way of determining the trading area of an existing store. A sample of charge accounts is selected and customer addresses are plotted on a map. This approach will only work if you keep your own credit records.

Customer survey

Probably the best way to determine the trading area for an existing store is to conduct or sponsor a customer survey. The survey can be done with a mailed questionnaire, a telephone interview, or a personal interview. Each of these ways has its good and bad points, as shown in Table 5–3. The interviews can be conducted at the store if they are personal interviews. A sample of respondents can be chosen from customer records and called on the phone or mailed a questionnaire. You may also be able to participate in a survey sponsored by the local chamber of commerce or a similar organization.

The customer survey will give you information on where people shop for items like you offer. For example, if you interview your own customers you can plot their addresses on a map to measure your own trading area. Also, you can do a survey of noncustomers and draw trading areas for your competitors. You probably should draw circles for one, two, and five miles away from your firm to see how far most of your customers travel to shop with you. If this is your first store, plot the information for an outlet as nearly like yours as possible. The results will give you an idea of what to expect.

A customer survey can give you other useful information as well. Such information might include, (1) *demographic data* (age, occupation, number of children), (2) *general shopping habits* (type of store preferred, how often consumers shop, area of town preferred), (3) *purchasing patterns* (who does the buying), and (4) *media habits* (radio, TV, and newspaper habits). A typical questionnaire is shown in Table 5–4 and might be used to get information in helping to start a women's shoe store.

HOW MUCH BUSINESS CAN BE DONE IN THE TRADING AREA?

You need five sets of data to help you estimate the amount of sales you may be able to obtain: (1) number of people in your defined trading area, (2) average household income, (3) amount of money spent each year by the households on the type of goods sold by your firm—i.e., groceries, drugs or apparel, (4) the total market potential available, and (5) the share of the total market potential you can expect to get.

The *number of people* in your trading area can be obtained from U.S. Census data in almost any public library. The data are reported by census

TABLE 5–3
Strengths of the three survey methods

	Criterion	Mail	Telephone	Personal
1.	Ability to handle complex questionnaires	Poor	Good	Excellent
2.	Ability to collect large amounts of data	Good	Fair	Excellent
3.	Accuracy of the resultant data	Good	Fair	Fair
4.	Control of interviewer effects	Excellent	Fair	Poor
5.	Time required	Poor	Excellent	Fair
6.	Probable response rate	Fair	Fair	Fair
7.	Cost	Good	Good	Poor

Source: Donald Tull and Del I. Hawkins, *Marketing Research* (New York: Macmillan Company, 1976), p. 388.

TABLE 5-4

Name of Interviewer_____   Address of Respondent_____

Name of Respondent_____   Sex of Respondent: (1)M_____ ;   (2)F_____

Good morning/afternoon/evening. I would like to speak to the youngest female member of the family who is over 18 years of age. I'm _____ with Marketing Research Associates. We are working with a local business which wants to do a better job of meeting your needs. I would like about five minutes of your time to ask you a few questions. Thank you.

General Shopping Habits

1. How frequently do you shop for shoes for yourself?
   a. Once every 3–4 months_____ ;   b. Once every 5–9 months_____ ;
   c. Once a year_____ ;   d. Once every 3–5 years_____ .

2. Please tell me the type of store at which you prefer to shop for the following types of shoes:

	Department store (1)	Boutique (2)	"Traditional" shoe store (3)
a. Dress shoes	_____	_____	_____
b. Casual shoes	_____	_____	_____
c. Evening shoes	_____	_____	_____
d. Sports shoes	_____	_____	_____

3. Do you normally shop (1) downtown_____ ; (2) shopping center_____ ?

Purchasing Behavior

4. How often do you shop out of town for shoes?
   (1) Never_____ ; (2) Every 3–4 months_____ ; (3) Every 5–9 months_____ ;
   (4) Once a year_____ ; (5) Less than once a year_____ .

5. Which of the following factors are most important to you in deciding where to shop for shoes?
   (1) Price_____ ; (2) Brands carried_____ ; (3) Quality of sales personnel_____ ;
   (4) Wide selection of styles and sizes_____ .

Media Habits

6. What is your favorite radio station? (1) WNPT_____ ; (2) WTBC_____ ;
   (3) WACT_____

7. Which daily paper do you usually read?_____

8. What TV stations do you normally view?
   (1) WCFT_____ ; (2) WAPI_____ ; (3) WBRC_____

Demographic profile

We are almost finished, but I would like to know a little about the people to whom I have talked.

9. Would you please tell me your age? (1) 18–24_____ ; (2) 25–34_____ ;
   (3) 35–44_____ ; (4) 45–54_____ ; (5) 55–64_____ ; (6) 65 or over_____

10. What is your approximate annual household income? (1) Under $10,000_____ ;
    (2) $10,000–$15,000_____ ; (3) $15,001–$25,000_____ ; (4) $25,001–$35,000_____ ;
    (5) Over $35,000_____

11. Are you a (1) White American_____ ; (2) Black American_____
    Thank you for your time.

tracts (small areas with 4,000–9,000 people) for all cities of 50,000 or more population. County data are reported in the *Sales Management Survey of Buying Power.*

The *average household income* in each census tract is published by the U.S. Bureau of the Census. The *Sales Management Survey of Buying Power* also reports this data for each county and large city in the United States.

The *amount of money spent each year* on the goods you sell can be found in several places. Data published by the U.S. Department of Labor is probably the best source. Table 5–5 shows an example of such data.

You now multiply the average annual household income by the number of people in your trading area to get *total sales potential.* Next, multiply total sales potential by the percentage of the average annual household income spent on the type of goods you will sell, for example groceries, to get total sales potential for the type of goods you will sell. You then add up sales potential for each tract to get total sales potential for the type of goods you plan to sell.

Now decide how much of the available sales potential you can get. Begin by plotting competitors in the trading area on a map and try to figure out the sales levels of each one. Use such indicators as number of checkouts, number of employees, square footage, and the like in figuring out their sales. Last, decide on how much business you need in order to make a profit. Now, you must make a decision on whether and how you can take the business away from competition. Figure 5–1 shows this five-step process.

Retail saturation

The idea of retail saturation can help you. If your trading area is not already filled with competing stores you have a better chance of success. You can make the calculations as follows:

$$IRS_1 = \frac{C_1 = RE_1}{RF_1}$$

Where:

IRS_1 = Index of retail saturation for area one.
C_1 = Number of consumers in area one.
RE_1 = Retail expenditures per consumer in area one.
RF_1 = Retail facilities in area one.

The data for the formula are readily available to you. Published census data can tell you how many potential customers are within your trading area. The Bureau of Labor Statistics expenditure data referred to above tells you how much each household with a certain income level spends yearly on the goods in which you are interested. The number of competitors within the trading area can be determined by counting them.

TABLE 5-5
Selected family characteristics, annual expenditures, and sources of income classified by family income before taxes
(all families with head 55-64 years)

	Family income before taxes						
	Complete reporting of income						
Item	$8,000 to $9,999	$10,000 to $11,999	$12,000 to $14,999	$15,000 to $19,999	$20,000 to $24,999	$25,000 and over	Incomplete income reporting
Current consumption expenses, excluding personal insurance, gifts and contributions							
Average annual expenditure	$6,357.76	$7,018.90	$8,106.24	$9,519.78	$11,669.81	$15,372.48	$9,606.51
Percent reporting	100.0	100.0	100.0	100.0	100.0	100.0	100.0
Food, total							
Average annual expenditure	$1,529.73	$1,718.98	$1,847.33	$2,081.63	$2,420.09	$2,850.37	$1,992.90
Percent reporting	100.0	100.0	100.0	100.0	99.5	100.0	98.5
Food at home							
Average annual expenditure	$1,256.42	$1,396.18	$1,468.41	$1,575.07	$1,818.55	$1,953.80	$1,503.39
Percent reporting	99.3	99.7	100.0	99.5	99.5	99.4	97.1
Food away from home, excluding trips							
Average annual expenditure	$250.24	$302.90	$365.48	$495.38	$585.48	$867.59	$463.67
Percent reporting	88.9	92.8	95.8	96.4	97.2	99.7	87.8
Meals as pay							
Average annual expenditure	$23.07	$19.90	$13.44	$11.18	$16.06	$28.98	$25.84
Percent reporting	8.7	9.9	7.1	5.4	9.1	8.3	7.5
Alcoholic beverages							
Average annual expenditure	$52.68	$58.44	$66.40	$86.96	$119.53	$150.93	$69.12
Percent reporting	51.9	60.4	66.3	70.2	77.0	87.8	58.4
Tobacco products							
Average annual expenditure	$144.27	$142.96	$145.50	$167.12	$174.52	$148.13	$145.69
Percent reporting	63.2	56.9	61.0	63.1	63.8	55.3	52.6
Housing, total							
Average annual expenditure	$1,751.25	$1,891.56	$2,072.77	$2,431.81	$2,963.08	$4,199.66	$2,672.10
Percent reporting	99.6	100.0	100.0	100.0	100.0	100.0	100.0
Shelter, total							
Average annual expenditure	$837.83	$987.32	$993.61	$1,154.39	$ 1,496.27	$ 2,129.68	$1,378.98
Percent reporting	97.2	100.0	99.5	98.9	99.6	99.6	96.5
Rented dwellings							
Average annual expenditure	$298.65	$338.31	$284.04	$287.88	$319.10	$363.58	$349.11
Percent reporting	24.5	22.7	16.7	14.7	14.3	11.0	19.8
Owned dwellings							
Average annual expenditure	$527.85	$644.92	$691.11	$820.27	$1,084.13	$1,669.65	$981.71
Percent reporting	75.3	80.3	85.1	86.4	88.6	92.6	78.4
Other lodging, excluding trips							
Average annual expenditure	$11.34	$4.09	$18.46	$46.23	$93.04	$96.45	$48.16
Percent reporting	7.7	3.5	8.5	13.1	18.5	22.6	11.6

Source: U.S. Department of Labor, Bureau of Labor Statistics, *Consumer Expenditure Survey Series: Interview Survey, 1972-73*, Bulletin 1985 (Washington, D.C.: U.S. Government Printing Office, 1978), p. 284.

FIGURE 5-1
Example of the method used to estimate the annual sales for a supermarket from one census tract located in the store's retail trading area

	A		B		C		D
Factor:	Number of households in a census tract in the retail trading area	×	Median annual income of the households in the census tract	×	Proportion of a household's annual income spent on items sold by the store	×	Proportion of money spent on that item that will be spent in the store	=	Revenue (sales) obtained from all households in the census tract by the proposed store
Method:	1,000 households	×	$3,000 per year	×	0.15*	×	0.50†	=	$225,000 per year

* The proportion of 0.15 means that 15 percent of the typical household's annual income of $3,000 is spent on groceries and meats.
† The proportion of 0.50 means that you believe that 50 percent of the groceries and meats purchased by all households living in this census tract will be from your proposed supermarket.

Source: William Rudelius. Robert F. Hoel. and Roger Kerin. "Assessing Retail Opportunities in Low-Income Areas," *Journal of Retailing*, vol. 48, no. 3 (Fall 1972). p. 106.

Consider the following example in analyzing supermarket potential in Market A:

The 10,000 consumers in Market A spend an average of $5.50 per week in food stores. There are 15 supermarkets serving Market A with a total of 144,000 square feet of selling area.

$$\text{IRS} = \frac{100,000 \times 5.50}{144,000} = \frac{550,000}{144,000} = \$3.82$$

The $3.82 per square foot of selling area measured against the dollars per square feet necessary to break even would provide the measure of saturation in Market A. The $3.82 figure would also be useful in evaluating relative opportunity in different market areas.[11]

HOW DO YOU GO ABOUT SITE EVALUATION?

In addition to choosing carefully the community and the general area in the community in which you want to locate, also be careful in selecting the exact site.

Site selection requires that you consider many factors, including the amount of automobile traffic, pedestrian traffic, and in some instances, public transportation. Also, look for a buffer against undesirable features such as noise. Evaluate the chances for future expansion, the adequacy of parking, and the physical characteristics of the land. Also, utilities and zoning are important. A checklist for such factors is shown in Table 5–6.

Let's now consider the special problems you face in going into a shopping center.

Restrictions on locating in a shopping center

Until recently, shopping center developers and the large stores were able to keep independent stores almost totally at their mercy if they wanted to locate in a shopping center. However, the Federal Trade Commission has ruled that shopping center developers and large tenants cannot unfairly limit what the smaller stores can sell, their advertising policy, the hours and days they are open for business, the expansion of their stores, and merchants association membership.

Even so, independent firms without a record of success are likely to have a hard time getting into a large shopping center. They are often viewed as a rent-loss hazard to developers.

Rental agreements

Rental agreements are also important in deciding whether you can afford a location in a shopping center. Rents may be on a flat dollar basis or a percentage of sales. The more successful the record of a store in drawing traffic to a location, the lower the percentage rent which is likely to be paid. Other guidelines are as follows:

1. As the gross leasable area increases, the percent rent decreases.
2. As the sales per square foot increases, the percent rent decreases.
3. As the profit margin increases, the percent rent increases.
4. As the shopping center size increases, the percent rent increases.[12]

TABLE 5-6
Checklist for site selection

	Rating			
	Excellent	Good	Fair	Poor

I. Trading area potential
    A. Public utility connections (residential) . . . .
    B. Residential building permits issued . . . .
    C. School enrollment . . . .
    D. New bank accounts opened . . . .
    E. Advertising linage in local newspapers . . . .
    F. Retail sales volume . . . .
    G. Sales tax receipts . . . .
    H. Employment—specific . . . .
    I. Employment—general . . . .

II. Accessibility
    A. Public transportation (serving site) . . . .
    B. Private transportation (serving site) . . . .
    C. Parking facilities . . . .
    D. Long-range trends (transportation facilities) . . . .

III. Growth potential
    A. Zoning pattern . . . .
    B. Zoning changes . . . .
    C. Zoning potential . . . .
    D. Utilities trend . . . .
    E. Vacant-land market (land zoned for residential use) . . . .
    F. Land use pattern (in areas zoned for other than residential . . . .
    G. Retail—business land use trend . . . .
    H. Retail—building trend (building permits issued for new retail business construction) . . .
    I. Retail—improvement trend (permits issued for remodeling expansion,
        etc., in existing properties) . . . .
    J. Retail—location trend (changes in occupancy of retail-business locations) . . . .
    K. Income trend for average family unit . . . .
    L. Plant and equipment expenditure trend . . . .
    M. Payroll trend . . . .

IV. Business interception
    A. Location pattern—competitive businesses between site and trade area . . . .
    B. Location pattern—competitive businesses between site and trade area (served by
        and sharing traffic arteries with site) . . . .

Source: Adapted from Richard Nelson, *The Selection of Retail Locations* (New York: F. W. Dodge Corporation, 1958), pp. 349–50.

Examples of rent averages for selected types of retail outlets are shown in Table 5–7.

SHOULD YOU BUILD, LEASE, OR BUY?

No right answer exists to the question of build, lease, or buy. If you build or buy, costs such as rent are eliminated. On the other hand, you may decide not to tie up working capital in a building but try to keep money working for you in other ways.

TABLE 5-7
Tenants most frequently found in super regional shopping centers

Tenant classification	Rank	Median GLA (sq. ft.)	Median sales volume per square foot GLA	Median total rent per square foot GLA
General merchandise:				
Department store (unknown)	11	173,064		$ 0.55
Food:				
Candy and nuts	15	750	$149.41	15.43
Food service:				
Restaurant without liquor	20	2,855	110.28	7.12
Restaurant with liquor	17	4,518	104.15	8.08
Fast-food/carryout	8	1,099	127.25	12.00
Ice cream parlor	18	850	133.96	11.35
Clothing:				
Ladies specialty	5	1,672	105.27	8.00
Ladies ready-to-wear	1	3,840	102.47	6.11
Menswear	2	3,158	103.73	7.00
Family wear	13	4,394	127.15	7.50
Unisex/jean shop	10	1,997	141.14	9.50
Shoes:				
Family shoes	3	3,377	101.94	7.56
Ladies shoes	7	2,915	94.51	7.99
Men's and boys' shoes	9	1,418	123.68	11.67
Home appliances music:				
Radio, TV, hi-fi	16	2,367	160.21	7.46
Gifts/Specialty:				
Imports	19	1,444	79.94	8.55
Cards and gifts	6	2,412	89.91	8.34
Books and stationery	12	3,707	103.12	8.00
Jewelry and Cosmetics:				
Jewelry	4	1,924	189.65	11.29
Offices:				
Medical and dental	14	899		5.67

Source: Urban Land Institute, *Dollars and Cents of Shopping Centers,* Washington, D.C.: Urban Land Institute 1978.

Building or buying, however, gives you the advantage of seeing your investment go up in value. Also, you are able to make whatever changes you want in the structure without worrying about getting the approval of the landlord. To build, buy, or lease simply depends upon your own situation. The advantages and disadvantages of each alternative are outlined in Table 5-8.

SUMMARY

Location is a key in the retailing mix. You should consider it as carefully as your pricing, promotion, and other policies such as store hours. Additionally, you need to understand the behavior of consumers and the information sources they rely on in shopping. To the extent that consumers are less

TABLE 5-8
Major characteristics of build, lease, and buy alternatives

Alternative	Advantages	Disadvantages
A. Buy a lot and build a facility upon it	1. Ownership 2. Flexibility in operations 3. New facilities 4. Constant mortgage payments 5. Appreciation of land value	1. High initial costs 2. Construction time 3. Lack of good available sites 4. Long-run commitment 5. Zoning problems
B. Leasing	1. Low initial costs 2. Quick occupancy 3. Good locations 4. Reduced long-run commitments 5. Limited zoning problems	1. Nonrenewal problems 2. Increased leasing terms 3. Inflexibility of operations 4. Age of facilities 5. Difficulties in resale of business
C. Buying an existing facility	1. Ownership 2. Flexibility in operations 3. Quick occupancy 4. Good locations 5. Limited zoning problems 6. Constant mortgage payments 7. Appreciation of land value	1. High initial costs 2. Long-run commitment 3. Adaptability of fixtures, etc. 4. Age of facility

Source: Barry Berman and Joel R. Evans, *Retail Management* (New York: Macmillan Company, 1979), p. 242.

inclined to physically search for most types of merchandise or that gas is too high to make shopping worthwhile, location is more important than ever.

The factors which influence retail location are dynamic and interacting. These forces, for example, have led to the decline of downtown areas as the most desirable retail location for many types of outlets. Likewise, suburban locations have increased in popularity. However, with the increased price of gasoline, central locations like downtown areas perhaps will be increasingly popular in the future. Regardless, many retailers appear to be willing to pay high rental costs to locate in a shopping center. They recognize that consumers try to keep the costs of shopping low by doing as much business as possible in a single location.

NOTES

1. Albert Bates, *Retailing and Its Environment* (New York: D. Van Nostrand Company, 1979), pp. 90–91.

2. "Daylin Outlets Go A-Clustering," *Chain Store Age Executive* (August 1978), p. 88.

3. "Ward Sticking Close to Home," *Chain Store Age Executive* (August 1978), p. 82.

4. "Home Centers: Slow But Steady Growth," *Chain Store Age Executive* (August 1978), p. 85.

5. "Kroger: Less Is Much Better," *Chain Store Age Executive* (August 1978), p. 55.

6. "No Rocky Mountain 'High' for Eckerd," *Chain Store Age Executive* (August 1978), p. 10.

7. "J. C. Penney's Fashion Gamble," *Business Week,* January 16, 1978, p. 68.

8. *Forbes,* December 1, 1977, p. 45.

9. "Growing Big in the Country," *Chain Store Age Executive* (January 1978), p. 60.

10. Barry Berman and Joel P. Evans, *Retail Management* (New York: Macmillan Company, 1979), p. 202.

11. Bernard LaLonde, "The Logistics of Retail Location," in William D. Stevens, ed., *1961 Fall American Marketing Association Proceedings,* Chicago: American Marketing Association, p. 572.

12. Robert L. Fitts and Bixby Cooper, "An Empirical Examination of Retail Rental Costs," in Barnett Greenberg, ed., *Proceedings,* Southern Marketing Association, 1974, p. 185.

DISCUSSION QUESTIONS

1. What are the factors which have led to the decline of downtown areas as desirable locations for many retail outlets? What can be done to overcome these problems?

2. What factors have caused shopping centers to be so popular with consumers? What are the likely effects of high gasoline prices on where consumers will shop?

3. What do you consider to be the important factors in selecting a site for a fast-food outlet? How do these contrast, if at all, with your notion of the key factors for the location of an outlet selling stereo components?

4. What factors can justify the retailer paying a higher rent for location in a shopping center than in a non-shopping center location?

5. Why is an outlet such as Kmart typically not located in a shopping center?

6. What are the advantages of following a policy of regional or city dominance in store location?

7. What factors make the Sunbelt a popular area for retailers to open new stores?

8. Why are some retailers turning to smaller communities in looking for new sites?

9. What are the key factors to consider in selecting a community in which to open a new retail outlet?

10. What can downtown areas do to better compete with the surburban shopping centers?

PROJECTS

1. Select a medium to large mall. Make a license plate survey of the cars on the lot (noting only the county and state symbols on the license plates) at three different times of the day as follows: midmorning; midafternoon; and evening. Make an analysis of your findings including such things as percentage analysis of the county by county license plates and do a map plotting. Compare and contrast the results of your finding for the three different times of the day.

2. Devise a questionnaire to obtain the following information:

   a. Shopping center frequented most.
   b. Distance traveled to the shopping center.
   c. Number of visits per week/month.
   d. Items usually purchased at this shopping center.
   e. Factors most liked about the shopping center.
   f. Dominant reason for shopping there.
   g. Opinion about the prices of merchandise.
   h. Opinion about the quality of merchandise.
   i. Opinion about selection of merchandise.
   j. Opinion about salespeople.
   k. Opinion about the convenience of location (open-end question).

l. Amount spent here on the average per week/month.

Expand this questionnaire to obtain similar information about the shopping center frequented second most.

Using the data obtained from your questionnaire, do an analysis to isolate the factors which determine the choice of shopping centers. Which factors are the most important? Which are the least important? Are greater dollar amounts spent at the shopping center visited most frequently? What meaning does this have for the retailer? What are the similarities and differences in the reasons given for the shopping center visited most and second most?

3. A topic of interest in many cities is the future of the central business district (CBD). If you are in a city which has gone through a downtown revitalization program, arrange to have interviews with the public servants (and volunteers) who were responsible for getting the project "going." Describe it; indicate the views of success; and indicate future directions. If you are not in such a situation, search the current literature for examples of cities which have done downtown revitalization jobs. Contact the chambers of commerce for information and indicate some of the national efforts along these lines.

4. Prepare a location and site analysis for a good quality cafeteria (other types of service retailer or tangible goods establishments may be used) for your local community based on the information in the text. Assume that the cafeteria is a regional chain with excellent regional recognition and acceptance but that it is not in your community. Prices are higher than "fast-food" outlets but lower than "service restaurants" of comparable quality food.

Minicase 5-1   The Mayfair Department store, located in a city of about 1 million people, added 300,000 square feet to its existing facility. The expansion was to the

firm's downtown, largest location. To get to the expansion property, Mayfair had to agree to lease part of the first floor addition to an existing drugstore outlet of a regional chain. The other part of the main floor was available for lease to another retail outlet. The size of the remaining space was approximately 40 feet frontage by 75 feet deep. The space available is the 100 percent location for shopping goods in the city. Speculate as to who should be interested in the available site. Consider such factors as rent paying capacity, and advertising expenditures necessary in 100 percent locations.

Minicase 5-2   Gorman's, a local department store in a medium-sized city, operates a number of branches. The first, opened in 1965 with a 25-year lease, is the smallest store. It is a part of a strip of high fashion stores located in the highest income area of the city. Within five minutes' driving time is the largest Gorman's. It is located in a fashion mall opened in 1980 with a long-term lease. Ten minutes' driving time in the other direction from the smallest store is another Gorman's branch. This store is also located in a mall but was opened in 1980 with a long-term lease. The area surrounding this mall is a blue-collar neighborhood.

Why does Gorman's have stores so close together? Aren't they competing with themselves? What do you predict will happen to these three branches over the next ten years?

Minicase 5-3

Taylors is a locally owned medium-priced women's clothing outlet in the downtown area of a city of 65,000 people. The downtown is like so many other downtowns today. Namely, few national merchants are located downtown and a number of store vacancies exist. The downtown area looks old and worn. But the Downtown Merchants Association is making a strong effort to revitalize the area. A large number of persons still work downtown in such places as banks, attorneys' offices, and local, state, and federal government offices.

Mr. Taylor opened a branch in a regional shopping center of the community about ten years ago. Recently a ground breaking was held for a 600,000-square-foot regional mall to be opened within two years. Major tenants include Sears, Penneys, and two popular regional department stores. Penneys is giving up its downtown location to go into the mall. Sears is giving up an older strip location to do likewise.

Mr. Taylor is confronted with a problem. He sees his competitors moving to the new mall. He has also talked to the leasing agent and knows that a large number of nationally known women's specialty shops will be in the mall. He is hesitant to go into the mall because rent will be high and he has a ten-year lease remaining on his downtown location. On the other hand, he fears a major loss of customers to the mall.

He has called in a consultant to help him think through the situation. Assume that you are the consultant. Outline for Mr. Taylor the advantages and disadvantages of remaining where he is. Assuming that he remains downtown, what are some of the recommendations which you might make to help him minimize the effects of the new mall on his business?

6

HOW TO PLAN YOUR STORE

This chapter is concerned with store planning and its purpose is to help you understand that subject by explaining:

- The meaning of store image and the closely related idea of atmosphere.
- How store layout affects atmosphere.
- What must be considered in layout planning.
- How you allocate total store space to various activities.
- The types of layout arrangements.
- What factors you consider in locating departments.
- Some suggestions for departmental display.
- The meaning of the following terms:

Store planning	Grid (gridiron) layout
Store design	Free flow layout
Store layout	Sales productivity method of allocating space
Modernization	Buildup method of allocating space
Atmosphere	Impulse merchandise
Image	Demand merchandise
Departments	

Look back at Figure I–1, "The Student's Guide to Retailing." Part I of our text focused on the following things (labeled A) useful to you as a retailer:

1. What retailing is like today.
2. How to understand the consumer.
3. How to start your own business.
4. How to make location decisions.

Let's now plan your store. Specifically the purposes of this chapter are to:

1. Help you understand the meaning of store planning, design, modernization, and layout.
2. Help you focus on the key things to consider in these activities.
3. Show you how store planning can be used as a sales tool in the retail mix.

KEY IDEAS

Think of your store as being planned to give you high levels of sales by helping customers to buy. But first you need to understand some key terms.

Store planning refers to exterior and interior building design, location of departments, and allocation of space to departments.[1]

Store design means planning the style of a store. The style or character tells the market what the store is all about. But you must first understand your consumer (or target market) and how your design should be a part of your retail strategy. Then you can plan your fixtures, windows, lighting, color, and store entrance requirements with confidence.[2]

Store layout means planning the arrangement of the store's departments, both selling and sales supporting, and deciding on the amount of space for each department. Think of the departments in relation to each other and to the building itself when doing your planning.

We also mentioned earlier that from time to time you need to check the "health" of your business. Thus, *modernization* may be a response to one of your checks. You may need to bring the store (or some parts of it) up to date to keep up with a competitor, or perhaps get ahead of it.

Figure 6–1 shows the relationships among the things you should consider as you plan your store. Store planning, design, layout, and modernization are

FIGURE 6–1
The store planning process

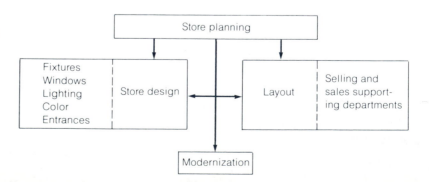

highly technical matters. Even a very large retail company calls in outside help in planning large jobs. Trying to handle your own design activities will cost you a bundle in the long run. Most retailers do not have the skills for such activities. They also don't know how to make their work meet the local building codes. Help is available to you from merchandise suppliers; local store planners and architects; engineers; and equipment firms.

Atmosphere and image

Think of store layout as part of a good marketing plan. Store planning (in the broadest sense) and design are really jobs for a different kind of expert. Remember, however, that store design (which is hard to separate from the layout of the store) affects store image. The image is the way in which consumers in your market think of your store. Image is the result of the blending of all of the items in the retailing mix (see Chapter 1). One of the most important factors in image is the atmosphere of your store. *Atmosphere* means the physical characteristics of the store that are used to help develop an image and to draw customers.[3]

Store design and layout greatly affect image. Figure 6–2 separates *atmosphere* into each of its elements and gives a brief summary of each element. The information in the figure highlights the role of store design and layout as a merchandising tool in developing image.

STORE LAYOUT

Layout is probably the most important part of atmospherics in creating desired effects on customers. Layout affects customer movement in the store. It also allows you to show merchandise as attractively as possible.

Macy's converted a dingy bargain basement into "The Cellar"—a modernization miracle creating a shopping street of food and items for the home

Courtesy Macy's

FIGURE 6–2
Elements that make up a store's atmosphere—Image related to design and layout

I. *Exterior store design factors which affect atmosphere-image*
    A. Storefront—The total physical exterior of the store; includes:
        1. Marquee—Sign used to display store name.
        2. Entrances—Must decide:
            a. Number of entrances.
            b. Types of entrances; e.g., regular doorway, revolving, open front, air curtain.
            c. Walkways; e.g., wide or narrow (affect image).
        3. Display windows—Must decide:
            a. Number and size.
            b. Shape (closed or open backs).
            c. Color.
            d. Theme and changes per year.
            e. Whether to have *any* (especially in shopping centers).
    B. Height and size of exterior building—Project a great deal about a store; e.g., a boutique "feels" small.
    C. Visibility—A store must be seen and the way the storefront, height, and size elements are handled, will contribute to total visibility.
    D. Uniqueness—Result perhaps from the way the prior elements are carried out.
    E. Surrounding stores and area—Attempt to be different, but must blend with neighbors and the general area.
    F. Parking—Adequate parking is a plus; inadequate parking detracts from total image.
    G. Congestion and crowding—In parking lot, walkways, and entrances likely to diminish positive atmosphere.

II. *Interior design factors which affect atmosphere-image*
    A. Flooring—The material from which floors are constructed affect image (vinyl in supermarkets).
    B. Colors and lighting—The psychedelic flashing colored lights in a disco-style junior department.
    C. Sounds—Disco music in the same department to create a feeling.
    D. Scents—Perfume scents in a cosmetics department.
    E. Fixtures—Chrome and glass for mod look; rustic woods for casual shop.
    F. Wall textures—Embossed texture for high fashion; barren walls for warehouse grocery store.
    G. Temperature—Mood of shopper affected.
    H. Width of aisles—Affect comfort and movement.
    I. Dressing rooms—The prestige of the store can be affected by how these are handled.
    J. Vertical transportation—The type of store atmosphere desired can be affected by the way customers are moved between floors.

III. *Store layout affects atmosphere-image*

Source: Much of this material is based on Barry Berman and Joel R. Evans, *Retail Management—A Strategic Approach* (New York: The Macmillan Company, 1979), pp. 398–407.

What are the things you must consider in layout planning? The following steps can guide you:

1. Allocate total store space to selling and sales-supporting activities.
2. Classify goods by department.
3. Shape customer flow to your advantage by your arrangements.
4. Allocate space to selling and sales-supporting areas.
5. Locate selling and sales-supporting activities within the store.
6. Decide on displays within the department.

**Allocation of
total store space**

Let's assume a superstore of 40,000 square feet. What things have to be done in that space, or what activities are carried out in *any* store?

1. *Selling* activities take place—merchandise is displayed; clerks move about and customers move their carts down aisles; produce is weighed, etc.
2. *Merchandise* which is not in refrigerated cases, shelves, meat coolers, etc. is *stored* in a stockroom or storage area.
3. Store *employees* must have certain space for personal needs; e.g., rest rooms, lunch area; executives need office space.
4. In some stores, *customers* need their own space other than aisles (e.g., in an apparel store, fitting rooms, lounges, etc.); in a superstore (a large store selling food and nonfood items together) customers need little space outside of aisles for movement.
5. Other *sales-supporting services* space—in a superstore, service area for check OKing, information; checkout stands; cart storage; etc. (Some authorities call *sales supporting* by the term *nonselling*—we like the positive sound of the former.)

Thus, your first task in layout planning is to decide how much space will go to each of the activities just noted. Management can use its experience with existing stores in allocating space. If you are involved in a single, new store, then the problem is tough. Our later discussions in this chapter will give you some guidelines to help in the decision.

As a general rule, except for specialty retailers, devote as much space to the sales area as possible. For example, mass merchandisers such as Kmart do *not* (1) try to develop a prestige image through wide aisles, (2) have only a few items on display to avoid a crowding effect, and (3) have large customer service areas. Instead, they try to have as much merchandise on display as possible. Their image is thus affected by their layout as much as by the other elements of store design (see Figure 6–2).

**Classification of
merchandise into
departments**

Place merchandise in the store *by* groupings or departments. The department as a planning unit is useful in planning for: (1) personnel requirements; (2) merchandising needs; (3) promotional efforts; and (4) accounting (e.g., allocating expenses).

In a superstore (our example here), consider the following possible groupings of merchandise. Figure out the bases for the arrangements.

1. Canned groceries (e.g., fruits, vegetables, juices). These are generic groupings—the goods *naturally* fit together.
2. Frozen foods (including vegetables, desserts, etc.). Grouping based on the need for refrigeration and *special handling* needs.
3. The deli department. Based on *customers motives* or preferences in

Private Lives—A department concept for up-scale bedroom items

Courtesy Macy's

purchasing, customers prefer a precooked meal on the way home perhaps.

4. The *gourmet* department or dietetic foods department. Based on serving a *target group* of customers, in these cases "prestige" and "diet concerns," respectively.

The second question is "how many departments should you have?" No "right" answer exists to this question. But trade associations can be helpful in this regard. A good rule of thumb is that you do not want so many departments that the cost of organizing them is greater than the benefits you get from having them.

What are the types of layout arrangements?

The two extremes in layout arrangement are (1) the grid or gridiron (straight) and the (2) free flow (or curving) patterns. The most common is the *grid*. Here counters and fixtures are at right angles to each other as on a football field (see Figure 6–3). Our superstore typically uses this arrangement. This arrangement is for store efficiency rather than customer convenience. The layout hinders free movement. Customer flow is guided by the layout of aisles and fixtures rather than demand for merchandise. In Figure 6–3, for example, 80–90 percent of all customers shopping in a supermarket with a

FIGURE 6-3
The grid layout

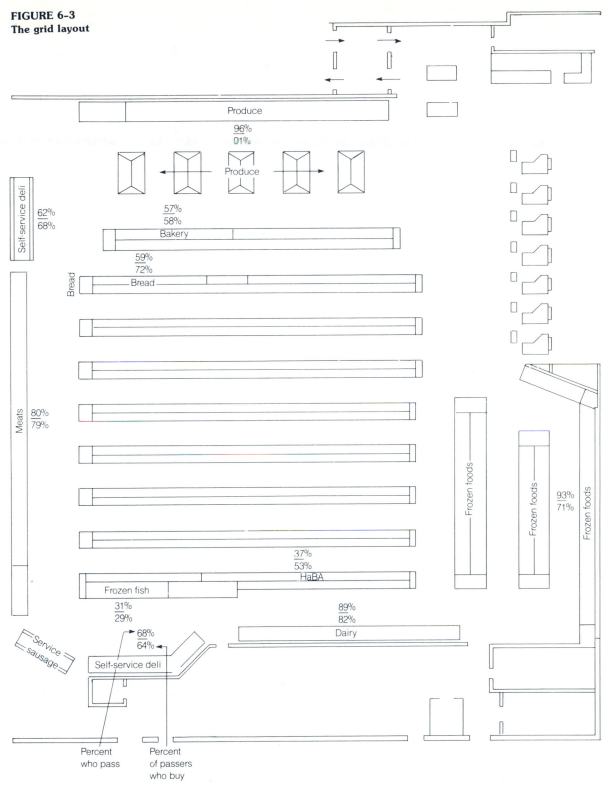

Source: "How Major Departments Pull Traffic through the Store," *Progressive Grocer*, January 1976, p. 72.

grid layout pass the produce, meat, and dairy counters. Fewer shoppers pass other displays because the grid forces the customers to the sides and back of the supermarket.

Figure 6–4 shows another example of a superstore. This one is a Jewel Grand Bazaar located in Chicago. The floor plan indicated in Figure 6–4 is actually prepared for customer convenience in the store. You can see that the floor plan of the store indicates the location by aisle of various major categories of merchandise. Then the listing of items in Figure 6–4A is an alphabetical list of items for the customer to use. Suppose a person wants to locate furniture polish. It is quickly apparent from the item list that this category is located on aisle 12.

The particular store which is represented in the figures is a combination grocery, drug, and general merchandise superstore. The layout plan and list of items, however, only include the grocery categories. The layout is classic grid with some freestanding categories such as a sausage shop, a floral center, and a fresh (scratch) bakery. It is interesting to note that this particular store has an impressive amount of space devoted to generics (no brand names). They had in April 1980, 139 generic items in stock. Note also on the alphabetical listing of items that *generic products* receive clear identification. Note that the entrance to the store is directly in front of the generic counters. Movement through the store is from aisle to aisle—classic grid movement— except for special-purpose shopping trips. Customers, for example, who want to visit only the bakery, will head in that direction. Passing the generic products counters may well cause an impulse purchase.

This Grand Bazaar store is comprised of 63,000 square feet (38,700 square feet of grocery lines and 24,300 in the Osco Drug section which includes the general merchandise). Figure 6–5 shows a floor plan of a combination store of 57,800 square feet (38,700 food and 19,100 Osco) with another classic grid design.

In department stores like Sears and departmentalized specialty stores like Lord & Taylor, the grid arrangement on the main floor usually forces traffic down the main aisles. Shoppers are thus more likely to ignore items along the walls. As a result, highly demanded merchandise (shopping goods) is placed along the walls and convenience goods in main parts of the store. Customer traffic is thus drawn to what could otherwise be slow-moving areas.

The *free flow pattern* is planned for customer convenience and exposure to merchandise. Free flow design lets customers move in just about any direction at their own speed. But space is less efficiently used in this type of layout.

Figures 6–6 and 6–7 are typical layouts for a department store unit in a national chain. These layouts show the most common layouts for first and second floors. The layouts are a combination of the grid and the free flow arrangements. As you can see, such shops as contemporary fashions and conservative fashions on the first floor bring together complete offerings in one department. You do not have to go to different departments for, say, shoes, suits, and similar goods. These merchandise groupings are called *boutique arrangements*. The customer with a certain lifestyle can shop in one location for all related items.

How do you allocate space?

Dividing total space between selling and sales-supporting areas is hard to do. Store design and layout affect your decisions. Let us assume that your best judgment indicates about 90 percent of your 40,000- (or 36,000) square foot superstore will be used for selling. Keep in mind that selling versus sales-supporting space relationships vary greatly by types and size of store. In a very large department store—over $50 million annual volume—selling space may account for roughly 65 percent of total space. Jewelry stores need almost no sales-supporting space. But a home improvement center may have more space for warehousing and storage than for selling. In general, the larger the store, the greater the percentage of sales-supporting space.

Specifically in our example how do you divide the 36,000 square feet of selling space among the various departments? Let's start with the health and beauty aids (HaBA) department.

You can use three basic methods for space allocation:

1. Use average industry figures by type of merchandise.
2. Sales productivity of product lines.
3. The buildup (or model stock) method.

Average industry figures. Here you find the "average" percentage of selling space that health and beauty aids nationally account for in superstores. Remember that "averages" can only be a guide since each store is different. Let's assume that HaBA account for 4 percent of total selling space as an average. Thus, in a store with 36,000 square feet of selling space, you would set aside 1,440 square feet for this department.

Sales productivity method. Sales productivity is measured by sales per square foot of selling space. Let's assume that the planned sales for HaBA is $144,000. If the average sales per square foot nationally for this department is $100, then you will allocate 1,440 feet to HaBA. ($144,000 ÷ $100).

The buildup or model stock method. Let's continue with our health and beauty aids department to see how this approach works. Go through the following checklist in planning space based on this method. Specifically decide on:

1. The ideal stock balance (*ideal* in terms of the number of items needed to reach your sales goal in the department—in Chapter 11 you will get

FIGURE 6-4

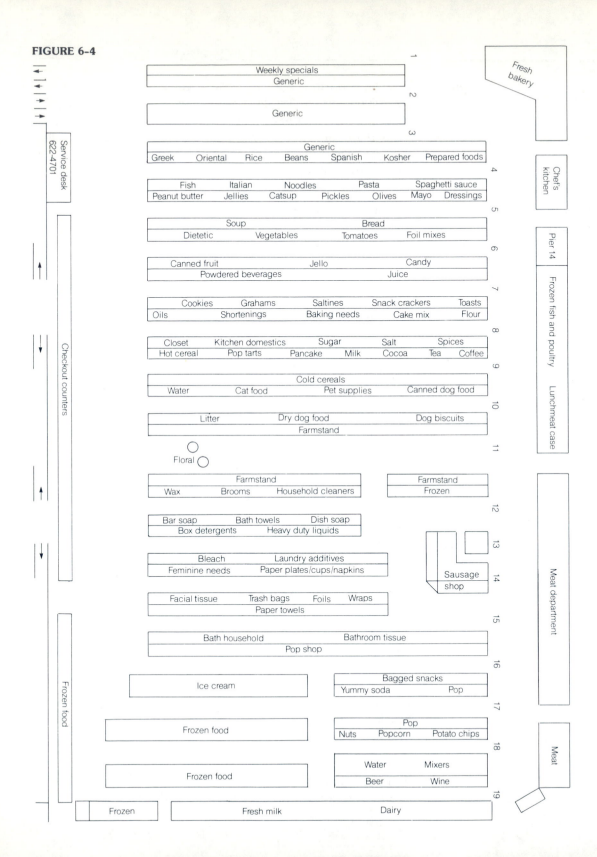

Fresh bakery

Service desk
622-4701

Checkout counters

Frozen food

1

Weekly specials
Generic

2

Generic

3

Generic
Greek — Oriental — Rice — Beans — Spanish — Kosher — Prepared foods

4

Fish — Italian — Noodles — Pasta — Spaghetti sauce
Peanut butter — Jellies — Catsup — Pickles — Olives — Mayo — Dressings

5

Soup — Bread
Dietetic — Vegetables — Tomatoes — Foil mixes

6

Canned fruit — Jello — Candy
Powdered beverages — Juice

7

Cookies — Grahams — Saltines — Snack crackers — Toasts
Oils — Shortenings — Baking needs — Cake mix — Flour

8

Closet — Kitchen domestics — Sugar — Salt — Spices
Hot cereal — Pop tarts — Pancake — Milk — Cocoa — Tea — Coffee

9

Cold cereals
Water — Cat food — Pet supplies — Canned dog food

10

Litter — Dry dog food — Dog biscuits
Farmstand

11

Floral

Farmstand
Wax — Brooms — Household cleaners

Farmstand
Frozen

12

Bar soap — Bath towels — Dish soap
Box detergents — Heavy duty liquids

13

Bleach — Laundry additives
Feminine needs — Paper plates/cups/napkins

14

Facial tissue — Trash bags — Foils — Wraps
Paper towels

Sausage shop

15

Bath household — Bathroom tissue
Pop shop

16

Ice cream

Bagged snacks
Yummy soda — Pop

17

Frozen food

Pop
Nuts — Popcorn — Potato chips

18

Frozen food

Water — Mixers
Beer — Wine

19

Frozen — Fresh milk — Dairy

Chef's kitchen

Pier 14

Frozen fish and poultry — Lunchmeat case

Meat department

Meat

FIGURE 6-4A

Jewel Grand Bazaar
6505 W. Diversey
Chicago, Illinois 60636

Aisle	Item	Aisle	Item	Aisle	Item
12	Air fresheners	14	Garbage bags	4	Rice
14	Aluminum foil	2-3	Generic products		
6	Applesauce	12	Glass cleaners	5	Salad dressings
12	Auto. dish detergent	7	Graham crackers	8	Salt
		6	Gravy mixes (foil)	7	Saltine crackers
5	Bacon bits			14	Sanitary napkins
14	Bags (lunch)	OSCO	Health and beauty aids	12	Scouring pads
14	Bags (trash)	5	Honey	5	Shake & Bake
8	Baking needs	4/5	Hostess cupcakes	8	Shoe polish
12	Bar soap	12	Household cleaners	8	Shortening
5	Bar-B-Que sauce			16	Snacks
15	Bathroom tissue	8	Ice cream cones/toppings	16/17	Soda
4	Beans (dry)	4	Italian food	5	Soup
4	Beans (in sauce)			4	Spaghetti sauce
13	Bleach	5	Jams/jellies	4	Spanish food
5	Bouillon cubes	6	Jello	8	Spices
12	Bowl cleaners	7	Juice (canned)	8	Sponges
5	Bread			14	Straws
5	Bread crumbs	5	Ketchup	5	Stuffing
12	Brooms	7	Kool-Aid	8	Sugar
		4	Kosher foods	9	Syrup (pancake)
6	Candy bars				
8	Cakemate decorating	13	Laundry soap	8	Tablecloths
8	Cake mixes	10	Litter	9	Tea
4	Canned fish			7	Toasts
6	Canned fruit	4	Macaroni	9	Toaster pastries
4	Canned gravy	6	Marshmallows	12	Toilet bowl cleaners
7	Canned juice	12	Matches	15	Toilet tissue
9	Canned milk	5	Mayonnaise	6	Tomatoes
6	Canned vegetables	9	Milk (evaporated)	14	Toothpicks
10	Cat food	9	Milk (powdered)	12	Towels — Bath
5	Catsup	12	Mops	8	Towels — Dish
9	Cereal	6	Mushrooms	15	Towels — Paper
4	Chinese foods	5	Mustard	14	Trashbags
12	Cleanser			4	Tuna fish
9	Cocoa	14	Napkins		
9	Coffee	4	Noodles	6	Vegetables
9	Coffee filters	8	Nuts (baking)	5	Vinegar
7	Cookies	18	Nuts (snack)		
7	Crackers			10	Water
9	Creamer	8	Oils	14	Wax paper
5	Croutons	5	Olives		
4	Cup-O-Noodles	4	Oriental foods		
		12	Oven cleaners		
6	Desserts				
6	Dietetic	9	Pancake mixes		
12	Dish soap	9	Pancake syrups		
10	Distilled water	14	Paper — Cups		
10	Dog food	14	Paper — Plates		
5	Dressings	1	Paper — Towels		
		4	Pasta		
6	Envelope mixes	5	Peanut butter		
8	E-Z Foil	10	Pet food		
		10	Pet supplies		
13	Fabric softeners	5	Pickles		
14	Facial tissue	6	Pimentos		
14	Feminine hygiene	12	Polishes		
4	Fish	16/17	Pop		
12	Floor wax	18	Popcorn		
8	Flour	9	Pop Tarts		
8	Foil bakeware	18	Potato chips		
14	Foil wrap	6	Potatoes (dry)		
6	Fruit (canned)	9	Placemats		
12	Furniture polish	4	Prepared foods		
		6	Pudding		

FIGURE 6-5

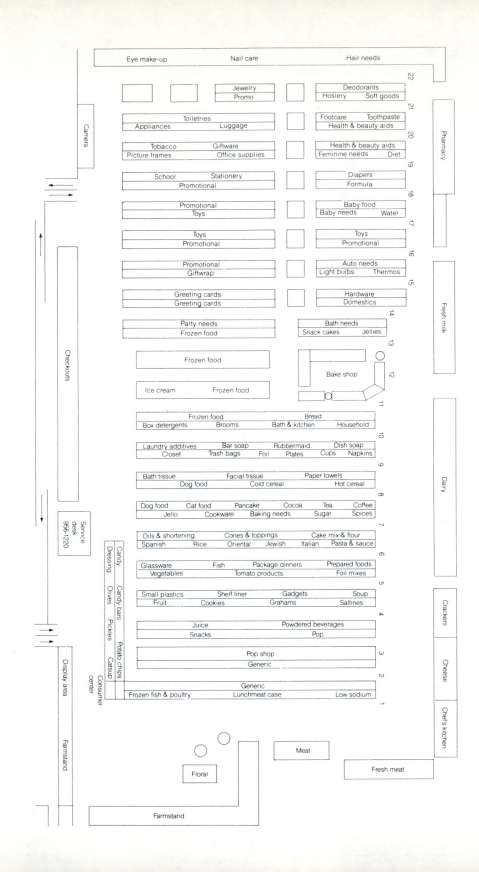

FIGURE 6-5A

Jewel
819 S. Elmhurst Road
Des Plaines. Illinois 60016

Aisle	Item	Aisle	Item	Aisle	Item
10	Air fresheners	10	Fabric softeners	8	Pancake mixes
9	Aluminum foil	21	Face creams	8	Pancake syrups
20	Analgesics	9	Facial tissue	21	Pantyhose
20	Antacids	19	Feminine hygiene	9	Paper — Cups
10	Auto. dish detergent	20	First aid	9	Paper — Plates
16	Automotive needs	6	Fish	9	Paper — Towels
		10	Floor wax	14	Party favors
18	Baby food	7	Flour	6	Pasta
17	Baby powders	7	Foil bakeware	13	Peanut butter
9	Bags (lunch)	9	Foil wrap	19	Pens/pencils
9	Bags (trash bags)	21	Foot preparations	8	Pet food
1	Bake & Fry	21	Footwear	1	Pickles
7	Baking needs	18	Formula	7	Placemats
20	Bandages	4	Fruit (canned)	9	Plastic housewares
1	Bar-B-Que sauce	10	Furniture polish	10	Polishes
10	Bar soap			3	Pop
9	Bathroom tissue	5	Gadgets	8	Pop Tarts
9	Bath towels	9	Garbage bags	3	Potato chips
15	Batteries	10	Glass cleaners	5	Potatoes (dry)
6	Beans (dry)	6	Glassware	6	Prepared foods
6	Beans (in sauce)	4	Graham crackers	6	Pyrexware
7	Birthday candles	5	Gravy mixes		
10	Bleach	15	Greeting cards	21	Razor blades
10	Bowl cleaners			6	Rice
11	Bread	22	Hair coloring	10	Rubbermaid products
1	Bread crumbs	22	Hair spray		
10	Brooms	21	Hand lotions	1	Salad dressings
10	Brushes (household)	15	Hardware	7	Salt
10	Bubble bath	20	Health & beauty aids	4	Saltine crackers
		11	Honey	19	Sanitary napkins
7	Cake mixes	21	Hosiery	19	School supplies
7	Candles			10	Scouring pads
5	Candy	12	Ice cream	20	Sewing notions
6	Canned fish	7	Ice cream cones/toppings	1	Shake & Bake
4	Canned fruit	6	Italian food	22	Shampoos
6	Canned gravy			21	Shaving creams
4	Canned juice	13	Jams & jellies	5	Shelf paper
8	Canned milk	7	Jello	9	Shoe polish
5	Canned vegetables	4	Juice (canned)	7	Shortening
8	Cat food			3	Snacks
1	Catsup	1	Ketchup	3	Soda
8	Cereal	5	Kitchen gadgets	5	Soup
6	Chinese food	4	Kool-Aid	6	Spaghetti sauce
10	Cleaners — Glass	6	Kosher foods	7	Spices
10	Cleaners — Household			10	Sponges
10	Cleaners — Oven	10	Laundry soap	19	Stationery
10	Cleanser	15	Light bulbs	9	Straws
8	Cocoa	FRONT	Litter	1	Stuffing
8	Coffee			7	Sugar
8	Coffee filters	6	Macaroni	8	Syrup (pancake)
20	Cold remedies	5	Marshmallows		
22	Combs	10	Matches	7	Tablecloths
4	Cookies	1	Mayonnaise	8	Tea
22	Cosmetics	7	Metal cookware	1	Toasts
4	Crackers	8	Milk (evaporated)	20	Tobacco
		8	Milk (powdered)	10	Toilet bowl cleaners
21	Dental needs	10	Mops	9	Toilet tissue
22	Deodorants	16	Motor oil	21	Toothpaste
19	Diapers	21	Mouthwash	9	Toothpicks
1	Dietetic	1	Mustard	14	Towels - Bathroom
10	Dish soap			7	Towels - Dish
7	Dish towels	9	Napkins	9	Towels - Paper
8	Dog food	6	Noodles	17	Toys
1	Dressings	7	Nuts (baking)	9	Trashbags
		3	Nuts (snacks)	6	Tuna fish
15	Electrical	21	Nylons		
7	E-Z foil			5	Vegetables
		7	Oils	1	Vinegar
		1	Olives	20	Vitamins
		6	Oriental foods		
		10	Oven cleaners	17	Water
				9	Wax paper

FIGURE 6-6
First-floor layout for a typical department store of a large national chain

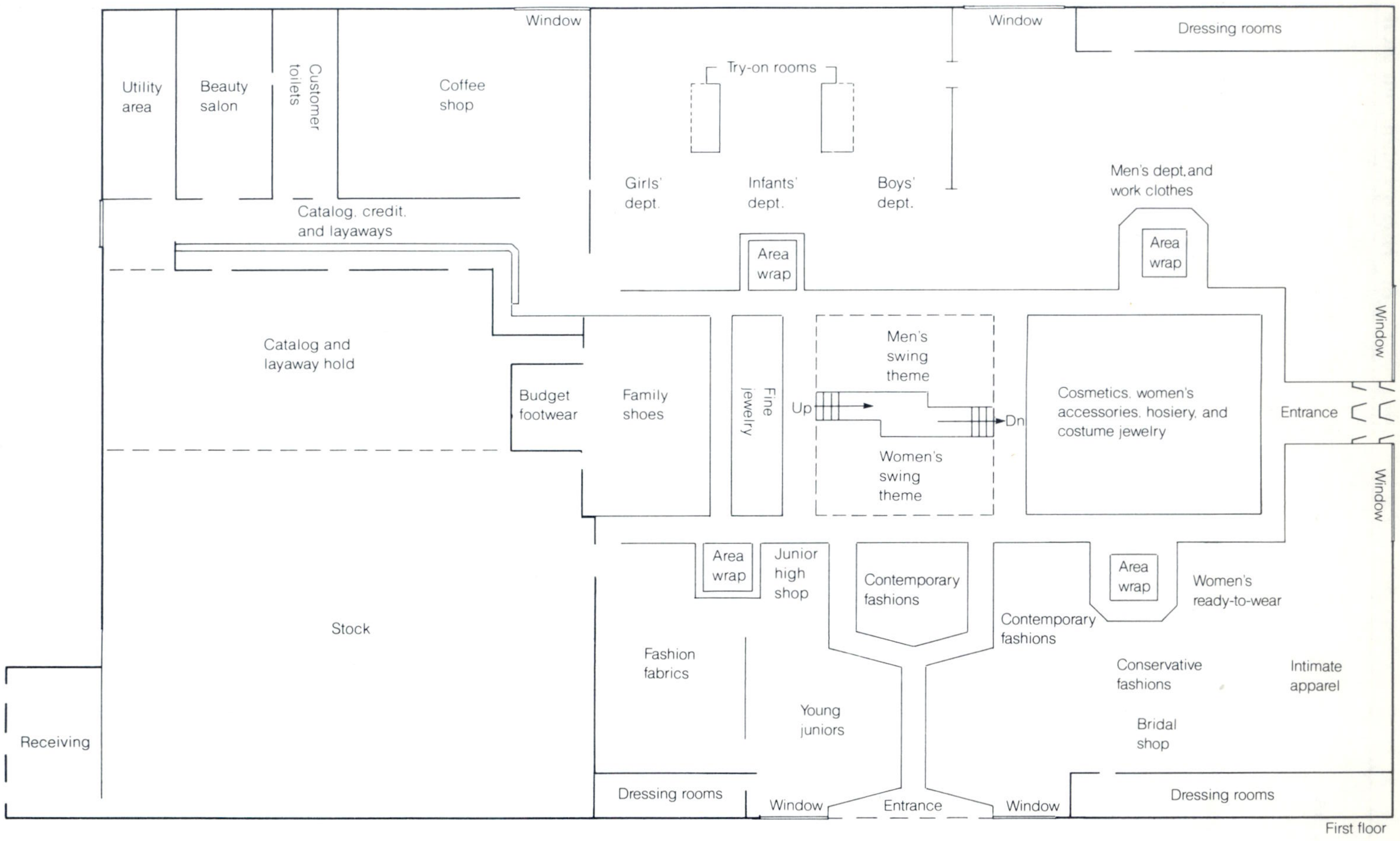

FIGURE 6-7
Second-floor layout for a typical department store of a large national chain

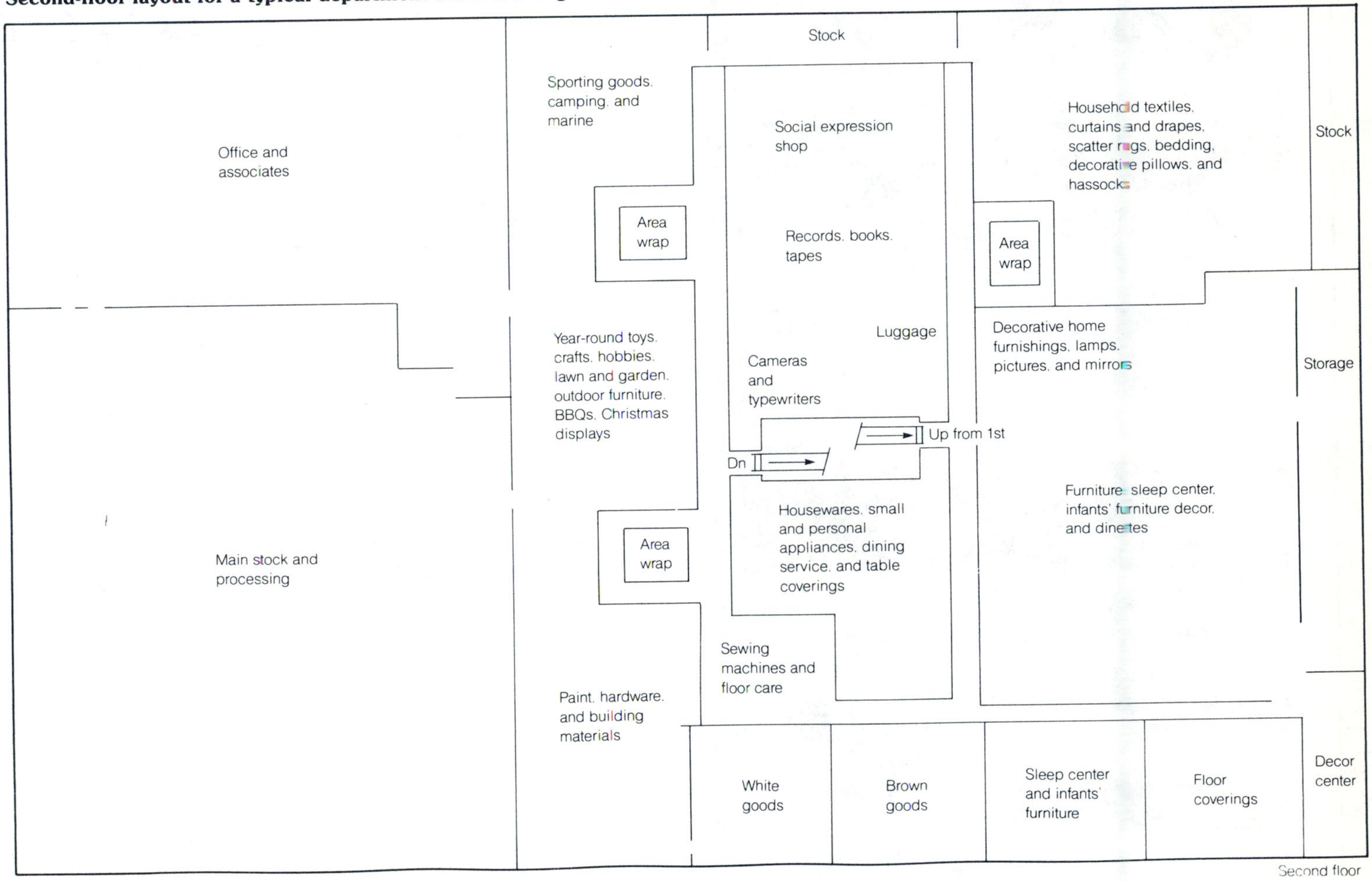

Macy's Herald Square modernized, elegant main floor with classic gridiron layout arrangement

Courtesy Macy's

some help on this issue). Does seasonal variation exist in HaBA? If so, the "peaks and valleys" must be considered in planning for the amount of space needed.

2. How many items (e.g., deodorants, toothpaste tubes, suntan lotion bottles and tubes, and so on) are needed for display. Also, how many should be kept in reserve stocks. Really, 100 percent of all items should be on display. Goods don't sell in storage! But it's probably not possible to have all merchandise displayed.

3. The best method of displaying merchandise. A great deal depends on the types of display equipment available.

4. How many of these "best display fixtures" are needed to display your items. Start by finding out how many units can fit into the fixtures you selected.

5. How you are going to handle reserve stock. Keep as much of reserve stock as possible under the displayed items (or behind, depending on the display fixture). If you need more backup stock than can be stored *on* the selling floor, plan on having space in the backup stockroom. (If you have a local supply source and good delivery, you may not need a remote stock area.)

6. The service needs which are necessary for the departments. In our example, you don't need any. If we're talking about a coffee classification, however, you might need space for coffee grinder.

A main floor using a free flow layout

Courtesy NCR

7.   The total space requirements. Find your total space needs by adding the space in steps 4, 5, and 6.

How do you locate selling departments?

You have now figured out how many square feet your health and beauty aids department needs to generate the planned volume of business. You also know that the store will have a grid layout arrangement. So now you have to decide where to locate the department within the total store. Let's look at the aids to help you make the decision.

1.   *Rent paying capacity.*   The departments with the highest sales per square feet (and best ability to pay a high rent) placed in the best store areas. If a number of departments are equally good, make your decision on the *gross margins* of the merchandise. (Gross margin = Sales − Cost of sales.)

2.   *Impulse versus demand merchandise.*   Impulse merchandise (bought on the basis of unplanned, spur-of-the moment decisions) normally gets the best location in the store. They are often located on the "home stretch"—on the way out. Demand merchandise (purchased as the result

of a customer coming into the store to buy *that* item) can be located in less valuable space because customers will look for the items.

3. *Replacement frequency.* Certain items (such as health and beauty aids) are purchased often and don't cost much. Customers want to buy these items as easily as possible. Place these items in easily accessible locations.

4. *Keep related departments together.* Place similar merchandise close together. In a superstore, for example, all household items (paper products, detergents, kitchen gadgets, and so on) are placed this way. Note also in Figure 6–3 that the deli department and the meat department are close together. You are hoping that customers will make combination purchases. The men's furnishings department (e.g., shirts, ties, underwear, and so on) is placed near the suit department in a department store. A new suit calls for a new shirt and tie. Combination selling is thus easier if the items are close together. In a self-service store location is even more important because no salesperson is around to help the customer.

5. *Seasonal variations.* Some departments are big sellers only a few months or weeks in the year. Toys and summer furniture are examples. You might well place such opposite (in sales) departments near (or next to) each other. Thus when toy sales expand at Christmas you can give them more space since summer furniture is "dead," and vice versa.

6. *Size of departments.* You may also want to place very small departments in valuable space. A very large department might need a less desirable location in the store. Its size makes it visible.

7. *Merchandise characteristics.* In a supermarket, bakery products (especially bread) should be near the checkout to avoid crushing in the carts if they are picked up early by a customer. Produce such as lettuce is usually displayed along a wall to allow more space and to better handle wiring for cooling.

8. *Shopping considerations.* Items such as suits and dresses, which are often tried on and "fitted," can be placed in less valuable locations away from heavy traffic. Also the items are "demand" not "impulse," and thus can be placed in out-of-the-way areas.

9. *New, developing, or underdeveloped departments.* Assume that you have picked up a new department (more "nonfoods" in superstores, for example.) You may want to give more valuable space to it to increase sales by exposing more customers to the items.

Where do you locate sales-supporting activities?

Sales-supporting activities (such as credit) can be thought of in the following ways:

1. Those that must be located in a specific part of the store.
2. Those that are related directly to some selling activity.
3. Those that involve direct customer contact.
4. Those that are in no way related to any of the above.

"See you later, Mom. We're going to the hardware store to shop for clothes."

Reprinted by permission The Wall Street Journal

Activities located in a specific part of the store. Receiving and marking areas should be located near the "dock" area, usually at the back of the store. Display windows need to be exposed to high traffic in order to call attention to the merchandise.

Some activities relate directly to selling. Cutting areas for fresh meat need to be close to the refrigerators. Both refrigeration and cutting need to be close to the display cases. Drapery workrooms in department stores need to be close to the drapery department.

Activities with direct customer contact. In a supermarket, customers often want to check parcels, cash a personal check, or ask for information about an item. Credit departments and layaway services are needed in department stores. Locate such activities in out-of-the-way places to increase customer movement in the store.

Activities that serve the store only. Such activities are personnel services (employees of the store), promotion, and display. Locate these activities in the least valuable out-of-the-way places.

How do you display within departments?

We can only give you some simple suggestions for planning the best arrangement of items in departments. Experience in display and layout is your best guide.

1. *Each item should earn the space it occupies.* By this we mean that the others should produce enough sales (or profit) to justify their location.
2. Consider the following things in deciding where to place items in relation to each other:

a. Place items so that good and easy choices can be made by customers. In an item with various sizes, group the merchandise *by size*.

b. Place items in such a way that "ensemble" (or related item) selling is easy. For example, in a gourmet food department, all Chinese food components should be together. In a women's accessories department, handbags, gloves, and neckwear should be together to help the customer complete an outfit.

c. Place items in a department so that trading up is possible. (Trading up means getting a customer to want a better quality, higher priced item.) Place the good, better, and best brands of shortenings, for example, next to each other so customers can compare them. Informative labels (information given on the package) make it easy to compare items displayed next to each other.

d. Place merchandise in a department in such a way that it stresses the wide assortments (choice of sizes, brands, colors, and prices) available.

e. Place items in a department so that inventory counting (control) and general stock keeping is easier. The importance of this factor is clearer after you study Chapter 18.

f. Finally, make your displays as attractive as possible.

RECAP

You now understand the concepts of store planning, design, modernization, and layout. You have some keys to work with on making these activities important merchandising tools for you.

The beginning is over! You *know* the things you must know before anything good can happen—before you are ready for the retail business . . . *but* you must also be aware of other important things in the world around you.

NOTES

1. William R. Davidson, Alton F. Doody, and Daniel J. Sweeney, *Retailing Management*, 4th ed. (New York: Ronald Press, 1975), p. 516.

2. R. Ted Will and Ronald W. Hasty, *Retailing, A Mid-management Approach* (San Francisco: Canfield Press, 1973), p. 355.

3. Barry Berman and Joel R. Evans, *Retail Management: A Strategic Approach* (New York: The Macmillan Company, 1979), p. 398.

DISCUSSION QUESTIONS

1. Explain the terms: store planning; store design; store layout; and modernization. How do they relate to each other?

2. How do "image" and "atmosphere" relate? How does "layout" relate to atmosphere?

3. Discuss some of the elements which make up a

store's atmosphere-image (i.e., elements related to design and layout).

4. What are the things you must consider in layout planning?

5. Explain the activities which must be carried out in any store.

6. What is a department and explain how it is a helpful planning unit.

7. Explain the two types of layout patterns and discuss the value of each pattern.

8. Explain how you might divide total selling space in a store among the various departments. (Discuss three ways.)

9. Use examples and illustrate how you would go through a checklist to use the "buildup" or "model stock" approach to planning selling space.

10. Discuss various aids you might use in deciding where to locate a department.

11. How do you consider the various sales-supporting activities in a store in making a decision about where they should be located?

12. Discuss some useful ideas which you can use in planning the best arrangement of items in departments.

PROJECTS

1. Use Figure 6-2 ("Elements That Make up a Store's Atmosphere") and select a particular store in your local community. Evaluate and describe the exterior and interior store design factors in that figure.

2. Select three different types of stores (e.g., a department store; a food store; and a boutique) and compare and contrast them in terms of layout, displays, and finally atmosphere-image.

Minicase 6–1   Robert Talbot owns and operates a ladies' ready-to-wear store, Talbot's, in the downtown business district. He is in the process of opening a branch of approximately 3,500 square feet in the new suburban mall. He has had no experience in opening branches. Sales are budgeted at $175,000 for the new store. He has asked the buyer of jewelry how much space she will need for her department, assuming that he wants 5 percent of budgeted sales from that department.

How much space does she need? How did you determine it? Why did you use that particular method?

Minicase 6–2   Smith and Son has merchandise arranged in a grid pattern which allows customers to move quickly through the store. The store is located on a New York City street with many office buildings. The store has an opening to the street and a second opening from the subway. Each day many people go through the store on their way to and from the subway. A few stop to look at the merchandise, but sales from this walk-through traffic are very low.

In an effort to increase sales from the walk-through traffic, the management has decided to change the layout of the store.

What method of arrangement would you recommend that it use? Why?

Store Planning: A Critique*

Specialists in the interior design profession, store planners, must solve problems in three areas:

1. *Layout.* Decisions regarding space allocation, arrangement, and location of sales departments, service areas, and circulation routes within and between areas of the store.
2. *Design.* Decisions regarding store atmosphere, including fixture design, decoration, architectural elements, finish materials, graphics, and lighting.
3. *Display.* Decisions regarding location, design, and illumination of areas for point of purchase and feature displays within the store.

The criteria used in evaluating the interior design features of the store environment are:

1. *Cost.* What is the cost of "extras," such as interior decor, display equipment, and space for customer lounge areas? Is the consumer willing to pay for the high quality of the design features?
2. *Convenience.* How easy is it to locate departments, merchandise assortments, and service areas such as checkout counters and credit departments? Is access to different store levels convenient? How easy is it to move among and within selling areas?
3. *Suitability.* Is the store atmosphere consistent with the target consumer's self-image? Is the decor appropriate to the quality of merchandise? Is the cleanliness of the store environment satisfactory?
4. *Performance.* Are salespersons able to serve the customer quickly and efficiently? Is stock easily inspected? Does the store lighting represent the true color value of the merchandise?

THE MEN'S DEN

Exhibits 1 and 2 illustrate an interior design concept for a men's clothing store. This design shows the potential for adaptive reuse of a building constructed in 1930. The architectural shell, containing approximately 2,400 square feet on the street level, is representative of many buildings in downtown business districts of American cities. The economic advantages of "recycling" older buildings for new uses is recognized by many retailing firms operating in today's highly competitive environment.

Store design

The Men's Den is designed to offer leisure and dress wear for persons in business and executive positions, typically 25–50 years of age. Traditionally styled clothing, footwear, and accessories all emphasize quality and styling.

---

* This critique is by Dr. Dennis James, assistant professor of Interior Design at The University of Alabama. The store plan was prepared by Carol Hoffman, an interior design student at Alabama. The critique shows the high level of expertise and of designer/retailer interaction needed for store planning.

EXHIBIT 1

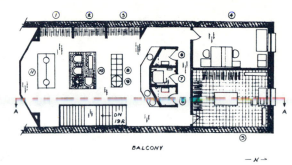

WINDOWS CONSTRUCTED
15'-0" ABOVE GROUND
FLOOR & ALIGNED
WITH EXISTING WIN-
DOWS BELOW

BALCONY

— N →

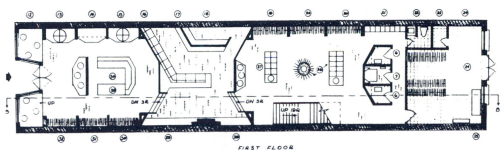

FIRST FLOOR

<u>FLOOR PLAN</u>

SCALE: 1/8" = 1'-0"

LEGEND

① SUITS
② SPORT COATS
③ DRESSY TOP COATS
④ OFFICE
⑤ ALTERATION AREA
⑥ DRESSING ROOM
⑦ FITTING AREA
⑧ DRESS SHIRTS
⑨ DESIGNER TIES
⑩ CUSTOMER LOUNGE AREA
⑪ DRESS SLACKS
⑫ WINDOW DISPLAY

⑬ TIES
⑭ SEASONAL ACCESSORIES (E.G. SCARVES, GLOVES)
⑮ BELTS
⑯ BANQUETTE SEATING
⑰ SHOE DISPLAY
⑱ FORWARD SHOE STOCK
⑲ CASUAL SHIRTS
⑳ CASUAL SLACKS
㉑ UNDERWEAR
㉒ RESTROOM
㉓ STORAGE FOR MAINTENANCE SUPPLIES

㉔ RECEIVING/STORAGE AREAS
㉕ PRICING AREA
㉖ SWEATERS
㉗ CASUAL SLACKS (DENIMS)
㉘ SHOE POLISHES & LACES
㉙ SOCKS
㉚ BATHROBES
㉛ RAINCOATS/SEASONAL JACKETS
㉜ HANGING SEASONAL WEAR (E.G. TENNIS OUTFITS)
㉝ SMALL, EXPENSIVE GIFT ITEMS (E.G. JEWELRY)
㉞ CHECK-OUT STATION

Brass, muted browns, and subtle changes in textures provide a visually rich yet relaxed setting for the featured merchandise. All areas of the store use similar styling. For example, the carpet is consistent throughout, as are the major wall finishes. The balcony level lounge seating is an appropriate contribution to the inviting and comfortable ambience of the store.

The main sales areas are distinctly angular, and help counteract the inherent tunnel effect created by the long and narrow building. Valance lighting in wall fixtures serves to highlight merchandise and visually widen the space. The design of all store fixtures compliments the architectural forms, thus providing primary emphasis on the clothing and not on the architecture or furniture.

EXHIBIT 2

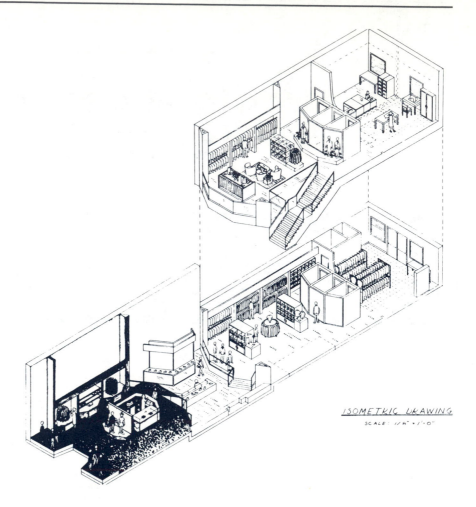

ISOMETRIC DRAWING
SCALE: 1/8" = 1'-0"

Changes in the floor and ceiling levels create a feeling of spaciousness. These changes invite the shopper to look throughout the store upon entry and help define various departments and service areas. Mirrored panels and walls are used primarily in inspection and fitting areas. Mirrors and other reflective surfaces are placed so as not to disorient customers who are walking within the sales areas.

The island fixtures are three-foot-wide modular units, each unit having casters and demountable dividers. This design provides flexibility in arrangement and permits the retailer to make adjustments for seasonal demands and changes in market strategy.

Store layout

A model stock program resulted from a study of stores similar in concept to the Men's Den. In addition to identifying generic classes of clothing to be featured in the store, the study established space needs and display requirements. A sampling:

Item	Average quantity for floor display	Optimal display	Fixture design/ space allocation
Dress slacks	300 units	Hanging, access from one or both sides of fixture.	Freestanding or wall fixture: 24 inches deep, 36 inches high per row, 40 inches wide per 40 slacks.
Dress shirts	150 units	Folded and stacked, access from one side.	Open bins: 16 inches deep, 14 inches wide, 16 inches high; 8 shirts per bin.
Ties	200 units	Hanging, access from one side.	Square or circular stand: 36 inches high; 24 ties per rod foot.

Thirty-seven hundred square feet of floor space is required to hold all sales departments and service areas. To provide convenient store operation, merchandise is arranged into five departments:

Gifts and accessories
  Jewelry
  Toiletries
  Leather goods

Service desk and checkout

Leisure wear
  Shirts
  Sweaters
  Denims
  Casual slacks

Dressing and fitting rooms

Shoes
  Dress shoes
  Casual shoes
  Laces
  Polishes

Forward stockroom

Dress wear
  Suits
  Shirts
  Ties
  Sport coats
  Dress slacks
  Top coats

Dressing and fitting rooms, lounge seating

Seasonal wear
  Raincoats
  Windbreakers
  Sportswear
  Swimwear

Service desk and checkout

The designer has not attempted to locate all accessory goods in one department. The decision was made to place these items near related merchandise. For example, belts and socks are placed near the shoe department on the assumption that sales of these accessory goods may be strengthened.

The checkout desk is placed near the entrance and is designed for display of smaller gift items, such as wallets and colognes. A very useful feature of the checkout desk is undercounter storage space for clothing which has had alterations and is ready for pickup. Feature displays, showing styles and coordinates, are in direct line of vision by incoming shoppers. The entry area serves effectively as a showplace for available merchandise and as the "operations center" for salespersons.

Generously wide (six–eight feet) circulation aisles are provided at no cost to stocking requirements. The balcony stairway is given prominent architectural emphasis and is easily visible from the main entrance. Movement through all areas and levels of the store is encouraged by this arrangement, which permits uncrowded two-way traffic.

The shoe department is placed between the entrance gallery and the leisure wear department. Luxuriously proportioned seating in this area is within easy view from other departments. This seating arrangement is intended to reinforce the comfortable and spacious store atmosphere. Forward shoe stock, conveniently accessible by salespersons, is provided in back of the shoe display cabinet. The lower section of the display cabinet is mirrored for customer use and is protected from breakage by a brass molding.

The value of lowering the floor level in the shoe department is questionable. Although it does help to define and set off the area, movement through the store is slowed—a problem perhaps more noticeable to salespersons than to shoppers.

Unlike purchases of many impulse and convenience goods, shoppers normally plan a store visit to purchase or compare shopping goods (suits, dress shirts, topcoats). Therefore, these items are located in the more remote areas of the store. Leisure wear is placed in the rear section of the first floor. Dress wear, the most expensive merchandise offered by the Men's Den, is placed on the balcony. Assuming that a low-rise stairway is not objectionable to the target market, the balcony appears to be an appropriately prestigious location for finer quality clothing.

Approximately 900 square feet of floor space is required for service areas in the store, including:

1. Alterations.
2. Bookkeeping.
3. Incoming stock.
4. Rest rooms and cleaning supplies.
5. Checkout desk.
6. Major and secondary circulation aisles.

Space allocations appear to be appropriate with the exception of the stockroom. Because many retailers prefer to price merchandise on the sales floor, space in the stockroom could be reduced and used to enlarge the leisure wear department. The alteration room is placed at the rear of the balcony and is separated from the sales area by two spacious dressing rooms and a semiprivate fitting area. Access to the alteration room is less convenient for salespersons in the leisure wear department (first floor). However, a closet for temporary storage of clothing to be altered is provided on this level.

Store display

Shoppers enter the store between two feature-display cases. These cases, on low platforms, are completely open to the sales floor in order to permit access to garments.

A similar design is used for ensemble displays on the balcony and at the entrance side of the sales desk. Store fixtures are designed to accommodate smaller point-of-purchase displays for such items as shirts and ties. This design encourages shoppers to stop and inspect merchandise—important first steps in the buying process.

All clothing displays are located adjacent to major traffic aisles and are placed at eye level. Recessed, directional lighting in the ceilings is used for point-of-purchase and feature displays. The light fixtures provide high intensity illumination for the merchandise and minimize eye glare and discomfort for shoppers and salespersons. The store's lighting is designed to provide variations in brightness within the sales and circulation areas. This variation in lighting is required to emphasize displays and enhance the general level of visibility throughout the store environment.

PART II

You are ready for the retail business . . . *but*

". . . you must also be aware of some other important things . . ." We refer you again to Figure I-1. "The Student's Guide to Retailing" is your road map to the next part of your trip. Part II is concerned with things you cannot control. Part I gave you a background for understanding the retail structure. You also looked at the consumer and then the specific decisions you had to make.

The factors you will study in this part really affect everything you have learned in the first part. They are outside your business, but they are always present. We are talking about:

1. The legal situation—how it may affect you.
2. Changes around you (economic and social).
3. Your people (staffing) problems.
4. How the explosion in technology can affect you.

These subjects are discussed in Chapters 7, 8, 9, and 10. The appreciation of these important outside factors is essential to your success in the "nuts and bolts" operations of your retail store (Part III).

7

THE LEGAL SITUATION

The purposes of this chapter are to help you understand:

- Restraint of trade.
- Unfair methods of competition.
- Trade regulation rules.
- Regulations affecting pricing, promotion, distribution, and products sold.
- How to spot potential legal problems.
- The meaning of the following terms:

Exclusive dealing	Trade regulation rules
Exclusive territory	Product warranties
Good faith defense	Product recalls
Unfair methods of competition	

Government regulation may be *the* toughest problem you face today. Local, state, and federal laws affect everything you do. The purpose of the laws is good. They try to (1) keep competition at a high level, (2) protect consumers from unfair business practices, and (3) provide consumers with enough information to make wise buying decisions.

This chapter looks at the areas to which you need to be alert as a retailer. These include issues involving (1) restraint of trade, (2) unfair competition, (3) FTC trade regulations, and (4) laws affecting the retail mix; i.e., pricing, promotion, distribution, and product practices.

WHAT IS RESTRAINT OF TRADE?

Restraint of trade means:

1. Putting pressure on suppliers to prevent them from selling products to competing retailers.
2. Acquiring other retail firms if you are trying to lessen competition or to create a monopoly.
3. Trying to fix the prices of goods that you and the competition sell. In other words, retailers cannot agree to stop price competition among themselves.
4. Underselling other retailers to gain control of a market. This prevents a large chain, for example, from lowering prices to drive smaller competitors in one area out of business while the chain maintains high prices in other areas.[1]

The key restraint of trade laws are (1) the Sherman Act, (2) the Clayton Act, and (3) the Federal Trade Commission Act.

The Sherman Act

The Sherman Act (1890) was the first law passed to maintain competition. It makes every action to restrain trade illegal. Such activities are almost limitless. However, they generally include price-fixing, dividing markets among competitors, forcing suppliers to give you the exclusive right to sell merchandise in a given area, or suppliers requiring retailers to purchase a variety of products in order to get one product which they really want. These activities are illegal only when they tend to create a monopoly or substantially lessen competition.

The Clayton Act

The Clayton Act (1914) was more specific than the Sherman Act. It declared certain practices illegal even if they did not actually restrain trade and even if they did not actually constitute a monopoly or an attempt to monopolize. Further, the practices were declared illegal even if they did not actually injure competition. The activities were held to be illegal if they *might* lessen competition or *tend* to create a monopoly.

The Federal Trade Commission Act

The Federal Trade Commission Act (1914) created an independent agency (the Federal Trade Commission) to help enforce the Clayton Act and other antitrust laws. The Commission was given the power of investigation and the power to issue cease and desist orders. Also, acts or practices which do not violate the Sherman or Clayton acts may be restrained by the FTC as unfair methods of competition. The Federal Trade Commission (the FTC) is primarily involved in activities which affect interstate commerce.

The philosophy behind such regulations is that by removing various restraints to trade, prices will be kept at reasonable levels. Stronger price competition and better consumer service are likely if all firms must compete with one another to survive. Recent actions by the FTC led to the lowering of the prices of eyeglasses and contact lenses.

Also, they have ruled that buyers of used cars must be told about defects in cars which they purchase. Finally, their actions have recently led to legality of advertising by such persons as attorneys, CPAs, and medical doctors.

WHAT ARE UNFAIR METHODS OF COMPETITION?

Unfair methods of competition are unethical business practices. They are policed by the FTC at the federal level. Each state or local area may have similar laws. For example, a city may require you to have a license to sell door to door. Some examples of unfair methods of competition are listed below.

Unordered merchandise. Consumers do not have to pay for items mailed to them which they did not order.

Push money. It may be illegal to "push" the sale of certain products by paying salespersons extra to sell the product. The practice is not per se illegal, but is always a likely candidate for FTC study.

Retailers who allow suppliers to pay retail salespersons to "push" certain items may also lose control over their sales staff. But a retailer may also decide to offer extra money to salespersons to sell slow-moving or unwanted items.

Some forms of so-called push money are clearly illegal. For example, record companies cannot pay disc jockeys to play their records. People believe that the records played the most often are the most popular.

WHAT ARE TRADE REGULATION RULES?

Trade regulation rules are guidelines issued by the FTC which must be followed in selling certain products or services. They are issued to affect specific industries and are not laws passed by Congress. For example, *retailers selling items by mail* must state the delivery dates for the items. If they cannot be delivered by the stated time, the buyer can cancel the order.

The FTC also requires *door-to-door sellers* to identify themselves as salespersons before entering a person's home.

Mispricing and out-of-stock advertised food items is another area covered by trade rules. They require retailers to have enough of the advertised item to meet a "normal" level of demand.

Other agencies also issue trade rules. For example, the Food and Drug Administration (FDA) has rules to be followed in *posting or advertising prescription drug prices.*

WHAT LAWS AFFECT THE RETAILING MIX?

The key elements of the retailing mix are the four ps—price, promotion, place, and product.

What do you watch out for in pricing?   Pricing is regulated at the state and federal levels by many laws. Pricing is one of the most important elements in the retailers marketing mix and can offer a major advantage over competition. On the other hand, cutthroat pricing by some retailers may drive smaller or less efficient firms out of business.

Price-fixing is always illegal.   You can't agree with competitors on the price that items will be sold. The practice is illegal under the Sherman Act and the Federal Trade Commission Act.

Still, retail price-fixing is not uncommon. The large number of retailers makes it difficult to control the practice. For example, three large New York retailers (Bergdorf Goodman, Bonwit Teller, and Saks Fifth Avenue) agreed to put up some $5.2 million to settle a series of price-fixing class action suits brought by credit card customers.

What is predatory pricing?   *Predatory pricing* means pricing in such a way as to try to drive competition out of business. Varying your prices by community is also illegal: (1) if you cannot justify it on the basis of your costs, or (2) if you are trying to get rid of competition. The FTC enforces this regulation.

What are sales below cost?

Several states have laws which do not allow the sale of items at less than their cost. These laws usually cover such product lines as milk and dairy products, cigarettes, or gasoline.

Some states allow sales below cost if they are necessary to meet the price of a competitor.

What about price discrimination?

The Robinson-Patman Act (1936).   This is the law to watch out for in price discrimination. We all know that suppliers do not always charge the same price to each retailer. For example, quantity discounts may be given to retailers who purchase in large volume. Also, wholesalers may get larger discounts from manufacturers than retailers. Finally, lower prices may be charged in one market area than in another to meet competition. Not all price discrimination is illegal under the Robinson-Patman Act. But you should always be prepared to justify price differences. Key areas to watch out for are as follows:

Price differences to various retailers, each ordering similar goods, are OK when (1) differences exist in the cost of manufacturing or delivery, and (2) the effect does not lessen competition.

A supplier can charge a different price to various retailers if done "in good faith to meet an equally low price of a competitor or the facilities furnished by a competitor"—the good faith defense.

Advertising allowances offered to you by a supplier must be available to all retailers on "proportionally equal terms."

Also, you cannot legally force a supplier to knowingly grant you a price lower than that given to your competition unless it can be justified as above. Thrifty Drugstores, a California chain, agreed for example to an FTC order in which it agreed not to seek special treatment from suppliers or overcharge them for promotional activities.

As a guide, price differences among retailers cannot exceed the savings to the supplier. Also, you and the seller must be able to justify the different price to you based on cost savings.

What are illegal promotion practices?

False advertising allowances by suppliers to lower the cost of goods to retailers are illegal. Also, misleading advertising is illegal. FTC regulations affect all media advertising, promotional items sent through the mail, price lists, and similar promotional material. Your ads cannot make false or misleading claims about prices, the value of goods, or guarantees. Levitz Furniture, for example, entered an agreement with the FTC to stop making false claims about price savings, comparable value, warranties, and furniture composition.

You must be prepared to prove the truth of your advertising claims. Advertisers can be required to submit data to the FTC to support claims about a product's safety, performance, or quality. Large national retailers with private label products have to run corrective ads if the FTC finds that their advertising is misleading.

You cannot do "bait and switch" advertising. Here goods are advertised at a very low price. The retailer then tries to "switch" the customer to a higher priced item. Sears was found guilty of this practice a few years ago in selling sewing machines.

What are illegal distribution practices?

Exclusive dealing can cause you problems. Exclusive dealing occurs when a supplier requires you not to sell the products of a competitor. This practice is only illegal when it lessens competition. Such agreements, when done in good faith, can help both you and your supplier. You may get a more stable source of supply. The supplier gets a sure market for the products.

Exclusive territories may also be bad news. Exclusive territories occur when a supplier limits the area in which you can sell a product. In return, the supplier agrees not to sell to any other retailer in your area. As a result you probably would give more time and attention to the product.

Many such agreements are illegal. Probably the only safe way for a supplier not to violate the law is to have an agency distribution system. Here the supplier keeps title to the product until you sell it.

You cannot unfairly eliminate competitors. Big "anchor" stores in shopping centers cannot say which other tenants can locate in a shopping center. They also cannot restrict the marketing practices of smaller tenants. The FTC recently obtained agreements with such retail firms as Federated, Gimble's, May Department Stores, and Sears prohibiting them from engaging in such practices.

Tying arrangements may cause you problems. Here a supplier agrees to sell you a product on the condition that you will purchase other products of the supplier. Sometimes you may have to carry an entire line of items to get the one item you want. Tie-in sales may be illegal under the Clayton or the Sherman acts as noted above.

Franchising has been hit hard because of tie-ins. Tying agreements sometimes are used to keep good quality control. Also, they are sometimes used in order to make bulk volume purchases possible. But the case against them is that franchisers sometimes sell the supplies at inflated prices.

WHAT ABOUT PRODUCT PROBLEMS?

Unsafe consumer products are being distributed in unacceptable numbers. Consumers are often unable to guard against the risk of such products. Both suppliers and retailers are being pressed to find better ways of informing consumers about these hazards.

Be careful what you do with warranties. A *warranty* is a guarantee by a seller as to the quality or performance of goods. *Express warranties* are in writing.

The Magnuson-Moss Warranty Act (1975) is the major warranty law. The law applies to written warranties about products. It requires that warranty information must be available *on the sales floor* for customers.

Many warranties are really those of a supplier. However, if you offer a warranty for parts or labor, this too comes under the act. Also, you cannot require that a consumer use only a certain brand of replacement items before you will honor a warranty.

The act also regulates some things in local commerce. For example, it allowed rules to be developed for warranties in the sale of used cars.

You cannot be required to give a warranty. But you can be required to state that you have no obligation for repairs. Study your media advertising for anything which might be thought of as a warranty.

In summary, you are now required to:

1. Give warranty information to consumers before they buy a product.
2. State warranty terms in "simple and readily understood language."
3. Establish a way to easily handle consumer complaints.

You must make warranties available to consumers in one of four ways: (1) in text material near the product; (2) in a binder available for consumers; (3) on a product package; or (4) on a sign displaying the warranty text.

"The motion has been made and seconded that we obey the law."
Reprinted by permission The Wall Street Journal

Product liability suits are another problem. The law is unclear whether you can be held liable for the unforeseen use of a product. If the use is not unexpected you and/or the supplier may be held liable. Regardless, when you are named in such a suit, odds are you'll lose. What can you do about this? Keep good records, carry liability insurance, and warn salespersons not to overstate product claims.

Figure 7–1 is a self-audit checklist that can help retail managers identify potential danger areas for product liability suits.

HOW CAN YOU MONITOR POTENTIAL LEGAL PROBLEMS?

A study of your internal records may help head off problems. The checklist in Table 7–1 is a start. For example, accounts receivable records and bad debt expenses can show potential problems in credit practices. Also, stay in contact with the local Better Business Bureaus to understand the type of consumer complaints about your firm.

SUMMARY

Many laws affect your decisions on pricing, promotion, distribution, and products. Always be alert to the rights of consumers and the options they have when displeased with you.

The retailer who is interested in serving the public by giving complete information and offering quality products at fair prices is less likely to encounter difficulties. In general, all laws and regulations seek to ensure fairness in competitive behavior and to protect the consumer from unethical sellers.

FIGURE 7-1
Self-audit survey

	Yes	No
1. I carry products that could generate a product liability lawsuit.	_____	_____
2. I always require proof of inspection and testing from the manufacturer of the products I sell.	_____	_____
3. The products I sell are properly labeled with adequate warnings and instructions.	_____	_____
4. My advertising and sales literature is up-to-date and accurate.	_____	_____
5. My sales personnel may make representations beyond those contained in advertising and sales literature.	_____	_____
6. My sales personnel only recommend the use or assembly of a product in accordance with product literature.	_____	_____
7. My sales personnel recommend substitute replacement parts manufactured by other manufacturers.	_____	_____
8. My sales personnel discuss with the customer the legal interpretation of warranties offered by the manufacturer.	_____	_____
9. I attempt to contractually arrange with the manufacturer to have the manufacturer defend and pay for lawsuits and judgments arising from products liability claims.	_____	_____
10. I include a conspicuous "hold harmless" clause in sales contracts with customers. Note: a "hold harmless" clause is a contractual agreement between the retailer and the customer where the customer agrees not to sue the retailer in the case of a product related injury.	_____	_____
11. I usually discuss product failures or defects with persons outside the marketing channel.	_____	_____
12. I promptly report all instances of product failures, product defects, product damage or bodily injury to the manufacturer.	_____	_____
13. It is necessary to quickly investigate and settle all product liability claims.	_____	_____
14. As part of my contingency recall program I keep complete records of all sales including names and addresses of purchasers.	_____	_____

Source: Lonnie L. Ostrom, Robert K. Banks, and Richard Gregg Maxon, "Product Liability: A Self-Audit of Distribution Exposure," *Retail Control*, September 1979, p. 19.

NOTES

1. R. Ted Will and Ronald Hasty, *Retailing: A Mid-Management Approach* (San Francisco: Canfield Press, 1973), p. 306.

DISCUSSION QUESTIONS

1. Why do some states have below cost laws which set prices below which it is illegal to sell merchandise?

2. Discuss the conditions under which price discounts are legal as defined by the Robinson-Patman Act.

3. What is meant by the term "good faith defense?"

4. Is exclusive dealing illegal? Can suppliers designate exclusive territories for a product or service to be sold by a particular retailer?

5. What is meant by the term "tying agreement?"

6. What precautions must a retailer take in advertising warranties on merchandise?

7. What are some of the steps which management can take in heading off legal problems?

8. What are the primary federal restraint of trade laws?

9. What is included in the term "unfair methods of competition?"

10. May a retailer legally engage in price-fixing? Explain.

TABLE 7-1
Potential legal problems in the selling process

Selling Stages	Activities	Potential legal problems	Internal indicators of potential legal problems
Presale	Media advertising	Deceptive advertising Nondisclosure of material facts Unfair advertising Deceptive pricing	Refunds and/or exchanges (if product purchased)
	Credit practices	Unfair credit practices Deceptive credit representations	Bad debts expense-customer failure to meet credit payment installments (if product purchased)
Point-of-sale	Selling practices	Deceptive packaging, labeling Nonavailability of advertised items Oral misrepresentations regarding product/service Unfair or deceptive games and contests	Retailer failure to fulfill customer product/service requests
	Contracts	Unfair contract terms Unclear contracts Deceptive contract terms Unfair or deceptive lease contracts	Number of contract cancellations by customer
	Product performance	Unreasonable consumer safety hazard Unsatisfactory performance/quality of product	Refunds and/or exchanges by customer
	Service adequacy	Failure to perform delivery Failure to perform refund/exchange Repair problems (guarantees/warranties)	Number of guarantee/warranty options used by customer
	Credit practices	Unfair or incorrect billing Unfair creditors remedies Unfair methods of debt collection	Accounts receivable and bad debts expense accounts

Note: Type and frequency of complaints may indicate problems in any of the above areas.
Source: James E. Stafford and William A. Staples, "Retailing: Potential Legal Problems in the Selling Process," *Tennessee Survey of Business,* September/October 1975, p. 27.

PROJECTS

1. Visit the manager of two or three of the retail outlets in your city. Find out the major problems with government regulation. What functions of the business seem most heavily affected? Does the manager think that the regulations serve a useful purpose? Try to find out if the manager has an active affirmative action plan.

2. Shop at several stores for a major consumer durable such as a dishwasher. Ask to see the warranties for the several models in the store. Are the warranties readily available to shoppers? Are the salespersons careful in the statements they make about the warranties? In your opinion, are they making oral statements which go beyond the written statements? Summarize in writing your view of the stores in terms of their compliance with the warranty regulations.

Minicase 7-1   Susan Martin is a regular shopper at Brown's Supersaver, a national food chain. Brown's Supersaver regularly advertises food items at reduced prices in the newspaper. But Susan has become increasingly upset in recent weeks when shopping in the store. She often finds that the store is out of the items which are advertised in the newspaper. Also, in checking the cash register tapes for the items she buys against the advertised price of the item, she regularly finds differences in the prices.

Susan recently read in the newspaper that Brown's Supersaver was one of the stores found guilty by the FTC of mispricing and unavailability violations of the FTC trade regulation rule. Now she is really mad and goes to the manager. She asks why the store cannot keep reasonable levels of advertised items in stock and why they make so many mistakes in their pricing policies. Besides she asked, "Where is the sign that deals with unavailability and rain checks which you are required to keep posted in the stores?" The manager is really upset. He knows Susan is a good customer and does not want to lose her. Outline some of the reasons which the manager probably gave Susan for the problems which are occurring. Do you think the answers could justify the situation? What can management do to reduce such problems?

Minicase 7-2   In a recent congressional session, the Department of Justice recommended changes in the Robinson-Patman Act. The department transmitted a 320-page report to Congress in which its Antitrust Division stated that evidence "seriously undermines historic claims" that the statute offered "any . . . economic protection to small business." Earlier the department had recommended to the president that Robinson-Patman be repealed in part and otherwise modified. The proposal met with a solid wall of opposition from retailers and other small business groups.

Assume that you are a small retailer. Prepare a letter to your congressman stating your position and give the rationale for your position.

THE WORLD AROUND YOU—
ECONOMIC AND SOCIAL

This chapter will help you to understand:

- The new consumer demographics.
- The mood of today's consumer.
- The effects of changes in the economy on your business.
- The effects of changes in competition on your business.
- The meaning of the following words and concepts:

Sunbelt	New economic realities
"The age of me"	Inflation
Traditional consumer values	The energy crisis
New consumer values	Foreign competition
Old economic realities	Scrambled merchandising

Don't make the mistake of thinking that retailing is simple and risk free. The brutal truth is that retailing is very competitive. Thousands of firms fail each year. They range from the smallest "mom and pop" operation to such giants as W. T. Grant.

Well-known giants who have had troubles in recent years include A&P and the Marshall Field department stores in Chicago.

Why is competition so fierce? (1) You can get started in retailing without much money; (2) most competing retailers carry the same items; and (3) most competing retailers operate the same way. Thus, it's no wonder that you can be easily wiped out if you don't read the warning signs of what is going on around you.

STRATEGIC SURPRISES

Under the best circumstances, however, some things can occur without warning. For example, in 1978 McDonald's was hit with several unfounded rumors which hurt their profits. One rumor was that McDonald's hamburgers contained worms. The owner of four McDonald's franchises in Atlanta said his business dropped 33 percent as a result. Another rumor was that the chain gave money to Satan's church in Los Angeles. This gave rise to several organized boycotts of McDonald's.[1]

The Hilton Hotel in Jerusalem lost its certificate of kosher status because the chief rabbi of Jerusalem felt the hotel was violating the law of the Sabbath. Removal of the kosher status was a terrible blow since the country has a half million Jewish tourists each year.[2]

Knowledgeable persons expected at least $20 million in claims following a power blackout in New York City.[3] Finally, consider the uninsurable nature of weather which can cost retailers hundreds of millions of dollars.

Still, major opportunities await alert retailers who can quickly spring into action to meet a new opportunity. The market for home insulation, solar energy, and improved furnaces/boilers will reach almost $14 billion by 1984. The market emerged because of the 1973 oil embargo. New laws caused a large increase in the sale of smoke alarms. Home video games have become very popular in recent years. Consider also the growth of sales in recent years for microwave ovens, CB radios, and jogging equipment.

WHAT ARE THE NEW CONSUMER DEMOGRAPHICS?

An understanding of changes in the consumer segments you want to serve is very important. Successful retailers seek to match product and service offerings to consumer preferences. This matching process is not possible without an awareness of basic trends in market structure.

The primary changes in the population that you need to be aware of include:

1. Smaller households.
2. Working wives.

3. Growth of suburbs.
4. Changing family relationships.
5. Age mix changes.
6. An older population.
7. Sunbelt growth.
8. Growth of smaller communities.

Smaller households

One- and two-person households now comprise 59 percent of all households. This group includes singles, widows, empty nesters, childless, and unmarried couples and younger couples planning to have children later.[4] These small households are good markets for town houses, condominiums, kitchen miniappliances, and packaged goods in single servings.

One- or two-person households earn more than $115 billion each year. SSWDs (singles, separated, widowed, and divorced) spend more money on travel and entertainment. But they save less and tend to buy more services.[5]

Working wives

Households with two or more wage earners account for more than 54 percent of all families. They have more than two thirds of total family buying power.[6] These households spend more for luxuries, even though many second wage earners are working to pay off family debts. Working wives offer many markets for new services. They especially want products and services which offer them convenience and save them time.

Growth of suburbs

Suburbs now account for more than half of all U.S. retail sales. During the 1970s more than 2 million Americans left such areas as New York and Chicago than moved into them. Younger and more affluent persons are the ones moving. Older and poorer groups stay behind but do not have enough money to support the retail structure.

The suburban population accounts for 60 percent of the population in metropolitan areas. During 1976–77 alone, 250 cities lost population and had a net reduction of $18 billion in residents' personal income.[7]

Changing family relationships

The new family relationships can be described as less marriage, later marriage, and more divorce. For every two marriages there is now one divorce. Clearly these factors mean more small households. The trends also affect consumer outlooks and values which in turn affect goods bought.

These shifts also bring new laws. For example, wives no longer can be denied credit simply because they aren't working outside the home. Also, divorced women can now use the credit record they established as a husband and wife household when applying for credit.

New shopping patterns in terms of who shops, when they shop, and the number of trips made are also emerging. One-stop shopping will increase.

Few persons are now at home during "regular working hours." Late night and weekend store hours for goods and services will be more common.

Age mix changes

The birthrate is declining. It stood at 1.76 in 1976—far below the population replacement level. The growth of the 18–24-year-old age-group, the darling of retailers in the 1970s, is slowing sharply.

As important as declining birthrates is the shift in age-groups. The shifts are shown in Figure 8–1. The baby boom following World War II is now moving through the population.

During the next 12 years the fastest growing age-group will be persons 24–44 years of age. And this is a group with high spending power. Seventy-eight million persons will be in this group by 1990. By 1985, the 45–54-year-old age-group will expand in size and by 1995 will swell the ranks of 55–64-year-olds.

The population is also older. The average age of the population in 1970 was 28 and will reach 30 by 1981. The median age in the year 2000 will be 35. These changes mean shifts in what is bought. People will be more conservative than today. The demand for health-related services will also rise.

Sunbelt growth

The Sunbelt and western states are growing faster than other areas. Many people are migrating from other states to these areas. Many Sunbelt and western states also have a higher birthrate because of the younger population. The growth in the Sunbelt and the West does *not* occur largely because of the people who are retiring.

Between 1970 and mid-1976, the Sunbelt increased by 7,114,000 persons, 63 percent of the total national increase. Florida, Texas, and Sunbelt California accounted for more than half the regional gain. Table 8–1 shows

FIGURE 8–1
U.S. population
projections*

Age-group (years)	1980 Number (000s)	Percent change 1975–80	1985 Number (000s)	Percent change 1980–85	1990 Number (000s)	Percent change 1985–90
Under 5	16,020	+ 0.9	18,803	+17.4	19,437	+ 3.4
5 to 14	33,896	−10.2	32,826	− 3.2	35,758	+ 8.9
15–19	20,609	− 1.6	18,007	−12.6	16,777	− 6.8
20–24	20,918	−10.0	20,510	− 2.0	17,953	−12.5
25–29	18,930	+12.4	20,581	+ 8.7	20,169	− 2.0
30–34	17,242	+23.8	19,278	+11.8	20,917	+ 8.5
35–39	14,033	+21.2	17,274	+23.1	19,261	+11.5
40–44	11,688	+ 4.6	14,102	+20.7	17,331	+22.9
45–49	11,030	− 6.4	11,526	+ 4.5	13,889	+20.5
50–54	11,668	− 2.6	10,931	− 6.3	11,422	+ 4.5
55–64	21,198	+ 7.2	21,737	+ 2.5	20,776	− 4.4
65 and over ...	24,927	+11.2	27,305	+ 9.5	29,823	+ 9.2
All ages	222,159	+ 4.3	232,880	+ 4.8	243,513	+ 4.6

* Includes Armed Forces abroad.
Source: U.S. Department of Commerce. Population Series P-25, as of July 1, 1977.

TABLE 8-1
Golden dozen metropolitan areas (top 100 metropolitan areas)

	Total retail sales (000)	Percent change 1978/1972	Per household sales		Adjust. index 78/72	Sales/income index	
			1978	1972		1978	1972
Las Vegas	$ 1,952,744	121.1%	$14,475	$8,488	171	134	118
Houston	11,693,453	121.0	12,832	7,716	166	95	114
Austin	1,983,056	115.2	11,651	7,857	148	104	126
Flint	2,639,689	114.6	15,537	7,868	197	138	113
Baton Rouge	1,837,861	110.3	12,834	7,644	168	125	118
Anaheim-Santa Ana- Garden Grove.........	8,250,080	110.2	13,050	8,111	161	89	103
Phoenix	5,711,768	106.5	12,289	7,928	155	123	121
Fort Lauderdale- Hollywood............	4,394,616	105.9	12,030	8,294	145	116	136
Tulsa	2,678,819	105.5	11,332	6,621	171	126	117
Fresno	1,996,226	104.2	11,763	7,001	168	106	115
San Diego	6,648,835	102.1	10,601	7,165	148	107	100
Sacramento	4,052,427	101.2	11,712	7,315	160	84	108

Source: *Advertising Age*, December 19, 1979, p. 72. Copyright 1979, *Market Economics Guide* 1979–80. Further reproduction without expressed permission is prohibited.

that all but two of the golden dozen metro areas are in the Sunbelt. In Florida alone, the population rose by 1,630,000, more than the combined increase in the 21 northeast and north central states.[8] The North has lost almost 2 million persons since 1970. But don't be blinded by growth. Look at market potential in considering a location. Table 8–2 shows some of these opportunities. Also, some areas in the Sunbelt are losers. Certain counties have been losing population since 1940 and probably will do so at least through the year 2000.

Growth in smaller communities

The largest growth is in the smaller market areas—cities with populations of 50,000–200,000. Consider, for example, the so-called golden dozen metro growth areas: Anchorage, Alaska; Boise, Idaho; Brownsville-Harlingen-San Benita, Texas; Bryan-College Station, Texas; Fort Meyers, Florida; Gainesville, Florida; Killeen-Temple, Texas; Lafayette, Louisiana; Laredo, Texas; Las Vegas, Nevada; McAllen-Pharr-Edinburg, Texas; and Richland-Kennewick, Washington. All of these markets except Las Vegas are in the smaller sized group as noted above. And all but three are deep in the fast-growing Sunbelt region. On the average, these areas had a population growth nearly four times that of the United States. Their retail sales growth rates is one- and one-half times the national average.[9] The best retail growth opportunities are in this area.

TODAY'S CONSUMER

Understanding shifts in ages and locations of markets isn't enough. You also need to understand the way in which people who are the markets for your products and services think and act.

TABLE 8-2
Population, income, retail sales of 100 top markets

Rank	SMSA	Population 1/1/79 (000)	Disposable personal income: 1978 (000)	Total retail sales: 1978 (000)	Per household income: 1978
1.	New York, N.Y.	9,265.7	$70,916,871	$26,237,272	$19,514
2.	Los Angeles-Long Beach, Calif.	7,197.6	48,870,925	28,529,774	17,310
3.	Chicago, Ill.	6,989.9	53,730,767	27,372,706	21,823
4.	Philadelphia, Pa.	4,741.1	33,559,849	16,061,649	20,378
5.	Detroit, Mich.	4,359.3	32,806,560	17,076,275	22,251
6.	Boston-Lowell-Brockton-Lawrence-Haverhill, Mass.	3,841.8	27,419,323	14,000,316	20,459
7.	San Francisco-Oakland, Calif.	3,164.4	26,006,270	13,187,165	20,867
8.	Wash. D.C.-Md.-Va.	2,998.1	30,318,505	12,339,382	28,872
9.	Nassau-Suffolk, N.Y.	2,697.9	23,627,176	9,900,294	28,171
10.	Dallas-Fort Worth, Tex.	2,676.3	19,543,426	10,727,128	20,364
11.	Houston, Tex.	2,626.6	22,393,276	10,656,904	24,573
12.	St. Louis, Mo.	2,374.6	16,368,829	8,760,791	19,776
13.	Pittsburgh, Pa.	2,278.0	15,842,078	8,073,171	19,443
14.	Baltimore, Md.	2,158.0	11,009,726	7,223,610	14,965
15.	Minneapolis-St. Paul, Minn.	2,017.5	15,461,153	8,292,770	22,538
16.	Newark, N.J.	1,952.0	14,618,329	6,668,984	21,300
17.	Cleveland, O.	1,923.1	13,613,038	7,475,665	20,016
18.	Atlanta, Ga.	1,848.0	11,842,048	7,680,795	18,687
19.	Anaheim-Santa Ana-Garden Grove, Calif.	1,826.2	16,811,464	8,250,080	26,609
20.	San Diego, Calif.	1,724.7	11,342,173	6,648,835	18,084
21.	Denver-Boulder Colo.	1,501.8	10,710,702	6,661,323	20,099
22.	Miami, Fla.	1,469.2	9,803,253	6,285,750	17,471
23.	Tampa-St. Petersburg, Fla.	1,458.1	8,744,183	5,159,388	14,286
24.	Seattle-Everett, Wash.	1,447.5	10,709,669	6,504,180	19,705
25.	Milwaukee, Wis.	1,412.3	10,230,471	5,176,000	20,981
26.	Riverside-San Bernardino-Ontario, Calif.	1,394.7	9,590,923	5,217,108	18,947
27.	Cincinnati, O.	1,378.2	11,067,280	5,170,946	22,895
28.	Phoenix, Ariz.	1,307.6	8,437,300	5,711,768	18,153
29.	Buffalo, N.Y.	1,294.1	7,246,198	4,155,122	15,968
30.	Kansas City, Mo.,-Kan.	1,286.1	9,746,270	5,405,883	20,614
31.	San Jose, Calif.	1,216.9	10,826,909	5,438,986	25,821
32.	Portland, Ore.	1,149.8	8,236,633	5,142,687	18,978
33.	Indianapolis, Ind.	1,146.9	8,206,768	4,913,639	20,374
34.	New Orleans, La.	1,133.2	7,582,624	4,097,342	19,670
35.	Columbus, O.	1,079.9	7,746,855	4,296,912	20,413
36.	Hartford-New Britain-Bristol, Conn.	1,055.0	7,732,165	3,844,860	21,006
37.	San Antonio, Tex.	1,028.0	6,061,536	3,419,509	18,073
38.	Rochester, N.Y.	956.3	6,192,519	3,455,815	18,652
39.	Sacramento, Calif.	955.0	8,927,318	4,052,427	25,801
40.	Fort Lauderdale-Hollywood, Fla.	904.1	6,917,855	4,645,928	18,937

TABLE 8-2 *(continued)*

Rank	SMSA	Population 1/1/79 (000)	Disposable personal income: 1978 (000)	Total retail sales: 1978 (000)	Per household income: 1978
41.	Louisville, Ky.	880.3	5,653,756	3,399,915	18,446
42.	Memphis, Tenn.	879.3	5,324,720	3,230,259	18,342
43.	Providence-Warwick-Pawtucket, R.I.	851.0	5,454,947	2,698,928	17,962
44.	Salt Lake City-Ogden, Utah	837.2	5,017,392	3,224,594	18,521
45.	Dayton, O.	827.7	5,183,996	2,981,744	17,907
46.	Birmingham, Ala.	825.1	4,889,325	3,133,604	16,779
47.	Bridgeport-Stamford-Norwalk-Danbury, Conn.	808.8	7,439,813	3,191,618	26,392
48.	Norfolk-Virginia Beach-Portsmouth, Va.	802.9	4,829,052	2,545,276	18,481
49.	Albany-Schenectady-Troy, N.Y.	791.8	4,697,419	2,701,663	16,362
50.	Nashville-Davidson, Tenn.	784.3	5,586,946	3,216,961	20,294
51.	Greensboro-Winston-Salem-High Point, N.C.	781.8	$4,923,364	$2,998,878	$17,968
52.	Toledo, O.	781.5	6,045,031	2,948,632	22,290
53.	Oklahoma City, Okla.	779.9	5,407,531	3,538,689	18,557
54.	New Haven-Waterbury-Meriden, Conn.	756.9	5,157,132	2,662,613	19,344
55.	Honolulu, Hawaii	711.9	5,166,433	2,840,932	29,985
56.	Jacksonville, Fla.	708.2	3,848,745	2,452,926	15,684
57.	Worcester-Fitchburg-Leominster, Mass.	665.7	4,064,562	2,140,092	17,565
58.	Akron, O.	656.4	4,149,586	2,411,996	18,345
59.	Gary-Hammond-East Chicago, Ind.	651.9	3,982,053	2,358,089	18,564
60.	Syracuse, N.Y.	639.7	3,689,343	2,165,646	16,793
61.	Northeastern Pennsylvania	633.2	3,613,288	2,168,638	15,494
62.	Tulsa, Okla.	630.2	3,862,824	2,678,819	16,340
63.	Allentown-Bethlehem-Easton, Pa.	629.2	4,261,024	2,290,308	18,502
64.	Orlando, Fla.	617.4	3,872,662	2,634,673	17,484
65.	Richmond, Va.	606.2	3,936,950	2,394,098	18,579
66.	Charlotte-Gastonia, N.C.	600.3	3,896,348	2,472,653	18,869
67.	Springfield-Chicopee-Holyoke, Mass.	598.2	3,634,572	1,896,554	17,291
68.	Grand Rapids, Mich.	595.1	4,844,329	2,383,908	24,295
69.	New Brunswick-Perth Amboy-Sayreville, N.J.	582.7	5,113,637	2,132,385	26,971
70.	Omaha, Neb.	573.8	3,759,633	2,109,587	18,931
71.	Jersey City, N.J.	567.2	4,122,827	1,365,081	18,843
72.	Youngstown-Warren, O.	544.6	3,284,196	1,885,872	17,629
73.	Greenville-Spartanburg, S.C.	537.9	3,168,430	1,810,090	16,989
74.	Wilmington, Del.	520.6	3,714,191	1,993,054	21,115
75.	Flint, Mich.	514.3	3,488,082	2,390,967	20,530
76.	West Palm Beach-Boca Raton, Fla.	504.3	3,572,071	2,333,760	17,657
77.	New Bedford-Fall River, Mass.	492.7	2,720,625	1,475,717	15,259
78.	Raleigh-Durham, N.C.	488.7	3,497,155	1,916,875	20,829
79.	Long Branch-Asbury Park, N.J.	487.1	4,192,412	1,893,356	25,332
80.	Fresno, Calif.	487.0	3,418,324	1,996,226	20,143

TABLE 8-2 *(concluded)*

Rank	SMSA	Population 1/1/79 (000)	Disposable personal income: 1978 (000)	Total retail sales: 1978 (000)	Per household income: 1978
81.	Oxnard-Simi Valley-Ventura Calif.	485.4	3,921,003	1,726,610	24,975
82.	Austin, Tex.	481.1	3,455,625	1,874,860	20,303
83.	Tucson, Ariz.	465.7	3,252,588	1,882,207	19,465
84.	Paterson-Clifton-Passaic, N.J.	459.0	2,656,783	1,621,124	16,082
85.	Knoxville, Tenn.	454.8	3,460,375	1,852,119	21,190
86.	Lansing-East Lansing, Mich.	454.1	2,853,791	1,702,627	18,899
87.	Baton Rouge, La.	444.3	2,670,305	1,687,349	18,647
88.	El Paso, Tex.	443.8	1,851,083	1,523,677	13,661
89.	Tacoma, Wash.	438.9	2,869,143	1,574,594	17,910
90.	Mobile, Ala.	434.6	2,111,941	1,444,804	14,769
91.	Harrisburg, Pa.	430.8	3,859,424	1,794,269	24,535
92.	Albuquerque, N.M.	426.2	2,370,508	1,744,900	16,690
93.	Johnson City-Kingsport-Bristol, Tenn.	409.9	1,896,604	1,407,483	13,153
94.	Chattanooga, Tenn.	408.8	2,222,998	1,444,818	15,331
95.	Canton, O.	404.9	2,376,852	1,543,384	16,798
96.	Charleston, S.C.	389.5	2,409,978	1,297,339	19,983
97.	Wichita, Kan.	388.3	2,433,706	1,699,839	17,211
98.	Fort Wayne, Ind.	381.2	2,658,552	1,519,271	20,095
99.	Columbia, S.C.	376.0	2,364,144	1,406,306	19,603
100.	Davenport-Rock Island-Moline, Ia./Ill. ...	374.5	2,903,610	1,541,998	21,685

Source: *Advertising Age*, December 19, 1979. Copyright 1979, *Marketing Economics Guide 1979–80*. Further reproduction without expressed permission is prohibited.

And what is the "age of me?"

The president of one of the nation's largest advertising agencies has labeled the current consumer mood as "The Age of Me." He sees it as "an age of self-interest, rather than self-sacrifice. It's an age of creativity, self-expression, individualism, instant reward and abandonment of all common goals."[10] People are seeking a higher quality of life. Consider the following evidence:

> The growing consumer tendency to reject the artificial in favor of the natural whether in ingredients, products, appearance or behavior.
>
> The election of a "people's" president, Jimmy Carter, against great odds when his campaign began.
>
> The decision by Colorado voters, based in part on environmental considerations, not to host the 1976 Winter Olympics which the state had previously been awarded.
>
> The growing number of middle-aged adults leaving well-paying jobs for a simpler life or refusing promotions because they mean relocation.
>
> The multiple efforts in communities throughout the nation to slow population growth and development.

The appearance of such books on the nonfiction, best-seller list as *Total Fitness, The Save Your Life Diet, TM: Discovering Inner Energy and Overcoming Stress.*

The march of females into the labor force, a trend only partly due to economic factors.[11]

According to the president of this large advertising agency:

1. We see things that influence lifestyles and brand images. We see a preoccupation with appearance, the body. People have become fanatical about jogging and bicycling.
2. We see a renewed preoccupation with status and personal achievement . . . sales of . . . Gucci, Cartier, and Yves St. Laurent products have grown rapidly.
3. Commercials exploiting the drive for personal success are quite acceptable.
4. Promises of convenience . . . are once again acceptable. There's nothing wrong with doing it the easy way.[12]

Consumers are not turning their backs on money and what it can buy. But their priorities have changed. They know that money may not bring personal happiness. The quality of their lives today is at least as important as material gain.

Today's consumer values are in contrast to the 1960s, as shown in Table 8–3. No one knows how long this mood will prevail. But you need to be aware of what's going on in the consumer's mind. How do you react to a consumer, for example, (who is concerned in buying food) about health, nutrition, convenience, speed, cost, and gourmet cooking all at once?

What are the new consumer segments?

One writer has observed that these changes in the things people value and in their behavior patterns have led to four diverse groups of consumers. He sees these new groups as:[13]

1. The buy-for-one consumer.
2. The stability-seeking consumer.

TABLE 8–3
The changing consumer

Traditional consumer values	*New consumer values*
Orientation toward "things"	Orientation toward "experiences"
Increasing quantity of possessions	Increasing quality (of life and of possessions/services); life simplification
Focus on acquisition costs ("bargains")	Focus on total "use" cost
Liberal use of credit	Greater caution
High expectations	Moderated (or lowered) expectations
"Growth at any price"	Emerging conservation ethic
Emphasis on conformity	Emphasis on individuality

Source: Leonard L. Berry and Dan H. Wilson, "Retailing—The Next Ten Years," *The Journal of Retailing,* Fall 1977.

3. The get-my-money's-worth consumer.
4. The time-buying consumer.

The *buy-for-one consumer* represents the rapidly expanding number of single-person households comprised of divorced persons, people living alone, and single-person elderly households. These individuals spend their time and money differently as one-person households. They seek food items packaged in single servings and utensils especially made for preparing meals for one person. They have more time for leisure and spend more on entertainment and travel. They are prime targets for town houses and condominiums but poor markets for insurance.

Many of these individuals are upwardly mobile professionals with high earning power and high expectations from the marketplace. They are good customers who expect quality products and quality salespersons to wait on them.

The *stability-seeking consumers* are normally blue-collar, middle-class households. They provide a good market for many products and services, including durables such as recreation equipment and equipment for various do-it-yourself activities.

These persons are somewhat overwhelmed by the rapid changes occurring around them. They seek (1) a return to yesterday, i.e., the "Happy Days" TV program; (2) a return to nature (by buying indoor plants, for example); and (3) life simplification as in hobbies and do-it-yourself activities which gives them a sense of control over their destiny. This group of consumers readily responds to friendliness, personal attention, the ethic of hard work, and the traditional American value and morality structure.

The *get-my-money's-worth consumer* is somewhat of a consumer activist, an admirer of Ralph Nader, and a supporter of various social activist causes.

These people look for good values—though not always the lowest price. They seek energy efficient homes and appliances and look for durability. They substitute consumer labor for consumer costs; i.e., they use self-service gasoline stations or are willing to use inferior goods and services—for example, powdered meat extender mixes and no-name products. They also look to goods with a hedge against inflation—land, diamonds, houses, but not savings.

The *time-buying consumer* reflects the rapidly growing number of two or more income households. Increasingly, females are entering the labor force either for reasons of self-fulfillment or economic necessity in helping to support the family. Increased time pressures are placed on households with two working persons. They also have to carry on the functions of maintaining a household in addition to their normal jobs. Thus, time is scarce. They are prone to use telephone shopping services, catalog shopping services, to purchase only well-known national brands, and to be receptive to such appliances as microwave ovens which save them precious time.

The growing shortage of time

Consumers do not have enough time to meet all the demands on them. The fast rising number of women working, over 50 million today plus many in school, creates problems. A woman working in and outside her home has a work week of 60–80 hours. The reasons women work are: (1) the shortage of women for certain jobs, (2) the women's movement, (3) economic hard times, (4) more single women, and (5) a lower birthrate.

A second drain is the time now devoted to physical and mental well-being, i.e., "me time." For example, only 100,000 Americans played racket ball in 1970 as compared to 500,000 today. Look at the increase in the number of joggers, outdoor gardeners, and meditators. Retailers must find ways to help today's consumer cope with the growing shortage of time.

The above statements reinforce the points made in Chapter 2 that all persons are not alike. As a retailer, you need to carefully think about those who will be likely customers for your product or service. The entire marketing effort must be designed to serve the needs of the customers whom you would like to attract to your outlet.

Now, let's turn and look at the economy which also can cause problems for you as a retailer.

WHAT ABOUT CHANGES IN THE ECONOMY?

The new economic realities today include problems with (1) energy, (2) inflation, (3) foreign competition, (4) shortages of money, (5) low labor productivity, (6) high building costs, (7) long delivery time for goods, and (8) new technology. The old and the new economic realities are contrasted in Table 8–4.

What are the effects of rising energy costs?

Rising energy costs are forcing consumers to make tough trade-off decisions. Markets are opening up for energy-saving products such as wood-burning stoves, storm windows, and insulation. Sales of all energy-saving products are growing. Americans are rethinking their travel patterns. Already we face waiting periods of up to six months for cars that will get 50 miles per gallon. Bicycle sales are up, as are sales of mopeds. Buying by mail and telephone is up. As observed:

TABLE 8–4
The changing economy

Old economic realities	*New economic realities*
Low inflation	High inflation
Low-cost energy	Higher cost of energy
Solid GNP growth	Lower gross national product growth
Fast rate of population growth	Slow rate of population growth
High levels of consumer confidence	Erosion of consumer confidence
The assumption of abundant resources	Uncertain resource availability
Freedom of land use	Resource conservation
"No questions asked" technology	Environmental protection
Abundant capital	Scarce and high-cost capital

Source: Adapted from a presentation by Leonard L. Berry at a conference on "Competitive Structure in Retail Markets: The Department Store Perspective," New York City, April 6, 1979.

The purchasing power of consumers will continue to decline as inflation outstrips increases in income. Consumers will adjust to this problem by seeking products that are:

1. Low in initial cost.
2. Resistant to obsolescence.
3. Durable and do not require much service.
4. Not heavy users of energy.

Consumers will seek advertising that is informative about these issues. They will be less willing to pay for packaging and product features that add somewhat to the usefulness of the product but increase its cost disproportionately. And they will increasingly seek informative labeling.

Among specific products, these trends will appear:

Cars—trends toward smaller cars using less gasoline.

Clothing—more sweaters and thermal underwear.

Insulation—for new and existing houses will be in greater demand.

Buses—more buses and fewer cars.

Travel—less individual travel and more group travel.

Less eating out—theater, movies, other out-of-home entertainment, visiting.

More work at home—less travel to work.

Plastics—less use of petroleum as a raw material for plastics, fertilizers, other products.

Computers—more demand for computers for controlling heat, light, and other energy uses.

Prices of all products will rise, especially of those that require a great deal of energy for their manufacture and transport. The same is true of materials. Prices of services also will rise, especially of those that require transportation of the service person.

To reduce costs, manufacturers will tend to standardize products. They will pay less attention to product differentiation and to catering to the needs and desires of individual market segments.

New products will be introduced that are more durable, require less service, and require less energy in their manufacture, distribution, and use. Still, smart retailers will see these times as an opportunity to practice creative marketing and keep their sales and profits high. Study Aid 8-1 illustrates this point.[14]

Other changes which are occurring include the following:

1. Consumers are shopping less; they are making fewer mall and store visits, larger transactions per visit and doing more group shopping.
2. A new concept of store loyalty seems to be emerging, as consumers are less willing to travel to a store simply because they have been loyal to it in the past.
3. Neighborhood stores of all kinds and neighborhood shopping centers are flourishing as shoppers leave their cars home and rely on walking or public transportation whenever possible.

STUDY AID 8-1

THE OIL SHORTAGE

Well, the fact is the energy crisis is here, apparently for some time to come, and this can be a major problem for retailers—especially suburban outlets.

Yet, this is a perfect time for many retailers to introduce into their sales promotion plans—Marketing. Now you might wonder how will marketing solve a retail oil shortage? The answer is simple: People will drive, and will pay 99.9 cents per gallon, if the need is justified, and the merchandise right for the times.

For example, insulation and insulating materials will certainly sell. Carpeting, properly promoted, will sell, if promoted as a floor warmer this coming winter. Sleepwear, outerwear, and underwear are great items to buy during a period of lower thermostats. And low energy-consuming air-conditioners are a natural item to promote this summer along with those appliances that consume less energy.

In the future, store planners will consider more efficient means to cool and heat stores. Lighting will certainly change as daylight supplies more of the stores' lighting needs. Clever visual merchandise directors will experiment with displays that require less light—with more lighting directed at selected merchandise.

The times are changing and retailers must become more energy conscious. With a strong marketing/sales promotion guide, plus clever interior and exterior design, retailers will continue to generate traffic and sell merchandise efficiently. But you must start planning NOW.

Source: John A. Murphy, "Marketing News," *Promotion Exchange*, April 1979, p. 7.

4. A sharp rise in catalog sales is occurring, evidence that shoppers are already more willing to buy certain items from their home.
5. Retailers are increasingly running advertising programs which advise shoppers to shop by phone and save fuel.

What about inflation? Many consumers are in danger of having to lower their standard of living. They are cutting back on such items as vacation, substituting lower quality products for higher quality products—hamburger for steak.

Consumers know about the effects of inflation and have adopted a "buy now because it will cost more later" way of thinking.

But first how are consumers changing their shopping habits? Table 8–5 shows some of the things which consumers are doing. All of these will affect you as a retailer. Consumers are also switching brands more often to take advantage of price specials, are using more coupons, and are trying more private labels. They are cutting down on or cutting out meat and snacks. They are buying no-name or generic products.

From the retailers' side, inflation also presents problems. You can only hold profit margins by one of three ways: (1) raising prices, (2) increasing

TABLE 8-5
Consumer reactions to inflation

Because of inflation we are	To a very great or great extent	To some extent	To a little or very little extent
In the purchase of grocery items:			
Buying different quality products than what we used to	43.5	35.8	19.9
Buying same quality products in smaller quantities	44.5	36.4	18.4
Changing brands because they are expensive	58.1	25.1	26.0
Buying large economy size packages	46.5	29.7	22.4
No longer buying certain items	50.7	29.2	18.9
More careful in the use of products	66.1	22.5	10.7
Making special efforts to eliminate waste of all kinds	62.9	22.5	12.8
In the purchase of clothing and other household products:			
Reducing the frequency of purchases	61.4	26.6	11.7
Buying lower quality items	25.5	25.6	48.1
Buying a different brand	27.6	30.7	40.9
Buying in smaller quantities than we used to	39.9	29.2	29.7
In the purchase of clothing and other household products:			
Paying more attention to sale announcements than in the past	61.4	22.5	15.3
Using discount coupons more often than in the past	49.6	20.5	27.6
Fixing and repairing things around the house more often than in the past	37.9	26.1	33.2
Buying more through mail orders	12.7	11.2	73.7
Buying more used items	13.7	17.4	67.1
Stocking up in large quantities as we expect the prices to go up further	24.0	21.5	53.7
Using and caring for the products more carefully	32.7	31.2	13.8
In the purchase of durable goods: (autos, appliances, small appliances)			
Generally postponing the purchase	57.9	24.1	17.3
Purchasing or considering buying a different model (or type) than what we normally like to buy	37.3	30.2	30.1
Using the present product although we would like to change it	48.6	28.2	21.4
Paying more attention to careful use and maintenance of the products	73.5	18.9	6.5
In relation to purchasing-related activities			
Doing *more* comparative shopping	70.7	16.9	11.2
Shopping in some stores more than we used to do	40.4	30.2	27.6
Shopping in some stores now which we did not shop in the past	35.3	22.5	40.4
Spending more time on shopping	35.8	30.7	32.2
Stopped shopping in some stores	36.8	28.2	32.7

Source: C. P. Rao and G. E. Kiser, "An Evaluation of Consumer Inflation Psychology and An Assessment of Income Efforts," in Henry Nash and Donald Robin, eds., *Southern Marketing Association Proceedings*, 1977, pp. 15–16.

productivity, and (3) reducing costs. All three are difficult in inflationary times.

The fast-food business, for example, took a real beating in recent years because they had to raise prices so much. Their prices, for example, jumped almost 50 percent in one year because of the rise in the cost of meat.

The annual increase in the minimum wage causes problems, as do runaway costs for energy. The high cost of borrowing money is also a problem.

WHAT ARE THE CHANGES IN THE COMPETITIVE ENVIRONMENTS?

Retailing increasingly has an international focus. Large retailers are now often importing directly from foreign countries. They do this to save money on the cost of the goods. But they may have problems with delivery, poor product quality, and political unrest.

What about foreign competition?

Some retailers are also in trouble for "dumping" foreign goods on U.S. markets. (*Dumping* is the sale of foreign goods in the United States at below their fair market value. The practice is illegal under federal law if it damages U.S. industries). Companies charged with dumping Japanese TV sets include Sears, Wards, Penneys, and other firms such as Western Auto. Dumping recently cost Sears, Roebuck several million dollars.[15]

Foreign firms are also buying out U.S. retail firms. Inflation is now as high here as in some other parts of the world. Also we have a more stable government. This country used to be the place for the homeless poor. Today it is the place for rich foreigners who want to keep their money!

Foreign investors usually buy regional firms, not those with national markets. They invest in stores in high-income areas in such cities as New York and Chicago. Or they may buy an interest in regional shopping malls in the Sunbelt. The purchase of 42 percent of the A&P Company stock by a German firm was a recent purchase of a national retailer by a foreign firm.

WATCH OUT FOR MONEY PROBLEMS

Tight money can also cause you problems. Small businesses, especially retailers, are hit the hardest and first by rising interest costs. Small retailers normally do not qualify as "best customers" for financial institutions. They usually pay 2 or 3 percent above the so-called prime rate for money. Borrowing is especially tough for retailers with annual sales less than $500,000 a year. Banks are often unwilling to lend money to these firms. Also, few retailers can issue stock to attract funds and they often do not have long-range lines of credit at banks.

The first reaction of many stores to tight money is to hold sales to get the needed cash. This often does not work because many other retail outlets are likely to have the same idea. The result is higher sales but lower profits. Retailers then are faced with the need to lay off part-time workers, reduce advertising, and perhaps cut back on their inventory. Some retailers may turn to the Small Business Administration (SBA) for help. Still, relief from the SBA is normally modest at best.

A good long-term commonsense strategy is to 1) always strive to maintain a good credit rating, 2) seek to maintain good relationships with suppliers through both good and bad times, and 3) always offer a quality product or service so you do not have to compete only on the basis of price when the competitive environment becomes tougher than usual.

HOW CAN YOU AVOID MERCHANDISE SHORTAGES?

Merchandise shortages are no longer uncommon. Also, delivery dates are long. Today, it may be better to do business with only a few suppliers. Suppliers pay more attention to their large accounts. Also, try to buy goods months in advance so they will be available when you need them.

Shortages present a good opportunity to look at your inventory. You may want to discard or cut back on low-profit margin numbers. Shortages may also lead to a blurring of seasons.

Your promotional strategies become more important during periods of shortages. You will need to manage shopper demand by stimulating or discouraging customer demand for certain product categories and brands, depending on both cost and supply problems.

How can you increase productivity?

Hold business costs down by taking over old buildings. Their rental costs may be less than 40 percent of the rent for new buildings. Modify your existing buildings to save energy.

Try to get more work out of the same people. Consider opening later and closing later. Then you are only open during high sales hours. Labor costs are more than half your total expenses in retailing. So, anything you can do to get more sales from the same people will help you make a profit.

WHAT ARE YOUR COMPETITORS DOING?

Competition is tougher than ever. Why? Population growth is slowing down, more stores are building in the same areas and management is getting smarter.

Regional firms are moving into smaller markets. They have large expert staffs to help select sites, to forecast sales, and to buy and price items right. Independents have a tough time winning against these firms.

But one of your biggest problems is that the same items are sold in so many different types of outlets today. This is known as *scrambled merchandising.* A supermarket may carry the fastest selling drugs at prices lower than a druggist and may sell liquors and even cooked food at prices below firms specializing in these items. Drugstores may sell hardware items and sports equipment. Thus, it's hard for you to know your real competition. For example, Table 8–6 shows that 32 percent of health and beauty aids are sold in grocery stores and 32 percent in drugstores. Less than 6 percent is sold in department stores!

Your toughest competition comes from people who are part of a merchandising system or chain. You know how tough competition would be for you as an independent if you had to face McDonald's, Sears, Wendy's, or other

TABLE 8-6
Sales of health and beauty aids, hardware products, and machine-made glassware by type of outlet

Health and beauty aids

Type of outlet	Percent of total sales
Grocery stores	32.2%
Drugstores	32.1
Discount stores	12.0
General merchandise and variety stores	8.4
Nonstore retailers	8.2
Department stores	5.7
All other	1.4
Total	100.0%

Hardware products

Type of outlet	Percent of total sales
Hardware and building material store	31.0%
General merchandise and variety stores	23.8
Discount stores	17.7
Home improvement centers	16.4
Department store	4.9
Nonstore retailers	2.0
Grocery stores	2.0
All other	2.2
Total	100.0%

Machine-made glassware

Type of outlet	Percent of total sales
Discount stores	27.8%
General merchandise and variety stores	24.6
Department stores	18.2
Grocery stores	11.8
Specialty stores	7.9
Drugstores	4.3
All other	5.4
Total	100.0%

Source: Albert D. Bates, *Retailing and Its Environment.* © 1979 by Litton Educational Publishing, Inc. Reprinted by permission of D. Van Nostrand Company.

national firms. These firms have better management, better promotion, lower prices, and better personnel. But you can still beat them at the local level by responding more quickly to trends in the local market and creating a strong local market image for yourself.

THE ENVIRONMENT AND SOCIAL ISSUES

Shopping centers are getting harder to put together. Society is concerned about their effects on air and water pollution and the loss of open space. Many communities today are trying to limit growth. They often refuse to zone land for business purposes and do not agree to provide access to water and sewage.

Provisions of new laws like the Occupational Health and Safety Act can increase costs to modify your buildings. You are subject to fines if you do not comply with the laws.

SUMMARY

Having to face constant change may shake you up. But it's a fact of life in retailing. Markets are always changing, new laws are passed, the consumer mood changes, and new types of competition come. You have to be alert in order to survive.

Growth will continue in the Sunbelt and in smaller cities. Inflation will remain high. Consumers may make fewer shopping trips and more purchases by mail or telephone. Goods for you to sell probably will also be harder to get. Consumers are clearly uncertain about the future.

We don't know what the future holds for the economy and the consumer. But you must keep a close eye on the economic and social changes if you are going to survive and prosper.

NOTES

1. "Rumors Hurt McDonald's," *Tuscaloosa News*, November 14, 1978 p. 2.
2. "Not Kosher," *Time*, November 13, 1978, p. 56.
3. "Protecting against Blackouts," *Chain Store Age Executive* (September 1977), p. 20.
4. "New Minority: The Average American Family," *Marketing News*, February 14, 1978, p. 3.
5. *The Wall Street Journal*, November 16, 1977, p. 1.
6. *Sales and Marketing Management*, November 14, 1977, p. 34.
7. "The Towering Rise in Downtown Construction," *Business Week*, March 5, 1979, p. 2.
8. Gurney Breckenfield, "Business Loves the Sunbelt (and Vice Versa)," *Fortune*, (June 1977), pp. 133–134.
9. *Advertising Age*, September 12, 1977.

10. "Age of ME Poses Many Problems for Marketers," *Marketing News,* June 30, 1978, p. 3.

11. "Leonard L. Berry and Don H. Wilson," Retailing—The Next Ten Years," *Journal of Retailing* (Fall 1977).

12. "Age of ME," p. 3.

13. Leonard L. Berry, "The New Consumer," Address at a conference on Competitive Structure in Retail Markets: The Department Store Perspective, New York City, April 6, 1979.

14. Leon Winer and J. S. Schiff, "Rising Energy Costs Will Alter Marketing Patterns," *Marketing News,* May 6, 1977, p. 4.

15. "U.S. Chains Face Heavy Fines for Dumped Japanese Televisions," *Chain Store Age Executive* (March 1979), p. 54; For additional reading, see "Direct Importing by Retailers Has Its Tradeoffs," *Chain Store Age Executive* (March 1979), pp. 52–54.

DISCUSSION QUESTIONS

1. What are the effects of inflation on the retailer? How can you adjust to these effects? What about the effects of recession?

2. What are some of the steps which you can take to handle such problems as materials and energy shortages?

3. How can you continue to grow and expand in the face of slowed population growth?

4. How are Americans adjusting their buying behavior to the environments of the 1980s? What can you do to make a profit?

5. What elements of consumer demand are likely to remain unchanged in the face of changes in the economy? Which parts of demand will likely be hurt the most?

6. Such measures of change as unemployment levels and the rate of inflation may present misleading information to a retailer. How can management avoid being misled by these indicators of change? What types of information would be useful at the store level? How can this information be obtained?

7. What are the types of products or services which are likely to be hurt as the population gets increasingly older? What products or services will benefit?

8. Why is the major growth in population occurring in the Sunbelt states? Will these changes increase the probable success of a retail outlet in these areas? Why or why not? Does this mean that opportunities for retailing will not continue to remain good in other parts of the United States? Discuss.

9. What best describes the consumer mood today? How does this affect merchandising patterns?

PROJECTS

1. Visit the downtown business district of your town and determine:
    a. How many vacant stores.
    b. Which particular types are vacant.
    Discuss the factors leading to this. If the downtown area in your town has been revitalized, how did they do it? How successful has it been?

2. Set up a research project to find out how the retailer believes the energy crisis may affect him or her. What plans are being made to cope? Is it being taken seriously? What do you predict will be the major impact in the long run on the retail structure in general of energy shortages?

Minicase 8-1   The Men's Shop in Mountainville, an industrial city of 75,000 people had enjoyed several years of successful business. Management thus expanded their offerings in both selection and depth. Then the economy took a sudden downturn which resulted in widespread layoffs at many local industries. Sales declined sharply and left the Men's Shop holding a rather large inventory. To make matters even worse, there were some major changes in men's fashions and several new styles were introduced which soon became very popular. It was only by drastic reductions in price that the old stock was sold. For the last couple of years the Men's Shop has kept inventories at a low level by offering only a few styles in depth.

However, most economic indicators now predict an upturn in the economy and many local plants are beginning to resume normal operation. The Men's Shop has been offered an excellent buy on a new line of good quality men's suits. However, in order to carry this line, it will have to make a substantial purchase as the supplier expects retailers to offer the full line in depth.

After thinking it over, management declined the offer and purchased a small selection of a less well-known, but good brand, from another supplier.

1.   What factors do you think caused the Men's Shop to make the decision they made?
2.   What are the major advantages and disadvantages of their decision?
3.   Do you feel that they were justified in making the decision they made?
4.   Was their decision based more on historical experience or future outlook? Which is more relevant for marketing decisions? Explain.

Minicase 8-2   Martin Jones is the owner of a local neighborhood service station. He has a full service operation and has been in business for 15 years. He provides various repair services for his customers and picks up and delivers vehicles for his customers. Also, he has a large number of female customers who still want the usual full service when they come to purchase gasoline.

The gasoline shortage in 1979 posed major problems for Mr. Jones. His allocation of gasoline was not sufficient to allow him to sell gasoline his usual 60 hours per week. He is considering several alternatives, including:

1.   Placing a dollar limit on the amount of gasoline which could be purchased by a customer.
2.   Selling gasoline only during certain hours of the day.
3.   Not opening on weekends.

During a recent period, long lines formed at the station and customers had to wait up to two hours to purchase a tank of gasoline. Mr. Jones noticed many strange faces in the lines. Additionally, his regular customers complained bitterly about having to wait in line with people who apparently had never made purchases at Mr. Jones' station before. He doesn't know what to do. On the one hand, he would like to limit sales to his regular customers or at least give them first priority. However, he likes the additional volume of the new customers. He hopes he can convert some of them to regular customers for some of the other services which he offers at the station. Besides he does not know how he can take better care of his present customers although he wants to do so. What would you advise Mr. Jones to do? Why?

9

PEOPLE (STAFFING) PROBLEMS

The purposes of this chapter are to show you how to:

- Recruit employees.
- Select employees.
- Train employees.
- Evaluate employees.
- Handle pay and benefits.
- Handle union-management problems.
- Motivate employees.
- Provide employee job enrichment.

- Define the following terms and concepts:

Equal Employment Opportunity Commission
Title 7, Civil Rights Act of 1964
Age Discrimination Act of 1967
Equal Pay Act of 1963
Discrimination

Job evaluation
Fringe benefits
Grievance procedures
Job enrichment

Retailing is a people business with tough people problems. The industry pays low starting wages to management and to salespersons. Also, too often only limited training is given. The results are low employee morale, high turnover, high payroll costs, and unhappy customers.

Everyone has probably walked out of a store because of poor salespersons. We think that such persons cause as many lost sales as lack of goods. The situation in Study Aid 9–1 is well known to all of us. Also, the person selling books doesn't read and the person selling tennis rackets usually doesn't play tennis!

Top management is now starting to give more attention to people issues. A good personnel office can avoid such problems as (1) wrong pay scales, (2) weak training programs, (3) hiring the wrong person for a job, and (4) violating affirmative action guidelines.

Retailing is often seen as a poor career choice. Young people often say "who wants low starting salaries, long working hours, and close contact all day with strangers?" Sure, these are drawbacks! But in fact, chances to move up in retailing are greater than in many other industries. Also, salaries and working conditions are improving.

HOW DO YOU RECRUIT, SELECT, TRAIN, AND EVALUATE EMPLOYEES

Good personnel planning involves the matching of management needs with human resources. Personnel planning occurs in all organizations, even though the planning is informal in small stores.

Your demand for employees depends upon the demand for your product and services. Thus, one way to determine your personnel needs is to think about the likely demand for your product and services during the next three to five years. Do you have plans for expansion, or perhaps plans to close a particular branch? You also need an analysis of peak traffic hours so that less coverage can be arranged during slow periods. Part-time people can play an important role in such instances.

Begin your process of personnel planning with job design and analysis. Job designs and/or descriptions help employee morale and help you plan. *Job designs* specify the methods and content of jobs. *Job analysis* then helps you determine the skills, the abilities, and responsibilities needed in an employee. *Job descriptions* can then be developed from your job analysis.

Careful consideration of job analysis and planning before you hire can thus help you determine your employment needs, the skills and attitudes you are seeking and pay levels which perhaps will be necessary to attract good employees. Think about the issues of recruiting, selection, and training only after you have given careful thought to the types of people you want to hire.

HOW DO YOU RECRUIT?

Recruiting in retailing is often haphazard. Management needs to give more attention to matching job needs with the interests and skills of a potential employee.

STUDY AID 9-1

A PERSONAL RECONNAISSANCE

Of the many problems that bother store managers and promotion people, the worst and most difficult to solve is sales personnel.

The salesperson who won't face you, won't approach you, won't ask "May I help you?" who is on the phone making a date, is almost standard. The success of everything that's been done to make a store known, appealing, and warm to the customer is dependent on this contact.

In one major shopping center in the Southeast, which cost the developer $20 million, I decided to try an experiment. I walked the mall at a time when I knew managers would be at dinner. I went into 21 stores before the first salesperson even noticed me. One woman was reading. I walked around her twice, walked over to a rack of clothing, picked up a jacket, sneezed, strolled back to her, asked her how much it was. No answer. I put the jacket down in front of her and stomped out.

Why is this? In many centers employees are lured from store to store with promises of small raises (even though, managers agree not to lure away from each other).

Have you ever tried to make a purchase at 8:30 P.M. in a center whose hours are 9 to 9? Forget it! "My register is closed." "Go to the next cashier." Don't be at the employee exit at 9 unless you want to be mobbed.

A center that officially closes at 9 is really out of business at 8:30, especially the major stores. Everyone is powdering her/his nose.

Something else that drives promotion people crazy is the "What's going on in the mall?" question. Most salespeople couldn't care less. Ask almost any employee. Answer: "Don't know." It doesn't matter if notices have been posted or managers have told employees. It could be a skating rink, an art show, a flower show—they don't know!

This situation is more than serious. The salesperson is the center's window to the world. All promotion, TV, radio, newspaper and circular advertising combined doesn't equal the person-to-person contact between the customer and the employee. A difficult problem, unending, with no good solution.

Source: *Chain Store Age Executive,* March 1978, p. 47.

Sources of applicants   The typical sources of applicants are walk-ins, referrals by employees, employment agencies, and recruiting programs in high schools and colleges as shown in Table 9–1. You need a way to make sure you get exactly the same information on all of the persons who apply for your jobs so that you can do a better job of evaluation and selection. Figure 9–1 is a commonly used application for employment which is designed to ensure that complete information is obtained on each applicant.

TABLE 9–1
The most frequent employee recruitment sources based on a national sample of retailers (percent)

Source	Salaried Employees	Hourly paid Employees
Walk-ins	43	88
Employee referrals	50	82
Newspapers	54	75
Radio	1	3
Private employment agencies	57	31
Public employment agencies	24	62
Minority media	16	25
High schools	3	29
Distributive Education programs	3	29
Two-year colleges	29	43
Four-year colleges	46	38

Source: Myron Gable and Charles Holton, *A Survey of Current Personnel Practices* (New York: National Retail Merchants Association, 1977), p. 15.

Recruiting

How do you avoid discrimination in recruiting? First, avoid stating that you prefer a person of a certain "race and/or sex" when advertising or posting job notices. Second, follow the "right procedures." Word-of-mouth recruiting by current employees may not be good enough. If the current work force contains only a few minority employees, this might limit the number of such applicants. Third, placing job ads where they may not reach minority group members may also violate the law. Fourth, make sure that the employment

"Are you sure you won't quit after a year or two to get married?"
Reprinted by permission The Wall Street Journal

FIGURE 9-1

APPLICATION FOR EMPLOYMENT

NAME _____ (_____) JOB PREFERENCE _____
First   Initial   Last   Maiden

ADDRESS _____ Full-Time _____ Part-Time _____ On Call _____
Street   City/State   Zip Code

SOCIAL SECURITY NUMBER _____ / _____ / _____   TELEPHONE NO. _____ MARITAL STATUS _____

EDUCATION: HIGH SCHOOL _____ DATE OF BIRTH _____
VOCATIONAL TRAINING _____   Month   Day   Year
COLLEGE _____ SPECIAL SKILLS _____
TYPING _____ SHORTHAND _____
Have you served in the Armed Services of the U.S.A.? _____ Branch _____
Dates _____ Type of Discharge _____

PLEASE COMPLETE ALL INFORMATION REQUESTED AS FULLY AS POSSIBLE

EMPLOYMENT HISTORY (Must include last 3 employers)

Present or Last	Nature of	Your
Employer _____	Business _____	Supervisor _____
	Position	Weekly
Street _____	Held _____	Salary _____
City & State _____	Dates:	Reason for
Telephone number _____	From _____ To _____	Leaving _____
Next Previous	Nature of	Your
Employer _____	Business _____	Supervisor _____
	Position	Weekly
Street _____	Held _____	Salary _____
City & State _____	Dates:	Reason for
Telephone number _____	From _____ To _____	Leaving _____
Next Previous	Nature of	Your
Employer _____	Business _____	Supervisor _____
	Position	Weekly
Street _____	Held _____	Salary _____
City & State _____	Dates:	Reason for
Telephone number _____	From _____ To _____	Leaving _____

PERSONAL REFERENCES (Not to include relatives)

Name _____ Address _____ Phone No. _____
Name _____ Address _____ Phone No. _____
Name _____ Address _____ Phone No. _____

Have you ever been employed by _____ Co.? _____ If so, please give dates _____
Who referred you to _____ Co.? _____ Do you have any friends or relatives presently employed by
_____ Co.? _____ If so, whom? _____
How many days have you lost in the last three years due to serious illness or injury? _____
What was the nature of the illness or injury? _____
Have you ever been arrested and convicted of a crime other than a minor traffic violation? _____
If so, when? _____ Please give details _____
Have you ever been arrested and convicted for shoplifting? _____
Have you ever drawn workman's compensation from a previous employer for a work injury? _____
If so, what was the nature of the injury? _____
In case of emergency, Contact _____ Phone No. _____

PLEASE COMPLETE INFORMATION ON THE OTHER SIDE

agencies you use do not discriminate in referring persons to you. The use of minority employment agencies is a good idea.

You probably should use a process which does the following:

1. Indicates in all job ads that the firm is "an equal opportunity employer" interested in attracting and hiring minority and women applicants.
2. Utilizes advertisements and media designed to reach minorities.
3. Uses state employment offices whose services tend to be used more by minorities.

FIGURE 9-1 (*continued*)

HEIGHT _____ Ft. _____ In.   WEIGHT _____ lbs.

CHECK ANY OF THE ILLNESSES BELOW THAT YOU HAVE OR HAVE BEEN SUBJECT TO IN THE PAST

Asthma _____   Nervous disorders _____
Back trouble or injury _____   Are you under Dr.'s care for this condition _____
Diabetes _____   Rheumatic Fever _____
Epilepsy_____controlled with medication_____   Skin Infections _____
Fractures _____   Tuberculosis _____
Heart trouble _____   Varicose Veins _____
Hernia _____
High Blood Pressure _____   None of the above _____

Have you ever been in an automobile accident? _____ If so, when? _____

  Nature and extent of injuries? _____

Check any defects you have in Hearing _____ Sight _____ Hands _____ Feet _____

Are you under a Doctor's care? _____ If so, reason _____

Is there any work you are physically unable to do? _____

I hereby apply for employment and certify that the facts set forth in the above in reference to my application for employment are true and

complete. I understand that false or dishonest answers or omissions shall be considered sufficient cause for rating me ineligible for

employment or discharge after hiring, my employment being based on the truth of answers made. I authorize the company to investigate all

statements made, information furnished, and all matters relevant to this application.

_____   _____   _____
APPLICANT'S SIGNATURE   Witnessed By   Date

FOR OFFICE USE ONLY - - - - - DO NOT COMPLETE BELOW THIS LINE

Interviewed by _____ Store _____
Considered for the following position (s) _____
           _____

References checked by _____
1. _____
2. _____
3. _____
Approved by: _____ Date _____
EMPLOYMENT INFORMATION

Employee number _____ Start Date _____ Store _____ Department _____
Full-Time _____ Part-Time _____ On Call _____ Position _____
Hourly rate _____ Weekly rate _____ Eligible for _____
Separation Date _____ Reason _____ Rehire _____
Re-employed _____ Position _____ Rate _____ Store _____

4. Works with groups in minority communities which try to locate employment for minority members.

Table 9–2 highlights the antidiscrimination laws in hiring.

HOW DO YOU SELECT EMPLOYEES?

A variety of selection methods are available to help you select among the applicants for your position. The selection process allows you to develop an objective way of matching the applicants with your needs. A useful way to handle this problem is by performance criteria. Begin by identifying the features of persons who have previously performed well the job for which you are interviewing. Then look for the same features in potential new employees. Normally you are only looking for a few such characteristics. Among the things you may evaluate are intelligence scores, tests of manual dexterity,

TABLE 9-2
Major federal fair employment practices regulations

Regulation	General coverage	Private employer jursidiction	Affirmative action requirements
Title VII of the Civil Rights Act of 1964, as amended	Discrimination in employment on the basis of race, color, sex, national origin, or religion.	Employers with 15 or more employees.	Affirmative action may be included in a conciliation agreement or by court order.
Age Discrimination in Employment Act of 1967, as amended	Age discrimination in employment of persons between the ages of 40–70.	Employers with 20 or more employees.	Affirmative action may be required after discrimination is found to exist.
Equal Pay Act of 1963, as amended	Discrimination in compensation on the basis of sex.	Employers under coverage of the Fair Labor Standards Act.	Affirmative action other than salary adjustment and back pay is not required.
Executive Orders 11246, 11375, and 11141	Discrimination in employment on the basis of race, color, religion, sex.	Employers holding federal contracts or subcontracts in excess of $10,000.	Written affirmative action plans are required of federal contractors and subcontractors with contracts in excess of $50,000 and 50 or more employees.
Vocational Rehabilitation Act Amendments of 1973 and Executive Order 11914	Discrimination in employment on the basis of physical or mental handicap.	Employers holding federal contracts or subcontracts in excess of $2,500.	Same as above.
Vietnam Era Veterans Readjustment Act of 1974	Discrimination against disabled veterans and Vietnam War veterans, but more of an Affirmative action order than antidiscrimination policy.	Employers holding federal contracts or subcontracts in excess of $10,000.	Same as above.

Source: Daniel Gallagher, "Fair Employment Practices Regulations Affecting Small Business Employee Recruitment and Selection," *American Journal of Small Business,* vol. 3 (January 1979), p. 7.

formal education, and related job experience. Other intangible, but important things are personality, overall physical appearance (including style of dress), and attitude.

Selection techniques

After building a pool of applicants, your selection process also has to be free of bias. As shown in Table 9–3, the most frequent helps in selection are the application blank, the interview, personal and business references. Each of these can cause problems.

You cannot discriminate on the basis of "race . . . and/or sex." So your job application forms, preemployment interviews, or selection tests may be illegal if they cause you to be less likely to hire certain groups of persons. For example, you can't hire only high school or college graduates unless you can show that your educational requirement is related to job performance.

Other things which the courts have held may be illegal include:

1. Refusal to hire persons because of their arrest record.
2. Refusal to hire persons because of a poor credit record.

TABLE 9-3
The most frequently used techniques in employee selection based on a national sample of retailers (percent)

Techniques	Salaried employees	Hourly paid employees
Application blank	78	92
Test	9	16
Interview	82	95
Polygraph test	4	7
Physical exam	14	14
Credit report	33	27
Police check	19	22
Business references	70	75
Personal references	56	62
Handwriting analysis	0	1
Assessment center	3	1

Source: Myron Gable and Charles Holton, *A Survey of Current Personnel Practices* (New York: National Retail Merchants Association, 1977), p. 24.

3. Rejection of persons based on adverse personnel reports from other companies without giving the person an opportunity to speak to the report.
4. Use of minimum height or weight requirements.
5. Denial of employment to unwed mothers.
6. Rejection of a person because of appearance or manner of speech if the appearance and manner of speech is peculiar to a race or national origin.[1]

Thus, in interviewing people you probably should not ask about their age, religion, financial status, whether they are married, their military discharge, or their arrest record unless you can prove that these things affect their ability to do a job. Questions about handicaps and health can be asked only if they relate to job performance. Other guidelines are shown in Study Aid 9-2.

Selection tests

Your selection tests also cannot discriminate on the basis of "race and/or sex." Also, the test must be job related. The burden of proof rests with you.

Even if your tests are valid, you may still have to show that no other way exists to select employees which would have less impact on certain groups.

HOW DO YOU TRAIN EMPLOYEES?

Training is an effort to improve employee skills. Every person you hire needs at least a minimum of training. Also, a basic orientation to job expectations and work requirements is necessary. During the training program stress that the firm is in business to serve the consumer and to help the consumer shop. Provide your employees with product knowledge and stress the need for positive attitudes toward customers. Many types of training are used (see Table 9-4). On-the-job training is used by more than 90 percent of retail employers. Salespersons expecially need skills in customer relations and product knowledge.

Tell your employees how they can move up in the company. Provide information on salary, benefits, and company policies. The benefits of training

STUDY AID 9-2

CHECKLIST ON THE HIRING INTERVIEW

1. Don't ask the applicant's age.
2. Don't ask the applicant's date of birth.
3. Don't ask the applicant what church he/she attends or the name of his/her priest, rabbi, or minister.
4. Don't ask the applicant what his/her father's surname is.
5. Don't ask the female applicant what her maiden name was.
6. Don't ask the applicant whether he/she is married, divorced, separated, widowed, or single (but you may ask Mr., Mrs., Miss, or Ms).
7. Don't ask the applicant who resides with him/her.
8. Don't ask the applicant how many children he/she has.
9. Don't ask the ages of any children of the applicant.
10. Don't ask who will care for the children while the applicant is working.
11. Don't ask the applicant where a spouse or parent resides or works (although you may ask whether relatives of the applicant are or have been employed by the company).
12. Don't ask the applicant if he/she owns or rents his/her place of residence.
13. Don't ask the applicant whether he/she ever had his/her wages garnisheed.
14. Don't ask the applicant whether he/she was ever arrested.

Source: *Checklist on the Hiring Interview* (New York: National Retail Merchants Association, 1976), p. 3.

include higher worker output (and thus better customer satisfaction), and improved morale.

HOW DO YOU EVALUATE EMPLOYEES?

All employees have a need to be recognized and to feel that they are an important part of the firm. Too often they feel that they do not get the recognition they deserve. Formal periodic evaluations are one way to overcome this problem. Retailers need to improve their ability to relate to their

TABLE 9-4
The most frequently used training methods for full-time hourly employees based on a national sample of retailers (percent)

Methods Used	25 employees or less	Over 5,000 employees
Lecture	28.3	81.5
Films	3.3	77.8
Role playing	8.3	40.7
Classroom training	5.0	88.9
Informal on-the-job training	91.7	92.6
Job rotation	30.0	40.7
Programmed instructional materials	11.7	59.3
Coaching	35.0	44.4

Source: Myron Gable and Charles Holton, *Personnel Practices of the Retail Industry* (New York: National Retail Merchants Association, 1977), p. 31.

employees. A regular evaluation process can do much to help this problem. Above all, make your evaluation more than simply techniques oriented.

Whatever the method of evaluation, management should hold evaluation interviews for employees and tell them the results of the evaluation. Both the supervisor and the employee should sign and/or witness the form. Employees who disagree should have the chance to put an explanatory statement in their personnel record.

Reasons for evaluation

Employees are evaluated (1) for wage and salary reasons, (2) for promotions, (3) for transfers, (4) to correct poor performance, and (5) to reward good performance.

Frequency of evaluation

Large retailers use formal evaluation systems. The objective evaluations are normally done once or twice a year. If a union is involved, criteria for evaluation should be developed with them.

For beginning employees, evaluation is usually twice a year. For higher level employees, evaluations are normally once a year. The immediate supervisor usually does the evaluation.

Techiques of evaluation

Many techniques exist to help you evaluate employees (see Table 9–5). But overall, only the rating scale is used by at least 50 percent of retailers. The checklist is also often used. Research has shown that over 50 percent of retailers do not use any type of formal employee evaluation.[3] Figures 9–2 and 9–3 illustrate employee job performance rating forms for selling and nonselling positions.

HOW DO YOU HANDLE EMPLOYEE PAY AND BENEFITS?

Compensation is the way employees are paid for their work. Methods of pay vary widely. Wage levels depend on market conditions, union contracts, and economic conditions. The federal and state governments also play a major role. The most familiar wage guideline is the minimum wage which must be paid to almost all employees.

TABLE 9–5
Techniques used in evaluating employees based on a national sample of retailers (percent)

Evaluation techniques	Salaried employees	Full-time hourly employees	Part-time
Ranking of employees	13.6	17.3	16.1
Rating scale	53.4	66.4	65.3
Field review	17.5	12.3	12.6
Forced distribution	1.0	2.3	2.5
Weighted checklist	12.6	14.1	15.6
Checklist	33.0	40.0	41.2
Critical incident	9.2	6.8	5.5
Free-form essay	32.0	17.7	16.1
Multiple techniques	26.7	19.5	20.6
Peer evaluation	15.1	16.8	17.6

Source: Myron Gable and Charles Holton, *Personnel Practices of the Retail Industry* (New York: National Retail Merchants Association, 1977), p. 48.

FIGURE 9-2

EMPLOYEE JOB PERFORMANCE RATING—*SELLING*

	RATER #1	
	RATER #2	

EMPLOYEE'S NAME	DEPT.	SALES NO.	DATE SENT TO DEPT. FOR RATING

Check below each factor the rating term which best represents your estimate of the employee's performance in that factor. Buyers are to rate with a red pencil. Service Managers will use a blue pencil.

REMINDERS
1. Do not rate hurriedly. Each factor and each employee must be given separate and complete consideration.
2. Ratings must be objective and factual.
3. In rating each factor, do not compare employees with each other but do rate each one against what you consider to be satisfactory performance.
4. Do not permit dollar volume to influence the rating.

DEFINITION OF RATING TERMS	Approaches perfection, leaves little to be desired.	Generally beyond expected requirements.	Meets expected requirements satisfactorily.	Inconsistent, or slightly below standards.	Consistently fails to measure up to standards.
1. CUSTOMER APPROACH Consider promptness, pleasant manner, courtesy, interest and enthusiasm.	Unusual interest and enthusiasm at all times. ☐	Prompt, alert and gracious approach. ☐	Reasonable prompt approach. Favorable attitude. ☐	Often slow and indifferent, rarely enthusiastic. ☐	Unsatisfactory, always slow, disinterested, bored manner. ☐
2. KNOWLEDGE OF MERCHANDISE Consider knowledge of sizes, styles, price lines, fabrics, and salespoints.	Extremely well informed, always eager to improve knowledge ☐	Has better than average knowledge of merchandise. ☐	Knowledge is adequate and meets requirements. ☐	Knowledge is spotty, lacks assurance. ☐	Lacks basic merchandise information makes no effort to learn. ☐
3. PRESENTATION OF MERCHANDISE Consider appreciative display (to customers) and treatment of merchandise, volunteering information, encouraging trying on and handling of merchandise by customer; presenting ample selections.	Unusual ability, finesse and enthusiasm in presenting merchandise so as to create most favorable impression ☐	Always displays sufficient merchandise, handles effectively, gives pertinent information. ☐	Usually displays merchandise with care and interest, volunteers information. ☐	Inconsistent, rarely volunteers information, lacks enthusiasm. ☐	Displays mdse. without interest, never volunteers information. ☐
4. SUGGESTIVE SELLING Consider degree of ability to increase sales by suggesting substitutes, multiple purchases, and or related merchandise.	Always makes effective suggestions. ☐	Usually makes effective suggestions. ☐	Often makes effective suggestions. ☐	Seldom makes effective suggestions. ☐	Never suggests. ☐
5. MAINTENANCE OF CLIENT BOOK Consider legibility, number of customer contacts, new clients made, purchase record and whether or not book is kept up-to-date.	Unusually well kept book. Always legible Client contacts made regularly. Unusual number of new clients ☐	Book well kept and legible. Good number of client contacts, and new clients made. ☐	Usually well kept and reasonably legible book. Average number of client contacts, and new clients made. ☐	Carelessly kept book and often illegible. Few client contacts. Almost no new clients. ☐	Extremely careless about book. Usually illegible. Does not contact clients. No new clients. ☐
6. ACCURACY Consider frequency of errors in salescheck procedure, special orders, monogram orders, etc., or in giving information or making promises to customers.	Unusual accuracy and thoroughness ☐	Quality high. Work very well done. ☐	Generally accurate and reliable — few errors. ☐	Sometimes careless and inaccurate. ☐	Extremely careless, inaccurate. ☐
7. COOPERATION Consider degree of willingness to accept and follow store policies and procedures; to comply with instructions; ability to accept constructive criticism.	Extraordinarily cooperative and enthusiastic in all respects. ☐	Very cooperative, flexible, sets good example. ☐	Usually conforms cheerfully to policies and instructions. ☐	Unreasonable at times, inconsistent. ☐	Chronic complainer, inflexible, seldom accepts criticism, belligerent. ☐
8. RELATIONSHIP WITH OTHER EMPLOYEES Consider disposition, helpfulness and ability to earn respect and confidence of co-workers.	Exceptionally pleasant, helpful, well liked. Sets example and earns esteem of others. ☐	Pleasant disposition, well liked, always helpful. ☐	Maintains effective cooperation and working relations ☐	Not well liked but tolerated. ☐	Irritating personality uncooperative, trouble maker. ☐
9. STOCKWORK AND HOUSEKEEPING Consider initiative, consistency and thoroughness in doing stock and maintaining good housekeeping at counter; effective utilization of free time.	Unusually efficient and dependable, assists others when own work is done. ☐	Makes extra effort to keep stock in good order, keeps counter neat and orderly throughout the day. ☐	Does assigned stock work satisfactorily. ☐	Needs occasional reminder. Sometimes careless. ☐	Evades when possible, needs constant supervision. Careless work ☐
10. APPEARANCE Consider conformance with dress regulations, good grooming, good posture.	Consistently excellent appearance, good style sense, good posture. ☐	Well dressed, good grooming and posture. ☐	Acceptable appearance and grooming, good posture. ☐	Occasionally careless. ☐	Untidy, unkempt, careless grooming, poor posture habits, often out of regulations. ☐
TO BE RATED BY PERSONNEL DEPT. **11a. ATTENDANCE**	No absence ☐	Missed 1 day ☐	Missed 2 days ☐	Missed 3 to 5 days ☐	Missed 6 or more days ☐
11b. PUNCTUALITY	No lateness ☐	Late 1 to 3 times ☐	Late 4 to 10 times ☐	Late 11 to 20 times ☐	Late 20 times or more ☐

IMPORTANT: After completing the rating, fill in information on reverse side.

RATER #1, SIGNATURE	DATE	RATER #2, SIGNATURE	DATE	EMPLOYEE'S RATING SCORE		
				RATER #1	RATER #2	AVE.

CA-1732

All persons who perform the same job and who have the same skills and seniority must be paid equally regardless of age, race, or sex. You need to be familiar with the Fair Labor Standard Act of 1937, as amended. Minimum pay, overtime pay, child labor, and equal rights are covered by the act.

More than 60 percent of all retailers use formal procedure to set wages and salaries. The typical process is as follows:

1. Job analysis—the content of each job.
2. Job description—describing what was found in the job analysis.

FIGURE 9-2 *(continued)*

General comments relating to employee's performance.

Outline employee's strong areas.

In what areas is improvement indicated?

Do you feel the employee is well suited for the type of work she/he is doing? If not, explain.

Outline employee's goals for the next review period.

What progress has the employee made toward achieving goals of last review?

What difference of opinion exists between Rater #1 and Rater #2?

_____
Employee's Signature

QUESTIONS TO BE ANSWERED AFTER DISCUSSION WITH EMPLOYEE

What was the employee's attitude toward the discussion of the appraisal?

What suggestions did you make to assist the employee in improving weak areas?

Do you consider the employee promotable? If yes, to what position or type of work?

_____   _____
Supervisor's Signature   Date of Interview

3. Job specifications—the skills needed to perform the job.
4. Formalized plan of job evaluation—the relative importance of jobs to you.
5. Wage survey—what others are paying for the same positions.

Decide on methods of compensation

When all of the above things are done, you still have to decide how to pay employees. An *hourly wage* (straight salary) is the most common method. It is useful when output is hard to measure.

Commissions may be paid (instead of straight salary) to employees whose

FIGURE 9-3

EMPLOYEE JOB PERFORMANCE RATING – *NON-SELLING*

			RATER #1
			RATER #2

EMPLOYEE'S NAME	DEPT	POSITION	DATE SENT TO DEPT. FOR RATING

Check below each factor the rating term which best represents your estimate of the employee's performance in that factor. Department Managers are to rate with a red pencil and Assistant Department Managers or Service Managers are to use a blue pencil.

REMINDERS

1. Do not rate hurriedly. Each factor and each employee must be given separate and complete consideration.
2. Ratings must be objective and factual.
3. In rating each factor, do not compare employees with each other but do rate each one against what you consider to be satisfactory performance.
4. Do not permit dollar volume to influence the rating.

DEFINITION OF RATING TERMS	Approaches perfection, leaves little to be desired.	Generally beyond expected requirements.	Meets expected requirements satisfactorily.	Inconsistent, or slightly below standards.	Consistently fails to measure up to standards.
1. JOB KNOWLEDGE Consider degree of understanding and familiarity with job functions; also various forms, reports, and procedures where they may apply.	Exceptional understanding of own job and all related work ☐	Well qualified in own job and several related jobs. ☐	Can handle own job satisfactorily. Has some knowledge of related jobs. ☐	Incomplete knowledge of present work. Has little or no knowledge of related jobs. ☐	Very poor job knowledge. Does not absorb instructions. ☐
2. ACCURACY Consider degree of lack of errors; neatness, legibility.	Unusual accuracy and thoroughness. ☐	Quality high. Work very well done. ☐	Generally accurate and reliable – few errors. ☐	Sometimes careless and inaccurate. ☐	Extremely careless, inaccurate. ☐
3. PRODUCTIVITY Consider the amount of work which the employee actually produces.	Very rapid and efficient; consistently produces unusual amount of work. ☐	Works rapidly, produces above average amount of work. ☐	Generally produces a satisfactory quantity of work. ☐	Often wastes time. Inconsistent and limited quantity of work. ☐	Extremely slow; inefficient, produces very little. ☐
4. COOPERATION Consider degree of willingness to accept and follow store policies and procedures; to comply with instructions; ability to accept constructive criticism.	Extraordinarily cooperative and enthusiastic in all respects. ☐	Very cooperative, flexible, sets good example. ☐	Usually conforms cheerfully to policies and instructions. ☐	Unreasonable at times, inconsistent. ☐	Chronic complainer, inflexible, seldom accepts criticism, belligerent. ☐
5. INITIATIVE Consider extent to which employee suggests good new ideas, thinks for himself and is a "self-starter."	Gives more to job than called for. Serious application of efforts. Always finds work to do. ☐	Diligent in work habits. Often goes ahead on his own. ☐	Generally performs routine or assigned duties only. ☐	Does no more than he is told. Requires close supervision. ☐	Must always be told what to do. Requires constant supervision and frequent prodding. ☐
6. RELATIONSHIP WITH OTHER EMPLOYEES Consider disposition, helpfulness and ability to earn respect and confidence of co-workers.	Exceptionally pleasant, helpful, well liked. Sets example and earns esteem of others. ☐	Pleasant disposition, well liked, always helpful. ☐	Maintains effective cooperation and working relations with others. ☐	Not well liked but tolerated. ☐	Irritating personality, uncooperative, trouble maker. ☐
7. DEPENDABILITY Consider extent to which employee can be counted on to carry out instructions, stay on the job and fulfill responsibilities.	Completely reliable, always carries out duties thoroughly and without prompting. ☐	Almost always carries out duties or gives good advance reasons for failure to do so. ☐	Generally does work satisfactorily and only occasionally needs to be reminded of duties. ☐	Avoids work if possible, must be constantly supervised. Finds alibis for delays and errors. ☐	Cannot be counted on to perform work correctly or on time. Does as little as possible. Negligent. ☐
8. INTELLIGENCE AND JUDGMENT Consider ability to learn and understand details of the job and instructions; judgment in making necessary decisions and handling unusual situations.	Unusually quick to learn, shows good judgment, extremely capable. ☐	Learns quickly, generally sound thinking. ☐	Learns and understands instructions satisfactorily. ☐	Slow to learn, often misunderstands. Frequent poor judgment, requires much guidance. ☐	Shows great difficulty in learning, poor understanding of work, frequent repeated instructions. ☐
9. APPEARANCE Consider neatness, good grooming. (Allowances to be made on basis of the demands of the individual job.)	Consistently neat, clean, and well-groomed. Sets a good example. ☐	Almost always well-groomed and acceptably dressed. ☐	Generally acceptable appearance and grooming. ☐	Occasionally careless, is often more untidy or dirty than the job requires. ☐	Regularly untidy, unkempt, unclean. ☐
TO BE RATED BY PERSONNEL DEPT. **10a. ATTENDANCE**	No absence ☐	Missed 1 day ☐	Missed 2 days ☐	Missed 3 to 5 days ☐	Missed 5 or more days ☐
10b. PUNCTUALITY	No lateness ☐	Late 1 to 3 times ☐	Late 4 to 10 times ☐	Late 11 to 20 times ☐	Late 20 times or more ☐

IMPORTANT: After completing the rating, fill in information on reverse side.

RATER #1, SIGNATURE	DATE	RATER #2, SIGNATURE	DATE	EMPLOYEE'S RATING SCORE		
				RATER #1	RATER #2	AVERAGE

output can be measured. More often, employees are paid a combination of an hourly rate and commission. This method helps avoid "hard" selling by some salespersons. A straight commission may cause salespersons to ignore people who look like they are not going to buy.

Employees may also be paid a *bonus* for all sales above a certain quota. Table 9-6 shows the more common ways of paying persons in sales and sales-supporting positions.

How are managers compensated? Management is normally paid a salary plus a percent of sales or profit. Plans may also include stock options.

FIGURE 9-3 (*continued*)

General comments relating to employee's performance.

Outline employee's strong areas.

In what areas is improvement indicated?

Do you feel the employee is well suited for the type of work she/he is doing?
If not, explain.

Outline employee's goals for the next review period.

What progress has the employee made toward achieving goals of last review?

What difference of opinion exists between Rater #1 and Rater #2?

_____
Employee's Signature

QUESTIONS TO BE ANSWERED AFTER DISCUSSION WITH EMPLOYEE

What was the employee's attitude toward the discussion of the appraisal?

What suggestions did you make to assist the employee in improving weak areas?

Do you consider the employee promotable? If yes, to what position or type of work?

_____   _____
Supervisor's Signature   Date of Interview

What about fringe benefits?

Most employers offer some fringe benefits, which are a form of tax-free income. The amount varies but may be 25 percent or more of salaries. Table 9–7 lists the common fringe benefits.

PROBLEMS IN UNION-MANAGEMENT RELATIONS

Unions are becoming important in retailing. Almost 17 percent of retailers today are covered by a union agreement.[4] Unions try to do several things for their members. The goals include job protection, safer working conditions, higher wages, and fair rules and policies in promotion, salary increases, and dismissal.

TABLE 9-6
Four common retail compensation plans (salespeople and sales-supporting)

Types	Basic formula	Common positions covered by such plan	Primary advantage(s)	Primary disadvantage(s)
Straight salary	Paid for stipulated pay period.	Office employees and nontechnical sales areas.	Easily understood and easy to calculate and administer.	Lack of incentive.
Salary plus commission	Base salary plus small additional percent.	Areas of goods where special effort might get plus sales (drapery, garden shop, etc.).	Incentive to sell more.	Somewhat complicated in dealing with.
Quotas	Different dollar levels of goals established at which varying percentages of sales are paid.	Selected big-ticket departments or departments in which money incentives usually produce extra effort. Examples—furniture, shoes, carpeting, etc.	Establishes a "target" for employees needing an incentive and can result in sales of more high markup, sell-up merchandise.	Can become complicated to administer—especially substantiating factors in establishing quotas.
Straight commission	This is truly the incentive plan. Based on percent of sales—usually percent goes up on price lines within a specific line of goods to encourage selling volume-profitable items.	Women's coats, men's suits, furniture, carpeting, outside drapery sales, major appliances, building supplies, etc.	From employer point of view sales performance directly tied to sales results. From employees point of view true incentive: compensated directly for efforts made: easy to understand.	Sales person often doesn't take care of "small-ticket" customer and uses high pressure to close sales.

Source: C. Winston Borgen, *Learning Experiences in Retailing* (Pacific Palisades, Calif.: Goodyear Publishing Co., 1976), p. 124. © 1976 by Goodyear Publishing Co. Reprinted by permission.

TABLE 9-7
Fringe benefits offered retailing employees based on a national sample (percent reporting usage)

Benefit	Salaried employees	Hourly employee
Discounts on merchandise	92.9	96.8
Basic medical plan	84.7	85.7
Dental plan	10.3	10.6
Major medical plan	84.4	80.2
Pension plan	55.8	55.8
Life insurance	78.8	76.5
Cost-of-living adjustment	5.3	6.6
Tuition reimbursement	27.5	21.7
Profit sharing	42.1	38.6
Paid vacation	91.3	94.7
Drug insurance	17.5	17.5
Holiday pay	88.9	91.3
Severance pay	50.5	43.4
Disability insurance	64.0	50.8
Sick pay plan	68.3	65.3
Stock options	13.5	5.0
Travel accident plan	44.7	26.5

Source: Myron Gable and Charles Holton, *Personnel Practices of the Retail Industry* (New York: National Retail Merchants Association, 1977), p. 77.

Management's dealing with unions

Management faces many laws in dealing with unions. The major one is the National Labor Relations Act *(Wagner Act),* as amended by the Labor-Management Relations Act of 1947 *(Taft-Hartley).*

Union contracts are for one or two years. Both you and your employees agree to abide by the contract terms until the next bargaining period. However, problems often occur anyway. The union then represents employees in trying to handle disputes.

EMPLOYEE GRIEVANCE PROCEDURE

An employee grievance procedure is needed even without a union. The procedure is a formalized way of handling complaints. If a firm is unionized, these procedures are contained in the contract.

Grievance procedures can help settle small problems. A grievance usually begins when an employee complains to an immediate supervisor. The supervisor then trys to settle the issue at that point. If this fails, the issue is then appealed to higher levels. With unions, the final step is arbitration before an independent outside group of persons.

Procedures for discipline

Formal procedures for discipline are necessary. Discipline should begin with an oral reprimand, followed by a written reprimand, and then a suspension with or without pay. Keep a written record. Also, protect employee rights at all times. For example, employees should receive copies of all letters or memos about the problem. Also, make sure they understand the meaning of the action taken.

A final word on unions

Managers usually don't like unions. They feel that an organized work force is not good in the company. The National Retail Merchants Association has

STUDY AID 9-3

DON'TS FOR STORE EXECUTIVES
IN DEALING WITH UNIONS

1. You cannot promise your employees special benefits if they stay out of the union or refuse to have anything to do with it.
2. You can't do anything that can be interpreted as "interfering, restraining, or coercing" employees in their rights to take part in union activities.
3. You can't ask employees to talk to you privately about the union.
4. You cannot threaten or actually discharge, or discontinue benefits of the employee who joins a union.
5. You cannot threaten or actually discharge, discipline, or layoff an employee because of his activities on behalf of the union.
6. You cannot discriminate in penalties. If you penalize "union-minded" employees, penalize "company-minded" employees in the same fashion.
7. You cannot give good assignments, choice of overtime, special privileges only to "company" employees and discriminate against "union-minded" employees.
8. You can't say that you won't deal with a union if it is recognized.
9. You can't deny employees who represent the union the right to solicit members during nonworking hours.
10. You cannot ask your employee if he or anyone else is in favor of or belongs to a union. If he volunteers you can listen but you have to be careful about interrogation.
11. You cannot stop an employee from soliciting membership on company property and even during working hours when you cannot prove that such activity interferes with the job.
12. You cannot spy on union meetings.

Source: *Store Executives—Their Role in Union Drives* (New York: National Retail Merchants Association, undated), pp. 3-4.

developed a list of "don'ts" in dealing with unions, as shown in Study Aid 9-3.

WHAT ABOUT MOTIVATION AND JOB ENRICHMENT?

What is job enrichment?

Too many companies today treat employees as throwaway assets. The retail investment in people is high, however.

Sharp managers view the employee as a total person. They are concerned both with what the employee does during working hours and off the job. They try to help employees get more education, sharpen job skills, and participate in worthwhile nonjob activities.

Many retailers provide job enrichment incentives. These include scholarship aids, employee art shows, alcoholism programs, shopping discounts, sponsoring sports teams, recognition dinners, and similar activities.

Keeping employees happy and motivated at work is more than a matter of salary. Employees today want to belong and to feel that the company cares about them as total persons. Figure 9-4 describes all of a person's needs in

FIGURE 9-4
**Maslow's Ladder of Needs
(is this the ladder to
success?)**

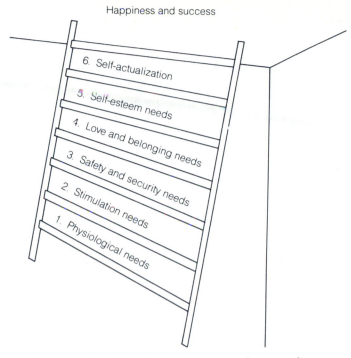

Happiness and success

6. Self-actualization

5. Self-esteem needs

4. Love and belonging needs

3. Safety and security needs

2. Stimulation needs

1. Physiological needs

Maslow identifies six levels of needs in man and arranges them on an ascending scale. He believes that people can attempt to satisfy a higher level need only after satisfying at least some of the needs on the ladder's preceding lower levels.

How many of the following levels of human needs have you been able to satisfy?

1. *Physiological needs.* The needs for air, water, food, and shelter are basic to man's survival and so rank as the first human needs to be satisfied.

2. *Stimulation needs.* Once people have the things that will keep them alive, they begin looking around for something to make life worth living. They explore, discover, get busy, and find activities and goals to keep them interested and active.

3. *Safety and security needs.* For many people, this is a difficult need to satisfy. People who live in earthquake or hurricane zones or in politically explosive areas, can never satisfy their needs for safety and security.

4. *Love and belonging needs.* In our society, where most people's lower need levels are at least minimally satisfied, many people spend their lives seeking to love and be loved.

5. *Self-esteem needs.* Needs near the top of Maslow's ladder are very difficult to satisfy. Because the need for self-respect underlines most accomplishments, individuals need to know and like themselves in order to know and like other people.

6. *Self-actualization needs.* The height of human achievement, according to the human needs approach, lies in an individual's understanding and respecting personal merits, recognizing the potential of these unique talents, and proceedings to develop it. The self-actualized person is sometimes referred to as being "fulfilled."

Source: Robert M. Fulmer, *Supervision: Principles of Professional Management* (Riverside, N.J.: Glencoe Publishing Co., Inc. distributed by Macmillan Co. 1979), pp. 20–21.

order to be self-fulfilled. Careful attention to these needs will contribute to higher employee productivity and less turnover.

How good is a job enrichment program? It's hard to say. You can't put a dollar value on these programs. But better productivity, less turnover, and higher morale are often the result.

How do you motivate employees?

Motivation and job enrichment cannot be separated. Motivation is normally related to work policies and supervisor attitudes. Motivated employees will devote their best efforts to company goals.

Competent supervisors are needed. Further helps include: (1) clear instructions, (2) fair policies, (3) incentives for imagination and creativity, (4) recognition for good performance, (5) merchandise or equipment necessary to do the job, and (6) feedback for both good and poor performance.

Many other things can be done to improve motivation, as shown in Study Aid 9–4. Not the least is good communication which takes many forms, as shown in Table 9–8.

STUDY AID 9–4

SPECIFIC IDEAS ON IMPROVING MOTIVATION

1. Attitude surveys and follow-up.
2. Individual bonus and commission arrangement.
3. More involvement of employees in management decisions that affect them.
4. Better explanation of company benefits program.
5. Setting up a procedure to handle grievances more effectively.
6. Updating rules and regulations so that your store is up-to-date.
7. Better orientation of new employees.
8. Recognize and utilize creativity.
9. Defining and communicating company policies.
10. Allowing employees to try different jobs on a trial basis.
11. Developing educational refund programs so that employees seeking improvement will not be penalized financially.
12. Better selection and training of supervisors.
13. Better counseling on an individual basis.
14. Updating an employee's records when he has done something that adds to his skills or potential.
15. Be sure that employees know what quality and what quantity of work you expect and that both time and cost are prime considerations.

Source: *Motivation—Key to Productivity* (New York: National Retail Merchants Association, 1977), pp. 5–6.

TABLE 9–8
A comparison of usage of communication techniques for employees—National sample (percent)

Techniques of communication	Less than $1 million in sales	$500 million or more in sales
Handbook	11.5	100.0
Regular newsletter	1.6	80.0
Meetings........................	49.2	100.0
Periodic announcements	27.9	86.7
Informal discussion	52.5	86.7
Annual reports	4.9	80.0
Benefit manuals	8.2	80.0
Pay envelope stuffers	9.8	46.7
Posters	8.2	80.0

Source: Myron Gable and Charles Holton, *A Survey of Current Retail Personnel Practices* (New York: National Retail Merchants Association, 1977), p. 102.

SUMMARY

The personnel function is a key to a good retail operation. Labor costs will be the largest category of your expenses. Yet, retailing still has the reputation of paying low wages, hiring mostly part-time employees and of having poor working hours. Many stores have gone to self-service in trying to avoid people problems.

Regardless, you still face the problems of recruiting, selecting, training, motivating, paying, and promoting employees. A good personnel manager is needed to cope with these problems.

Motivation remains a problem. Money alone is not a sufficient motivator. Employees need the chance to realize higher level needs.

NOTES

1. Daniel Gallagher, "Fair Employment Practices Regulations Affecting Small Business Recruitment and Selection," *American Journal of Small Business,* vol. 3 (January 1979), pp. 11–12.

2. District of Columbia Human Rights Law, Council Regulation 73–22, November 11, 1973. Codified under Title 43 of the District Rules and Regulations.

3. Myron Gable and Charles Holton, *A Survey of Current Retail Personnel Practices,* (New York: National Retail Merchants Association, 1977), p. 42.

4. Gable and Holton, *Survey of Personnel Practices,* p. 6.

DISCUSSION QUESTIONS

1. What are the key federal and state laws which affect recruiting, selection, and compensation? What are the likely effects on you as a result of these types of regulations?

2. Offer explanations for why the major problems of retailing continue to be people problems.

3. What are the desirable characteristics of a supervisor?

4. Discuss the ways of paying employees. Which is likely to be the most effective for (1) a retail salesperson, (2) an accountant, (3) a department buyer?

5. What do you see as the keys to increased productivity among retail employees?

6. Assume you are the owner of a small retail firm and that rumors are circulating that efforts will be made to unionize your outlet. What steps can you take to deal with this problem? Discuss the likely long-run effects of the courses of action which are open to you.

7. What are the special needs in retail employment of minorities, women, and the aged? What can be done to make these people feel that they are a valued part of the firm?

8. What are the likely effects on the personnel function of the trend toward increased numbers of Sunday openings and longer daily hours, including outlets that are open 24 hours each day?

9. Assume you are the manager of a men's clothing outlet located close to a major university campus. What would be the basic elements of a training program for the outlet? How would your program likely differ from the type of training which might be offered for new employees who have recently been hired by Sears Roebuck?

PROJECTS

1. Devise a format and interview at least five people who have worked in the retailing industry in some capacity. Determine the individual's honest views on wages, working conditions, superior-subordinate relationships, and so on. Prepare a report for class discussion on what you have discovered.

2. Secure an employee evaluation form from a local business. What types of specific criteria are used, and for what purpose. Do you think that the criteria are valid? Can you suggest others?

3. Select several different retail companies (differing in organizational arrangement, number of stores and sales volume, and product line) and make an appointment with the executive responsible for the personnel functions. Describe the employment process of each (include selection, training, and benefits including compensation) and draw comparisons among the group. See if you can explain the differences in apparent effectiveness of the programs. See if you can get them to discuss affirmative action.

4. Arrange through your college or university placement office to have a few minutes with all the recruiters coming to campus to interview people for retailing companies. Structure a questionnaire to administer to each recruiter to find out what he (she) is looking for in a student; how does the interview on campus enter into the selection process; what kinds of questions are asked of the interviewee; what does the recruiter expect the interviewee to know about the company; what are the variables considered in evaluating the student; and what are the subsequent steps in the employment process.

Minicase 9-1   Sally Bright has just received her M.B.A. degree and wants to enter the junior executive program with Austin's Department Stores, a large department store chain. Sally has heard that Austin's wants to hire women for this program, so she arranges for an interview.

Later during her interview, Sally learns that the main reason Austin's has for hiring women into its Junior Executive Program is to comply with federal equal opportunity requirements. Sally resents this, but takes the job with Austin's anyway as opportunities look promising.

After she has worked at Austin's for a while, Sally meets Jim Sharp, who also has an M.B.A. and is in the Junior Executive Program. They have several dates and Sally learns that Jim is making $100 more per month from Austin's than she is, yet they both were employed at approximately the same time. Sally is furious about this. She thought that discrimination in pay because of sex was a thing of the past. She announced that she is going to confront the personnel manager about this.

If you were the personnel manager, how would you handle Sally's case?

Minicase 9-2   Louise Fisher accepted a job with The Vanity, a major department store in a medium-sized southern town. She is a high school graduate and has decided she does not want to go to college. On the first Monday she reported to work she was introduced to the other people in housewares, her department, shown how to operate the POS terminal, and made aware of store guidelines concerning employee behavior. On Tuesday, Ms. Smith, the head clerk, was to help her get adjusted. Tuesday turned out to be a disaster. There had been an ad in Monday night's paper for a sale in housewares and customers were waiting for the doors to open. The first transaction was a charge sale but the woman did not have her card. The customer was in a hurry to get to work and was asking technical questions about the coffee pot she had selected. Louise explained that the head clerk was sick and that she had just started but the woman began to get aggravated. In addition to this, the department manager was in a staff meeting. Louise forgot how to use the terminal and amid all the bustle she burst into tears, went to the personnel office, and quit.

Do you think this situation is common? What steps could be taken to avoid it?

10

WHAT IS THE NEW TECHNOLOGY OF RETAILING?

The purposes of this chapter are to explain:

- The impacts of the electronic cash register and the point-of-sale terminal on retailing.
- The meaning of the universal product code (UPC) for food retailers.
- The OCR-A system of merchandise marking in general merchandise retailing.
- The importance of universal vendor marking (UVM).
- The meaning of electronic funds transfer systems (EFTS).
- The effects of the move to metrics on retailing.
- The meaning of the following terms:

Point of service system	Universal vendor marking
Electronic cash register	Scanning
Universal product code (UPC)	Metrication
OCR-A	Wanding
EFTS	Debit card

The old mechanical cash register served the retailer for many years. About all you could do with this register was to ring up sales and make change. The original purpose of the cash register was to cut down on employee theft.

The first machines were really adding machines set on top of a cash drawer. A clerk pushed buttons and cranked an arm to enter information into the register. Later versions displayed the price of each item purchased in large numbers for both the clerk and the customer to read. Even later registers printed a record of each sale and calculated the amount of change due.

The basic electronic cash register (ECR) came on the market in the 1960s. They use electric light beams to enter the information at a very high rate of speed. Things haven't been the same since! They are used in almost all retail stores today. More and more they are being used as a computer system to provide up-to-date reports for management. You call the ECR in this situation a *POS terminal.*

This new electronic technology has brought about changes in (1) the way you mark merchandise, (2) the way you handle money and credit, and (3) the way you work with your bank—closely, on a daily basis.

Clearly, the electronic dimensions of the new equipment are complicated. Computers can calculate the process data at high speeds with great accuracy. Still, the functions performed are very simple; namely, subtraction and addition plus the ability to transfer information from one location to another and the ability to store data.

Advances in electronic data processing in retailing have been slower than that in many other areas of business. Various reasons exist for this slowness. First, the dollar investment in the equipment is quite high, particularly for retail outlets which carry several thousand items. Second, transactions are complicated, particularly in general merchandise retailing. Thus, not unexpectedly, the supermarket industry has made greater advances in use of data processing than other sectors of retailing. Third, personnel problems still abound in training people to work with the new equipment.

However, recent advances in the technology have brought the prices down to the point where many outlets, including the smallest ones, can afford the equipment. The increased savings from better inventory management, reduction of under-rings at the cash register, less shrink at the point of sale, and the need to increase labor productivity have led to rapid advances in the use of the computer.

THE ROLE OF THE COMPUTER AND ELECTRONICS IN RETAILING

The computer is no longer a glorified payroll clerk. Rather, it functions as an important source of information for management. Let's look at the various applications of computer-based data today to better appreciate the potential of the computer to management.

Sales analysis

One of the most useful reports for management is a daily sales report which provides an analysis and count of departmental sales dollars and units.

FIGURE 10-1
Daily sales report

DAILY SALES REPORT		ITEM COUNT	REGISTER TOTALS	
START #52 PROGRAM CHANGE/RESET COUNTER CUSTOMER COUNTER/NO SALE	X	51	361	C
	X	621	22	C
Hamburger	X	112	39.78	1C
Deluxe Hamburger	X	61	35.99	2C
Double Hamburger	X	23	18.17	3C
Cheese Burger	X	74	36.26	4C
Double Cheese Burger	X	19	16.81	5C
Whopper	X	12	11.88	6C
Super Burger	X	8	7.92	7C
Beef	X	31	27.59	8C
Chili Burger	X	10	5.90	9C
Ribs	X	18	35.82	10C
Chicken	X	29	46.11	11C
White Chicken	X	5	8.45	12C
Dark Chicken	X	5	7.45	13C
Barrel	X	3	14.67	C
Bucket	X	7	25.	54C
			5.50	55C
Mashed Potatoes	X	14	4.20	56C
Potato Salad	X	21	6.30	57C
Salad	X	32	16.00	58C
Bread	X	36	3.60	59C
Rolls	X	21	2.10	60C
Soup	X	3	.90	61C
Pie	X	32	14.40	62C
French Fries	X	123	36.90	63C
Iced Tea	X	41	6.15	64C
Hot Chocolate	X	6	.90	65C
Coffee	X	179	17.90	66C
Cola	X	312	62.40	67C
Milk	X	26	7.80	68C
Hot Tea	X	4	.60	69C
Orange	X	41	6.15	70C
NET PRESET SALES	X		926.09	71C
MISCELLANEOUS	X	3	11.85	72C
SPECIAL	X	1	4.50	73C
TOTAL NET SALES	X		942.44	74C
GROSS SALES	X		971.15	75C
	X			
CONSECUTIVE # / STORE & REGISTER # / DATE	X	2280	12 4/02/7–	

Source: NCR Corporation, Dayton, Ohio.

Departmental Sales and Count*

An automatically printed report shows net sales and unit count for programmed departments. This report provides the information necessary to analyze the contribution of each menu item toward gross profit. Knowing sales by dollars and units per menu item also helps in the planning of additions to or deletions from the menu.

The report illustrated not only shows net sales and units for 70 categories, but it also shows:

Net total sales for the combined 70 categories.
Net sales for two open departments.
Total net sales.
Gross sales total.

*This report is for illustration only and does not represent the daily sales volume of an average fast-food restaurant.

Figure 10–1 illustrates such a daily sales report for the food service industry. In addition to a daily sales report, sales analysis reports can also be generated to measure the sales performance of individual items by department or category within specified time intervals. As shown in Figure 10–2, unit price, units sold, extended dollar value, and percentage of items by sale are readily available.

A similar report is the sales activities report which can provide a more in-depth picture of sales transactions and employee timekeeping activity to help increase sales in selected time periods (Figure 10–3).

Inventory control

Merchandise on hand is another important item of information for management. Inventory ties up a large amount of the firm's capital. Thus, man-

FIGURE 10-2
Sales analysis report

```
X        SALES ANALYSIS REPORT        40
    ITEM     PRICE SOLD  $ VALUE   %
DEPT 0001
   DELX BRGR   .85  114    96.90  5.95
   CHZ BRGR    .60 1023   613.80 37.90
   DBL BRGR    .70   79    55.30  3.39
   HAMBURGR    .50  265   132.50  8.13
   SUPR BRGR  1.05   14    14.70   .90
     DEPT TOTALS   1595   913.20 56.09

DEPT 0003
   FISH SDW    .50   18     9.00   .55
   FISH BSK   1.65   43    70.95  4.35
   FISH PLT   1.95   67   130.65  8.02
   SHRIMP     2.50   12    30.00  1.84
   OYSTERS    3.15   19    59.85  3.67
     DEPT TOTALS    159   300.45 18.45




DEPT 0030
   COLA        .25  245    61.25  3.76
   COLA        .30  105    31.50  1.93
   COLA        .35   47    16.45  1.01
   CHOC SHK    .45   15     6.75   .41
   CHOC SHK    .65   63    40.95  2.51

     DEPT TOTALS    475   156.90  9.63

     REPT TOTALS   2325  1627.85

1200        21/MAY/78        10:50PM
```

Source: NCR Corporation, Dayton, Ohio.

Sales Analysis Report

This report enables management to measure sales performance of individual menu items by department or product category within certain time intervals. Unit price, quantity sold, extended dollar value, and percentage of sales by item are shown.

The sales analysis report provides management with the ability to track individual item sales, analyze product acceptance, and monitor advertising and sales promotional efforts.

FIGURE 10-3
Sales activity report

```
X           ACTIVITY REPORT        01
08:30AM - 10:00AM
   TRAN COUNT      14 BONUS 1        10
   NET SALES    36.21 BONUS 2         7
   AVRG CHECK    2.59 EMPLOYEES       6
   CASHIERS         2 LABOR HRS    2:02
   CSTMR/MNHR    6.90 LABOR COST    6.64
   SALES/MNHR   17.84 % OF SALES   18.34
10:00AM - 11:00AM
   TRAN COUNT     196 BONUS 1       113
   NET SALES   519.21 BONUS 2        90
   AVRG CHECK    2.65 EMPLOYEES       8
   CASHIERS         2 LABOR HRS   17:34
   CSTMR/MNHR   11.16 LABOR COST   72.16
   SALES/MNHR   29.55 % OF SALES   13.90
11:00AM - 11:15AM
   TRAN COUNT      49 BONUS 1        22
   NET SALES   163.13 BONUS 2         4
   AVRG CHECK    3.33 EMPLOYEES       8
   CASHIERS         3 LABOR HRS    6:00
   CSTMR/MNHR   24.50 LABOR COST   30.24
   SALES/MNHR   81.57 % OF SALES   18.53
11:15AM - 03:00PM
   TRAN COUNT     854 BONUS 1       125
   NET SALES  2528.10 BONUS 2       184
   AVRG CHECK    2.96 EMPLOYEES       6
   CASHIERS         5 LABOR HRS   77.88
   CSTMR/MNHR   43.17 LABOR COST  376.04
   SALES/MNHR  127.81 % OF SALES   14.87
```

Activity Report

This report provides an in-depth picture of sales transaction and employee time-keeping activity during preselected time periods. Highlights of this report include:

1.   Number of customer transactions.
2.   Number of cashiers on duty.
3.   Average check amount, customer count and sales per man hour.
4.   Number of bonus items sold.
5.   Percentage of sales to total sales.
6.   Employee hours and labor cost.

agement needs to know the composition of the inventory. Merchandise not on hand can result in lost sales. On the other hand, having too many wrong items will lead to excessive markdowns. The use of computer-generated reports is really the only efficient way to keep up with inventory and to answer the questions of what to buy, when to buy, how to buy, and from whom to buy.

Figure 10–4 illustrates a series of inventory analysis reports on an item-by-item basis for a retail liquor outlet. Such information can be developed each day to allow buyers to decide on how much to reorder or to transfer between stores. Figure 10–4 shows a daily inventory analysis indicating the day's sales and the number of items on hand which will signal the number of items to be purchased.

FIGURE 10-4
Complete inventory control

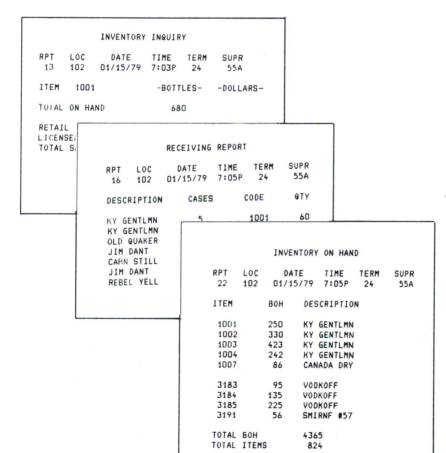

```
                INVENTORY ACTIVITY

   RPT    LOC     DATE     TIME   TERM    SUPR
    23    102   01/15/79   7:15P   24     55A


          CUR      RET      LIC     TOTAL
   ITEM   BOH     SALE     SALE     SALES

   10001  150     200      100      300
   10002  330      30       50       80
   10003  423     500      200      700
   10004  242      50       30       80

   30183   95     125      225      350
   30184  135      55       60      115
   30185  225     220      190      410
   30191   56      10       15       25


   BOH              44,365
   ITEMS             2,156
   INV. RECEIVED    29,500
   INV. ADJUSTED       225
   RET. SALES       12,345
   LIC. SALES       16,550
   TOT. SALES       28,895
```

Inventory Activity Report

This report provides store management with information relating to those items which have had activity within a specified period of time. The report provides vital data, such as current bottles on hand, sales by type of sale, inventory receipts and adjustments.

```
              INVENTORY INQUIRY

   RPT   LOC     DATE     TIME   TERM   SUPR
    13   102   01/15/79   7:03P   24    55A

   ITEM   1001         -BOTTLES-   -DOLLARS-

   TOTAL ON HAND         680

   RETAIL
   LICENSE
   TOTAL S
```

```
              RECEIVING REPORT

      RPT   LOC     DATE     TIME   TERM   SUPR
       16   102   01/15/79   7:05P   24    55A

   DESCRIPTION    CASES      CODE      QTY

   KY GENTLMN       5        1001      60
   KY GENTLMN
   OLD QUAKER
   JIM DANT
   CABN STILL
   JIM DANT
   REBEL YELL
```

```
              INVENTORY ON HAND

   RPT   LOC     DATE     TIME   TERM   SUPR
    22   102   01/15/79   7:05P   24    55A

   ITEM      BOH      DESCRIPTION

   1001      250      KY GENTLMN
   1002      330      KY GENTLMN
   1003      423      KY GENTLMN
   1004      242      KY GENTLMN
   1007       86      CANADA DRY

   3183       95      VODKOFF
   3184      135      VODKOFF
   3185      225      VODKOFF
   3191       56      SMIRNF #57

   TOTAL BOH          4365
   TOTAL ITEMS         824
```

Other Inventory Reports

Inventory On-Hand, Inventory Inquiry, Receiving, and Inventory Summary reports are always current and up-to-the-minute through the last completed transaction.

They provide these management benefits:

1. Complete inventory-on-hand listing.
2. A detailed record of inventory merchandise receipts.
3. Reports can be produced by any terminal within the store, whenever needed.
4. Reports provide store management with complete inventory price lookup control.
5. Management can selectively analyze the in-stock inventory level of any given item at any time.
6. Inventory data is in terms of bottles-on-hand and associated dollar value.

Source: NCR Corporation, Dayton, Ohio.

Sales forecasting

Inventory data is necessary as an aid in forecasting sales. Analysis of previous sales levels can point out trends which can be a clue to future sales. Remember, however, that inventory reports can only give you trends in past sales. They cannot forecast the future. You will have to modify your sales reports on the basis of judgment to make them the most useful. For example, a major strike in your community can be a clue that sales will be more in the next quarter than in the quarter in which the strike occurred. Likewise, if you believe that your area is going into a recession, your forecasted sales levels would probably be lower than trends in the computer reports alone would indicate.

Such detailed analysis for sales forecasting purposes requires more complex reports than we have talked about thus far. Figure 10–5 illustrates some of the information processing reports possible. Specifically, it shows detailed sales analysis reports, salesperson productivity reports, and a retail inventory management report for several stores. Such information analysis can be used as a tool in merchandise management. Such reports should be viewed as part of a retail reporting system to control the business and improve profitability.

Managing credit

The computer can allow you to handle two important elements of credit—credit authorization and credit control—more effectively. In *credit authorization* management wants to make sure that the customers do not make purchases over their approved credit limits. Today, a salesperson normally will dial the credit authorization extension for the computer and dial in the customer's account number and the dollar amount of the sale. The computer then issues an OK for the sale or indicates that the customer will need to discuss the sale with the credit department.

Credit control involves a series of issues, including outstanding credit by customer, the mail-out of monthly bills, up-to-date reports on delinquent accounts, reports on accounts to be turned over to an attorney for collection and similar reports which can be readily generated using today's technology. Figure 10–6 illustrates some of the key reports in managing the credit functions.

SOURCES OF DATA

The process of changing from the more traditional mechanical cash registers to a computerized system which can generate reports like those above is costly and time consuming. However, companies such as National Cash Register (NCR), which sell the necessary equipment and softwear programs to generate the reports illustrated will help install the systems, train store personnel, and provide maintenance and upkeep on the equipment. Figure 10–7 illustrates the information flow with the new equipment, beginning with basic decisions which might be needed as input to the information management needs for decision making all the way to the final reports produced.

FIGURE 10-5
Information Processing—An integral part of a retail control system

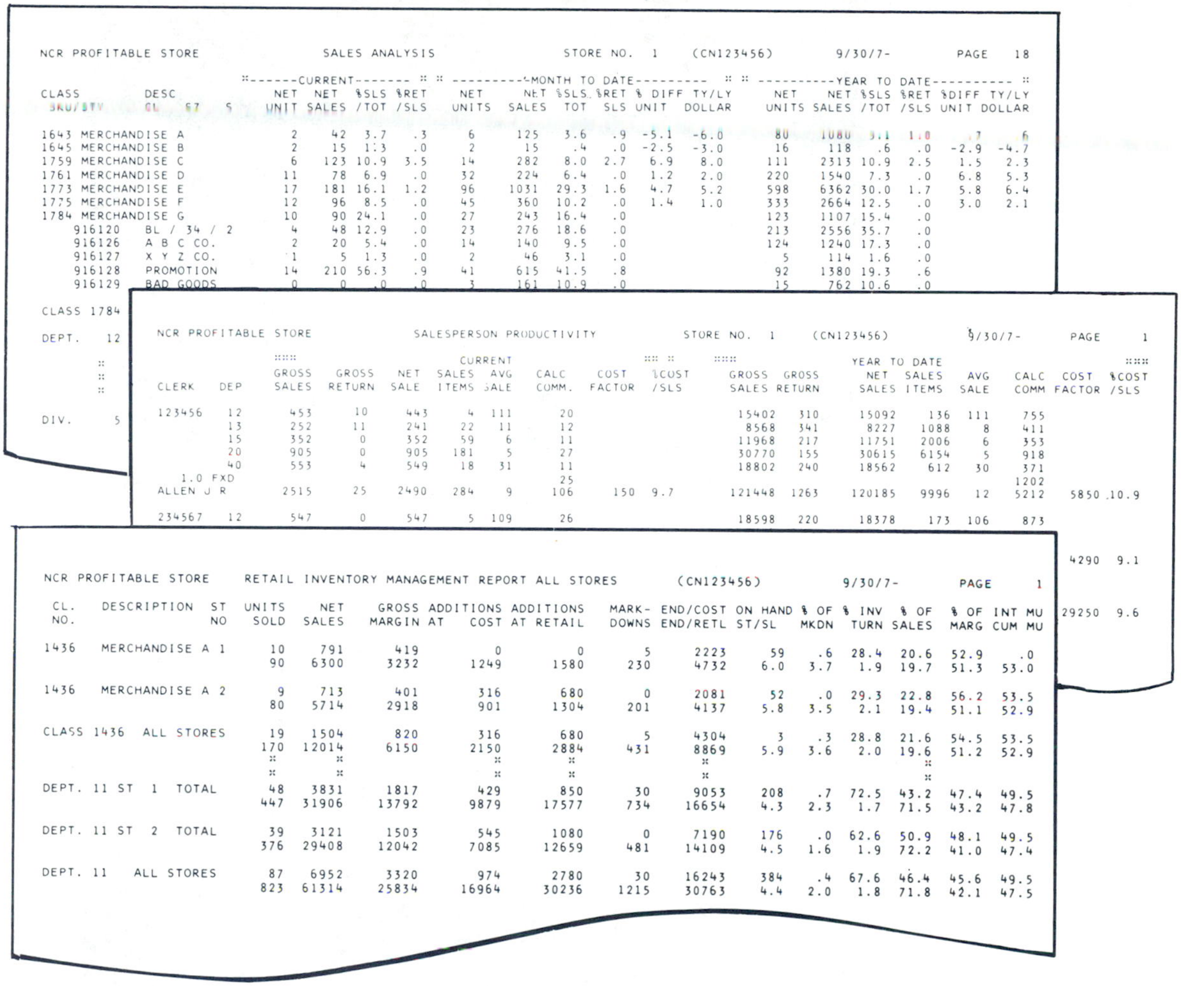

```
NCR PROFITABLE STORE          SALES ANALYSIS              STORE NO.  1    (CN123456)        9/30/7-         PAGE   18

                      ::------CURRENT------- :: :: --------4MONTH TO DATE--------- :: :: ----------YEAR TO DATE---------- ::
CLASS      DESC        NET   NET  %SLS %RET   NET    NET %SLS %RET % DIFF TY/LY   NET    NET %SLS %RET %DIFF TY/LY
SKU/STV    CL  57  5  UNIT SALES /TOT /SLS   UNITS  SALES TOT /SLS UNIT  DOLLAR  UNITS  SALES /TOT /SLS UNIT DOLLAR

1643 MERCHANDISE A      2    42  3.7   .3      6    125  3.6   .9  -5.1  -6.0     80   1080  3.1  1.8    .7    6
1645 MERCHANDISE B      2    15  1.3   .0      2     15   .4   .0  -2.5  -3.0     16    118   .6   .0  -2.9  -4.7
1759 MERCHANDISE C      6   123 10.9  3.5     14    282  8.0  2.7   6.9   8.0    111   2313 10.9  2.5   1.5   2.3
1761 MERCHANDISE D     11    78  6.9   .0     32    224  6.4   .0   1.2   2.0    220   1540  7.3   .0   6.8   5.3
1773 MERCHANDISE E     17   181 16.1  1.2     96   1031 29.3  1.6   4.7   5.2    598   6362 30.0  1.7   5.8   6.4
1775 MERCHANDISE F     12    96  8.5   .0     45    360 10.2   .0   1.4   1.0    333   2664 12.5   .0   3.0   2.1
1784 MERCHANDISE G     10    90 24.1   .0     27    243 16.4   .0                123   1107 15.4   .0
     916120   BL / 34 / 2    4    48 12.9   .0   23   276 18.6   .0              213   2556 35.7   .0
     916126   A B C CO.      2    20  5.4   .0   14   140  9.5   .0              124   1240 17.3   .0
     916127   X Y Z CO.      1     5  1.3   .0    2    46  3.1   .0                5    114  1.6   .0
     916128   PROMOTION     14   210 56.3   .9   41   615 41.5   .8               92   1380 19.3   .6
     916129   BAD GOODS      0     0   .0   .0    3   161 10.9   .0               15    762 10.6   .0

CLASS 1784

DEPT.   12
```

```
       ::    NCR PROFITABLE STORE        SALESPERSON PRODUCTIVITY       STORE NO.  1   (CN123456)        9/30/7-        PAGE    1
       ::
       ::            :::::             CURRENT           ::: ::  :::::          YEAR TO DATE           :::::
            CLERK  DEP  GROSS  GROSS   NET  SALES AVG  CALC  COST  %COST  GROSS  GROSS   NET  SALES  AVG  CALC  COST %COST
                        SALES  RETURN  SALE ITEMS /SALE COMM. FACTOR /SLS  SALES  RETURN  SALES ITEMS /SLS  COMM FACTOR /SLS
DIV.    5   123456  12   453    10     443    4   111   20                 15402   310   15092  136   111   755
                    13   252    11     241   22    11   12                  8568   341    8227 1088     8   411
                    15   352     0     352   59     6   11                 11968   217   11751 2006     6   353
                    20   905     0     905  181     5   27                 30770   155   30615 6154     5   918
                    40   553     4     549   18    31   11                 18802   240   18562  612    30   371
                1.0 FXD                           25                                                        1202
            ALLEN J R 2515    25    2490  284     9  106   150   9.7      121448  1263  120185 9996    12  5212   5850 .10.9

            234567  12   547     0     547    5   109   26                 18598   220   18378  173   106   873
```

```
                                                                                                             4290  9.1
NCR PROFITABLE STORE    RETAIL INVENTORY MANAGEMENT REPORT ALL STORES    (CN123456)       9/30/7-       PAGE   1
CL.    DESCRIPTION  ST  UNITS   NET   GROSS ADDITIONS ADDITIONS  MARK- END/COST ON HAND % OF % INV % OF % OF INT MU  29250  9.6
NO.                 NO  SOLD   SALES  MARGIN AT   COST AT RETAIL DOWNS END/RETL ST/SL MKDN TURN SALES MARG CUM MU

1436  MERCHANDISE A 1   10     791    419      0         0       5    2223     59    .6  28.4 20.6 52.9   .0
                      90    6300   3232   1249      1580     230    4732    6.0   3.7   1.9 19.7 51.3 53.0

1436  MERCHANDISE A 2    9     713    401    316       680       0    2081     52    .0  29.3 22.8 56.2 53.5
                      80    5714   2918    901      1304     201    4137    5.8   3.5   2.1 19.4 51.1 52.9

CLASS 1436  ALL STORES 19   1504    820    316       680       5    4304      3    .3  28.8 21.6 54.5 53.5
                     170  12014   6150   2150      2884     431    8869    5.9   3.6   2.0 19.6 51.2 52.9
                       ::     ::            ::         ::              ::                             ::
                       ::     ::            ::         ::              ::                             ::
DEPT. 11 ST  1  TOTAL  48   3831   1817    429       850      30    9053    208   .7  72.5 43.2 47.4 49.5
                     447  31906  13792   9879     17577     734   16654    4.3  2.3   1.7 71.5 43.2 47.8

DEPT. 11 ST  2  TOTAL  39   3121   1503    545      1080       0    7190    176   .0  62.6 50.9 48.1 49.5
                     376  29408  12042   7085     12659     481   14109    4.5  1.6   1.9 72.2 41.0 47.4

DEPT. 11  ALL STORES   87   6952   3320    974      2780      30   16243    384   .4  67.6 46.4 45.6 49.5
                     823  61314  25834  16964     30236    1215   30763    4.4  2.0   1.8 71.8 42.1 47.5
```

Information Processing

Early information capturing techniques expanded traditional inventory control to a technique of merchandise management. Then, due to expanded volumes, dispersal of outlets, mass merchandising, and competitive pressures, retailers could no longer survive with just merchandise management; they required a total information system offering control in the areas of personnel, finances, and customers. And much of the data needed for control in these areas is available at the point of service.

Computer reports are not ends within themselves; they are not capable of making strategic decisions. Modern retailing is a never-ending decision-making responsibility; and timely, accurate reports are essential for profit-making decisions.

Through the use of the data capturing ability, management is able to implement a Total Information System which produces up-to-date reports with which to scientifically plan and control the business to improve profitability.

Source: NCR Corporation, Dayton, Ohio.

FIGURE 10-6
**Credit management—
increase productivity
and efficiency**

FIGURE 10-6 *(continued)*

```
3072659529-0                    COLLECTOR 0021   -STATUS-      -OTHER ACCTS-
JOHN A. TRENT                   NODE      0001   RETURN MAIL   5408848131-0
DOROTHY TRENT                   LAST LTR     2   COLLECTION
118 FRANKLIN AVE                SKIP-CBR    01
                                CUR DUN      4
GRANVILLE KY 40310

RESIDENCE   (502)293-9427
POE NAME-1  (502)419-6817    TV REPAIR       METROPOLIS TV
POE NAME-2  (502)271-2458    SECRETARY       ADAMS & SMITH INC
RELATIVE    (502)253-4961
IN COLL   04578 NEXT REV 10/12/78 H-PAY  50-09  M-BAL  264.40  H-BAL   324-00
OPN-BILL  22-20 PROM PAY 10/09/78 P-PAY  40.00  M-DUE   80.00  CRLMT   00500
MSIC-TIC  13-03.LAST PAY  9/10/78 L-PAY  30.00  M-PAY   40.00  LMTCH   14-2

ATTORNEY  00016    IN ADJUST 07/27/78    HI BAL  300.00
AGENCY    00202    ADJUST       50.00    HI PAY   75.00
                   ID ADJUST       04    CR LMT  500.00
                   SR ADJUST       10    MOS CL      03
                   REV STAT        03
                   DUN LTR-T       02
```

CRT display terminals provide direct people-to-computer interface for rapid data entry and retrieval. These terminals are easy to understand, and easy to operate, while performing a wide spectrum of processing functions.

The integrated data base of delinquent accounts, bill adjustments pending, and border-line accounts is literally at the collector's fingertips. Collection personnel can interact with the data base in a conversational manner. They can, based on security codes, inquire into the files, create new records, update records, and even control processing of data. Data entry is easily verified to eliminate errors and to maintain file integrity.

The interactive video display is the control center for the system. There is no need to wait for a printed report. The displayed information can be used to provide instantaneous collection follow-through and credit authorization at the various levels of responsibility.

Collection Account Displays

A series of collection account displays allow the terminal operator to examine a collection account in an orderly fashion. These displays provide up-to-date information that includes customer identification, review dates and actions taken, current month financial history, and 12-month financial history.

Source: NCR Corporation, Dayton, Ohio.

What is a POS?

The point-of-sale (POS) cash register is the key as an input device for all the systems. A POS system simply records a variety of data at the time a transaction occurs. The information is then stored and can be called up at the end of the day, or whenever, to reveal which merchandise, styles, and colors of which manufacturers are selling most rapidly. The ability to identify slow- and fast-moving items is a key to good merchandise management.

Retailing thrives on a large variety of merchandise, minimal inventory and rapid turnover. The new systems thus allow frequent and up-to-date informa-

**FIGURE 10–7
The electronic data
processing system**

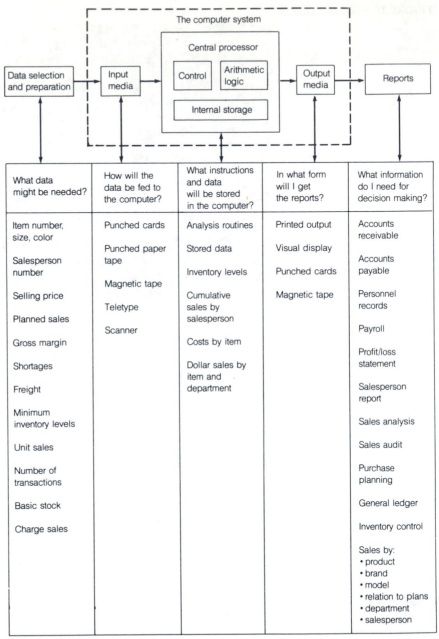

What data might be needed?	How will the data be fed to the computer?	What instructions and data will be stored in the computer?	In what form will I get the reports?	What information do I need for decision making?
Item number, size, color	Punched cards	Analysis routines	Printed output	Accounts receivable
Salesperson number	Punched paper tape	Stored data	Visual display	Accounts payable
Selling price	Magnetic tape	Inventory levels	Punched cards	Personnel records
Planned sales	Teletype	Cumulative sales by salesperson	Magnetic tape	Payroll
Gross margin	Scanner	Costs by item		Profit/loss statement
Shortages		Dollar sales by item and department		Salesperson report
Freight				Sales analysis
Minimum inventory levels				Sales audit
Unit sales				Purchase planning
Number of transactions				General ledger
Basic stock				Inventory control
Charge sales				Sales by: • product • brand • model • relation to plans • department • salesperson

Source: R. Ted Will and Ronald W. Hasty, *Retailing* (New York: Canfield Press, 1977), p. 126.

tion on product sales rates, stock outages, sales patterns, and similar information which can be grouped for buyers by department.

Benefits for customers from the systems include quicker completion of sales transactions, fewer cash register errors, faster credit approval, and easier departmental interselling by store personnel.

ITEM MARKING

The new equipment has caused many changes in retailing. One of the major changes is in item marking. Items can be marked in what is known as a *machine readable format* for use with a POS terminal (some formats can also be read by humans).

You are probably familiar with the black and white bar format on supermarket items. The bars are codes which contain information about the product and the manufacturer (see Figure 10–8). These bar codes are passed over a "scanner" at the checkout. The information from the bar codes goes from the scanner into the POS system. Computers can then automatically update the store's inventory, "look up" the price of the item in question, and print a receipt for the customer.

You need to be familiar with two different types of item marking. The first is the *universal product code (UPC)* used for food and health and beauty aids (again, look at Figure 10–8). The second is OCR-A, used in marking nonfood items.

Universal product code (UPC)

Let's look first at the UPC. Much of the information about the benefits of the universal product code for food retailers is also true for general merchandise (nonfood) marking. Thus, it is not necessary to repeat the benefits of OCR-A marking (for general merchandise items) when we discuss that format.

A scanning checkout in a supermarket

Courtesy NCR

FIGURE 10–8

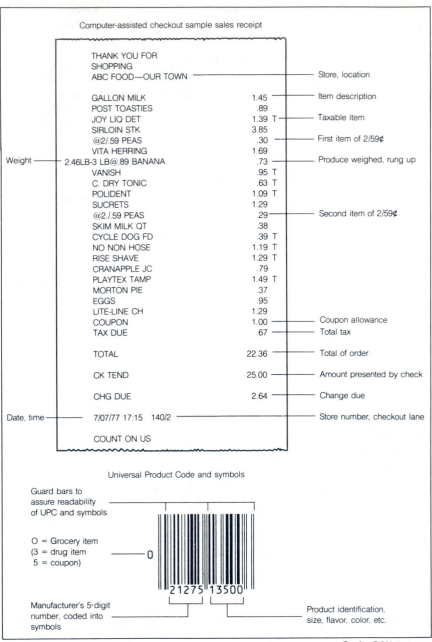

Computer-assisted checkout sample sales receipt

THANK YOU FOR
SHOPPING
ABC FOOD—OUR TOWN ————————— Store, location

GALLON MILK	1.45	Item description
POST TOASTIES	.89	
JOY LIQ DET	1.39 T	Taxable item
SIRLOIN STK	3.85	
@2/.59 PEAS	.30	First item of 2/59¢
VITA HERRING	1.69	
2.46LB-3 LB@.89 BANANA	.73	Produce weighed, rung up
VANISH	.95 T	
C. DRY TONIC	.63 T	
POLIDENT	1.09 T	
SUCRETS	1.29	
@2./.59 PEAS	.29	Second item of 2/59¢
SKIM MILK QT	.38	
CYCLE DOG FD	.39 T	
NO NON HOSE	1.19 T	
RISE SHAVE	1.29 T	
CRANAPPLE JC	.79	
PLAYTEX TAMP	1.49 T	
MORTON PIE	.37	
EGGS	.95	
LITE-LINE CH	1.29	
COUPON	1.00	Coupon allowance
TAX DUE	.67	Total tax
TOTAL	22.36	Total of order
CK TEND	25.00	Amount presented by check
CHG DUE	2.64	Change due

Weight ———— (2.46LB-3 LB@.89 BANANA)

Date, time ———— 7/07/77 17:15 140/2 ————————— Store number, checkout lane

COUNT ON US

Universal Product Code and symbols

Guard bars to
assure readability
of UPC and symbols

O = Grocery item
(3 = drug item
5 = coupon)

O

21275 13500

Manufacturer's 5-digit
number, coded into
symbols

Product identification,
size, flavor, color, etc.

Credit: GGX Associates

How did it all start? The idea of mechanizing the checkout has been around since 1920 when the founder of Piggly Wiggly stores introduced self-service.[1] He spent the rest of his life trying to develop an "automatic" store called the Keedoozle.

Today, checkout efficiency is critical. Checkers who use conventional equipment earn $6 or more an hour so the "front end" accounts for 40 percent of supermarkets' labor costs. And losses through mis-rings and cheating may run as high as 1.5 percent of sales. This percentage is as much as the average supermarket makes before taxes. And not only is the checkout a source of retailer dissatisfaction, but more importantly, of shopper resentment.

Potential benefits to consumers and retailers. Early tests of UPC scanner systems promised much help for supermarket woes:

1. *Accuracy of checkout.* In a 15-month test in a Kroger store in Kenwood, Ohio, checker error dropped by 75 percent.
2. *Customer satisfaction.* Speed, accuracy, quietness, and the detailed shopping tape are consumer pluses. (See Figure 10–8).
3. *Time and labor savings.* Some stores report productivity gains of up to 45 percent when item price marking (no longer necessary since the price is carried in the computer) is eliminated. Even *with* price marking, other savings make scanner investment worthwhile.
4. *Improved inventory* and financial control.

Then what's taking so long?

1. The full-scale switch to scanning—$80,000–$160,000 per store—represents an enormous dollar investment in equipment by a retailer. The recession/inflationary period hasn't helped either. Retailers' capital crunch is worse with more pressure on volume and profits.
2. Some persons failed to realize that scanner systems are *not* simply an advance on previous technology. They require entirely new operating procedures and management systems. Food retailing is a service- and customer-oriented industry. Thus, the new technology is a major roadblock to adoption.
3. Some unions and consumer groups are opposed to nonprice marking. Legislation barring price elimination on packages has passed in some states and localities. You can see that this clouds the outlook for scanning and makes retailers hesitate to invest.
4. Relatively slow rate of coding (other than national grocery brands) concerned retailers at first; they also had problems coding such items as produce in hard-to-scan poly bags.
5. There were doubts about the equipment (was this the final version?) and also problems. Check stand height and scanner windows were so

scratched by products passing over them that one store was replacing them every three days.

New push to scanning.   There are a number of factors pushing retailing faster into scanning:

1. The fast rise in wages (labor now represents over 67 percent of food retailing costs, up from 55 percent in the mid-60s) encourages retailers to automate their operations. It's a key way to remain competitive in an industry for which slowing growth is forecast.
2. Retail leaders are falling in line. Until recently, most scanning test activity was limited to the medium-sized organization. The giants are now getting involved.
3. Further push for retailers to go the scanner route: many different kinds of products are being imprinted with the UPC by manufacturers. Other industries are interested in supermarket or chain drug distribution for their products and are jumping aboard. Latest to organize for bar coding: the greeting card and long-playing record industries.

What's in it for "retailers"?   A good question. Many manufacturers who expended time, money, and effort on bar coding wonder what, if any, concrete benefits they will realize—and when.

One area with potential: policing cents-off couponing. Recent data suggest that consumer misredemption alone accounts for a third of all coupons cashed in. Such misuse could be costing marketers well into the hundreds of millions of dollars.

The coupons can be UPC coded for scanning to correspond to the products and cents-off amounts involved. Thus the computer can validate the transaction. It will reject coupons which are not to be used.

Reprinted by permission The Wall Street Journal

Totally new data breakthroughs. Probably scanning's greatest long-term benefit is its ability to generate totally new marketing information.

Scanners could provide retailers with:

1. The first ever accurate reading, item by item, of actual item movement at the point of sale.
2. Readings, overnight, store by store, of consumer buying behavior.
3. Fast, accurate feedback on test market experiments.
4. Measurement of the effects of marketing and promotional activity.

What is OCR-A?

OCR-A (optical character recognition—the A identifies the style of the character) is becoming the most widely used format for general merchandise. It is the recommended ticket marking method by the National Retail Merchants Association (NRMA). Sears has switched to OCR-A and Wards and Penneys are in the process of doing so. The OCR tickets are cheaper and more easily human-read than other tickets (see Figure 10–9.)

The OCR tickets are read with *wands* which are passed over the items. *Remember,* the UPC codes are read by fixed (slot) scanners at the checkout in supermarkets in contrast to wands. Wand readers greatly reduce the average error rate. They are needed because most general merchandise (e.g., goods on hangers) would be difficult to scan with a fixed scanner. Instead, a wand containing a light beam is moved across the tag. Except for this the system is the same as in a supermarket.

An OCR-A price ticket being "read" by a wand

Courtesy NCR

FIGURE 10-9
Examples of OCR-A and
UVM merchandise tickets

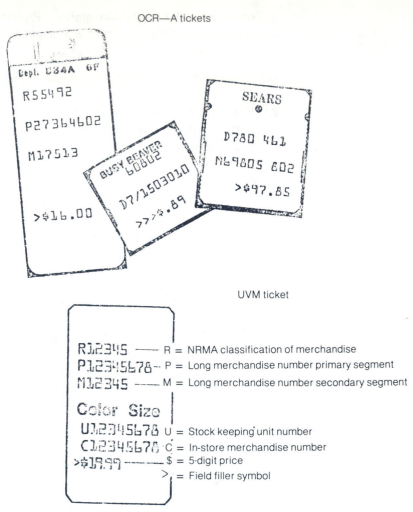

OCR—A tickets

UVM ticket

R12345 ——— R = NRMA classification of merchandise
P12345678 -- P = Long merchandise number primary segment
M12345 ——— M = Long merchandise number secondary segment

Color Size
U12345678 U = Stock keeping unit number
C12345678 C = In-store merchandise number
>$19.99 ——— $ = 5-digit price
> = Field filler symbol

Source: Copyright © 1978 by Creative Strategies, Int'l. Not to be reproduced without permission.

WHAT IS UNIVERSAL VENDOR MARKING (UVM)?

UVM refers to universal vendor marking. It involves a standard vendor-created identification system. The need to mark the items when they are received by each store would be eliminated. Much of the ticketing for Sears, Wards and Penneys is now done at the vendor level.

The highest advances in labor productivity will not occur until at least 70 percent of all general merchandise is marked at the vendor level. Also the differences between the OCR-A system and the UPC system need to be worked out. Supermarkets, for example, now carry nonfood items which cannot be read by scanners that can only read the UPC bar code. Examples of OCR-A and UVM are shown in Figure 10-9.

Premarked items identified by manufacturer, style, size, and color will speed the items through the retailer's receiving and marking functions. If a

A POS terminal with salesperson "wanding" a price ticket

Courtesy NCR

more complete item stock record is needed, the items can be store-marked with information as to department, class, season, and price. This type of information could be quickly handled with a small quick-stick.

WHAT IS AN ELECTRONIC FUNDS TRANSFER SYSTEM (EFTS)?

Most of you have read newspaper articles which refer to the cashless/checkless society. Well, the system may soon be upon us.

One of the advantages of an electronic funds transfer system (EFTS) is that by use of a terminal in the retail outlet, contact can be made with a bank to: (1) get a customers credit OK, (2) process credit card sales, (3) verify checks, and (4) shift money from the customer's account to the account of the merchant.

Food stores have a problem in approving checks and in collecting on bad checks. A check guarantee card is helping. Some stores are experimenting with customer-operated terminals. This removes the process of OKing the checks away from the check stand. The customer deals with a bank in getting the OK.

The use of the *debit card* (a card which allows funds to be shifted from the customer's account to the merchant's account) has possibilities. The lack of a standard account numbering system for all cards is a problem, however. Progress is being made in developing a standard card format.

Finally, retailers like to reduce their float—the time between when the customer presents a check and when the funds are deposited to the retailer's account. Thus, automatic authorization of credit and electronic funds transfer from one account to another would eliminate part of the problem with float.

Still some problems exist with this concept. Consumers, for example, don't like the instant switch of funds from their account to that of the retailer. They prefer to have the several days which now pass before a check clears the bank. Some consumers also simply do not trust computers, especially when it comes to their checking accounts.

THINK METRIC

Only a half dozen countries, including the United States, have not gone to the metric system. However, the United States will soon have to do so to compete in world trade. Many countries had gone to the metric system by the late 1800s.

The metric system is making steady progress in the United States. Many of you have seen labels, signs, and instructions in both metric and inch-pound units. Today, wine and soft drink bottles, for example, are printed either in metric units or expressed in both metric and inch-pound units.

The most common metric units are shown in Table 10–1. As you probably

**TABLE 10–1
Common metric units**

	Name	Symbol	Approximate size
Length	Meter	m.	39½ inches
	Kilometer	km.	0.6 mile
	Centimeter	cm.	Width of a paper clip
	Millimeter	mm.	Thickness of paper clip
Area	Hectare	ha	2½ acres
Weight	Gram	g.	Weight of a paper clip
	Kilogram	kg.	2.2 pounds
	Metric ton	t	Long ton (2,240 pounds)
Capacity	Liter	l.	One quart and 2 ounces
	Milliliter	ml.	1/5 teaspoon
Pressure	Kilopascal	kPa	Atmospheric pressure is about 100 kPa

Units of *time* and *electricity* will not change.

The Celsius *temperature* scale should be used, familiar points on which are:

	°C	°F
Freezing point of water	0	32
Boiling point of water	100	212
Normal body temperature	37	98.6
Comfortable room temperature	20–25	68–77

Source: Christine Hager, "The Move to Metric," *National Food Review*, December 1978, p. 53.

know, many consumers and businesses have no interest in going to the new program. But many major companies are making the metric change when they redesign packages and labels. You can see the metric method of measurement in some advertising. You might as well get used to the idea of thinking metric. It's on its way into our everyday lives and will be going full force in the late 1980s.

The views of the various groups involved in the shift to metric are shown in Figure 10–10.

SUMMARY

Three major electromechanical inventions have occurred in the history of retailing. These are the cash register, the computer, and the point-of-service terminal. The new technology is affecting almost every aspect of retailing including merchandise management, buying, pricing, promotion, location, operations, and personnel.

The point-of-service (POS) terminal allows all sales data to be captured in the terminals at the point of sale and to be transmitted to a back office system.

FIGURE 10–10
How four groups anticipate metric conversion

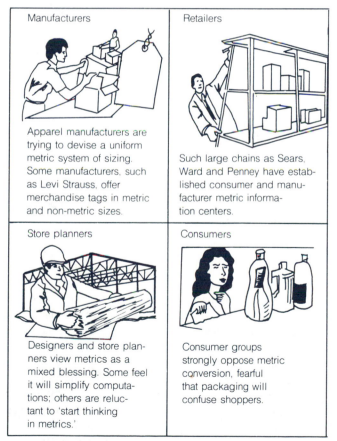

Source: "Chains Disagree on U.S. Metrics Switch," *Chain Store Age Executive* (March 1976), p. 52.

The data can then be recalled for processing and analysis. The resulting data gives you timely, detailed information to help offset a decline in profit margins caused by such factors as lack of inventory control, rapid growth of credit, rising labor costs, and proliferation of merchandise.

Keys to the acceptance of point-of-service terminals are the universal product code (UPC) in the food stores and the OCR-A in general merchandise retailing. These are machine readable codes which allow greater productivity and efficiency at the point-of-service. It also allows merchandise to be marked by the manufacturer and not at the retail level.

The use of electronic cash registers and POS systems is spreading rapidly. Electronic scanning in both food and general merchandising is coming along more slowly, however. Another problem yet to be completely resolved is electronic funds transfer systems (EFTS). This way of doing business would allow the automatic transfer of funds from the customer's account to that of the store.

NOTE

1. All of this material on the universal product code is either quoted or paraphrased from *Grey Matter,* vol. 48, no. 2 (1977), pp. 1–5. Used with permission.

DISCUSSION QUESTIONS

1. What are the advantages of the electronic cash register over mechanical cash registers?
2. What is the meaning of the term optical character recognition?
3. Explain the differences between the UPC and the OCR-A.
4. What is universal vendor marking and what are its advantages?
5. What is a point-of-sales terminal? What are the advantages to you as the retailer?
6. What is meant by wanding?
7. What are the advantages and disadvantages of a debit card to a retailer?
8. Why is it important for you as a retailer to think metric?

PROJECTS

1. Interview the managers of a large department store, a local outlet of a supermarket chain, and a fast-food store. Determine the type of system (electromechanical cash registers, electronic cash registers, or POS) employed in each. How many terminals are there? Are there any plans to change the type of system currently used? Has this change occurred already? If they plan to change, to what type of system will they go? Why? What savings are associated with the change?

2. Electronic funds transfer systems (EFTS) are "hot" topics for management today in retailing. The impetus is perhaps coming from the banking community. Make contacts with local banks and see what is going on in your area relative to "thinking" and "planning" for the era of EFTS. Has there been any impact yet? What forms have EFTS taken in general? Then go to the retail community and see what the status of their knowledge is about the issue. If they are knowledgeable, "pick their brains" about future plans.

3. What is the state of technological advances within your local community? Do a careful survey of the state of adoption of POS systems in the area. Find out from management what equipment is being used; what functions are being performed by the equipment on hand; what are future plans for expanding functions or adopting the new technology in any form. Make a summary chart, comparing companies by kind of business.

4. Check in your area on the "state of the art" relative to technology in the specific area of vendor marking (UPC in grocery trade and OCR-A in general merchandise). What plans are being made for scanning in the stores at this time? If plans are being made, when will implementation be accomplished? What problems are seen in the scanning process? To what uses will the input be put? Do a convenience sample of customers to see what they know about vendor marking and how they react to the "nonhuman readable" portion of the code in grocery stores. How do they react to the detailed tape received from the new terminals? What are your general conclusions from such a study?

Minicase 10-1   Al Smith's Supersaver recently converted to a scanner system. All prices for the food items are stored in a backroom computer. When the item to be purchased is passed over the scanner, the computer automatically looks up the price and adjusts store inventory. The new system prints for the customer a detailed receipt describing the items purchased and the prices of the items.

This process has eliminated the need for marking the price on each individual item. This appealed to Mr. Smith since he looked upon it as a way of lowering his costs. Now he has two major problems. The union to whom his employees belong are picketing the store. They claim the new system will eliminate jobs without lowering costs to the consumers. Consumers are also unhappy because they want the price marked on each item. Somehow they don't trust the computer or the salesperson. They want to be able to look at the price on the item and make sure that is the price which is rung up by the cash register. Mr. Smith has explained the advantages of the new system to both groups and told them how he hoped it will help him to hold down price increases. They are still unhappy. Analyze the situation from the point of view of the union, the customers, and Mr. Smith. What should Mr. Smith have done in the beginning to avoid these problems?

Minicase 10-2   Mrs. J. W. Brown was visiting a major metropolitan city in the East. She was from the Midwest and had a charge card from her "favorite department store" at home, which had an eastern affiliate. In the past when she visited the eastern mecca she went to customer services and received a temporary shopping credit card which made it possible for her to be charged directly so that she did not have to carry cash with her. In addition, her major bank credit cards were not accepted, so that the only way she could take advantage of the elegant new gourmet department about which she had heard so much was to work out her usual arrangement.

She went to customer services, took a number from a spindle, and waited

30 minutes while other customers were involved in what appeared to be a series of confrontations with the service representatives. She wondered whether that was what "services" were all about. Finally her number came up and she presented her hometown card. After she had explained to the representative that the store was a member of the same ownership group, the representative disappeared behind a rather dismal looking partition. After some 20 additional minutes, a temporary card was given to Mrs. Brown. Since it was getting rather late, Mrs. Brown dashed to the men's furnishings department to get her husband a wallet. She found just what she wanted and handed it to the salesperson together with her newly acquired temporary charge card. She was testily informed that the wallet could not be purchased since the store was in the midst of inventory taking and instructions had been given that nothing which had been counted and segregated could be sold. Mrs. Brown was annoyed but anxious to get to the gourmet section, so she left disgruntled but in anticipation of the pleasures to follow.

The visit to the new "shop" was a delight. The assortments of unusual gourmet foods and accessories were up to all expectations. Her cart was brimming with imported Brie, crackers from England, flat bread from Sweden—her hotel room would be a veritable food hall in a few minutes! At the checkout, she anxiously handed her temporary card to the checker—the items were entered in the shiny new POS terminal, and the clicks sounded like music to Mrs. Brown. As the card number was entered into the terminal, a red light flashed, the sale was voided, and the checker rather rudely said to Mrs. Brown, "Move the cart to the side and go up to customer services." Mrs. Brown was horrified and stated that she had no intention of going back to customer services since she had just come from there. The line behind her was growing, and the checker became rather adamant about the procedure. Mrs. Brown said that she wanted to see a management representative. The checker said that she was too busy to look for one, so Mrs. Brown asked the checker to call credit and see what was wrong. The checker very angrily picked up the store phone, dialed a number, and quickly slammed down the receiver. She said that she had been told that if a sale were voided, as Mrs. Brown's had been, the only recourse was to go to customer service. "Next customer, please," the checker said.

Mrs. Brown looked around the department for someone with an identifying tag which indicated that the person was "official." She finally found a young floor manager who was very pleasant, but after Mrs. Brown had calmly related her story, the floor manager said, "The only thing you can do is go to customer services and find out what is wrong. Credit won't answer me any better than they did the checker. I'm sorry, but that's the way the system works since we went on the 'new computer.'" Mrs. Brown was furious. She asked the store representative if there were not some higher authority to whom they could appeal. She was assured that nothing more could be done.

Normally, Mrs. Brown would have walked out of the store, never to return. Instead, because of the potential pleasures sitting against the far wall in an unattended cart, Mrs. Brown made the long trip to customer services. After taking her second number and waiting her 30 minutes, she got the same surly service representative who seemed never to have seen her before. She explained the occurrences of the past hour or so; the service representative again disappeared into the "back room," came out a short time later, and without a word of apology told Mrs. Brown, "Well, it was very simple. Someone, and it wasn't me, forgot to 'put your new number into the system,' so when you tried to charge, the sale was automatically voided. I don't know why you came back here! Why didn't you call credit?"

Analyze the above situation and see how many errors were caused by technology, misunderstanding, and lack of customer orientation. What should the floor representative have done? If you were the operating vice president of the store, what would you do if Mrs. Brown had got to you?

PART III

The things you must know and do to make a profit

"'Whatever happened to W. T. Grant?' That is a sadly familiar question throughout the business community. The well-known chain, once the country's 17th largest retailer, went bankrupt in 1975. The briefest and most obvious answer is 'bad management'. . ."[1]

"Bad management" means little unless contrasted to *good* management. And it makes you wonder just exactly what *is* management. Over 80,000 people were thrown out of work in the W. T. Grant case. Over 1,000 stores were closed, and $234 million was lost by banks and suppliers as a result of the failure.[2]

So, what is retail management? Stated simply, retail management is an activity or process. The process helps management use the *resources* of the firm to meet agreed-on objectives. What resources—people, money, inventory, building, and equipment? What objectives?—*profit* is the major reason a retailer is in business. (There may also be other reasons.)

What are the activities (or functions) that all retail managers at whatever level perform? They are:

1. Planning.
2. Organizing.
3. Directing.
4. Controlling.

When you as a retail manager *plan,* you work out your objectives, and how to reach them. In Chapter 11 we will show you *how* to plan to make a profit.

Once you have plans, you must *organize* your human resources to carry out these plans. In Chapter 12, we will look at some to see how this might be done.

You *direct* when you try to get your people to work efficiently and willingly. Look back in Chapter 9. The management function of directing is really discussed there.

You *control* when you do all you can to make sure that your objectives are being met. If they are not, then you need to take action to improve the situation. You will practice control in Part IV.

We have included Appendixes A and B at the conclusion of this part of the book. We believe that the Small Business Administration (SBA) Aids will be very valuable to you. After studying this part of our text, the *Business Plan for Retailers* (Small Marketers Aid No. 150) and *Marketing Checklist for Small Retailers* (SMA Aid No. 156) should be used as practical summaries of the materials in our book. These checklists not only complement our discussions, but they give you another way of looking at "the things you must know and do to make a profit."

We must make one point at this time. In the checklists which are included at the end of this part, some of the things to "check" are actually discussed in

Part I (especially that portion relating to your customers). Also, information which you will be studying in Part IV (control and accounting) is included in these two appendixes. We believe, however, that Part III is the natural time to introduce these valuable management guides. We suggest that such checklists could be placed at the beginning, the middle, or the end of this book. They would be valuable at any time. Use them well!

NOTES

1. David J. Rachman and Michael H. Mescon, *Business Today*, 2d ed. (New York: Random House, 1979), p. 67.
2. Rachman and Mescon, *Business Today*, p. 76.

11

HOW DO YOU PLAN FOR PROFITS?

The specific purposes of this chapter are to explain to you:

- The steps in merchandise planning.
- How you can look at stock balance.
- How you can understand stock turnover.
- How you can set up your merchandise budget to find out *how much* to spend.
- How sales, inventory, reductions, and purchases affect your profits and how you plan each one.
- How you find out *what* to spend your dollars *for* and *how much* to buy.
- The need for planning your expenses.
- The meaning of the following terms:

Product	Cost of sales (cost of goods sold)
Product line	Stock-sales ratio
Variety	Reductions
Assortment	Employee discounts
Width (breadth)	Shortages (shrinkage)
Support (depth)	Markdowns
SKUs	EOM and BOM inventories
Stock balance	Expense budget
Turnover	Maintained markup

This is the first of seven chapters to point out what you need to *know and do* to make a profit. So get ready, since profit interests all of us!

The broad *purposes* of this chapter are:

1. To show you *how to* set up a merchandise budget.
2. To illustrate *how* budgets affect profits.

Budgets are the key to profit planning. They are the blueprints for merchandise planning.

KEY TERMS

In the introduction to this part of the book, we briefly defined *management* and *planning*. We feel, however, that a more detailed definition would help you dig into this material which is so important. *Management* in retailing involves planning, organizing, controlling, staffing, leading, motivating, communicating, and decision making. By whom? The top executive. Why? To make sure that the resources (land, labor, capital, buildings, and equipment—the salespersons in the store utilizing the registers, e.g.) are used so that profit results. This chapter is concerned with the *planning* activity of management. What is it—making tomorrow's decisions today—deciding where you intend to be in the future and how you should get there. That's planning!

Make sure you understand the terms below or you may have problems understanding the chapter.

A *product* is what you are selling—a physical object (a dress), or a service (suit cleaning). The *product line* includes *all* of the products or services you sell.

A product line consists of "variety" and "assortment." *Variety* means the kinds of goods in a product line. Let's take *food* as a product line in a supermarket. In the food line you can find bread, canned vegetables, frozen juices, and cheese among others. Another product line might be paper products. In that line you would see napkins, towels, and toilet tissue.

Assortment is the variety available for each item in your product line. Imagine you are looking for coffee. Coffee is one item in the food *product* line. In the coffee section your assortment might include: (1) regular, instant, and freeze-dried coffees; (2) in regular, ground, or coffee beans; (3) sizes in regular grind: 13 ounces, one pound, or two pounds; (4) Folgers, Maxwell House, or a private brand (the retailer's own brand); and other choices.

As you may have guessed by now, this chapter is concerned with *merchandise assortment planning* for profit. Merchandise assortment planning helps you balance your *stock* (inventory of merchandise) with sales.

Figure 11–1 is a diagram for merchandise planning. This figure is a guide for the rest of the chapter. We will refer to it from time to time. Pay close attention now to points 1, 2, and 3—these are the key terms discussed above. Don't let Figure 11–1 turn you off. We will continue to break it into several parts for discussion.

FIGURE 11-1
How to understand the merchandise planning process

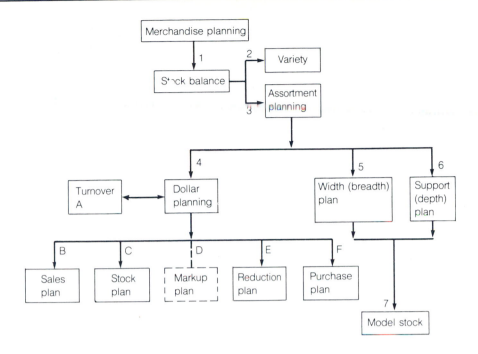

HOW CAN YOU LOOK AT STOCK BALANCE?

Keep in mind the following three points which go together in planning stock balance:

1. Width (or breadth).
2. Support (or depth).
3. Total dollars.

Width (or breadth)

In *width,* think about the assortment you need (1) to meet the demands of your market, and (2) to meet competition. Here the idea of SKUs (stock keeping units which are specific items you want to plan and control) is helpful in planning the width of your coffee offering:

Brand (Folgers, Maxwell, private) . . . . 3 SKUs
×
Types (regular, instant, freeze-dried) . . . . 3 = 9
×
Sizes (3 in each can of coffee) . . . . 9 = 81 SKUs

Thus, 81 SKUs are needed to meet customer wants and what is offered by the competition.

Support (or depth)

You have now decided how many SKUs you need. Now, decide on how many one-pound, Folger's, regular grind cans of coffee versus 13-ounce automatic drip coffee you need.

The answer to how many depends on the *sales importance* of each factor.

If 10 percent of your sales are in Folgers one-pound, regular grind, then you may want 10 percent of your "support" to be in that SKU. It sounds simple, but the "art" of merchandising enters here. Only experience in planning your stock (discussed later in this chapter) will give you confidence.

Dollars

Let's assume you need 1,000 cans of coffee for your ideal stock level. How many dollars do you need in stock at any one time?[1] Here *merchandise turnover* comes into play.

Merchandise (or stock) turnover means the number of times your average inventory of an item is sold each period (week, month, or year)—point 4A, Figure 11–1. Your turnover can be figured out based on (1) your cost for an item, or (2) its retail selling price. (Figure 11–2 shows how to figure your turnover.) For example, assume . . .

You want a turnover that is: (1) fast enough to give you a good return on your money tied up in inventory, and (2) not so fast that you are always out of stock.

FIGURE 11–2
How to understand stock turnover

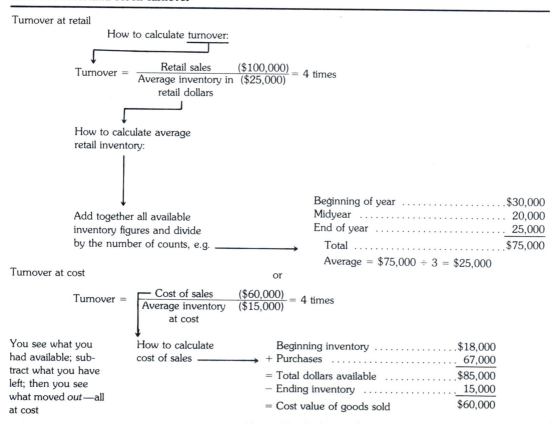

Turnover at retail

How to calculate turnover:

$$\text{Turnover} = \frac{\text{Retail sales} \quad (\$100,000)}{\text{Average inventory in} \quad (\$25,000)} = 4 \text{ times}$$
retail dollars

How to calculate average retail inventory:

Add together all available inventory figures and divide by the number of counts, e.g.

Beginning of year	$30,000
Midyear	20,000
End of year	25,000
Total	$75,000

Average = $75,000 ÷ 3 = $25,000

or

Turnover at cost

$$\text{Turnover} = \frac{\text{Cost of sales} \quad (\$60,000)}{\text{Average inventory} \quad (\$15,000)} = 4 \text{ times}$$
at cost

You see what you had available; subtract what you have left; then you see what moved *out*—all at cost

How to calculate cost of sales

Beginning inventory	$18,000
+ Purchases	67,000
= Total dollars available	$85,000
− Ending inventory	15,000
= Cost value of goods sold	$60,000

FIGURE 11-3
How to look at stock balance

Ways to look at stock balance	Examples	Things to consider in assortment planning
Width (or breadth)	Number of brands, sizes, prices	1. What customers want. 2. What competitors offer.
Support (or depth)	How many units needed to support expected sales of each size, e.g.?	3. The sales importance of each size.
Total dollars	How many dollars needed in inventory?	4. Look at turnover— *a.* Fast enough to get good return. *b.* Not so fast that out of stocks occur.

Summary

Figure 11-3 recaps what we have said so far. Go back over the first few pages of this chapter if you don't understand everything shown.

Now, let's figure out how to set up a merchandise budget.

HOW DO YOU PLAN YOUR MERCHANDISE BUDGET?

Merchandise budgeting means *dollar planning.* (Figure 11-1, points 4A-F.)

In deciding how many dollars to spend on merchandise you need to:

1. Decide on the things which affect your profits.
2. Set up a merchandise budget based on these factors.

What factors affect your profits?

The items to be included in your merchandise budget are:

1. Sales—4B.
2. Stock (inventory)—4C.
3. Reductions—4E.
4. Purchases—4F.

Figure 11-4 is your guide to a merchandise budget. Keep coming back to it as you follow our discussion.

Sales planning. Begin your merchandise budget with a seasonal sales plan. (Point 4B in Figure 11-1). Let's work with men's ties.

FIGURE 11-4
A guide to the merchandise budget

	Profit factors to be budgeted					
	Sales		Stock (inventory)	Reductions		Purchases
	Season	Month		Season	Month	
Information available for planning						
Judgment applied in certain issues						

Note in Figure 11-4 that you plan sales by season and then by month.

By season. A *season* is the typical planning period in retailing, especially for fashion. Let's assume you are planning the budget for the spring season (February, March, April, May, June, and July) 1981. You start planning in November 1980.

For convenience, "blow up" a section of Figure 11-4 and call it Figure 11-5. This figure gives you the outline for your seasonal sales plan.

Sticking with Figure 11-5, assume that you had sales of $15,000 for spring 1980 in your tie classification. Sales for the fall season, 1980 have been running about 5 percent ahead of fall 1979. You expect the trend to continue. So, you plan for spring sales of $15,750 ($15,000 × .05 = $750).

But you can't stop here. Now, use your judgment and look at the forces outside the firm which can affect your plan. Assume: (1) a new men's store is opening next door and will carry similar tie assortments; (2) the new store is part of a national chain with excellent management; (3) a major manufacturing plant in your area is planning a large expansion; and (4) the "disco craze" is bringing ties of all kinds into fashion.

Finally, you plan to move the tie display to a more valuable store location. Also, more space will be available.

You can't put *exact* numbers on the factors above. You must, though, factor them into your sales forecast. So, now you decide that sales will go up by 10 percent. Your sales plan for the 1981 spring season thus is now $16,500 ($15,000 × .10 = $1,500).

By month. Now divide your planned season sales into months. Again (Figure 11-5), your starting point is spring 1980. Assume the following sales distribution by month for spring 1980: February—10 percent; March—20 percent; April—15 percent; May—15 percent; June—30 percent; and July—10 percent. Based on this breakdown, your planned season's sales plan by month for spring 1981 would look like that in Figure 11-6.

FIGURE 11-5
Diagram of the sales budget, 1981

	Sales	
	Season	*By month*
Information available for planning	1. Sales for spring of 1980. 2. Recent trends in sales. 3. Check trend against published trade data.	1. Sales percentages by month, 1980. 2. Check distribution against published trade data.
Judgment applied in certain issues	1. Factors outside the store such as new competition. 2. Internal conditions such as more space available.	1. Factors outside the store such as new competition. 2. Internal conditions such as more space available.

FIGURE 11–6
Spring sales plan, 1981

Month	Percent of total season's business in 1980	× Seasons sales forecast	= Planned sales for months of 1981 season
February	10%	$16,500	$1,650
March	20	16,500	3,300
April	15	16,500	2,475
May	15	16,500	2,475
June	30	16,500	4,950
July	10	16,500	1,650
Total	100%		$16,500

Stock planning. Stock planning is point 4C in Figure 11–1. Another expansion from Figure 11–4 is now in order. Figure 11–7 is your guide to planning your inventory.

You begin by planning your *beginning of the month inventories* (the amount of stock you need to meet your sales plan). The inventory on hand at the *end* of the month becomes the beginning of the month inventory for the next month. You know based on Figure 11–6 that your planned sales for January are $1,650. Also, you know based on past experiences and industry trade data that you need 7.6 times more dollars in inventory than your planned sales. Your BOM stock is thus $12,540 ($1,650 × 7.6).[2]

Figure your stock to sales ratio by dividing your *turnover* (number of times you sell and replace your average inventory during a period such as a year) into 12 (the number of months in a year). For example:

If turnover is:	Divide turnover into 12 (number of months in year)	Then average stock sales ratio is
4.0	12 ÷ 4.0 =	3.0
2.5	12 ÷ 2.5 =	4.8
30.0	12 ÷ 30.0 =	.4

As you can see the *lower* the turnover, the *higher* the stock-sales ratio.

Figure 11–8 gives you needed BOM stocks for spring 1981 using planned sales for spring 1981 from Figure 11–6 and your stock-sales ratios for past years.

FIGURE 11–7
Diagram of inventory budget, 1981 (by month)

Concrete information available for planning	1. Stock-sales ratios based on past history 2. Trade stock-sales ratios or your own performance
Judgment applied to planning	1. Compare actual turnover with turnover goal

FIGURE 11-8
BOM stock, spring 1981

Month	Planned sales ×	Stock-sales ratio	= Planned BOM stock
February	$ 1,650	4.7	$ 7,755
March	3,300	4.2	13,860
April	2,475	4.3	10,640
May	2,475	4.4	10,890
June	4,950	3.4	16,830
July	1,650	6.9	11,385
	$16,500		$71,360

You next want to adjust the above figures a little based on what you think may be different from last year. Also, remember that in some situations such as in a grocery store, you may want to plan inventory by the week, not by the month.

Reduction planning.   What are *reductions?* They are anything other than sales which reduce inventory (point 4E in Figure 11-1).

Employee discounts are reductions. If an item sells for $100 and employees receive a 20 percent discount, the employee pays $80. The $80 is recorded as a sale. The $20 reduces the inventory dollar amount but is *not* a sale. It is an employee discount—a reduction.

Shortages (shrinkage) are reductions. A shoplifter takes a $500 watch from a jewelry department. Inventory is reduced by $500 just as if it were a sale. But no revenues come from shoplifting. A salesperson takes another watch (called internal pilferage). The results are the same. A $1,000 watch is received into stock and by mistake is *marked,* "$500." A clerical error. Fewer inventory dollars are in stock than you think.

Markdowns are reductions (and the only type of reduction we will focus on). For example, assume a $25 tie does not sell during the season. So you mark it to $15. The $10 markdown is counted as a reduction of inventory. Only $15 is counted as a sale.

Why plan reductions as a part of your merchandise budget? Suppose as in Figure 11-8 you planned a BOM stock of $13,860 for March to support March sales of $3,300 (with a 4.2 stock-sales ratio). But suppose you have marked down, during February, an amount approximating $5,000. Your EOM inventory in February (BOM—March) is $5,000 less than if no markdowns had been taken.

So, plan your reductions in order to have sufficient BOM inventory to make your planned sales.

Assume that reductions for the spring season in the tie department are planned at 8 percent or $1,320 ($16,500 seasons sales × 0.08). Figure 11-9 shows how to plan the monthly reductions using historical monthly patterns. Reductions normally vary by month.

Planned purchases.   You have now planned (1) sales, (2) stocks, and (3) reductions. Now, you are ready to plan the dollar amount of your purchases (point 4F in Figure 11-1).

FIGURE 11-9
Planned reductions,
spring 1981

Month	Planned sales	Planned percentage reductions (8 percent season)	Amount of reductions
February	$ 1,650	20%*	$ 264
March	3,300	10	132
April	2,475	10	132
May	2,475	10	132
June	4,950	20	264
July	1,650	30	396
	$16,500	100%	$1,320

* 20% × $1,320 = $264, etc.

Figure planned purchases as follows:

A. You *need* dollars of purchase to ... 1. Make sure we have enough EOM inventory to be in business the following month.
2. Make sure you have enough to support your sales plan.
3. Take care of your planned reductions.

and

B. You *have* dollars to contribute to the above needs in the form of .... 4. Retail BOM inventory.

Thus, *planned purchases* are found by:

Planned purchases = Planned EOM stock + Planned sales + Planned reductions − Planned BOM stock.

Look back at Figures 11-8 and 11-9 to get the information. Let's determine the purchases for March:

Planned
purchases = $10,640 (EOM March or BOM April) —Figure 11-8
+ 3,300 (Planned sales, March) —Figure 11-9
+ 132 (Planned reductions, March) —Figure 11-9

= $14,072 (Dollar *needs,* March)
−13,860 (BOM March—what you *have*) —Figure 11-8

= $ 212

You now have gone through the dollar merchandise budget process and know how to set up such a budget.[3] But look back at Figure 11-1. You will see that we still have to plan the width and support factors of stock balance *(points 5 and 6).* The following section shows you how to set up these parts of the merchandise budget.

How do you plan the width and support of assortments?

Now that you know how much to spend for your stock you have to decide (1) "what to spend your dollars for *(width)*" and (2) "in what amounts *(depth).*" Width and depth make up stock balance.

Your basic goal is to set up a model stock (see point 7, Figure 11–1). That is your best prediction of the assortments you need to satisfy your customers.

Width plan. Figure 11–10 is a model stock plan for your tie classification. Assume that only two customer-attracting features are important—a bow tie or a four-in-hand tie. (A four-in-hand tie is the regular man's tie as opposed to a bow tie.) This is a simple illustration. Even so, you can see that to offer your customers only *one* tie in each assortment *width* factor (in both four-in-hand and bow) you would need 270 ties ($2 \times 5 \times 3 \times 3 \times 3$)—column 1 of Figure 11–10.

Depth plan. Your next job is to decide on the depth plan (column 2). How many ties do you need in each of your five assortment factors? You

FIGURE 11-10
Model stock of ties

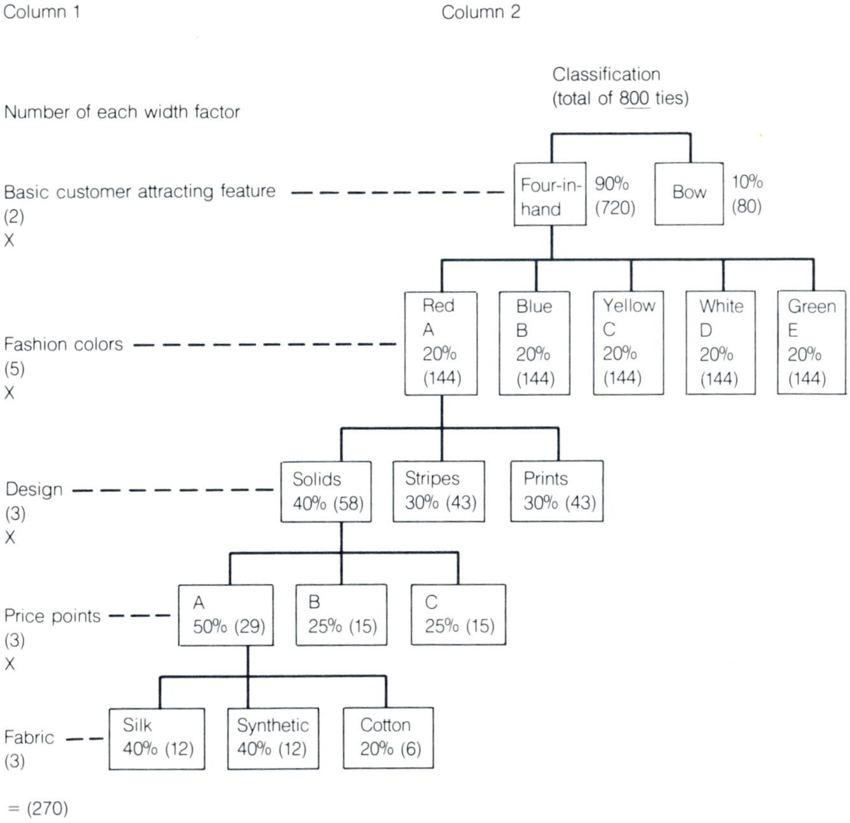

Column 1   Column 2

Classification
(total of 800 ties)

Number of each width factor

Basic customer attracting feature — — — — — — —   Four-in-hand 90% (720)   Bow 10% (80)
(2)
X

Fashion colors — — — — — Red A 20% (144)   Blue B 20% (144)   Yellow C 20% (144)   White D 20% (144)   Green E 20% (144)
(5)
X

Design — — — — — Solids 40% (58)   Stripes 30% (43)   Prints 30% (43)
(3)
X

Price points — — — A 50% (29)   B 25% (15)   C 25% (15)
(3)
X

Fabric — — Silk 40% (12)   Synthetic 40% (12)   Cotton 20% (6)
(3)

= (270)

Note: The percentage in each factor is the expected importance of that assortment factor. Numbers in parenthesis represent the share of the 800 tie total; for example, 90% × 800 = 720; 20% × 720 = 144, and so on.

decide that you need 800 ties for one turnover period. (If your turnover is to be 3, then you need ties for four months—12 ÷ 3 = 4). Also remember that you are planning your dollars at the same time as your assortments. Those dollars will also affect your support.

You believe that 90 percent of your sales will be in four-in-hand ties. So 90 percent × 800 = 720 ties. Following Figure 11-10 on down, you see that you will have 144 fashion color A; 58 solids in that color; 29 at price point A, and finally 12 silks.

The act of planning. Merchandise planning requires a "feeling" about many things. Here is the "art" of retailing. In this chapter we have stressed the "how to" rather than the "what" and "why." Experience is the only real teacher here.

EXPENSE BUDGETING

You now need to plan your expenses. Expenses need to be forecast for a specific period just like the merchandise budget. Both the merchandise and the expense budgets are based on planned sales. *The main purpose of merchandise budgeting is to maintain a balance between inventories and sales. The main purpose of expense planning is to balance planned expenses with planned income.*

Think of income as "maintained markup." (Much more on that in Chapter 13.) The maintained markup must cover operating expenses and profits. Maintained markup is the difference between retail sales and the cost of sales. The following diagram shows these relationships.

If your expenses were $17,000, for example, instead of the planned $15,000, your profits would be cut to $3,000. That would probably not be enough to satisfy you as a return on your investment. You should see how important it is to plan (and control) expenses because of the impact they have on profits.

The kinds of expenses which must be planned vary by type of retail store. Just as an example, the following expense classification is used by members of the Super Market Institute.

Labor expenses.

Advertising and promotion expense.

Trading stamp expense.

Store supply expense.

Store occupancy expense (rent and utilities).

Equipment depreciation or rental cost.

Maintenance and repairs.

All other store expenses.

Remember, the expense budget (just like the merchandise budget) is just a plan. Periodic review is necessary to see whether the budget is effective. The use of periodic reports comparing planned and actual expenses is sound. (Chapter 18 will explore this control aspect.)

Many technical questions of expense management exist which we will not cover here. We are merely introducing you to the importance of expense planning in the profit planning process.

SUMMARY

We wonder if any chapter can be more important than one discussing "how to plan for profits." We urge you to look back at the "specific purposes" of this chapter and review the things which you should know now. Figure 11–1 is a good summary of the way the merchandise planning process operates. You can see that you look at stock balance in three ways: dollars, width (breadth), and support (depth). The concept and importance of turnover to dollar planning is important to review. The merchandise budget for planning your dollars was given a complete treatment. The items you planned are: sales, stocks (inventory), reductions, and purchases. The guide to merchandise budgeting is important to you for planning purposes. Review it. The idea of a model stock and an example of the width and support plan are important in your study. Again, review it.

You now have reviewed a process for finding out *how much to spend and for what and how many.*

Finally, while the merchandise budget provides a way to balance your stocks and sales, the expense plan is to balance planned expenses and planned income.

NOTES

1. Obviously dollars invested in inventory relate to width and support. In fact the dollars planned become the controlling decision. How many dollars you have will determine your investment in SKUs. Clearly, also, planning width, support, *and* dollars does not guarantee the optimal stock. Many of your questions about how well you are doing the planning will be answered when you study Chapter 18; the control function of management.

2. You may wonder *why* 7.6 more dollars of inventory than sales is needed. The fact

really relates to the support factor. An example can help illustrate. *If* customers were individually predictable, that is if we could know that we only needed *one* tie to satisfy all of our demand, then we might get by with a 1 to 1 ratio. But people want to select from many colors, designs, fabrics, and so on. Thus, we need many more SKUs to support our planned sales. The more fashion-oriented the merchandise (or the less stable), the more stock you will need to support your sales.

3. In Part IV you will see how to set up a control system to measure how well your plan is working. Some of you might want to look at that part now. It is a logical way to look at the process.

DISCUSSION QUESTIONS

1. By using examples distinguish among: product; product line; variety; and assortment. How do they all relate to "merchandise (assortment) planning?

2. What are the three points which go together in planning stock balance?

3. Explain width (or breadth) in terms of SKUs. What considerations are important in planning width?

4. Diagram the "merchandise planning process."

5. What do you consider in planning stock support or depth?

6. Explain "merchandise turnover" and indicate how it is useful in planning your total dollars in inventory. What do you consider in setting a turnover goal?

7. What things must you consider in deciding how many dollars to spend on inventory?

8. What factors affect your profits (or what are the items that should be included in your merchandise budget)?

9. Diagram a "guide to the merchandise budget."

10. Discuss the following: sales planning; stock planning; reduction planning.

11. Explain "stock-sales" ratios and explain how they are a guide to stock planning in the budget.

12. Explain the relationship between stock-sales ratios and turnover.

13. What are "reductions?"—Give specific examples of the various types.

14. Explain why you should plan reductions as a part of your merchandise budget.

15. How do you plan purchases? Give a "common-sense" example of the process.

16. Contrast (or compare) merchandise budgeting and expense budgeting.

PROBLEMS

1. If net sales for the season are $640,000 and the average monthly retail stock on hand for the season is $350,000, what is the annual stock turnover rate?

2. Given the following figures, what is the stock turnover rate for the season?

	Retail stock on hand	Monthly net sales
Opening inventory	$342,000	
End of 1st month	339,000	$135,000
End of 2d month	345,000	127,400
End of 3d month	336,000	131,900
End of 4th month	328,000	128,700
End of 5th month	305,000	114,000
End of 6th month	294,000	106,500

3. If the average inventory at cost is $20,000 and the cost of goods sold is $100,000, what is the stock turnover rate?

4. What is the rate of stock turnover if the average inventory at cost is $15,000, net sales are $100,000, and the markup on retail is 40 percent?

5. What is the average stock if the stock turnover rate is three and net sales are $90,000?

6. A new store shows the following figures for its first three months of operation; net sales, $32,000; average retail stock, $64,000. If business continues at the same rate, what will the stock turn be for the year?

7. The merchandising executive in a retailing organization is continually thinking in terms of stock turnover

rates. The following problems are illustrative of matters that receive frequent attention. Calculate the answers to the following problems:

	Given	Find
a.	Average inventory at cost, $20,000; cost of goods sold, $85,000	Rate of stock turn
b.	Average inventory at retail, $60,000; net sales, $280,000	Rate of stock turn
c.	Average inventory at cost, $30,000; net sales, $200,000; gross margin as percentage of sales, 25 percent	Rate of stock turn
d.	Stock turnover, 5; average inventory at retail, $140,000	Sales
e.	Stock turnover, 4; net sales volume, $160,000	Average retail stock

8. Last year a certain department had net sales of $60,000 and a stock turnover rate of five. A turnover rate of six is desired for the year ahead. If sales volume remains the same, how much must the average inventory be reduced in dollar amount and in percentage?

9. A hardware store has net sales for the year of $142,500. The stock at the beginning of the year is $45,000 at cost and $75,000 at retail. A stock count in July showed the inventory at cost as $47,500, and at retail as $72,500. End-of-year inventories are $50,000 at cost and $77,500 at retail. Purchases at cost during the year amounted to $97,500. What is the stock turnover rate (a) at cost? (b) at retail?

PROJECTS

1. Make a contact with a local buyer of a line in which you are interested. If you can work out such a relationship, allow the buyer to let you do a full six-months merchandise plan for a specific merchandise classification. Utilize the text format for your process of planning.

2. The text gives much attention to formal merchandise planning. Select certain stores which are available to you and find out how they handle this function in reality. How much planning? Levels of sophistication? Does the degree of planning differ by merchandise lines? See whether you can develop some generalizations from your investigations.

Minicase 11-1   Thomas Mason was asked by his merchandise manager to compute the turnover in one of his classifications; namely, men's dress shirts. Thomas, who had just been assigned the position of assistant buyer in the men's department, was anxious to do a good job on this first "real" assignment. He poured over the recent records and found that the average inventory at cost for the last six months was approximately $20,000. He had figures for each month and he added them up and divided by the number of months. He then took his total sales for the same period—$100,000—and began writing his report to the boss. He was pleased to report that the turnover in the department for the period was five. He was amazed when the merchandise manager came in the next day and was less than pleased with the information he had received.

What was the cause of the displeasure? What can be done now to give a happy ending to Thomas' problems.

Minicase 11–2   Jane Rich was a new trainee in a department store. Her assignment was to assist the junior sportswear buyer. Her buyer was in New York when a call came from the market asking Jane to do some quick figuring so that the amount of planned purchases could be computed. The buyer also said to Jane, "Tell me how you can help me get some more purchase dollars." Jane was perplexed—Would she have to go to the bank? Give Jane some good advice.

12

HOW DO YOU ORGANIZE FOR PROFITS?

This chapter is designed to introduce you to and explain:

- The various ways you can organize a retail firm.
- The key functions of a retail store.
- Recent trends in organization.
- The role and responsibilities of the buyer.
- Who your merchandise resources can be.
- How you make your market contacts.
- What things you must consider in getting the best prices from vendors.
- Things you must know about when you negotiate with vendors.
- The meaning of the following terms:

Five-functional organization plan	Leased department
Unity of command	List price
Tandem management	Trade discount
Fashion coordinator	Quantity discount
Comparison shopping	Seasonal discount
Central market	Cash discount
Resident buying office	Promotional allowance
Group buying	Cash datings
Central buying	Future datings
Buying committees	Anticipation
Consignment	FOB

In the introduction to this part of the book—"The Things You Must Know and Do to Make a Profit"—we said all managers must plan and *organize*. We have just completed, in the previous chapter, a planning discussion. We stressed merchandise planning (or budgeting).

In this chapter we will follow the management functions logically. In the organizing function you will see how to organize human resources.

We will continue our merchandising emphasis in this present chapter. Also we will continue our focus on relatively small firms.

This chapter spends a lot of time on the *buyer*. This person is management's representative at the operating level for the merchandising activities. Most people think of the buyer as responsible for buying and selling all of the merchandise in the store or in a department. But this definition is not always accurate.

Two terms used in this chapter should be clearly understood now. In retail management, *organizing* is simply the bringing together of all the firms resources (labor, capital, and so on) to make sure the goals of the firm are accomplished. The *organization chart* is just a picture which shows the functions of a firm and the lines of authority and responsibility. A good organization chart shows a clear picture of the organization.

Let's see how this relates to profits. . . .

HOW ARE RETAIL FIRMS ORGANIZED FOR PROFITABLE OPERATIONS?

The management function of organizing is most easily understood in an organization chart. So, in this section we will use several to stress the points we consider important.

Remember though that differences do exist (1) between stores of different sizes and (2) between stores carrying different types of merchandise. The organization of Macy's, for example, is quite different from a small "mom and pop" boutique in a regional mall or from Kroger. *But,* the differences are primarily a matter of degree and department identification. The same basic functions have to be carried out. We attempt to vary our examples so that you can see how interchangeable the ideas are.

Key functions of a retail store

The two functions which probably will first be "organized" are (1) merchandising and (2) operations (or store management). Such an organization would look like the one in Figure 12-1.

The *operations manager* is responsible for building upkeep, delivery, stockroom(s), service, supplies, equipment purchasing, and similar activities.

FIGURE 12-1
The simplest organization

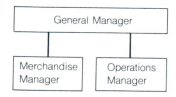

The *merchandise manager,* in addition to being responsible for buying and selling, has other functions to direct. This executive supervises and/or also prepares merchandise budgets; advertising, displays and other promotions; and inventory planning and control.

As a store continues to grow in size, other specialization occurs. The process may begin to look like Figure 12-2.

As you can see, the next managers who will probably be added are financial, promotion, and personnel.

The controller (financial manager) handles the finances of the firm. The person is probably accounting oriented. The organization in Figure 12-2 is typical of department stores. But a food operation, for example, performs the same functions.

Unity of command.   A basic principle of management is that no person should report to more than one supervisor. The organization plan in Figure 12-2 violates this principle. You can't see it, but under the plan, salespeople report to several supervisors. They interact with representatives in the merchandise division, operations division, and personnel division. Each manager feels that the salesperson can be directed in certain activities. So, the poor salesperson has a variety of bosses. That's bad! Put yourself in that position. The "orders" can be different. That places the salesperson in a no-win position.

Trends in organizing

After World War II, the shopping center became the key way of expanding in retailing. "Downtown" stores "branched" to the shopping centers.

We noted earlier that the merchandising division in the "typical" plan (Figure 12-2) was ordinarily responsible for buying and selling in the store. When branches were added, the merchandiser in the downtown (or "main") store also merchandised for the branches.

Try to imagine that you were managing (handling buying and selling responsibilities) in a downtown store. Suddenly you find yourself with not one, but *three* stores to buy for, supervise sales, and generally manage. How can you do a good job in the main store and in several branches? You can't!

So a trend developed during the "branching" era to *separate* the buying and selling functions.

FIGURE 12-2
Five-functional
organizational plan

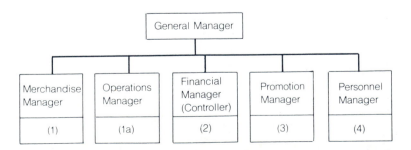

FIGURE 12-3
Separation of buying and selling

They should not be separated	*Counter arguments*
1. Buyer must have contact with the consumer to interpret needs.	1. With technology, reports, etc., it is not necessary.
2. Persons who buy merchandise should be responsible for selling it.	2. Buying and selling require two different job skills.
3. Should be single responsibility.	3. Separate buying and selling activities, essential as firm adds units.

Separation of buying and selling. Some people argue that buying must be under the same manager as selling. Their arguments (and our answers) appear in Figure 12–3.

We believe that the arguments against separation are not as strong as the counterarguments. The branch store problem itself seems to demand separation. Thus, the trend is to separate! Figure 12–4 shows a department store which is organized for the separation of buying and selling. The general merchandise manager is responsible for buying. Selling is the responsibility of the vice president for branch stores.

Food stores could have the same problem, but their expansion history has really solved their problems. Rather than "branching," these companies ex-

FIGURE 12-4
Organization for separation of buying and selling

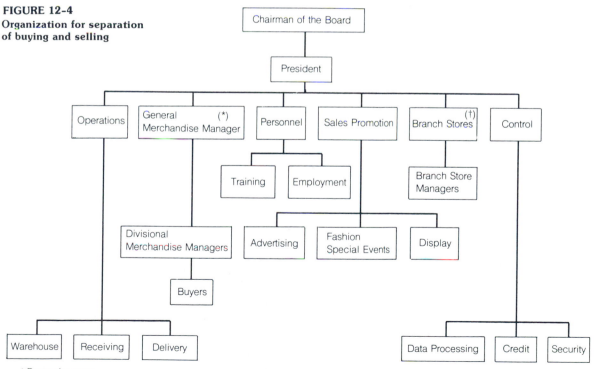

° Buying functions.
† Selling functions.

panded as chain store organizations. By the nature of this type of firm, buying and selling were separated. No "main" stores exist in a chain organization. Buying and selling are always separated.

Chain store organization. Certain features of a chain should be explained. Major differences exist between chain and branch store organizations.

Let's compare a chain store organization with an earlier (before separation) branch store (or even a single-store) organization:

1. In a chain, responsibility is more centralized in the headquarters (or home office).
2. More divisions exist in a chain organization; e.g., real estate, transportation, warehousing, public relations, legal.
3. The chain organization has tighter supervision of store activities.
4. The chain probably has more reports for control purposes.

Vice president, marketing. While we do not plan to make a big issue of it, in large, multiunit, department stores you can find today the vice president, marketing as a key executive.

This person handles marketing research and promotion for the various regions. As time goes on, you will find more of the major companies appointing marketing vice presidents. With our smaller company focus, we will not spend more time on this trend.

Tandem management. A new organization arrangement is now emerging. This trend is primarily occurring in the department store industry.

The top executive has such time pressures that a new plan was needed. *Tandem management* offers one solution. *Two* chief executive officers (CEOs) operate "in tandem." One of the persons has responsibility for the merchandising and promotional activities. The other CEO is more of an "operating and control" person.

Ideally, "two can live 'better' than one." Only time will tell. But it appears to be a trend you should be aware of.

HOW CAN THE MERCHANDISING FUNCTION BE ORGANIZED?

Many stores still are organized with buying and selling under the general merchandise manager. Figure 12–5 shows an organization with this view of management. With only one or two branches such a plan might work.

The major difference in a firm where buying and selling are separate can be shown by looking again at Figure 12–5. All of the staff (advisory) functions remain (merchandise budgets, unit control, fashion, comparison, and testing). The branch store, main store, and basement store managers report to a sales manager or a branch stores manager (as in Figure 12–4). The buyers and assistant buyers remain in the structure and report to a general merchandise manager. Of course the salespeople and stockpeople report to the store managers rather than to the assistant buyers.

FIGURE 12-5
The merchandising division

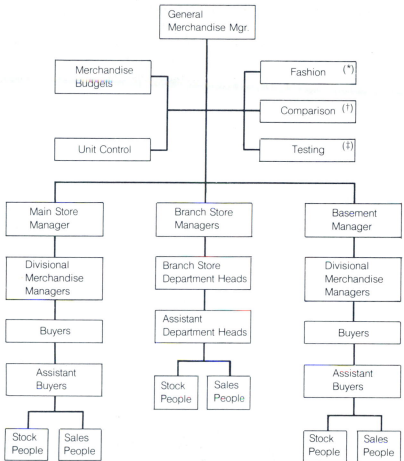

° Fashion coordination—makes sure a consistent fashion "story" is told.
⁺ Comparison shopping—compares competitive offerings with own store.
⁴ Testing laboratory for safety and quality.
Source: Ralph D. Shipp, Jr., *Retail Merchandising Principles and Applications* (Boston: Houghton Mifflin Company, 1976), p. 4.

ROLE AND RESPONSIBILITIES OF THE BUYER

As we indicated in the first part of this chapter, the *buyer* is our focus. This person is the operating manager in the merchandising division. Let's forget, for the moment, the problem of separation of buying and selling. Assume that the buyer has buying responsibility. No selling responsibilities are of concern here. (Regardless of who has the responsibility, this function is discussed in Chapter 15.)

What merchandise to buy

This responsibility of the buyer was discussed in detail in Chapter 11. You remember that you were concerned with *planning*. And planning *what* to buy was a major concern.

When to buy

The *what* and *when* are closely related. For your own ease in studying retailing, however, we hold off on the *when* until Chapter 18. The "when" you buy is so closely related to the control function of management, that we hold off on that until we get to that function. We think you will appreciate that as you move through this text.

How much to buy

Just as you decide *what* to buy (width of assortments and total dollars), you must decide *how much* to buy. Remember we discussed "support" (or depth) of assortments in Chapter 11. That is another duty of the buyer. You are already familiar with that job.

What to charge

This duty of the buyer is complicated. We devote an entire chapter (Chapter 13) to the problem. We will not go into it in this chapter.

Where to buy and how to get the best price possible

These responsibilities are discussed in the remainder of this chapter. These issues fit easily into our concern with the operating level of management (buyer).

But before we face these questions, you should be aware of the qualifications needed by a buyer. It may have some career benefits.

A buyer following up on delivery with a merchandise resource

Courtesy NCR

Qualifications of the Buyer. Buyers must be merchandise *specialists*. They should be able to recognize quality, judge workmanship, and have knowledge regarding materials, color, and design. Although buyers should be able to appreciate the aesthetic appeal of merchandise, they must be prudent enough to buy what they think will sell rather than what might be in good taste in their opinion . . . Experience plus a natural talent will aid buyers. . . .

Buyers must learn how to be traders. The profit margin of their departments will be bigger if they can negotiate low purchasing prices and take advantage of vendor helps as well. . . .

Buyers should be good managers. . . . Too often buyers get bogged down in paperwork or become too involved in the details of running their department. The ability to delegate authority . . . should be developed early in their careers. Otherwise they will soon find themselves on a treadmill leading nowhere.

. . . A successful buyer must exhibit an uncommon amount of drive and a will to succeed. Buying is a highly competitive and exhausting job. Although the rewards are many, some persons cannot take the daily strain of meeting people, bargaining with vendors, placating customers, and pleasing superiors. Buyers are more subject to "ups and downs"; than are persons in many other lines of endeavor. Buyers must be firm and decisive because quick decisions are part of their everyday lives. In order to cope with these tensions, buyers should enjoy conflict. People who are not aggressive and whose feelings are easily hurt will probably find that buying and merchandising are not for them.

Finally, buyers should possess personal integrity. Because they sign purchase orders amounting to hundreds of thousands of dollars, buyers are under great temptations to make "deals" with vendors. . . . Word quickly spreads if a buyer is on the "take," and professional reputations are easily ruined. High personal and business ethics cannot be measured in dollars and cents.[1]

WHAT ARE YOUR MERCHANDISE RESOURCES?

You often have a wide choice in the types of resources you select. Try to continue relationships over a period of time. It is convenient and economical to do so.

Wholesalers. Wholesalers are a major source. Most retailers do not buy directly from the manufacturer. "Probably almost half of all . . . goods go through the hands of wholesalers."[2]

Manufacturers. Goods may be purchased from manufacturers. The larger you are and the more bargaining power you have, the more likely you are to deal directly with them.

HOW DO YOU MAKE MARKET CONTACTS?

Vendor contacts. Vendor contact with retailers may begin through catalogs and price lists. These documents are made available to all potential retail customers.

Another source of vendor contact is the sales representative who calls on the retailer. In such lines as groceries and drugs, item turnover is very fast. Salespersons may call on the retailer almost weekly in such cases.

If you buy men's suits, the representative will only call on a seasonal basis.

The central market. A *central market* is a place where a large number of suppliers concentrate. It may be a large, single building. An example of this is the Merchandise Mart in Chicago. Usually only large retailers and fashion goods retailers buy in central markets.

New York City is still the primary central market for many types of merchandise especially women's fashion goods. Chicago and High Point, N.C., are well known for furniture.

Not all central markets are permanent. For example, the fine jewelry central market is held in New York periodically (January and July). Such central market events are called "trade shows."

Resident buying offices. Resident buying offices are becoming more important. Persons here are experts in market information. They remain in constant contact with central market suppliers and know what's new; what's "hot," when prices are changing, and they have market "clout" because they represent many buyers.

The most common types of resident buying offices are shown in Figure 12–6.

The key role of resident buying offices is to provide advice and information when you are in the market and when you cannot be present. The offices range from one-person operations to large firms which may provide space, secretarial help, and in fact become the buyer's "home away from home."

GETTING THE BEST PRICE FROM YOUR VENDORS

Group buying. *Group* (or cooperative) *buying* is the joint purchasing of goods by a number of noncompeting stores. Buy combining their orders into one large order, the stores hope to get lower prices. These group ar-

FIGURE 12-6
Four primary types of resident offices

Title or type	Controlled by	Examples
Cooperatively owned— associated type	Stores that own it Stores it serves Directors are usually executives of member firms	Associated Merchandise Corp. Specialty Store Association Frederick Atkins, Inc.
Divisional resident office— syndicated type	A division of a corporation that owns a chain of department stores	Allied Purchasing Corp. Associated Dry Goods Corp. Gimbel's, Macy's, May Co. buying offices
Specialty—independent buying office	Completely independent relationship, sets own policies, handles both hard- and soft-line goods	Arkwright Independent Retailers Syndicate Felix Lilienthal and Co. Mutual Buying Syndicate
Company-owned buying office	Controlled by its management (buying primarily women's, men's infants', children's wear)	Jack Braustein, Inc. S. Irene Johns, Inc. William Van Buren, Inc.

Source: Winston Borgen, *Learning Experiences in Retailing* (Pacific Palisades, Calif.: Goodyear Publishing Co., 1976), p. 156.

rangements can benefit in other ways too. The noncompeting buyers can share knowledge on markets, fashion trends, and so forth.

Group buying can be handled through resident buying offices. Some buyers have a hard time entering into group buying. They give up some of their individuality, and that hurts. Mass merchandisers can sometimes buy from manufacturers' stocks which have already been produced and thus get a good price. Fashion merchants find cooperative buying difficult because they feel their customers are unique.

Central buying. Central buying is most often practiced by chains. As branch store organizations grow in size, central buying is also logical for them. *Central buying* simply means that the buying of specific goods for all units of the firm is handled by one person. This person's full-time job is buying a merchandise category from vendors for all stores.

In firms where central buying occurs, most of the authority for buying lies outside any one retail outlet. In some firms, store managers are given a little authority to purchase locally produced items. For example, in a food store, locally grown produce might be bought by the local store instead of by the central buyer.

Central buyers hope, because of large quantity orders, to get favorable prices. Technology is important in central buying. The buyer must have adequate and rapid information from individual stores. Such information is necessary to make buying decisions.

Buying committees. *Committee buying* is a version of central buying. You want to achieve the savings of central buying but have more than one person share the responsibility. This type of buying is common in firms selling staples. Hardware stores are an example.

Consignment. In *consignment,* suppliers guarantee the sale of merchandise and will take it back from you if it does not sell. You have no risk in this kind of deal. If you have overspent your budget or if you are unsure about the item, consignment can be attractive. But, would vendors offer consignment if the goods could be sold any other way? It's a good question.

Leased departments. If you do not have the skills to operate a specialized department, you may choose to lease it. Typical *leased departments* are camera, beauty salon, restaurant, and optical. If you lease to an expert you can give your customers the specialized products or services without fear of failure which inexperience might cause.

Leased departments are common in mass-merchandise stores. History has shown that after the mass merchandiser "learns" how to run the department, however, it is taken over as a normal department.

NEGOTIATIONS

The good relationships that you establish with your vendors may be the most important asset you have in your business. It may seem trite, but you must treat a vendor as you would like to be treated. Never be too busy to see the representative of the supplier. You may not be interested in actually buying at the time, but remember, the salesperson expects courtesy from you. Every person has that right.

If you have strong, friendly relationships with your suppliers, negotiations can go smoothly. "Friendly" does not imply a lack of professionalism. Only experience in dealing with vendors will give you comfort in dealing at that level.

Be prepared to "give" on something during a negotiation. Regardless of what you are trying to "get," you should have something you will give up. In that way, you can then ask your supplier, "What are you willing to give up?" Remember, you are trying to get the best "deal" and the vendors are trying to hold the line to protect their profits.

Retailers normally attempt to negotiate on the following elements:

1. Cost price of the items.
2. Discounts and datings.
3. Transportation charges.

Cost (list) price

Certain laws affect the amount of "dealing" you can do to get a "good" price from a vendor. Bargaining does not begin, though, until you are sure that the items are truly what are needed for your store.

But some vendors will not negotiate. You will learn this. You can't "experience" negotiation in cost (or list) price from a text. Believe us—experience is the best teacher. Also, never forget that market memories are long. If you take advantage of a vendor, the word gets around. Always be professional.

Let's assume that the gross wholesale list price has been established with no further bargaining. Still other elements for negotiation exist as noted above. The purpose of the next discussion is to help you understand the various elements. If you don't understand them, you can't strike a bargain.

Discounts

You may be offered identical list prices by various vendors, but different discounts and different provisions as to who will be responsible for paying transportation costs. An understanding of the purchase terms or terms of sale is necessary if you are to negotiate the best price.

Trade. A trade discount is a reduction of the seller's list price and is granted to a retailer who performs functions which are normally the responsibility of the seller.

Illustration. A trade discount may be offered as a single percentage off list price or as a series of percentages in determining the net or real price to be paid by the retailer. Let's assume a list price on a sport shirt of $14.95, with a trade discount of 40 percent. The retailer will thus pay $8.97 for the shirt ($14.95 − $5.98); the $5.98 ($14.95 × 0.40) is the trade discount. The same buyer might be offered an identical sport shirt from another manufacturer at a list price of $14.95 less 30 percent, 10 percent, and 5 percent. The net price in this case would be computed as follows:

$$
\begin{array}{rll}
\text{List price} &= \$14.95 & \\
&- \underline{4.48} & (\$14.95 \times 0.30) \\
&= 10.47 & \\
&= \underline{1.05} & (\$10.47 \times 0.10) \\
&= 9.42 & \\
&\times \underline{0.47} & (\ \$9.42 \times 0.05) \\
\text{Net price} &= \$\ 8.95 &
\end{array}
$$

Quantity.   A quantity discount is a reduction in cost based on the size of the order.

Seasonal.   A seasonal discount is a special discount which is given by vendors to retailers who place orders for seasonal merchandise in advance of the normal buying period.

Promotional allowance.   Vendors offer discounts to retailers to compensate them for money spent in advertising particular items or for preferred window and interior display space for the vendor's products.

Cash.   A premium is often granted by the vendor for cash payment prior to the time that the entire bill must be paid. The three components of the cash discount are: (1) a percentage discount; (2) a period in which the discount may be taken; and (3) the net credit period, which indicates when the full amount of the invoice is due.

Illustration.   Assume that in the above example of a trade discount the cash discount is stated (in addition to the trade discount) as 2/10,n/30. This means that the retailer must pay the invoice within ten days to take advantage of the discount of 2 percent. The full amount is due in 30 days.

Returning to the $8.95 net bill for the sport shirt, assume that the invoice is dated May 22. The retailer has ten days to take the discount. Full payment is due June 1 (nine days in May and one in June). If the invoice is paid within this time, the retailer will remit $8.77 instead of $8.95 ($8.95 × 0.02 = $0.18). If the retailer does not discount the invoice, then the bill must be paid in full by June 21.

Cash datings

The agreement between the vendor and the retailer as to the time the discount date will begin is known as dating. Technically, if the terms call for immediate payment, the process is known as cash dating and includes c.o.d. (cash on delivery) or c.w.o. (cash with order). Cash datings do not involve discounts and consequently do not present any problem here. This statement should not be interpreted as meaning that cash datings do not pose problems of any kind, however. Two reasons may cause a negotiation to include cash terms. First, the seller may have a cash flow problem and must insist on cash on delivery (or even with the order) in order to meet the bills incurred in the processing or distribution of the goods. Second, the retail buyer's credit rating may be such that the only way a seller will deal with the firm is on a cash basis. In periods of "tight" money, retailers who must pay cash for orders may be in a very bad cash flow position. C.o.d. or c.w.o. terms are dangerous and when a retailer is faced with them, serious examination of all the elements of the business should be undertaken. It may be a symptom of much more serious problems in the future.

Future datings

The focus of this section is "future datings," which include end of month, date of invoice, receipt of goods, extra dating, and anticipation.

End of month (EOM).   If an invoice carries EOM dating, the cash and net discount periods begin on the first day of the following month rather than on the invoice date. To allow for goods shipped late in the month, an invoice dated after the 25th of the month may be considered as having been dated on the 1st of the following month. Thus, on a 2/10,n/30, EOM billing dated May 26 the ten-day discount period begins on July 1, not June 1. As a result, dating is further extended.

Illustration.   Let's assume that the terms in the above illustration now read "2/10, n/30, EOM." If the $8.95 invoice were dated May 22, the retailer would have until June 10 to pay the invoice and take the 2 percent discount (that is, pay $8.77). If, on the other hand, the invoice were dated May 26 (with the same EOM terms), then the retailer would have until July 10 to take the 2 percent discount.

Date of invoice (DOI).   Date of invoice, or ordinary dating, is self-explanatory. Prepayments begin with the invoice date, and both the cash discount and the net amount are due within the specified number of days from the invoice date. The DOI method is not particularly favorable to the retailer. If the vendor is slow in shipping the merchandise, payment may actually be due before the merchandise arrives.

Receipt of goods (ROG).   Certain vendors are more distant from their customers than are their competitors. Rather than be at a competitive disadvantage with ordinary datings, they may offer receipt of goods (ROG) datings. These indicate that the time allowed for discounts and for payment of the net amount of the invoice begins with the date that the goods are received at the buyer's place of business.

Extra.   Extra datings allow the retailer extra time to take the cash discount. An example might be 2/10-60 extra, n/90, which means that the buyer has 70 days to take the cash discount and that the net amount is due in 90 days.

Illustration.   Returning to our example, if the invoice were dated May 22 with ordinary dating, the invoice would be due (assuming 2/10, n/30) on

June 1. However, with 2/10-60 extra, n/90, the retailer could take the 2 percent cash discount through August 1 (10-day discount period through June 1, 29 additional days in June, and 31 days in July).

Anticipation. Anticipation is a discount offered in addition to the cash discount if an invoice is paid prior to the expiration of the cash discount period. For many years anticipation was at the rate of 6 percent per annum. Anticipation is most common with extra datings to those retailers who are able to pay the invoice in advance of the expiration of the discount period.

Illustration. In the prior example of extra datings, assume that the retailer pays the invoice on June 1, or 60 days prior to the expiration of the cash discount period. The 2 percent discount on the $8.95 will bring the cost to $8.77. The anticipation at 6 percent will allow the retailer to deduct the following additional discount (or anticipation):

$$\$8.77 \times \frac{6}{100} \times \frac{60}{360} = \$0.08, \text{ or a net bill of } \$8.69$$

This may seem like a small amount. However, if we are ordering 1,000 shirts, then $0.08 per shirt would mean an additional discount of $80 off the total price.

Transportation charges. Who pays the shipping costs? The most favorable terms for the retailer are f.o.b. destination. In this arrangement, the seller pays the freight to the destination. A more common shipping term is f.o.b. origin, in which the vendor delivers the merchandise to the carrier, and the retailer pays the freight charges.

Small retailers typically do not have the power to bargain with a vendor over the nature of the discount or the transportation schedule. On the other hand, large retailers may be able to obtain price concessions from the supplier by bargaining on discounts even though the list price of the merchandise does not change.

SUMMARY

Your success in retailing depends largely on how well you buy goods for your firm. Buying is more or less specialized. It depends on the size of the firm.

Regardless of the size of the firm or the items sold, certain functions must be carried out. Over a period of time, organizing for such operations changes. You must keep up with the changes which occur and choose the best for your own store.

The functions of a buyer are deciding: (1) what to buy, (2) when to buy, (3) how much to buy, (4) what to charge, and (5) where to buy and (6) how to get the best cost possible from the vendor. The last function was the major concern of this chapter.

Wholesalers and manufacturers are major merchandise resources. You can be contacted by the vendors at your own place of business or you may contact them in the central market or through a resident buying office.

Many factors need to be considered in trying to get the best cost from vendors. You must decide on the best method of buying; and the best way to negotiate cost, discounts, datings, and shipping costs.

NOTES

1. Ralph D. Shipp, Jr., *Retail Merchandising: Principles and Applications* (Boston: Houghton Mifflin Company, 1976), pp. 12–14.

2. Delbert J. Duncan, Charles F. Phillips, and Stanley C. Hollander, *Modern Retailing Management: Basic Concepts and Practices,* (Homewood, Ill.: Richard D. Irwin, 1972), p. 254. © 1972 by Richard D. Irwin, Inc. Also see the Appendix to this chapter, "Your Wholesalers' Services," SBA's *Small Marketers Aids No. 140* for an excellent review of the range of services available.

DISCUSSION QUESTIONS

1. What are the two "key" functions in a retail store which probably will be "organized" first? Show a chart of this simplest of organizations.

2. Describe the "five-functional" organizational plan by using an organization chart.

3. Explain what is meant by "unity of command" and relate that concept to the five-functional plan.

4. Discuss the advantages and disadvantages of separation of buying and selling. Why has the trend developed in retailing?

5. Draw an organization chart which separates buying and selling.

6. Explain the differences between a "chain store" and a "branch store" (or single-store) organization.

7. What does the vice president—marketing do? Where do you typically find this executive?

8. Explain tandem management. Why has it developed? Where?

9. Discuss the role and responsibilities of the buyer.

10. Discuss how you can make market contacts.

11. What is a resident buying office; what are its functions; what are the various types?

12. Describe the different methods of buying.

13. What are the elements which buyers normally attempt to negotiate?

14. Explain the types of discounts which may be available.

15. Explain the types of datings which may be available.

16. What are the most favorable transportation terms for the retailer? Explain.

PROBLEMS

1. A manufacturer of mattresses in Connecticut offers terms of 2/30, n/60. A furniture store places an order for six mattresses at $38 each and receives an invoice dated August 7. The invoice is paid October 6. Failure to obtain the discount is equivalent to paying what annual rate of interest? (Use 360 days as a year.)

2. Willmette Mills, Inc., a textile manufacturing firm in New England, sells on terms of 3/10, 2/70, n/90, ROG, no anticipation allowed. A dry goods store in Denver, Colorado, received an invoice dated September 8 for ten dozen, 81-inch × 108-inch plain hem sheets at $49.08 per dozen. The merchandise arrived on September 18, and the invoice was paid

on September 28. What was the net cost per sheet to the store?

3. A Wisconsin manufacturer of kitchen utensils quotes terms of 2/10, n/30. The company grants chain store trade discounts of 25, 20, and 10 percent. The list price of a five-quart stainless steel mixing bowl is $48 per dozen. A chain of general stores receives an invoice dated November 19 for five dozen of these bowls. The invoice is paid November 20. What is

(a) the net cost to the chain per bowl? (b) the amount of the cash discount the chain receives?

4. A manufacturer of men's shirts, pajamas, and sportswear offers terms of 3/10 EOM or 2/10—60 extra. Stores may choose either set of terms. Anticipation is allowed at the rate of 6 percent with either set of terms. An invoice for a billed amount of $482.29 is dated October 26 and is to be paid on November 5. Which set of terms should be chosen? Show why.

PROJECTS

1. To clarify the relationships between the buyer and the supplier, the text approaches the subject from the retail point of view. It may be valuable to approach the subject from the other point of view. Make contacts with local suppliers (wholesalers, agents, or local manufacturers who sell to retailers), and see what they attempt to do to strengthen their relationships with their customers. What problems do they incur in these relationships? What efforts do they make to "improve" the relationships?

2. Select a product line in which you are particularly interested. Spot merchants in your area who handle this line. Set up interviews after you have devised a questionnaire which is to determine how important the merchants believe relationships with suppliers are and administer the questionnaires to the managers of the stores. Attempt to find out how these managers implement their "philosophy" or relationships with vendors. If you can get measurements of the "success" of the various stores, see whether you can attribute some of that success to the "programs" for vendor relationships which you discover. This will be a difficult project, but attempting to carry it out will be a good experience, regardless of the outcome.

3. In interviews with retailers with whom you can establish good rapport, attempt to find out: (1) what special problems have been encountered with vendors, (2) what kinds of special "concessions" are offered to the retailers (give your reactions to these concessions; (3) whether any particular plans have been effective in improving relations; and (4) why vendors are dropped.

4. Arrange a visit with a local retailer. In discussions with that person, attempt to draw an organization chart of the firm. If it is multiunit, make sure you show all the interrelationships. If the firm is not one in which all functions are divided among executives, show where they are performed in the organization.

5. Do a field investigation of the similarities and differences among retail companies of differing types by kind of business, size, and number of units. See how the actual structures compare with what is "typical," and see how and why each type of company differs from the others.

Minicase 12-1   Sally Jones, a salesperson in linen and domestics, is told by the department buyer to push a certain towel combination, number 3440, since it is a high-margin item. A few days later the floor manager tells her she is spending too much time around the towels and directs her to circulate around the entire department. Later the same day, Sally is reprimanded by the personnel manager for violating the store's dress code by wearing slacks. (Sally had been told by the department's buyer that dress slacks were acceptable dress.) Sally becomes frustrated since she apparently can't do anything right and decides to quit.

What does this case say about the store's organizational structure?

Minicase 12–2   Allen Noble and John McPherson graduated from State University in May 1976 with degrees in marketing and accounting, respectively. They have been friends for years. Both are from Billings, and they attended the same high school. Billings is an industrial town of about 50,000 with a small junior college. While attending the university, Allen and John often ate lunch at a natural foods store called Sunflower Seeds. They returned home after graduation and decided to open their own health food store, organized as a partnership. Capital would be supplied by an inheritance received by Allen upon the death of his favorite uncle. They had scouted around and located what they considered an "ideal" site and had already lined up their suppliers. Their store, *Kelp Korner,* would be open from 11:00 A. M. to 2:00 P. M. and serve lunch only.

Which duties do you think each of the two should perform? Speculate on the outcome of this venture. Be sure to support your position.

APPENDIX   Your Wholesalers' Services*

If you haven't checked the management services which your wholesalers offer, you should. Because their business depends on you and the other retailers to whom they sell, they are natural sources of assistance.

Depending on the types of assistance he offers, your wholesaler, or wholesalers, may be able to help you "butter your bread." Some wholesalers offer services on sales promotion, buying and new developments in products. Others try to "think retail" and also provide services that help to increase profits as well as sales. They also offer assistance with financing and accounting, to mention two other examples.

The types of services and the extent to which they are available varies with wholesalers and lines of merchandise. Your wholesaler-distributor may or may not provide all of the services discussed in this *Aid* but reading about them should help you when you investigate his offerings.

PROMOTION

Wholesalers often offer help in promoting the products they sell to retailers. Some of these services are free, others carry a price tag. However, as a rule, the price tag is

---

* Richard M. Hill, *Your Wholesalers' Services,* Small Business Administration, Small Marketers Aids No. 140 (Washington, D.C.: U.S. Government Printing Office, 1977).

not great because the wholesaler spreads the cost of his sales-building program over a number of retailers.

Featured items. One of the most effective forms of promotional assistance is preselected merchandise which you can feature cooperatively with other independent retailers. By pooling customer orders for such items, your wholesaler can often secure price concessions or other favorable terms from manufacturers or processors. Generally, the wholesaler passes these savings on to his customers to help them counter the price appeals offered by large retailers who buy directly from the manufacturer in large quantities and thereby get price concessions. In other cases, a wholesaler-distributor will sell these preselected items at cost in an effort to have you concentrate a major part of your buying with him.

Stock control. In some lines of goods, the wholesaler provides help with stock control. He sets up a system, for example, whereby his salesman, with a minimum of attention from you, can keep your stock at the level you need for supplying your customers.

One drug wholesaler uses pressure-sensitive labels on his products and a computer to help his retailers with stock control. When the retail druggist sells an item, he peels off the label and pastes it on a card. When he returns the cards, the wholesaler runs them through a computer for automatic maintenance of the retailer's inventory. This practice helps the retailer to avoid tying up money in merchandise that doesn't move.

Point-of-sale promotional aids. Some wholesalers are major sources of display material which is designed to stimulate "impulse buying" for both nationally advertised and private brands. Because much of this material is furnished by manufacturers, the wholesaler keeps retailers informed about what is available and tells retailers how the aids can be used most effectively. In some instances, the wholesaler helps his retailers in building effective window, counter, and bin displays. In other cases, he may send an employee to work on the retail sales floor during special promotions.

In some lines of business, wholesalers offer another type of promotional aid—showrooms. For example, they allow their dealers to bring retail customers to their showrooms to inspect models which the dealers do not carry as regular stock.

Co-operative advertising. Advertising on a co-operative basis with a wholesaler-distributor can be a reasonably economical way for featuring your merchandise and building customer loyalty. For this type of advertising, many manufacturers give the wholesaler an advertising allowance on his purchases. This practice reduces costs which are shared on a percentage basis. Depending on the type and number of potential customers, the media most often used by wholesalers are radio and television, newspapers, and handbills.

MARKET INFORMATION

Wholesalers often supply market information which can help a small retailer in attracting customers and satisfying their wants. In his numerous contacts with local businesses and distant suppliers, the wholesaler accumulates information about consumer demand, prices, supply conditions, and new developments in the trade. He generally relays the information to his retailers through bulletins, newsletters, order books, invoices, and salesmen.

As one small retailer sees these services on marketing: "The wholesaler is in a good position to tell whether things are slowing down or changing, and he does keep us aware of these changes."

Consumer demand. The wholesaler's position between national and regional suppliers and local buyers enables him to "feel the pulse" of consumer demand. He can recognize, for example, events at the national and regional levels which are likely to bear on the amount of local consumer spending. Through his numerous contracts with local retailers, the wholesaler learns which items have attracted the attention of consumers and which items have not. By reviewing his orders, he can sense when demand for a product is changing and advise his customers to adjust their buying and inventories accordingly.

Price. Often you can get comprehensive and up-to-date price information from your wholesaler. Most wholesalers can collect competitive price information from their customers much more economically than the individual retailer could collect it for himself.

Suggested retail prices are also supplied by many wholesalers, particularly those offering co-operative advertising plans or those who sell their own private brands.

Supply conditions. You can usually depend on your wholesaler to keep you informed about primary market conditions which would affect the supply of a particular product. Information concerning the possible scarcity or superabundance of consumer goods or expected major shifts in its price are of particular importance when they reach you in time to be reflected in your buying plans.

New developments. One of the easiest ways to keep abreast of new methods, new products, and new ideas, is through the bulletins, newsletters, and other publications circulated by many wholesalers. These media often provide condensed versions of articles appearing in the trade or business press, lists of new products being introduced by manufacturers, pictures or descriptions of new equipment, and suggestions for improving merchandise displays and selling performance.

FINANCIAL AID

Many wholesalers provide a type of financial aid that retailers take for granted, if they think about it at all. By making prompt and frequent deliveries, wholesalers enable their customers to keep inventory investment small in relation to sales. This indirect financial aid reduces the amount of operating cash needed by the retailer.

Another type of indirect financial help is "open book" or trade credit. When the wholesaler-distributor extends it, he bills you for merchandise purchased and allows a discount for payment within a specified number of days.

In some trades, though, wholesalers extend direct financial assistance through the practice of delayed billing. For example, some wholesalers of lawn and garden supplies deliver seed to retailers in January but do not bill them for it until May. Nor is it unusual for wholesalers handling toys and Christmas decorations to ship merchandise to their retailers in June and July but delay billing until December.

ACCOUNTING SYSTEMS

A number of wholesalers help their retail customers to maintain adequate accounting systems. Several types of accounting assistance are available through wholesalers who offer this service. Some wholesalers have compiled forms and manuals which retailers can use as the basis for goods records.

A few wholesalers have retail accounting departments which perform virtually the entire accounting function for their customers. Retailers who use such a system supply operating information to the wholesalers at periodic intervals.

Other wholesalers have negotiated "umbrella" contracts with private accounting firms. These firms, in turn, do the accounting work for a given group of retailers—often at a smaller fee than the accounting firm could offer an individual retailer.

POLICY AND METHODS

Many wholesalers offer guidance and counsel which retailers can use in setting policies and in improving methods. Some of the areas covered are public relations, housekeeping methods, and administrative procedures, to mention three examples. Such assistance is usually available for the asking through the wholesaler's salesmen. In some instances, meetings are held to discuss such subjects, and retailers are kept abreast of new developments through bulletins and newsletters.

Many wholesaler-distributors belong to a trade association which specializes in their commodity line. These associations often publish monthly magazines as well as brochures aimed at helping the retailer.

Suggestions on setting policy and improving methods can be helpful because many small retailers get involved in the day-to-day tasks of keeping the business moving along. When this happens, they lose sight of the big picture. Often they overlook opportunities to improve their operations. For example, they know the value of good public relations but do nothing about it. In other instances, they may not know how to build a favorable image and their time and money are spent uselessly. Because he is not involved in the routine of a store, the wholesaler can often detect such management weakness of his customers and suggest ways for correcting them.

LOOKING AHEAD

Many wholesalers go beyond day-to-day operating assistance and offer services that are designed to help their customers with long range problems. They offer help on real estate problems, financing, insurance and personnel.

Real estate. Some wholesalers pass on to their retailers tips on stores that are for rent or for sale. These tips are given to their customers when they are considering a branch store. These wholesalers usually maintain up-to-date real estate files by gathering information from their salesman, customers, newspapers, and/or real estate agencies.

Depending on your wholesalers, you may be able to get help in analyzing the suitability of various locations, including an evaluation of the market potential. Some wholesalers keep a finger on the direction and character of urban development and offer advice about desirable future locations. They help the retailer establish a priority rating for each location. New locations, particularly in shopping centers and other large-scale trading area developments, may involve complicated leasing arrangements.

Finance. In some cases, wholesaler-distributors help their retailers with long-range financing. For example, a wholesaler may lend his own funds to enable a retailer to modernize an old building, acquire a new site, and/or erect a new building. The need for this type of financial assistance is especially evident in the retail food business. Here the trend toward costly supermarkets coupled with the inability of banks to help any but the best credit risks has greatly increased the importance of wholesalers as sources of direct financial aid.

Indirectly, a wholesaler often can help you with financial needs by supporting you at the bank or insurance company. The loan is made on his recommendation, and he generally guarantees part, or all, of its repayment.

In long-range financing, the retailer who deals with a relatively few wholesalers is in a better position than the retailer who buys small amounts from many wholesalers. In investing his funds in others, the wholesaler naturally looks for retailers who have proved themselves and whose business offers him growth possibilities.

Insurance counsel. A number of wholesalers try to help their customers secure adequate protection against risks from theft, fire, smoke, and water damage. This assistance may involve: (1) keeping you alerted to your insurance needs, (2) making sure that your insurance is kept in force, and (3) helping to get your claim settled as quickly as possible if a loss does occur.

Personnel. Your wholesaler-distributor through his salesmen can help you obtain qualified store personnel in informal ways. For example, he might tell you of an outstanding salesperson who wants to change jobs. Some of the larger wholesalers have even set up auxiliary personnel departments. Such departments maintain files on persons seeking retail employment and refer prospective employees to retailers on request.

WHICH SERVICES CAN YOU USE?

Not all of the services available from your wholesaler are equally important to you. Some may be indispensable. Others you can handle more effectively yourself. Some services carry charges, and you must decide whether they are worth their cost.

The first step in determining which services you can use in finding out what your wholesaler offers. Get all the details you can about each service that is available to you. Find out what advantages a service has for you. Find out what obligations it carries.

First things first. At this point, a few words of caution are in order. As far as you are concerned, the main duty of a wholesaler is to supply you with items which you can sell at a profit. Success in retailing starts with shelves and displays full of goods which customers need and want. Thus, in accepting management assistance from a wholesaler, you must be sure first that he is a reliable source of merchandise.

A small retailer, however, should know his customers better than the wholesaler. In mutual assistance, such as special promotion, the retailer should prevail. Resist the temptation to overbuy on attractive offers. For example, is there enough profit in using a missionary salesman to train salespeople and sell customers when you have to buy in gross lots rather than the usual case lot? It is your loss when the item doesn't move as fast as was thought. Try to schedule special promotions that are offered by the wholesaler to suit your plans for promoting sales and profits. Use cooperative advertising when it is to your advantage, but don't be a slave to it.

In fact, don't be a slave to outside assistance whether it is from a wholesaler or another source. Regardless of a wholesaler's good intentions—to help you sell more at a profit to both you and himself—never forget that one of the reasons you went into business was to be your own boss.

Compare services. When you have the details on the wholesaler's services, compare them with what you already have. If he can provide, for example, an accounting service, how does it compare with yours? Is his easier to use? Harder to use? Cheaper than yours? Higher?

You should also check the possibility of improving your method if it is not as good as what your wholesaler can provide. What is involved in the upgrading and what will it cost?

Follow through.   When you sign on to use services from your wholesaler, follow through with your end of the agreement. Provide him with the information and direction he needs to render the services you request from him. For example, when you use a wholesaler's accounting service, you need to send him daily expense and revenue data on a given schedule and format so his accounting staff can include your data in its work load.

Matters that can cause misunderstandings should be pinned down. For example, the order form should spell out prices, terms, dates of shipment, and liability for shipping costs. When an agreement is written, often mistakes can be corrected without damaging your relationship with the wholesaler. But a verbal agreement may be another story.

If you want him to help in selecting and training personnel, you will need to give the wholesaler job descriptions. His staff will use them to identify the types of employees you want and to determine whether applicants have the necessary skills.

13

HOW DO YOU DETERMINE PRICES?

This chapter is to help you understand what prices you should charge by explaining:

- The *existing things* which affect the prices you charge.
- The *store policies* which affect the prices you can charge.
- The kinds of price changes you may make after you make your original pricing decisions.
- A simple way to handle the arithmetic of pricing.
- The meaning of the following terms:

Market structure	Price lining
The "five rights"	Single-price policy
"Level of prices" policy	Leader pricing
One-price policy	Loss leaders
Variable-price policy	Additional markup
Private (distributor) brands	Markdowns
Manufacturer's (national) brands	Original retail price
Generic merchandise	Sales retail
Psychological pricing	Initial markup
Trade-in allowance	Maintained markup

In this "nuts and bolts" part of the book, this chapter is one of the *most* practical. Remember, we are looking into "the things you must *know* and *do* to make a profit."

You have just finished studying the role of the buyer/manager. "What price should I charge?" is one of the key questions a buyer has to answer. You have also now worked through the merchandise and expense plans. Setting the right price is as much a part of planning as budgeting is. Pricing clearly is the most visible result of planning. At least that's true from the customer's point of view. The consumer never "sees" a budget—but prices are seen. The price is one key thing which causes a customer to buy.

WHAT FACTORS AFFECT THE PRICES YOU CHARGE

When you place a specific price on a piece of merchandise you are doing one of your five "rights" activities. As a merchant (buyer) you are merchandising. And merchandising is having the *right* merchandise, at the *right* place, *right* time, in the *right* quantities, and at the *right price!*

You may have performed all of your other merchandising functions successfully. *But,* if your price is wrong (instead of right), it's like fumbling the ball on the one-foot line. It's almost a touchdown. But no score is on the board. If the price is not right, no sale is made. The cash register does not ring (or hum, or click!).

You must first consider in attempting to set the *right* price all those things that could affect your decision. These factors "exist." You did not set up the conditions. They may be results of some things you (or other management persons) did, but at the time you are pricing, they *do* exist.

Type of goods

If you offer goods which the customer views as convenience goods (that is, they are purchased almost anywhere, like cigarettes), prices are usually about the same in all stores. In such goods, customers don't feel it's worth their time to shop around for a better price (or quality). So the retailer has some latitude in pricing. Items for which customers are willing to shop in order to save money are called shopping goods. One of the bases for shopping may be price. Quality differences may also be evaluated. So, you have more leeway in pricing shopping goods.

Type of store (store image)

You must be familiar with your customers' viewpoints if you want to price profitably. Customers may come to your store because of its quality image or because of its low-priced reputation. In the quality stores, customers expect to pay more, but also expect more service and a better environment (atmosphere). Of course, these "extras" cost money and the price must cover these extras. We don't want to mislead you. Other factors affect patronage (convenience, location). You must know this.

Profit wanted

Also, be sure your price will be high enough to cover *all* costs of doing business. This includes the original cost of the goods plus the expenses of doing business. Of course the price must also provide the profit you want to earn. (This point will be discussed further in the section on "The Arithmetic of Retail Pricing.")

Customer demand

If you are selling an item where the demand exceeds the supply, a higher price can be charged. Just think of pricing actions when items are in short supply and demand is high. Objects of art fit this factor neatly. A fine painting by a well-known, deceased artist can be priced at whatever level the customer will pay. There is great pricing flexibility in this type of item. At a different level, the same has been true of gasoline in recent years.

Market structure

The degree of competition in your market will greatly affect your pricing decisions. If you have little competition, then your pricing decisions are easier than if you have a lot of competition. For example, if you have an "exclusive" on a brand in your market area, you can probably price with greater freedom.

Suppliers' policies

Suppliers will often suggest prices to you. If you need the supplier more than the supplier needs you, it's easy to guess what will happen. The supplier will have a lot of input in your pricing decisions. But many retailers are gaining more control over their pricing decisions. In some lines, strong manufacturers have effective suggested retail (or resale) price programs. These lines are usually sold to consumers and the manufacturer is able to "dictate" to retailers. In such cases, you give up pricing flexibility in order to carry the brand.

Economic conditions

Also, you must be superconscious of the economy. Probably in periods of inflation, increases in prices are *expected* by consumers. (This is not to imply that higher prices are welcomed!) You must be aware of any voluntary or required governmental price controls which can limit your price decisions.

In times when we are in a recession, prices often go down. You must be sensitive to such economic changes since they cause price adjustments.

An important element here is *competition* again. Be aware of what competitors are doing. Also the type of good and the store image can affect your decisions. Changing economic conditions make pricing more and more complex.

Governmental regulation

Retailers have been restricted from certain kinds of pricing actions since 1890. That was the year the Sherman Act was passed. (See Chapter 7 for a full discussion of legal impacts. This discussion just includes some of the things a merchant must think about which can affect pricing decisions.)

The laws most likely to affect pricing include:

Unfair Trade Practices Acts. If you are operating in one of the some 20-odd states with such laws you will be required to charge a certain minimum percentage above your cost.

Robinson-Patman Act You can legally receive favorable prices from vendors if the vendor can justify that "better" price on savings in cost. As a retailer, you can then price within your policies. You may simply have a better cost and can perhaps "undercut" your competition.

The Sherman Act. Under this act, price-fixing (different parties agreeing to certain prices) was declared illegal. During the many years since 1890 price-fixing has been interpreted differently. For many years (from the 1930s) fair trade (or Resale Price Maintenance) affected retailers' pricing decisions. In 1976, legal fair trade nationally ceased to exist. Many economic and social reasons lay behind the checkered history of fair trade. Here it is enough to say that retailers are now free to price without vendors "fixing" a price at which you must sell a branded item. Really, at this time, we're right back were we were under the original Sherman Act. Price-fixing is not legal in interstate commerce (between states).

WHAT STORE POLICIES AFFECT PRICES YOU CAN CHARGE?

In the section just completed, we considered the factors which you can't do anything about. These factors clearly affect what you can charge your customers.

In this section, we want to look at store *policies* (guidelines for actions) which management supports. These policies certainly exist, but they can be adjusted. They are *internal* to your store and your pricing actions, while the factors we just looked at are *external* to your pricing decisions.

"Level of prices" policy

Any decision you make when you are deciding on prices to charge are affected by your policy on "price level" desired. Your three choices are: (1) at the market, (2) below the market, or (3) above the market.

At the market. Most retailers are "competitive pricers." The prices they offer are roughly the same as their competitors. With a policy like this, you would probably try to make your store different in ways other than price. We call this "nonprice competititon." Superstores, for example, try to be competitive in prices with other superstores. But they may try to make themselves different by carrying more brands, having a "better" deli; offering different services; and the like.

A department store is typically an "at the market" pricer. Management attempts to meet discount store prices on identical merchandise. An extra service may be offered by the department store that the discount store does not offer—for example, alterations on a dress or delivery of a TV. If alterations or delivery are offered, then the department store will charge for these extra services.

Below the market. Discount houses, warehouse grocery firms, or other low margin, high turnover retailers, typically price below the market. Competition in these operations is almost entirely on a price basis.

Above the market. Some merchants price above the market without great concern for how customers are going to react. Some of the reasons stores are able to follow this policy are: they carry unique (exclusive) merchandise; they cater to customers who are not price-conscious and want highest quality goods; they offer convenience of location and time (convenience stores); they provide many unusual services; they take greater risks on credit terms; or they have an overall prestige image which customers are willing to pay for.

One-price versus variable-price policy

The majority of retail firms in the United States offer goods at one, take-it-or-leave-it price. There is no bargaining with customers. If you travel out of the United States in countries like Mexico and Italy, varying prices with "haggling" are expected. In this country in some types of stores in certain lines of goods (big ticket durable goods such as appliances and furniture and automobiles) one-price policies are *not* typical. If some retailers in your area haggle and you don't, your image can be damaged.

You can see that certain advantages exist in a store with a one-price policy. Customers do not expect to bargain so salespersons save time (as do customers); salespeople are not under pressure to reduce prices; and self-service would not work where there is bargaining.

Private brand policy

Major retailers (like Sears, Wards, Penneys, and Safeway) often have their own private brands. Wholesalers also may offer retail customers their private brands. *Private brands* (often called distributor brands) are *owned* by the

BURBANK

"It's Mrs. Hawthorne. She wants to know what sirloin opened at today."

Reprinted by permission The Wall Street Journal

retail or wholesale firm rather than by a manufacturer. The *manufacturer's brand* (or national brand) is *owned* by a manufacturer. A private brand may only be carried by the owner or someone the owner allows to carry it. A national brand may be carried by anyone who buys from the manufacturer of the brand. Bokar is a private brand of coffee owned by A&P. Maxwell House is a national brand owned by General Foods Corp.

If you feature private brands, you may offer them at below-the-market prices. You can do this (and still make a good profit) because you probably paid less for the private brand merchandise than you would have paid for a comparable national brand. Of course, you have more pricing freedom in private brand items.

The question of *generic* merchandise and pricing is important. Generics are "no-brand name" goods. For example, if a supermarket offers generic paper products, an identification might read "paper napkins." Customers may be willing to pay lower prices for lower quality in some types of goods. They rely on the reputation of the store and figure, "If my supermarket has generics for sale, they must be OK for the price."

You may be able to make *even* more profit with lower prices on generic items than on private brand goods. Watch the progress of generic brands, particularly in food stores. They may also become important in drugstores.

Psychological pricing

You can price merchandise too low. A blouse might not have sold at $5, but when marked up to $7 it might sell. The reason for this strange behavior is that for some goods, customers believe that *price* reflects *quality* (or value).

Odd-price endings are believed by many to have psychological value. Odd endings ($10.98 instead of $11.00) seem lower than the even ending price. But we really are not certain here. Some retailers prefer the even endings, wanting the extra markup, even if it is only a few pennies. Many transactions of a few cents *could* be important over time.

Trade-in allowance policy

If you decide to have a trade-in policy, plan your original pricing very carefully. If you carry such lines as tires, batteries, and automobiles your customers expect trade-ins. If they are good bargainers, you will find yourself actually taking a lower price. Trade-in allowances are similar to varying price policies discussed earlier.

Price-line policy

If you practice *price lining* you feature products or services at a limited number of prices. You may have a "good," "better," and "best" price structure. Let's take men's suits. Your "good" price is $125; your "better" price is $175; and your "best" suit is priced at $225. You thus have a price-lining policy. Some retailers use "price zones" instead of rigid price points. For example, suits fall between $125 and $140.

Price lining offers certain advantages. Many customers are confused when they see too many prices. Customers can't make up their minds when they see so many prices. Shopping is easier with fewer prices for customers to consider.

The merchant can offer greater assortment width and support with fewer price points. You can control inventories better with price lining.

The salesperson can learn the stock more easily with price lining. It is also much easier to explain differences between the merchandise when it is carefully planned and priced to show differences. Also, the buyer does not have to shop as many vendors if specific retail prices are sought.

Certain problems do exist in price lining. Some flexibility can be lost as you may feel "hemmed in" by the price line. Also, selection may be a little limited. If wholesale prices rise and fall rapidly, it may be difficult to maintain price lines. This is a reason for zones.

Single-price policy

Small, specialty stores might have single-price policies. You may see a "$5.00 tie store," or a $19.95 budget dress store." Clearly with such a policy, the variety of offerings is limited. Also fewer assortments are possible. The real strength of such a policy is that you can "target" in on a specific customer group. That customer in turn knows what to expect in your store.

Leader pricing policy

Some retailers use *leader pricing* with selected product categories. This policy is one where you decide to get less than a normal markup or margin on an item to increase store traffic. Some call this *loss leader* pricing. The "loss" implies "loss of the normal amount of markup or margin."

When you use leader pricing you are trying to attract customers to your store who will also purchase items carrying normal profit margins. If customers only buy the "leaders," you are in trouble!

Supermarkets and mass merchandisers often use leaders. They use items as leaders which are: (1) well known and widely used; (2) priced low enough to attract a lot of buyers; and (3) not usually bought in large quantities and stored. You may be wise to limit the quantity of leader items which can be bought at any one time by customers.

Grocery items which have proved to be good leaders are shortening, coffee, dishwashing liquid, and toilet tissue.

KINDS OF PRICING ADJUSTMENTS MADE AFTER YOUR ORIGINAL PRICING DECISION

In practice you may raise or lower prices after your pricing decisions have been made.

Additional markups.   In inflationary periods, additional markups may be needed. Such adjustments are made when costs to you are increasing.

Markdowns.   Most retailers take some markdowns. *Markdowns* (reduction in the original selling price of an item) are the most widely used way of moving items which do not sell at the original price. Other things you *might* do instead of taking a markdown are: (1) give additional promotion, better display, or a more visible store position to the item; (2) store the goods until the next selling season; (3) mark the item *up* (discussed in "Psychological Pricing"); or (4) give the goods to charity.

One of the most famous retail department store organizations in the United States is Filene's Basement in Boston. This firm has "made its name" through its widely known "automatic markdown policy." The policy operates as follows.

When an item has been in the store for 12 days it is marked down to 75 percent of list; after 6 more days it is reduced to 50 percent; 6 more days to 25 percent; and then after 30 days it is given to charity. Very little merchandise is given to charity!

Markdowns are also used for promotional reasons. The goods may not be slow moving, but markdowns create more activity. In the next section you will see that smart merchants *plan* certain amounts of markdowns. (In Chapter 11 you saw this.) In that way you protect your profit. It will be clearer shortly.

Avoid excessive markdowns. If your markdowns are too high, find out the reasons. The causes can come from buying, selling, or pricing errors. Once you find the cause, then a plan can be worked out to correct your errors.

THE ARITHMETIC OF RETAIL PRICING

This section presents a simple plan to help you understand the arithmetic of pricing. Every retailer is faced with the issues explained in this section. We admit that the field of retailing has been provided with "crutches" in the form of "profit flashers" and "markup equivalent tables" (see Table 13–1). You need, however, to understand the relationships we stress here. When you finish this section you will be ahead of many practicing retailers.

First let's look at some basic terms and then work the kinds of problems you will face. For those who are "formula oriented" we present those too. But if you look at the entire "plan" as a puzzle, it can be fun to play with the relationships. Remember always that it's all common sense. Don't fight it. If you can add, subtract, multiply, and divide (or have a calculator with you) it is a snap!

Retail price

Price can be looked at as follows:

The $100 original retail price is the first price at which you offer an item (or a group of items). The sales retail of $80 is the final selling price, or the price which the customer paid. Before the item was sold, there were $20 in reductions. These reductions may be markdowns or employee discounts. (In a

TABLE 13-1
Markup table

To use this table find the desired percentage in the left-hand column. Multiply the cost of the article by the corresponding percentage in the "markup percent of cost" column. The result, added to the cost, gives the correct selling price.

Markup percent of selling price	Markup percent of cost	Markup percent of selling price	Markup percent of cost	Markup percent of selling price	Markup percent of cost
4.8	5.0	18.5	22.7	33.3	50.0
5.0	5.3	19.0	23.5	34.0	51.5
6.0	6.4	20.0	25.0	35.0	53.9
7.0	7.5	21.0	26.6	35.5	55.0
8.0	8.7	22.0	28.2	36.0	56.3
9.0	10.0	22.5	29.0	37.0	58.8
10.0	11.1	23.0	29.9	37.5	60.0
10.7	12.0	23.1	30.0	38.0	61.3
11.0	12.4	24.0	31.6	39.0	64.0
11.1	12.5	25.0	33.3	39.5	65.5
12.0	13.6	26.0	35.0	40.0	66.7
12.5	14.3	27.0	37.0	41.0	70.0
13.0	15.0	27.3	37.5	42.0	72.4
14.0	16.3	28.0	39.0	42.8	75.0
15.0	17.7	28.5	40.0	44.4	80.0
16.0	19.1	29.0	40.9	46.1	85.0
16.7	20.0	30.0	42.9	47.5	90.0
17.0	20.5	31.0	45.0	48.7	95.0
17.5	21.2	32.0	47.1	50.0	100.0
18.0	22.0				

Source: *Expenses in Retail Business*, a publication of NCR Corporation, Dayton, Ohio.

classification of merchandise, you can also have shortages or shrinkage. See Chapter 11, "Reduction Planning" to review these concepts.)

Markup

The following diagram shows you the various ways to look at markup:

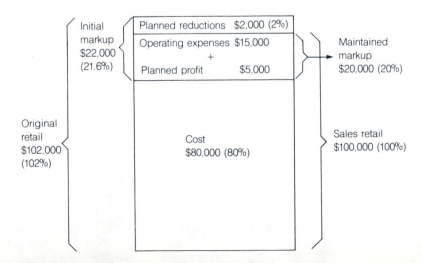

As you can see, *initial markup* is the difference between the cost of the merchandise and the *original retail price.* ($102,000 − $80,000 = $22,000.) If you express initial markup as a percentage, relate it to *original retail price* and you will see it is 21.6 percent ($22,000 / $102,000). You use the idea of initial markup when you are planning your total classification or department. (See Figure 11–1.) We said that you would plan your markup goals. This is what we were referring to.

Maintained markup is the difference between cost and *sales retail.* ($100,000 − $80,000 = $20,000.) In percentage terms, maintained markup is related to sales retail and is $20,000 / $100,000 = 20 percent. As you can see, maintained markup covers operating expenses and provides you with a profit.

Maintained markup and initial markup differ by the $2,000 reduction. For purposes of this discussion, maintained markup can be considered the same as gross margin. (In Figure 19–4 you will note a technical difference. Unless you are an accountant this difference is not important.)

Planning required initial markup

The following diagram is useful in this discussion. You can see that it is really a "separation" of the information in the foregoing diagram. To understand the process of initial markup planning we'll work backward. You have a planned sales figure in your department of $100,000, expenses of $15,000, and a planned profit of 5 percent of sales, or $5,000. The *results* expected from operations with these planned figures is a maintained markup of $20,000, or 20 percent of sales. You can also see that with planned reductions of 2 percent of $2,000, you will need an initial markup of $22,000, or 21.6 percent to maintain the $20,000 planned. This kind of planning forces you to consider everything that affects profits.[1]

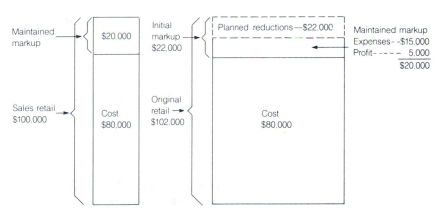

You cannot expect to have a uniform initial markup policy. That kind of policy would suggest that every item brought into a department will carry the same initial markup. Too many factors exist for such a policy to make sense. Look back to the first part of this chapter and you will see why.

Your planned initial markup figure does, however, become a good *check*. You can check your actual performance in markup during an operating period against what you have planned.

Computations   Everyone (students and merchants) needs practice in figuring the relationships among cost, initial markup, and original retail price. Don't *memorize*— you don't have to learn complex formulas (even though we'll follow examples with a formula for those who like them). All you need to remember is that Cost + Initial markup = Original retail price. Here is the plan, or puzzle box, you need to figure it all out:

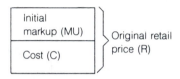

Given—Cost and retail.   A color TV costs the retailer $500. The original price charged is $800. What is the initial markup in dollars and percent computed on both cost and retail bases?

```
┌─────────────┐ ⎫
│ MU = ?      │ ⎬ R = $800
├─────────────┤ │
│ C = $500    │ ⎭
└─────────────┘
```

The difference between R and C is $300 ($800 − $500). Based on cost, the markup would be $300/$500 = 60 percent; based on retail price, the markup is 37.5 percent ($300/$800).

$$\text{Formula: } MU\% \text{ on } C = \frac{\$MU}{\$C}; \ MU\% \text{ on } R = \frac{\$MU}{\$R}$$

The following chart will help you visualize the difference between markup based on retail and cost.

Cost	Markup	Retail selling price
$160	$40	$200
80%	20%	100% (Markup based on retail)
100%	25%	125% (Markup based on cost)

Conversion of markup—Retail to cost.   You will often face the problem of converting a markup on retail to a markup on cost. If you are used to thinking in terms of cost and the vendor quotes in terms of retail, you need to know how to make the switch. As we noted earlier, conversion tables do exist. See Table 13–1 for a typical "crutch."

A supplier quotes you an initial markup of 42 percent on retail. What is the same markup on cost?

```
MU/R = 42%
MU/C = ?
              } R = 100%
C = 58%
```

If the retail markup is 42 percent, then retail is 100 percent and cost must be 58 percent. So, markup as a percentage of cost is 0.42/0.58 = 0.724 or 72.4 percent. In other words, 42 percent markup on retail is the same as 72.4 percent on cost. Clearly, markup on cost will always be larger than markup on retail. The cost base is smaller than the retail base. Markup is a constant.

$$\text{Formula: } MU\% \, / \, C = \frac{MU\% \, / \, R}{100\% \, - \, MU\% \, / \, R}$$

Cost to retail.   A vendor quotes you an initial markup of 60 percent on cost. What is the equivalent markup on retail?

```
MU/C = 60%
MU/R = ?
              } R = 160%
C = 100%
```

If the cost markup is 60 percent, then cost must be 100 percent. And then retail has to be 160 percent. So, markup on a retail base is 0.60/1.60 = 37.5 percent. Or, 60 percent markup on cost is the same as 37.5 percent on retail.

$$\text{Formula: } MU\%/R = \frac{MU\% \, / \, C}{100\% \, + \, MU\% \, / \, C}$$

Other relationships.   To give you a chance to see other types of situations you may face, study the following.

1.   A chair costs a retailer $420. If a markup of 40 percent of retail is desired, what should the retail price be?

```
MU/R = 40%
                    } R = 100% and $?
C = 100 - 40 =
60%; $420
```

If 60 percent = $420, then 100 percent = 420 ÷ 0.60, or $700, the retail price needed to achieve the desired markup of 40 percent on retail.

Formula: Whenever the retail price is to be calculated and the dollar cost and markup percent on retail are known, the problem can be solved with the following:

$$\$Retail = \frac{\$cost}{100\% - Retail\ markup\ \%}$$

2. A dryer retails for $300. The markup is 28 percent of cost. What was the cost of the dryer?

If 128 percent = $300, then 100 percent = $300 ÷ 1.28, or $234.37; the cost which is needed to achieve the desired markup of 28 percent on cost.

Formula: Whenever the cost price is to be calculated and the dollar retail and markup percentage on cost are known, the problem can be solved as follows:

$$\$cost = \frac{\$retail}{100\% + Cost\ markup\ \%}$$

3. A retailer prices a sport jacket so that the markup amounts of $36. This is 45 percent of retail. What are the cost and retail figures?

If 45 percent = $36, then 100 percent = $36 ÷ 0.45, or $80. If retail is $80 and markup is $36, then cost is $80 − $36 = $44.

Formula: Whenever the dollar markup and the retail markup percentage are known, the retail price can be determined as follows:

$$\$retail = \frac{\$\ retail\ markup}{\%\ retail\ markup}$$

SUMMARY

All retail pricing decisions require judgment. A lot of trial and error exists in planning prices. Be conscious of the external factors that affect your judgment. Also be aware of your own store policies which can affect the prices you can charge.

You can easily fall into the trap of applying a uniform markup on all items in your store. You have so many to price, that you can't consider each one separately. Or so you think. That's a mistake. If you are an "at the market" pricer, competition will force you to consider each price very seriously.

A major lesson of this chapter is *not* to consider pricing as routine. Planning your prices is as important as any planning you do.

We are enthusiastic about the value of the Small Business Administration, Small Marketers Aids. Consequently we are including as an appendix to this chapter Aid Number 158, "A Pricing Checklist for Small Retailers." You will find this checklist a fine accompaniment to the material in this chapter. There are some new ideas and you will find many familiar ones as well. We encourage you to use all of the governmental materials available for assistance in making sound management decisions.

NOTE

1. For those who like formulas, you can express this as follows:

$$\text{Initial markup percentage} = \frac{\text{Expenses} + \text{Profit} + \text{Reductions}}{\text{Sales retail} + \text{Reductions}}$$

DISCUSSION QUESTIONS

1. What is merchandising? How does the pricing decision relate to merchandising?
2. What "existing" factors affect the prices you charge as a retailer (i.e., external factors)? Discuss.
3. What store policies affect the prices you can charge? Discuss.
4. Discuss "level of prices" policy. Give examples of each one.
5. Contrast one-price versus variable-price policies. Evaluate the two policies.
6. Compare and contrast: private, manufacturer's, and generic "branding."
7. Explain and evaluate odd-price endings.
8. Illustrate price lining and evaluate the policy.
9. What do you think of "single-price" policy? Explain.
10. Explain the kinds of pricing adjustments which are made after the original price decision is made.

PROBLEMS

1. A retailer who used markup on cost in pricing her goods misplaced her list of retail equivalents. The cost percentages most commonly used in the store were 20 percent, 25 percent, 35 percent, 40 percent, 50 percent, 60 percent, 75 percent, and 100 percent. What retail equivalents should she have calculated for each of the cost percentages?
2. Men's hose may be purchased for $9.50 per dozen and women's hosiery for $13.50 per dozen.
   a. If the hose are marked up 70 percent on cost, and the hosiery are marked up 90 percent on cost, what retail price will be set per pair?
   b. If a markup of 45 percent on retail were applied, what prices would be set per pair?
3. An item carries a markup on retail of 37 percent. What is the equivalent markup percent on cost?
4. A retailer prices a chair so that the markup amounts to $36. This is 42 percent of retail. What are the cost and retail figures?
5. A snowsuit costs a retailer $4.80. If a markup of 45 percent of retail is required, what must the retail price be?
6. A cotton blouse costs a retailer $6.60. If a markup of 30 percent on cost is desired, what will the retail price be?
7. A retailer has been pricing merchandise at 45 percent on cost. What is the equivalent markup percent of retail?

8. A markup of 38 percent retail is equivalent to what markup percent on the cost base?

9. The retail price is $92; the cost markup is 34 percent. What is the cost?

10. A retailer prices a dress so that the markup amounts to $72. This is 50 percent of retail. What are the cost and retail figures?

11. What should the initial markup percent be in a department that has the following planned figures: expenses, $12,000; profit, $3,000; sales, $45,000; markdowns, $700; stock shortages, $300?

12. An item has been marked down to $3.95 from its original price of $5. What is *(a)* the markdown percentage and *(b)* the off-retail percentage?

13. Department A has taken $2,100 in markdowns to date. Net sales to date are $70,000. What is the markdown percentage to date?

14. Sales of $60,000 were planned in a department in which expenses were established at $18,000; employee discounts, $600; and markdowns and shortages, $3,400. If a profit of 4 percent were desired, what initial markup would be planned?

15. An item that was originally priced at $14.00 has been marked down to $11.50. What is *(a)* the markdown percentage? *(b)* the off-retail percentage?

PROJECTS

1. Devise a questionnaire to get consumer reaction to the practice of raising the price of goods already on display. (Grocers frequently do this by putting the higher price tag directly on top of the former price.) Do consumers feel that this practice is fair or unfair? Why? Allow room for individual consumer comment on your questionnaire.

2. Devise a method for determining whether people perceive odd or even prices as being lower. This can be done, for example, by interviewing store managers or consumers or by observing behavior in a store. Visit two types of stores, such as a hardware store and a clothing store; what pricing strategy does each follow? Why?

3. Assume that you are a management trainee for a major supermarket chain. Select a market basket of products which are available in all stores and easily comparable (for example, no private brands), and compare prices (including specials) in a conventional supermarket (that is, your own), a "warehouse-type" outlet, and a convenience store (a 7–11). Keep your record over a period of time, present your data in an organized format, and draw conclusions about the pricing philosophy of the different types of food operations.

4. Health and beauty aids are carried in many different kinds of retail establishments (for example, conventional drug stores, supermarkets, discount drugstores, and department stores), and often each type of establishment promises "lower prices," better "assortments," and so on to establish a differential. Prepare a list of selected items available in each store (by comparable size), and compare and contrast the items among the various types of stores. See what you find to be the "real" strategy of the competing stores in the market. Why is the lowest priced store able to price as indicated? What are the specials? Are they similar for all stores?

5. Since meat is such an important item in the family purchasing budget, focus a project on the pricing strategy of competing food stores relative to key meat items. You will have to interview butchers to determine what kinds of meat items you should investigate to make your comparisons. Include different types of "image" stores, and see how "in fact" meat prices follow the images projected by the stores. Charts comparing the prices by type of meat item may show an interesting relationship. Watch for "specials"—try to use the "regular" prices for your comparisons. Come up with some strategy conclusions from your study.

Minicase 13-1   Del-Ray Supermarket had been enjoying a profitable operation for several years. Recently Discount Foods, a new-type grocery store, opened nearby. The new store emphasized low prices and fewer customer services. Del-Ray Supermarket immediately experienced a drastic reduction in business—a nearly 50 percent decline the first week. Del-Ray Supermarket's manager is desperate and decides to employ a loss leader strategy to regain his lost customers. He decides that he will use Discount Foods feature items for his loss leaders. Business picks up, but most of the volume is on the loss leader items, resulting in profitless sales.

What actions should be taken by Del-Ray Supermarket's manager?

Minicase 13-2   During a recent trip to Dallas, Texas, Lynn Brown went shopping in Neiman-Marcus. She saw a beautiful cut glass bowl and inquired about the price. "$500," said the salesperson. "Ridiculous," Ms. Brown replied, "I can get the same thing at home for about half that amount." "Perhaps," said the salesperson, "but *this* is Neiman-Marcus." Is the bowl worth $500? How can retailers such as Neiman-Marcus charge above the market for the bowl if this woman can indeed get it at home for $250?

Appendix	"A Pricing Checklist for Small Retailers"*

A retailer's prices influence the quantities of various items that consumers will buy, which in turn affects total revenue and profit. Hence, correct pricing decisions are a key to successful retail management. With this in mind, the following checklist of 52 questions has been developed to assist small retailers in making systematic, informed decisions regarding pricing strategies and tactics.

This checklist should be especially useful to a new retailer who is making pricing decisions for the first time. However, established retailers, including successful ones, can also benefit from this Aid. They may use it as a reminder of all the individual pricing decisions they should review periodically. And, it may also be used in training new employees who will have pricing authority.

THE CENTRAL CONCEPT OF MARKUP

A major step toward making a profit in retailing is selling merchandise for more than it costs you. This difference between cost of merchandise and retail price is called *markup* (or occasionally *markon*). From an arithmetic standpoint, markup is calculated as follows:

---

* Bruce J. Walker, "A Pricing Checklist for Small Retailers," Small Business Administration, Small Marketers Aids No. 158 (Washington, D.C.: U.S. Government Printing Office, 1976).

$$\text{Dollar markup} = \text{Retail price} - \text{Cost of the merchandise}$$

$$\text{Percentage markup} = \frac{\text{Dollar markup}}{\text{Retail price}}$$

If an item costs $6.50 and you feel consumers will buy it at $10.00, the dollar markup is $3.50 (which is $10.00—$6.50). Going one step further, the percentage markup is 35 percent (which is $3.50 ÷ $10.00). Anyone involved in retail pricing should be as knowledgeable about these two formulas as about the name and preferences of his or her best customer!

Two other key points about markup should be mentioned. First, the *cost of merchandise* used in calculating markup consists of the base invoice price for the merchandise *plus* any transportation charges *minus* any quantity and cash discounts given by the seller. Second, *retail price,* rather than cost, is ordinarily used in calculating percentage markup. The reason for this is that when other operating figures such as wages, advertising expenses, and profits are expressed as a percentage, all are based on retail price rather than cost of the merchandise being sold.

TARGET CONSUMERS AND THE RETAILING MIX

In this section, your attention is directed to price as it relates to your potential customers. These questions examine your merchandise, location, promotion, and customer services that will be combined with price in attempting to satisfy shoppers and make a profit. After some questions, brief commentary is provided.

1. Is the relative price of this item very important to your target consumers?   **Yes No**   ☐ ☐

The importance of price depends on the specific product *and* on the specific individual. Some shoppers are very price-conscious, others want convenience and knowledgeable sales personnel. Because of these variations, you need to learn about your customers' desires in relation to different products. Having sales personnel seek feedback from shoppers is a good starting point.

2. Are prices based on estimates of the number of units that consumers will demand at various price levels?   ☐ ☐

Demand-oriented pricing such as this is superior to cost-oriented pricing. In the cost approach, a predetermined amount is added to the cost of the merchandise, whereas the demand approach considers what consumers are willing to pay.

3. Have you established a price range for the product?   ☐ ☐

The cost of merchandise will be at one end of the price range and the level above which consumers will *not* buy the product at the other end.

4. Have you considered what price strategies would be compatible with your store's total retailing mix that includes merchandise, location, promotion, and services?   ☐ ☐

5. Will trade-ins be accepted as part of the purchase price on items such as appliances and television sets?   ☐ ☐

SUPPLIER AND COMPETITOR CONSIDERATIONS

This set of questions looks outside your firm to two factors that you cannot directly control—suppliers and competitors.

6.   Do you have final pricing authority?   ☐   ☐
With the repeal of fair trade laws, "yes" answers will be more common than in previous years. Still, a supplier can control retail prices by refusing to deal with nonconforming stores (a tactic which may be illegal) or by selling to you on consignment.

7.   Do you know what direct competitors are doing   ☐   ☐
pricewise?

8.   Do you regularly review competitors' ads to obtain in-   ☐   ☐
formation on their prices?

9.   Is your store large enough to employ either a full-time or   ☐   ☐
part-time comparison shopper?
These three questions emphasize the point that you must watch competitors' prices so that your prices will not be far out of line—too high *or* too low—without good reason. Of course, there may be a good reason for out-of-the-ordinary prices, such as seeking a special price image.

A PRICE LEVEL STRATEGY

Selecting a general level of prices in relation to competition is a key strategic decision, perhaps the most important.

                                                                                            Yes   No
10.   Should your overall strategy be to sell at prevailing
market price levels?   ☐   ☐
The other alternatives are an above-the-market strategy or a below the market strategy.

11.   Should competitors' temporary price reductions ever   ☐   ☐
be matched?

12.   Could private-brand merchandise be obtained in order   ☐   ☐
to avoid direct price competition?

CALCULATING PLANNED INITIAL MARKUP

In this section you will have to look *inside* your business, taking into account sales, expenses, and profits before setting prices. The point is that your initial markup must be large enough to cover anticipated expenses and reductions *and* still produce a satisfactory profit.

                                                                                            Yes   No
13.   Have you estimated sales, operating expenses, and re-
ductions for the next selling season?   ☐   ☐

14.   Have you established a profit objective for the next   ☐   ☐
selling season?

15.   Given estimated sales, expenses, and reductions, have   ☐   ☐
you planned initial markup?

This figure is calculated with the following formula:

$$\text{Initial markup percentage} = \frac{\text{Operating expenses + Reductions + Profit}}{\text{Net sales + reductions}}$$

Reductions consist of markdowns, stock shortages, and employee and customer discounts. The following example uses dollar amounts, but the estimates can also be percentages. If a retailer anticipates $94,000 in sales for a particular department, $34,000 in expenses and $6,000 in reductions, and if the retailer desires a $4,000 profit, initial markup percentage can be calculated:

$$\text{Initial markup percentage} = \frac{\$34,000 + \$6,000 + \$4,000}{\$94,000 + \$6,000} = 44\%$$

The resulting figure, 44 percent in this example, indicates what size initial markup is needed *on the average* in order to make the desired profits.

16. Would it be appropriate to have different initial mark-up figures for various lines of merchandise or services? ☐ ☐
You would seriously consider this when some lines have much different characteristics than others. For instance, a clothing retailer might logically have different initial markup figures for suits, shirts and pants, and accessories. (Various merchandise characteristics are covered in an upcoming section.) You may want those items with the highest turnover rates to carry the lowest initial markup.

STORE POLICIES

Having calculated an initial markup figure, you could proceed to set prices on your merchandise. But an important decision such as this should not be rushed. Instead, you should consider additional factors which suggest what would be the best price.

17. Is your tentative price compatible with established store policies? Yes No
☐ ☐
Policies are written guidelines indicating appropriate methods or actions in different situations. If established with care, they can save you time in decision making and provide for consistent treatment of shoppers. Specific policy areas that you should consider are as follows:

18. Will a one-price system, under which the same price is charged every purchaser of a particular item, be used on all items? ☐ ☐
The alternative is to negotiate price with consumers.

19. Will odd-ending prices, such as $1.98 and $44.95, be more appealing to your customers than even-ending prices? ☐ ☐

20. Will consumers buy more if multiple pricing, such as 2 for $8.50, is used? ☐ ☐

21. Should any leader offerings (selected products with quite low, less profitable prices) be used? □ □

22. Have the characteristics of an effective leader offering been considered? □ □

Ordinarily, a leader offering needs the following characteristics to accomplish its purpose of generating much shopper traffic: used by most people, bought frequently, very familiar regular price, and not a large expenditure for consumers.

23. Will price lining, the practice of setting up distinct price points (such as $5.00, $7.50, and $10.00) and then marking all related merchandise at these points, be used? □ □

24. Would price lining by means of zones (such as $5.00–$7.50 and $12.50–$15.00) be more appropriate than price points? □ □

25. Will cent-off coupons be used in newspaper ads or mailed to selected consumers on any occasion? □ □

26. Would periodic special sales, combining reduced prices and heavier advertising, be consistent with the store image you are seeking? □ □

27. Do certain items have greater appeal than others when they are part of a special sale? □ □

28. Has the impact of various sale items on profits been considered? □ □

Sale prices may mean little or no profit on these items. Still, the special sale may contribute to *total* profits by bringing in shoppers who may also buy some regular price (and profitable) merchandise and by attracting new customers. Also, you should avoid featuring items that require a large amount of labor, which in turn would reduce or erase profits. For instance, according to this criterion, shirts would be a better special sale item than men's suits that often require free alterations.

29. Will "rain checks" be issued to consumers who come in for special-sale merchandise that is temporarily out of stock? □ □

You should give particular attention to this decision since rain checks are required in some situations. Your lawyer or the regional Federal Trade Commission office should be consulted for specific advice regarding whether rain checks are needed in the special sales you plan.

NATURE OF THE MERCHANDISE

In this section you will be considering how selected characteristics of particular merchandise affect planned initial markup.

	Yes	No
30. Did you get a "good deal" on the wholesale price of this merchandise?	□	□

31. Is this item at the peak of its popularity? ☐ ☐

32. Are handling and selling costs relatively great due to the product being bulky, having a low turnover rate, and/or requiring much personal selling, installation, or alterations? ☐ ☐

33. Are relatively large levels of reductions expected due to markdowns, spoilage, breakage, or theft? ☐ ☐

With respect to the preceding four questions, "Yes" answers suggest the possibility of or need for larger-than-normal initial markups. For example, very fashionable clothing often will carry a higher markup than basic clothing such as underwear because the particular fashion may suddenly lose its appeal to consumers.

34. Will customer services such as delivery, alterations, gift wrapping, and installation be free of charge to customers? ☐ ☐

The alternative is to charge for some or all of these services.

ENVIRONMENTAL CONSIDERATIONS

The questions in this section focus your attention on three factors outside your business, namely economic conditions, laws, and consumerism.

		Yes	No

35. If your state has an unfair sales practices act that requires minimum markups on certain merchandise, do your prices comply with this statute? ☐ ☐

36. Are economic conditions in your trading area abnormal? ☐ ☐

Consumers tend to be more price-conscious when the economy is depressed, suggesting that lower-than-normal markups may be needed to be competitive. On the other hand, shoppers are less price-conscious when the economy is booming, which would permit larger markups *on a selective basis.*

37. Are the ways in which prices are displayed and promoted compatible and consumerism, one part of which has been a call for more straightforward price information? ☐ ☐

38. If yours is a grocery store, it is feasible to use unit pricing in which the item's cost per some standard measure is indicated? ☐ ☐

Having asked (and hopefully answered) more than three dozen questions, you are indeed ready to establish retail prices. When you have decided on an appropriate percentage markup, 35 percent on a garden hose for example, the next step is to determine what percentage of the still unknown retail price is represented by the cost figure. The basic markup formula is simply rearranged to do this:

$$Cost = Retail\ price - Markup$$
$$Cost = 100\% - 35\% = 65\%$$

Then the dollar cost, say $3.25 for the garden hose, is plugged into the following formula to arrive at the retail price:

$$\text{Retail price} = \frac{\text{Dollar cost}}{\text{Percentage cost}} = \frac{\$3.25}{65\% \text{ (or } 65)} = \$5.00$$

One other consideration is necessary:

39. Is the retail price consistent with your planned initial markups?

ADJUSTMENTS

It would be ideal if all items sold at their original retail prices. But we know that things are not always ideal. Therefore, a section on price adjustments is necessary.

	Yes	No
40. Are additional markups called for, because wholesale prices have increased or because an item's low price causes consumers to question its quality?	☐	☐
41. Should employees be given purchase discounts?	☐	☐
42. Should any groups of customers, such as students or senior citizens, be given purchase discounts?	☐	☐
43. When markdowns appear necessary, have you first considered other alternatives such as retaining price but changing another element of the retailing mix or storing the merchandise until the next selling season?	☐	☐
44. Has an attempt been made to identify causes of markdowns so that steps can be taken to minimize the number of avoidable buying, selling, and pricing errors that cause markdowns?	☐	☐
45. Has the relationship between timing and size of markdowns been taken into account?	☐	☐

In general, markdown taken *early* in the selling season or shortly after sales slow down can be smaller than *late* markdowns. Whether an early or late markdown would be more appropriate in a particular situation depends on several things: your assessment of how many consumers might still be interested in the product, the size of the initial markup, and the amount remaining in stock.

46. Would a schedule of automatic markdowns after merchandise has been in stock for specified intervals be appropriate? ☐ ☐

47. Is the size of the markdown "just enough" to stimulate purchases?

Of course, this question is difficult—perhaps impossible—to answer. Nevertheless, it stresses the point that you have to carefully observe the effects of different size markdowns so that you can eventually acquire some insights into what size markdowns are "just enough" for different kinds of merchandise.

48.   Has a procedure been worked out for markdowns on price-lined merchandise?

49.   Is the markdown price calculated from the off-retail percentage?

This question gets you into the arithmetic of markdowns. Usually, you first tentatively decide on the percentage amount price must be marked down to excite consumers. For example, if you think a 25 percent markdown will be necessary to sell a lavender sofa, the dollar amount of the markdown is calculated as follows:

Dollar markdown = Off-retail percentage × Previous retail price
Dollar markdown = 25% (or 0.25) × $500 = $125.

Then the markdown price is obtained by subtracting the dollar markdown from the previous retail price. Hence, the sofa would be $375.00 after taking the markdown.

50.   Has cost of the merchandise been considered before setting the markdown price?

Yes   No

This is not to say that a markdown price should never be lower than cost: on the contrary, a price that low may be your only hope of generating some revenue from the item. But cost should be considered to make sure that below-cost markdown prices are the *exception* in your store rather than being so common that your total profits are really hurt.

51.   Have procedures for recording the dollar amounts, percentages, and probable causes of markdowns been set up?

Analyzing markdowns is very important since it can provide information that will assist in calculating planned initial markup, in decreasing errors that cause markdowns, and in evaluating suppliers.

You may be weary from thinking your way through the preceding sections, but don't overlook an important final question:

52.   Have you marked the calendar for a periodic review of your pricing decisions?

Rather than "laying an egg" due to careless pricing decisions, this checklist should help you lay a solid foundation of effective prices as you try to build retail profits.

14

HOW DO YOU PHYSICALLY HANDLE MERCHANDISE?

The objectives of this chapter are:

- To introduce you to the physical handling process and functions.
- To point out the differences in physical handling in a large store and a small one.
- To answer the following questions about physical handling:
- Should it be centralized?
  - Where should the responsibility be?
  - What determines receiving layout and equipment needs?
  - What are accepted receiving procedures?
- To have you think about the problems of quantity and quality checking.
- To investigate the various aspects of marking.
- To discuss distribution as the final physical handling responsibility.
- To help you understand the following terms:

Receiving	Nonmarking
Marking	Remarking
Checking	Preretailing
Distributing	Source marking
Bulk marking	

In your *planning* for profits up to this point you have worked out your budgets. You have *organized* your human resources to carry out your basic functions. We were especially concerned with showing you how to organize the merchandising function. We carefully studied the role of the buyer.

Another important function of the merchandising division we reviewed was pricing. You need to know how much to charge for the items in your firm.

The major concern of this chapter is the physical handling of the goods when they arrive at your store. This is the final step in the buying process. Figure 14–1 indicates the critical importance of physical handling of merchandise to the broad subject of Part III of this text. As a reminder, we're concerned with *planning for profit.* The "Merchandise Cycle" puts all the pieces together—you will be introduced to selling and analysis in subsequent chapters. We feel this is the proper time to restate where we are *now.*

FIGURE 14–1

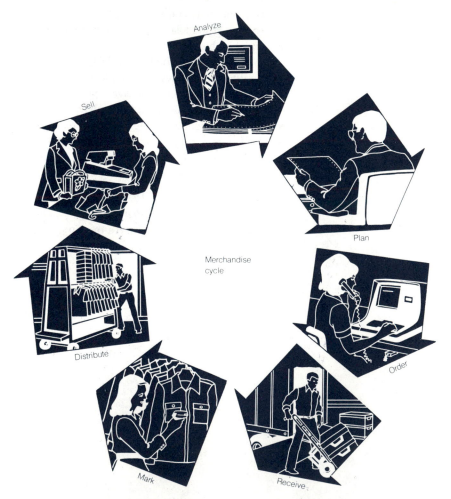

Source: NCR Corporation (SP-1813-01 0978) "OCR Reader . . . Changing the World of Business."

WHAT PHYSICAL HANDLING FUNCTIONS MUST YOU PERFORM?

After you have purchased goods from a supplier, they must be moved to you. When the goods arrive at the store, the *physical handling* functions start.[1] The shipment must be examined to make sure that it is (1) the quantity and (2) the quality ordered. Then the goods must be marked, prepared for sale, and displayed in the selling area. You need to keep tight control at all points during the physical handling of the goods from receipt at the store to the selling floor. Such controls hold down pilferage and damage.

The physical handling *process can be broken down into the following areas:* (1) receiving, (2) checking, (3) marking, and (4) distributing. The various sections of this chapter briefly look at each of these to accomplish functions.

We are concerned with physical handling *only* after the goods "hit the store docks" not when they are in transit. Let's admit that a good buyer will want to be involved with traffic management. But since traffic management is a specialized function, we are not going to get involved in it. Small merchants depend on suppliers' traffic managers to decide on best routings. Large retail firms have their own specialists.

Also, we are assuming that once the goods move to the selling floor, the physical handling function ends. Of course, customer "delivery" is movement and handling. Again, since it is a specialized function, we will not go into the questions of delivery here.

DOES STORE SIZE AFFECT PHYSICAL HANDLING?

In a small store the entire physical handling process is simple. The goods are most likely delivered directly to the sales floor where someone, probably a salesperson, performs all of the functions without actually knowing that they can be separated as we will do here.

In a very large retail firm the volume of goods handled is tremendous. As a result they have specialized personnel to perform the physical handling functions. This brings up the questions of centralization versus decentralization of the physical handling activities and of where to locate them.

Centralization?

As we said earlier, physical handling is actually the final step in the buying process. So, should the buyer also be responsible for receiving, checking, marking, and distributing?

In the small store where the functions are handled in a "back room" or on the selling floor, it is reasonable to say that the buyer should be responsible. The buyer is probably the manager of the floor too and that person can, and should, complete the buying role.

But, in the large organization, it is probably best to take these functions from the buyer and centralize them under the operating (or management) division. (See Chapter 12 for organization structure.)

Several reasons for centralization are:

1. If the buyers have the responsibility, controls might be neglected.
2. Salespersons resent having to do the job and are often careless and negligent. Specialized personnel do a better job of performing the operations. Controls are better. There is chance of "lost papers" in decentralization. In turn, selling is likely to be done better without additional responsibility.
3. Expensive equipment can be used if centralized operations exist. Each merchandise department could not afford its own.
4. Specialization should result in a better job done more efficiently.

Location?

Except in the very small store, physical handling activities are centered in a part of the store building which is not good for selling. Of course, the structure of the building will affect the decisions.

When you are making the decision of "where to locate" keep several factors in mind.

1. The value of the space should be low (as suggested above). If the space is "expensive" it should be used for selling. The value is related to the traffic it generates. An upper floor with enough room is not unusual in a large store. Of course, you need vertical transportation facilities to get the goods to receiving and marking.

2. Depending on the kinds of goods, you may need to consider how close the receiving and marking area is to the sales floor or the stockrooms. Handling costs are high and must be considered. We know of a small merchant who opened a ready-to-wear boutique and in planning the layout, no space was allocated for physical handling. The first few months found the washroom being utilized for marking. The store was small, but moving goods from the washroom (remote) to the selling floor was inefficient. Planning and organizing are essential management functions, no matter what the size of the business.

3. The merchandise must be received from carriers. Is there a receiving area which is easily accessible to such delivery vehicles?

PROBLEMS OF RECEIVING, EQUIPMENT, LAYOUT, AND OPERATIONS

Receiving, is really taking possession of the goods and then moving them for the next phase of the process, checking.

As we have suggested throughout this discussion, the very small store has little need for specialization and thus for any special equipment or layout concerns. There is probably a back room somewhere where goods are received (or maybe a washroom) and unpacked. It is just as likely that the activity is handled right on the sales floor.

In the larger stores, specific care with layout and equipment can make a more effective operation.

The following ten ideas will improve the effectiveness of any receiving department:[2]

1. Straight-line movement of all materials with as little backtracking as possible.
2. Movement of all material through the shortest possible distance and with the fewest possible motions.
3. Maximum machine operation, minimum hand operation.
4. Determination of the most efficient methods of performing specific re petitive operations, and standardization of these methods.
5. Careful attention to working conditions.
6. Careful selection and training of personnel.
7. Adequate supervision.
8. Sufficient equipment.
9. Standby equipment.
10. Enough records for adequate control.

While the layout depends on the system used in handling the items received, four methods are widely employed:[3]

1. *Stationary or checkmarking tables.* Tables placed in a room large enough to allow cases to be brought in and unpacked.
2. *Portable table.* Goods are placed on tables with wheels where they are sorted and checked for quantity. The tables are moved to another section for marking.
3. *Bin method.* The receiving room is divided into two sections. One is used for checking and one for marking. There is a series of bins or openings which divide the sections. Merchandise is checked on tables in one section and then shoved through the bins onto tables in another section for marking.
4. *Mechanical conveyor belts or roller conveyors.* Merchandise is moved mechanically from receiving point through the checking and marking operations. Technology allows overhead trolley systems for hanging merchandise. Some stores employ the overhead rail for all merchandise. They utilize hanging baskets for goods which cannot be hung. The goods can even be moved to stockrooms or selling area by mechanical means.

Receiving procedures   Once the goods have been received at the store, certain operations are needed to get goods ready for sale.

Each shipment must be inspected to make sure that there is no damage to the packing container (before the goods are unpacked). This activity should be done before the driver who brought the shipment leaves the store. At this point there is no inspection of the merchandise, merely the package itself. If damage is discovered, however, a claim settlement will be easier later.

The *receiving record* is an essential part of the procedures. Typically the record includes: date and hour of arrival; weight; form of transportation;

number of pieces; receiving number; invoice number; condition of packages; delivery charges; name of deliverer; amount of invoice; department ordering goods; and any other remarks.

WHAT MUST YOU KNOW ABOUT CHECKING?

Checking, as you must know by the prior discussion, concerns matching the buyer's purchase order with the vendor's invoice (bill); opening packages containing goods, removing the items from the packages, sorting the items, and finally comparing the quantity and quality of the shipment with what was ordered.

Quantity

There are four accepted methods of quantity checking:

1. *Direct check.* The shipment is checked against the vendor's invoice. The goods under this system cannot be checked until the invoice arrives. This method is simple but may cause carelessness in checking. It can also result in items accumulating in the checking area if invoices have not arrived.
2. *Blind check.* This system is designed to avoid the carelessness and merchandise accumulation problems of the direct check. The checker lists the items received without the invoice in hand. The system is slower than the direct check. The list prepared by the checker has to be compared to the invoice, so it is more time consuming.
3. *The semiblind check.* The checker is provided a list of the items in a shipment, but the quantity of these items is omitted. The time saved may be offset somewhat by the time required in preparing the list for the checker.
4. *The combination check.* A combination of the blind and direct checks, this system attempts to get an accurate count of goods received and speed up the movement to the sales floor. If the invoices are available when the goods arrive, the direct check is used. If the invoice has not come in, the blind check is used.

Quality

Checkers are not merchandise specialists. Buyers are. So, the responsibility for quality checking, when it is considered important, must be assumed by the buying staff. The decision to "check or not to check" for quality is the buyer's.

WHAT MUST YOU KNOW ABOUT MARKING?

Marking is putting information on the goods, or on some container nearby, to assist customers and to aid the store in the control functions.

Goods must either be marked within the store or by a vendor. Of course, if the retailer can shift the marking function to the supplier, it can be less costly.

Marking is being greatly affected by UPC (Universal Product Code in the supermarket industry being supported by vendors who premark merchandise) and by OCR (in the general merchandise field) with its voluntary vendor marking program. A discussion of this is in Chapter 10.

Manufacturers of marking equipment and price tags can be very helpful in assisting you in decisions relative to procedures and equipment.

Various methods exist for getting price information to place on the goods. A common method is *preretailing*. The buyer places the retail price on the store's copy of the purchase order. The buyer may also *retail the invoice*. In this practice, the buyer places a retail price on the copy of the invoice in the receiving room.

Also, as suggested, the store tries to shift the marking function to the vendor whenever possible. This is known as *source marking*.

Bulk marking

Items which sell at very low prices and subject to rapidly changing prices may be "bulk marked." They are not marked until they move to the selling floor. The shipping carton is marked when the goods arrive. When the item is moved to the floor, the individual prices are placed on the items. This is useful in goods where price changes are frequent and it avoids remarking. Some call this system "delayed marking."

Nonmarking

Some goods are unnecessary to mark. At the checkout, the person at the counter is supplied with the prices of such goods. In some categories, the shelf, or bin, can be marked with the price. Very low-priced items may be more costly to mark than the value derived. For example, individual nails would be impossible to mark.

Remarking

Prices change. Goods are marked up and they are marked down. How should these price changes be handled? These questions must be handled by management in line with the store image. Some stores always insist on new price tickets rather than merely marking through the old price. You must decide this issue. There is no rule.

CONTROLLING THE RECEIVING, CHECKING, AND MARKING ACTIVITIES

Every company selects the best method for controlling the physical handling functions. You will find many variations, but the essential information must be collected by all retail managers. The JC Penney system is explained for illustrative purposes; the company, of course is large, but what is done there must be done by all retailers. Also, we are simplifying the discussion by merely pointing up those elements of the system which could be adapted by store management of any type; stores of any size.

The basis of the Penney system is the purchase order form. We strongly believe that every retail company should have its own purchase order form and should never use suppliers' forms. Only in this way can the physical handling functions be controlled. The simplest way to see the control feature of the purchase order is to note that each order has a discrete number (in this case number 01518). If you write orders on a supplier's form, you have too many chances to lose track of them. Your control will be uncertain at best.

The "original" form goes to the supplier. (See Figure 14–2.) You should see all of the important information which is contained on this form. Of course you see the supplier's name and address. Immediately above that information the buyer will place the supplier's number—another control feature. Each supplier has a specific number. The terms of sale (payment period) are specified in the box "terms." The box labeled "Mail" tells the mail room whether the original and/or duplicate (Figure 14–3) should be sent to the supplier or to a distribution point within the company. The remainder of the purchase order is fairly clear. Obviously the "company retail" price will not be filled in on the original which goes to the supplier.

The "triplicate" or *office* copy (Figure 14–4) is for accounts payable. The "receiving" copy (Figure 14–5) is utilized in the marking room. The buyers

FIGURE 14-2

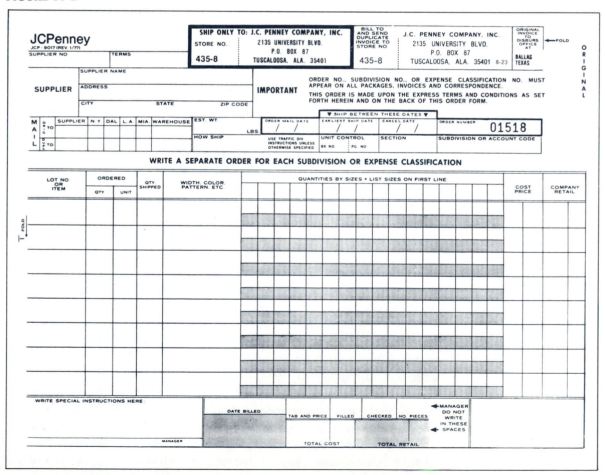

FIGURE 14-3

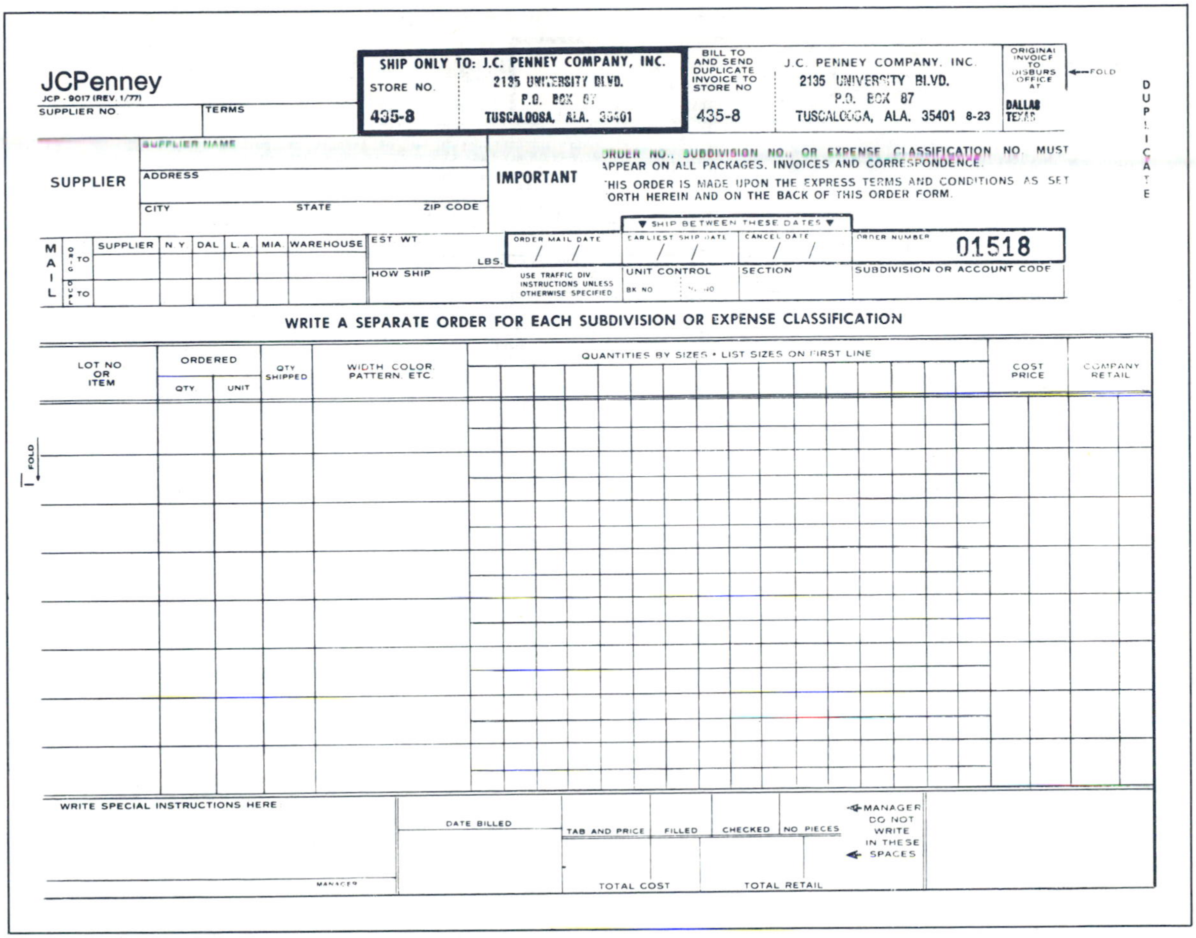
JCPenney
JCP - 9017 (REV. 1/77)
SUPPLIER NO
TERMS
SHIP ONLY TO: J.C. PENNEY COMPANY, INC.
STORE NO.
435-8
2135 UNIVERSITY BLVD.
P.O. BOX 87
TUSCALOOSA, ALA. 35401
BILL TO AND SEND DUPLICATE INVOICE TO STORE NO
435-8
J.C. PENNEY COMPANY, INC.
2135 UNIVERSITY BLVD.
P.O. BOX 87
TUSCALOOSA, ALA. 35401 8-23
ORIGINAL INVOICE TO DISBURS OFFICE AT
DALLAS TEXAS
FOLD
DUPLICATE
SUPPLIER
SUPPLIER NAME
ADDRESS
CITY
STATE
ZIP CODE
IMPORTANT
ORDER NO., SUBDIVISION NO., OR EXPENSE CLASSIFICATION NO. MUST APPEAR ON ALL PACKAGES, INVOICES AND CORRESPONDENCE.
THIS ORDER IS MADE UPON THE EXPRESS TERMS AND CONDITIONS AS SET FORTH HEREIN AND ON THE BACK OF THIS ORDER FORM.
MAIL
ORIG TO
DUPL TO
SUPPLIER
N.Y.
DAL
L.A.
MIA.
WAREHOUSE
EST. WT
LBS.
HOW SHIP
ORDER MAIL DATE
USE TRAFFIC DIV INSTRUCTIONS UNLESS OTHERWISE SPECIFIED
SHIP BETWEEN THESE DATES
EARLIEST SHIP DATE
CANCEL DATE
ORDER NUMBER
01518
UNIT CONTROL
BK NO
SECTION
SUBDIVISION OR ACCOUNT CODE
WRITE A SEPARATE ORDER FOR EACH SUBDIVISION OR EXPENSE CLASSIFICATION
LOT NO OR ITEM
ORDERED
QTY
UNIT
QTY SHIPPED
WIDTH COLOR PATTERN, ETC.
QUANTITIES BY SIZES • LIST SIZES ON FIRST LINE
COST PRICE
COMPANY RETAIL
FOLD
WRITE SPECIAL INSTRUCTIONS HERE
MANAGER
DATE BILLED
TAB AND PRICE
FILLED
CHECKED
NO PIECES
MANAGER DO NOT WRITE IN THESE SPACES
TOTAL COST
TOTAL RETAIL

preretail the purchase order and whether the store uses direct or blind check, this copy is used to show receipts. If back orders exist (incomplete shipments which will be shipped at a later date) the purchase order will be kept "open." If the shipment is complete, the receiving copy of the purchase order is sent to the office for payment.

WHAT ABOUT DISTRIBUTING?

Distributing is moving goods from the receiving, marking, and checking area to the sales floor and/or the stockrooms. In a multistore organization it is concerned with moving goods from some central point to the branches or units of a chain.

Mechanization is probably the answer for efficiency. The problem is most serious for multiunit organizations.

FIGURE 14-4

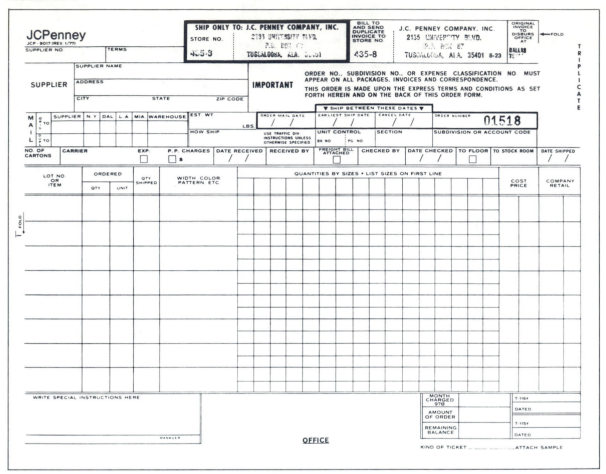

SUMMARY

The physical handling function is a technical and specialized function in retail stores. This chapter has stressed the things you must know to cope with the activity. Professional assistance is needed in large stores for mechanization. Small stores have to do the same jobs, but the degree of specialization is less.

Basically the physical handling functions are: receiving, checking, marking, and distributing.

We were concerned with centralization versus decentralization of the activities and where they should be located. Size is a great determiner of the answers to these questions.

The problems of checking for quantity and quality were discussed as were the marking problems. Finally we looked at the problems faced by single- and

FIGURE 14-5

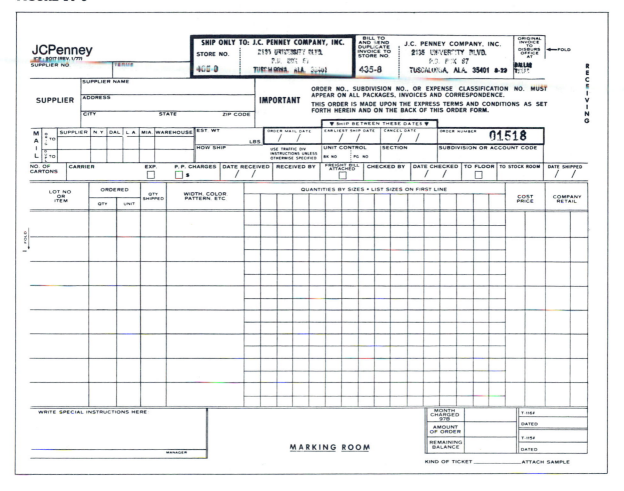

multiunit organizations in distributing the goods from the receiving and marking areas to the remainder of the store and the other units of the group.

NOTES

1. Physical handling in a retail store is a specialized function. The basic functions exist in every store. The best information for the technical aspects of systems, procedures, and equipment can come from professional consultants and suppliers of merchandise handling equipment. For the student who wants a more complete discussion of the subject, see: Delbert J. Duncan and Stanley C. Hollander, *Modern Retailing Management,* 9th ed. (Homewood, Ill.: Richard D. Irwin, Inc., 1977), pp. 370–92; Gerald Pintel and Jay Diamond, *Retailing* (Englewood

Cliffs, N.J.: Prentice-Hall, Inc., 1971), pp. 198–216; and Karen R. Gillespie and Joseph C. Hecht, *Retail Business Management,* 2d ed. (New York: Gregg Division, McGraw-Hill Book Company, 1977), pp. 256–68.

2. Pintel and Diamond, *Retailing,* pp. 201–3.

3. Duncan and Hollander, *Modern Retailing Management,* pp. 373–74.

DISCUSSION QUESTIONS

1. Into what specific areas can "physical handling" process be broken down? Discuss each one briefly.

2. Should the buyer be responsible for the physical handling functions? Explain.

3. Discuss the considerations you must be aware of in deciding on the location for the physical handling functions.

4. Explain the four accepted methods of quantity checking.

5. Distinguish among the following: preretailing, retailing the invoice; source marking; bulk marking; nonmarking; and remarking.

PROJECTS

1. Make a contact with a local retailer (preferably one which is rather large, e.g., a department store). Ask if the store manager will set up an appointment for you (or work through your professor) with the person in charge of receiving and marking. Write a report on "how it is done"—diagram the movement of goods from the truck to the customer's home.

2. Visit several different types of stores in your area. Describe the various ways merchandise is marked. Be sure you go to some food stores as well as department stores.

Minicase 14–1   The excitement of opening her own fashion shoe boutique had made Pam giddy during the weeks before the formal opening. No one thought that the old dentist's office near the campus could be transformed into such a "charming" experience. Everyone who stopped in before the doors were finally opened to the public (that included her many friends—she had worked in a local family shoe store in the town for many years) was amazed that the old "smelly" office had taken on such a glamorous look. Pam invited a good friend—a college professor teaching retailing at the university—for a last look at the fixtures and layout before the merchandise started rolling in prior to opening. He was complementary about the atmosphere and commented about how amazing the shop looked—one could hardly remember having a tooth filled in the spot where the cash register now stood. In looking at the sales-supporting parts of the store, Pam proudly noted where the backup stock would be stored and was delighted to note that no merchandise would be "piled" on the floor. One pair of shoes would be displayed on sophisticated fixtures throughout the small area. One problem bothered Pam's professor friend. He had to say it—"Pam, where are you going to receive and mark the merchandise?'' Pam almost froze in her tracks. She had utilized every square inch in the store for sales or storage. ''How could they have let me do such a thing?'' Pam exclaimed. Her friend scratched his head—he saw a stunning coffee service in the rear of the store for customer's to relax while enjoying the merchandise and conversation; he saw the small rest room with fancy gold fixtures just to the right of the opening in the rear which went out into the alley where the goods would come in—but obviously would have to be put into stock directly from the carrier without being checked or marked—unless it was done ''on the floor'' in sight of everyone. What would that do to the atmosphere Pam had worked so long and hard to create? If you were the professor, what would you recommend?

Minicase 14–2   Jim Taylor had been in charge of receiving and marking for some time. He liked working for Fashion Center, the city's most prestigious department store. He liked his job, but he had experienced some difficulties lately with his boss's buyers. Mr. Friedman, the general merchandise manager, not only had responsibility for all the buying and selling, he also was responsible for the physical handling of the goods from the dock to the selling floor. It was Jim's understanding of store policy that no merchandise could be marked until the vendor's invoice had arrived and then the merchandise could be checked and marked against the invoice. Several times lately, Ms. Perry, an attractive but ''tough'' buyer of fashion separates, had given him a hard time. Just yesterday she had said to Jim, ''Don't tell me I can't have my merchandise until the invoice comes in. I need it on the floor *now*. See that it moves up—I'll tell you the proper prices.'' Jim did not like scenes, especially with Ms. Perry, so he just nodded. She gave him the prices and he proceeded to call Mr. Friedman. As usual, Friedman was polite and kind. He told Jim that he understood Perry's attitude—she was really a terrific buyer, you know—and to go ahead and release the merchandise without the invoice this time—he just warned about doing it all the time. And he cautioned Jim to make careful notes about what he had done. Jim had to say, ''OK'' but he felt ''used.'' He recalled several times lately that Mr. Friedman had told him the same thing about other buyers. Just what was store policy and what did it really mean? Jim thought, ''Mr. Friedman wants the goods on the floor just as much as the buyers!'' Jim wondered what to do. He certainly didn't want to go over his boss's head. But he knew eventually they'd all get into a bad situation. Jim discussed this problem with Tom Franks, an old friend who was in charge of the warehouse. Assume you are Tom. What advice do you have for your old friend?

15

KEYS TO SUCCESSFUL SELLING

The purposes of this chapter are to help you understand:

- The types of selling needed in retailing.
- The steps in the selling process.
- Ways of increasing sales force productivity.
- The need for sales training programs.
- How to help people buy.
- The meaning of the following terms:

Routine selling	Emotional buying motives
Transaction processing	Sales force productivity
Creative selling	Add-on sales
Rational buying motives	

The first impression a customer likely will get about your firm is from contact with your salespersons. Everything else in your business may be great but a poor sales team can cost you many sales. Building a good sales force is probably one of the hardest jobs you will face.

Your problem is harder because retail salespersons are usually paid low wages and have low job status. Such things do not attract high quality persons. Try to promote retail sales as a career in order to attract bright people. Work closely with educators you know in trying to do this.

SELF-SERVICE OR FULL SERVICE?

The key to a good sales force is the right interaction between the (1) merchandise, (2) the customer, and (3) the salesperson. Some items such as groceries can be sold by self-service. Or you may want to have a fully staffed store if you are selling such items as expensive furs. A third possibility is a combination of self-service and full staffing. This is the policy of most stores. Consumers will serve themselves for certain items—for example, in supermarkets and gasoline stations. They do such things to avoid higher costs.

When are salespersons needed? A salesperson is needed when, (1) your customers have little knowledge about the product they plan to buy; (2) arguing over price is likely, as when buying a car; (3) the product you are selling is complex—for example, stereo equipment.

Remember, the sales force represents the store and in the eyes of the consumers is the store. In many respects the image projected by salespersons is one of the most important facets of the entire retail operation. Far too often the key role of the retail salesperson in this context is played down.

WHAT ARE THE TYPES OF RETAIL SELLING?

Several kinds of selling occur in retailing. A different type of person and different skill levels are needed for each.[1]

Transaction processing. The easiest selling task is *transaction processing.* Here employees simply serve as checkout clerks or cashiers and do little selling. Typical examples are salespersons in discount department stores or supermarkets.

Routine selling. *Routine selling* involves more product knowledge and a better approach to the sales task. Often persons in routine selling are involved in the sales of nontechnical items such as clothing. These salespersons help the shopper to buy by giving them confidence in their judgment.

Persons involved in routine sales should be trained in the techniques of suggestive selling. They should then be monitored closely to make sure that they practice the concepts they have learned. Such techniques can help increase sales by 10 percent or more. These additional sales are almost pure profit since they add very little if anything to the cost structure of the firm.

Creative selling. *Creative selling* requires the use of more skill by salespersons. Your salespeople need complete information about product lines, the uses of the product, and an understanding of technical features.

These persons are often called sales consultants. They may, for example, work as interior designers in a furniture store. Creative selling also occurs when the product is highly personalized such as in the case of expensive clothes or of cosmetics.

Above all, regard retail selling and the sales simulation functions as part of the total communications mix for your firm. Many "plus" sales can be made through creative sales efforts. The cost of retail selling is high, in spite of the fact that firms pay low wages to sales personnel. These costs can only be offset by high levels of sales per worker. A trained and effective sales force can be a major advantage for a firm. Competing firms can duplicate price cuts and promotion, but they will have difficulty in developing a quality sales force. Table 15–1 shows the minimum product-related information which all salespersons need in order to do an effective job of retail selling, for example.

THE SELLING PROCESS

A basic concept in retail sales is that a sale must first occur in the mind of the buyer. The job of the salesperson is thus to lead the customer to a buying action. Successful retail salespersons normally think of retail selling as a process. This process consists of the following steps:

1. Prospecting (pre-approaching).
2. Approach.
3. Determining customer needs and wants.
4. Demonstrating and handling merchandise.
5. Meeting objections and answering questions.
6. Closing.
7. Follow-up.[2]

Prospecting

Prospecting involves identifying possible sales prospects. Promotional programs are the normal way for identifying prospects by attracting people to the firm. Telephone and direct mail programs are also useful. Likewise, word of mouth can also be effective as satisfied customers refer their friends to the store.

The most successful retail salespersons try to know as much about their customers as possible before approaching them. Such a process at first may seem difficult. However, the concept of market segmentation we talked about earlier can help you identify the most likely persons who will come to the store. The type of promotion program featured by the store is also a key. For example, most persons shopping a Kmart or Woolco expect good price/value relationships and normally buy on the basis of price. They are often presold on products through national brand advertising and probably do not expect many services. On the other hand, the customers of an exclusive dress shop expect you to offer personalized attention, the salesperson to

TABLE 15–1
Summary of merchandise information needed by salespersons

The salesperson should know:	
Uses of the product	Primary and secondary uses Suitability Versatility
How the product will perform	Durability Degree of color performance Shrinkage or stretchage (in case of textiles) Breaking strength Resistance to water, wind, wear, heat, light Cost of upkeep
What the product is made of	Kinds of materials used Quality of materials used Cost of materials used Sources of materials used Available supplies of materials used
How the product is made	Size Weight Weave (in case of textiles) Finish Handmade or machine made Pressed, molded, stamped, inlaid, etc. Conditions under which goods are made Packaging

How to use the product	How to operate it, wear it, prepare it,
	    eat it, apply it, arrange it,
	    assemble it, display it, place it

How to care for the product	How to handle and adjust the product How to clean the product How to store the product How to oil and grease the product How to refrigerate the product
Appearance of the product	Beauty Style Ensemble possibilities
Background of the product	History of the article History of the manufacturer History of its uses History of competing articles Rarity Prestige
Services available with the product	Credit terms Shipping terms Speed and cost of delivery Transportation methods

Source: Kenneth H. Mills and Judith E. Paul, *Successful Retail Sales* (Englewood Cliffs, N.J.: Prentice-Hall, Inc., 1979, pp. 82–83. © 1979. Reprinted by permission of Prentice-Hall, Inc., Englewood Cliffs, New Jersey.

have a high level of product knowledge, and a wide variety of services to be available.

Finally, some firms keep lists of good customers and their likes and dislikes. Salespersons often call them when a new shipment of merchandise arrives which they think the customer will like.

Approaching the customer

The initial approach is quite crucial in getting the sale. The salesperson in approaching the customer should quickly (1) gain the person's attention, (2) create interest, and (3) make a smooth transition into a presentation. Various approaches to customers are possible. Commonly used approaches are the service approach, the merchandise approach, and the friendly, informal approach:

The service approach. The service approach, namely, "May I help you?" is weak if a customer is simply browsing. It gives the customer the opportunity to quickly say "no." However, such an approach is quite useful when (1) the customer has apparently made a selection, (2) the customer needs a salesperson to explain something about the merchandise, or (3) the customer needs someone to ring up a sale. Above all, always make the customer feel welcome, let them know that you are willing to serve them, and that you have the needed level of knowledge about the merchandise.

The merchandise approach. This approach begins with a statement about the merchandise such as "The style you are looking at is very popular this year." The salesperson in this approach waits until a potential customer seems to have decided on an item before approaching the individual. The salesperson then begins talking to the customer about the merchandise without asking whether the person would like to be waited on.

The informal approach. The informal approach is a friendly, personalized one. It lets the customers know that they are remembered, liked, and a valued part of the store's business. However, make sure you keep up-to-date information on your customers if you use this approach. Don't make the mistake of asking Mr. Jones about his wife a few days after their divorce! Above all, the tone in approaching the customer should always be friendly and cordial.

Table 15–2 outlines 11 basic types of customers you are likely to meet. The information in the table describes their characteristics and how to respond to them so as to make more sales.

Determining customer needs and wants

After the greeting, try quickly to discover the customers needs and wants. Good listening skills are the key here. A clear understanding of customer needs and wants will ensure greater levels of sales. Once you have the customer's attention and understand their needs, you can quickly move them into the interest and desire stage and hopefully to the buying stage. Motives for buying generally can be grouped into either emotional or rational buying motives. Such motives are highlighted in Table 15–3.

TABLE 15-2
Recognizing customers of all types

	Customer			Salesperson—
Basic types	**Basic characteristic**	**Secondary characteristics**	**Other characteristics**	**What to say or do**
Arguer	Takes issue with each statement of salesperson	Disbelieves claims, tries to catch salesperson in error	Cautious Slow to decide	Demonstrate Show product knowledge Use "yes, but . . ."
Chip on shoulder	Definitely in a bad mood	Indignation Angry at slightest provocation	Acts as if being deliberately baited	Avoid argument Stick to basic facts Show good assortment
Decisive	Knows what is wanted	Customer confident his choice is right	Not interested in another opinion—respects salesperson's brevity	Win sale—not argument Sell self Tactfully inject opinion
Doubting Thomas	Doesn't trust sales talk	Hates to be managed	Arrives at decision cautiously	Back up merchandise statements by manufacturers' tags, labels Demonstrate merchandise Let customer handle merchandise
Fact finder	Interested in factual information—detailed	Alert to salesperson's errors in description	Looks for actual tags and labels	Emphasize label and manufacturers' facts Volunteer care information
Hesitant	Ill at ease—sensitive	Shopping at unaccustomed price range	Unsure of own judgment	Make customer comfortable Use friendliness and respect
Impulsive	Quick to decide or select	Impatience	Liable to break off sale abruptly	Close rapidly Avoid oversell, overtalk Note key point
Look around	Little ability to make own decisions	Anxious-fearful of making a mistake	Wants salesperson's aid in decision—wants advisor—wants to do "right thing"	Emphasize merits of product and service, "zeroing" in on customer-expressed need and doubts
Procrastinator	I'll wait 'till tomorrow	Lacks confidence in own judgment	Insecure	Reinforce customer's judgments
Silent	Not talking—but thinking!	Appears indifferent but truly listening	Appears nonchalant	Ask direct questions—straightforward approach Watch for "buying" signals
Think it over	Refers to need to consult someone else	Looking for another adviser	Not sure of own uncertainty	Get agreement on small points "Draw out" opinions Use points agreed upon for close

Source: C. Winston Borgen, *Learning Experiences in Retailing* (Pacific Palisades, Calif.: Goodyear Publishing Co., 1976), p. 293. Copyright © 1976 by Goodyear Publishing Company. Reprinted by permission.

**TABLE 15–3
Buying motives**

Rational considerations	Emotional considerations
Cost	Ease and convenience
Durability	Safety and protection
Depreciation	Play and relaxation
Efficiency	Pride and prestige
Economy	Love and affection
Degree of labor necessary	Sex and romance
Saving of time and space	Adventure and excitement
Length of usage	Esthetic pleasure
Profit and thrift	Urge to create

Source: From C. Winston Borgen *Learning Experiences in Retailing* (Pacific Palisades, Calif.: Goodyear Publishing Co., 1976), p. 271. Copyright © 1976 by Goodyear Publishing Co. Reprinted by permission.

One way to develop information on customer needs and wants is to ask the customer what they want to use the merchandise for. This knowledge will help you better understand their buying problem and how the merchandise can help solve the problem. Such information indirectly will also provide insight to the price, styles, and colors which a customer may find preferable.

Demonstrating and handling merchandise

The above questions will help you determine what goods to show the customers and to point out how the merchandise will help to solve the problem they face. Good salespersons have a mental outline which they follow in presenting the merchandise. This mental outline differs from a canned sales presentation. The salesperson is free to deviate from a fixed statement but still keeps key points in mind as a sort of "checklist." Such a guide stresses the following points:

1. *Begin with the strongest features of the product.* These features might be price, durability, performance, and so forth.

2. *Obtain agreement on small points.* This helps the salesperson to establish good rapport with the customer.

3. *Point out the benefits of ownership to the customer.* Try to identify with the customer in making these points.

4. *Demonstrate the product.* This helps the customer to make a decision based on information other than that contained in the salesperson's presentation.

5. *Let the customer try the product.* Get the customer involved as much as possible. This will help the customer make the sale.[3]

Other useful techniques include testimonials of persons who have used the product, discussion of research results, discussion of product guarantees, and perhaps case histories.

Meeting objections and answering questions

Customers often object to a point during the sale process. Try to find out the real reasons for the objection. The objection may be based on price, quality of the product, service available, or various other reasons. Above all, don't argue with the customer. You will get nowhere. Also, avoid the "yes, but" approach, because that might also lead to an argument. Instead, try to get the customer to see the situation in a different way. Agree that you can understand why the person holds a particular view but try to provide information which can overcome the objection. For example, reaction to high price might be overcome by pointing out that the purchase is really an investment. Also, point out that the price of the product probably has not gone up any more than other items which the consumer has recently purchased.

Closing the sale

Salespersons often have the most difficulty with the close. Far too often they simply wait for the shopper to buy the goods instead of trying to close the sale. The customer often gives signals to an alert salesperson that a buying decision is at hand. Such signals may include questions about the use of the item, delivery, or payment. Facial expressions may also indicate that the customer is close to the buying stage. Several specific closing techniques are often used.[4]

The assumptive close. The assumptive close is a frequently used technique. Such questions as "Will this be cash or charge?" "Which color do you prefer? or "Would you like this delivered before this weekend?" can help you determine quickly whether the customer is ready to close.

Special sale or timing. Point out to the customer that the special sales offer is only good for today or perhaps for several more days. You also can point out that a good selection may not be available for very long because the items are quite popular and are selling fast. Try closing on a special concession. For example, offer to allow the customer to take the merchandise home over the weekend or for some other specified period for trial use.

Follow-up

Make sure that the merchandise is delivered on time, is in good condition, and that installation, if needed, is satisfactory. Take this opportunity to try to sell the customer an extended warranty on the merchandise, for example, if you did not do so in the process of initially closing the sale.

Above all, think back over the sale to determine what you have learned that will help you in your future sales efforts. Also, think about why some sales were not made and what you perhaps could have done to overcome the lack of a sale. Table 15–4 shows the most common reasons for losing a sale.

HOW CAN YOU INCREASE SALES FORCE PRODUCTIVITY?

Good management of the sales force means planning for increased sales. With selling expenses around 8 percent of sales, as shown in Table 15–5, and assuming pretax profits of 4 percent, a 10 percent increase or decrease in your selling expense ratio can affect your pretax profits as much as 20 percent! Also, selling costs are the most flexible payroll expense item in the short run.

The level of selling expense varies from store to store. The expense will even vary by department because of differences in merchandise and cus-

TABLE 15–4
Why sales are lost

Very often sales are lost through carelessness or indifference on the salesperson's part. Here are some reasons why:

1. **Disinterest.** Don't conduct a conversation with a fellow employee or another customer while waiting on someone. Give the customer your complete attention. Deadpan expressions, daydreaming, or "take it or leave it" attitudes leave merchandise unsold.

2. **Mistakes.** If you show the wrong item or make a mistake in change, acknowledge it and make the customer feel you are genuinely sorry.

3. **Appearing too anxious.** Show customers you want to serve their interests. Overinsistence and high-pressure tactics are objectionable to customers.

4. **Talking down other brands.** Talk up the brand you want to sell. Do not make unfair remarks about a competitive brand.

5. **Arguing.** Never argue with a customer. If it appears that an argument might develop, shift the conversation to another topic. There's little profit in winning an argument and losing the customer. If a customer makes an absurd statement, don't laugh or argue. You may anger the customer, and an angry customer is a lost customer.

6. **Being too long-winded.** A flood of words doesn't make many sales. Some people take time to make up their minds, and silence at the right time allows the customer to think and decide. Being a good listener often makes more sales than being a fast talker.

7. **Lack of courtesy.** Discourteous salespeople rarely last long on a job; they lose too many customers.

8. **Showing favoritism.** Never wait on your friends or favorite customers before taking care of customers who were there first.

9. **Being too hurried.** Take time to find out what a customer wants and then take time to show the merchandise properly.

10. **Embarrassing the customer.** Never laugh at a person who speaks with a foreign accent or correct a person who mispronounces words or product names.

11. **Misrepresenting merchandise.** Never guarantee any cures or make any claims for products that cannot be backed up by facts.

12. **Lack of product information.** Salespeople who are not well informed cannot expect to build a steady clientele for their store.

13. **Wasting customers' time.** When a customer is in a hurry, finish the sale as quickly as possible.

14. **Getting too personal.** Assume a professional attitude. Be sincere and friendly, but keep a touch of dignity and formality in all customer contacts. Never let familiarity creep into the conversation, for it is usually resented.

Source: R. Ted Will and Ronald Hasty, *Retailing* (New York: Canfield Press, 1977), p. 305.

tomer service needs. Regardless, your goal should always be to hold down selling costs without reducing sales.

What are your ways of increasing productivity in sales? You should always be trying to figure out how to meet customer service requirements without going over your expense budget. The typical activity of salespersons can be broken out as follows: 35 percent selling, 25 percent sales-supporting, 20 percent delay-idle, and 20 percent out of the area.[5] The percent of selling time thus can clearly be increased. How? One problem is overscheduling employees and not knowing how many salespersons are needed at a given time. Consider having less overtime and more part-time. Avoid peak "offs"

TABLE 15-5
Comparison of selling costs and total expenses of retail firms

	Selling costs as a percentage of sales	Total expense as a percentage of sales	Selling costs as a percentage of total expense
Department and specialty stores	7.73%	31.76%	24.3%
Furniture stores	7.21	36.41	19.8
Gift and novelty shops	9.79	26.74	36.6
Jewelry stores	9.8	38.5	25.5
Appliance and radio-TV dealers	5.0	28.3	17.7
Menswear stores	9.7	25.1	27.6

Source: David J. Rachman, *Retail Strategy and Structure,* 2d ed. (Englewood Cliffs, N.J.: Prentice-Hall, Inc., 1975), p. 263. Copyright 1975. Reprinted by permission of Prentice-Hall, Inc., Englewood Cliffs, New Jersey.

such as lunchtime. Think about split schedules. Also, use your salespersons for selling only. Such tasks as wrapping and shelf stocking can be done by lower cost nonselling persons.

Study Aid 15-1 provides some keys to good customer service and higher sales. Also, sales per person can be increased by:[6]

1. Better employee selection, training, and supervision.
2. Improved departmental layout.
3. More self-selection by customers.
4. Streamlining sales processing.
5. Improved merchandising and promotion.
6. Making sure salespersons fully know and understand the products they are selling.
7. Following up where necessary after the sale (for example, with the service department).

Better training and supervision

Sales training programs too often look only at the store system for ringing up sales. You need to understand how to complete the sale, but why ignore the selling process? Learning how to sell by trial and error results in many lost sales. Rarely are retail salespersons taught how to increase the amount of a sale, how to handle customer objections, good sales closing techniques, and how to handle several customers at once.

Often sales training programs do not even provide a basic knowledge of the items to be sold or focused on the need for good manners by the salespersons. A good training program also teaches them how to move from one area to another without losing sales effectiveness. Such movements require knowledge of items in the various departments. Training your sales personnel so they can move from one department to another in slack periods will also increase their earnings. The extra commissions earned will also help improve

STUDY AID 15-1

KEYS TO GOOD CUSTOMER SERVICE

1. Have an overall concept that customers are very important—that their actions will make or break the store.
2. Analyze what each customer is like before you try to make the sale.
3. Avoid assuming preconceived ideas on who will buy and who won't buy. (Stories are told of the barefoot oil heiress who was turned away from one store and spent thousands in the store of a competitor.)
4. Make each customer feel important regardless of the size of the sale.
5. Have patience with an irate customer. Do you react quickly in anger or do you respond quietly and calmly until the problem is settled?
6. Avoid talking to your friends while the customer waits impatiently.
7. Show courtesy to the people who are with the customers. A chair for a husband while his wife or daughter is trying on a dress is a small courtesy that may help increase your sales considerably.
8. Extend other courtesies such as explicit directions as to how to reach other departments or facilities.
9. Avoid being impatient on returns. Direct the person to where you know he/she will really be helped.
10. Know how to refuse credit without upsetting the customer. This means knowing what your credit regulations are.
11. Know when to trade up or use suggestive selling without badgering the customer.
12. Avoid acting hurriedly and impolitely when closing time is near and perhaps lose the last big sale of the day.
13. Listen carefully to what the customer really wants.
14. Try not to waste the customer's and your own time by useless chitchat.
15. Remember to thank the customer and ask her/him to come back.

Source: National Retail Merchants Association, *Checklist on Customer Service* (New York: National Retail Merchants Assoc., 1977), p. 3.

job satisfaction. Knowing when and how to handle returned items is important. But training in good sales techniques is even more important.

Improved departmental layout

Departmental layouts should be planned to allow the salesperson to ring up sales most easily. Keep the distances your salespersons have to move to a minimum. Arrange items so that your salespersons can locate them quickly and so that the customer can easily compare items.

More attention to self-selection

You can vary your level of sales staffing by department in this way. Good visual selling can occur by showing complete selections of items together, using signs, tags, and other labels to provide needed facts and selling points, including instructions for use.

Also try to know your customers' shopping habits. Some customers prefer to wait on themselves at their own pace. Salespersons should then be available to answer questions only if they arise.

Faster sales processing

Figure out ways to simplify the checkout. Use pre-wrapping whenever possible. Simplify the process of accepting customer checks by setting an amount below which back office clearance is not needed. Be aggressive in getting your customers to obtain and use a store credit card. Try to increase telephone sales.

WHAT ABOUT SALES TRAINING PROGRAMS?

You might wonder why the training of salespersons is necessary. Training makes good sense because it can increase employee sales levels, lead to better morale, higher job satisfaction, and lower job turnover. Also, training or retraining allows you to give your employees more knowledge about the items they sell and make them feel more a part of the firm.

Budget dollars for training just as you budget dollars for hiring salespersons. Look at training as a way to increase sales, not simply as another expense. Probably you agree that most people aren't lazy and want to succeed. But they can't succeed if you don't show them how through training. Customers will show their appreciation by increased levels of buying. Also add-on sales by your employees are almost pure profit since they add nothing to your expenses.

What should training include?

1. *Personnel should know something about the company for which they work.* Who started the company? How long has it been in business? What are the lines of merchandise it sells?

2. *What is expected of the salesperson?* Outline such things as your dress code, job skills which you expect, goals to be met by the personnel, and how you measure performance.

3. *Provide basic training in selling techniques.* Will your personnel need technical skills? Help your employees to understand their nonselling duties. We will look at training in sales techniques a little further in the chapter.

4. *Explain the company's promotion and fringe benefit policies.* Show your salespersons how the company can help them to advance. Does the company pay for education for the employees? What are the sick leave and annual leave policies? What benefits such as health and life insurance does the company provide?

What about training in sales techniques?

Let's look briefly at points to be included in the training of salespersons.

1. *Teach sales personnel how to greet customers.* The customer needs to feel welcome and know that the salesperson is ready and willing to provide information and assistance when needed.

The greeting can be used to help the salesperson find out what the customer is looking for. The salesperson can then begin to discuss such things as price, color, and selection.

2. *Train salespersons in how to present items.* Usually salespersons should begin with the medium-priced item and then watch for the customer's reaction in deciding whether to trade the customer up or down. Trading-up means trying to sell the person a higher quality (and higher priced) item. Trading-up can only be done if the customer knows the added benefits of the better product.

3. *Stress basic selling techniques.* Your salespersons must know the features of the product that will best meet the customer's needs. Train them to always think in terms of customer benefits. Help customers to buy with confidence. Point out the product guarantee, the brand of the item, and similar information.

4. *Train salespersons in how to overcome objections.* Get them to anticipate the objections the customers will have and to respond to them before they are raised. For example, talk about the good value and high quality of a product before the customer objects to the price.

5. *Train your personnel to ask for the sale.* Often closing the sale can be a hard moment for the salesperson. Such questions as "Would you like to pay cash or charge the item?" or "Which color do you prefer?" can often lead to a sale. But above all, salespersons should not rush or argue with the customer. Also, teach them to respond directly to customer's questions and objections. Or else the customer may lose confidence in the store.

6. *Train your salespersons to seek add-on sales.* Add-on sales are a result of suggestion selling. For example, if a customer purchases a suit, find out if he or she also needs items such as a tie or socks. In the case of appliances remind customers that service contracts can be purchased.

7. *Don't forget the follow-up.* Persons selling major items like cars or appliances should call the customer a few weeks after the sale to find out if the customer is still satisfied. This effort probably will impress the customer and may cause them to refer other persons to the firm.

8. *Remember to use telephone selling.* For example, salespersons may call a list of regular and preferred customers when new merchandise arrives which they think the customer will like.

Study Aid 15–2 outlines some other things salespersons should know before going on the sales floor.

**MANAGING RETAIL
SALES PERSONNEL**

One of the problems, especially in small stores, is that often no one person is in charge of sales personnel. Rather, you may fall into the trap of expecting your management people to do a little of everything. Try to have all of your sales-related functions handled by one office or person. But you may have several persons under this one individual who can supervise the selling in various parts of the store.

STUDY AID 15-2

THINGS TO KNOW BEFORE GOING ON THE SALES FLOOR

1. Know your store's policy on customer relations. Is the "customer always right?"
2. Know how to handle charge accounts and cash sales.
3. Know the credit cards your store honors.
4. Know the physical layout of the store. Where the different departments are, where exits, rest rooms, and other facilities are.
5. Know where to order more merchandise.
6. Know your store's policy on layaways.
7. Know your store's policy on returns.
8. Know where to get help immediately when you see someone shoplifting.
9. Know your store's policy on your own personal behavior and how you should dress for work.
10. Know your store's policy on lateness, absenteeism, sick leave, vacations, and holidays.
11. Know the disciplinary policy of the store.
12. Know where you fit in the whole picture—what authority you have.
13. Know the rules and regulations of the store on safety, energy conservation, checkout of packages, and so on.
14. Know the mechanics of the machines with which you will be working.
15. Identify *yourself* with the *store*.

Source: National Retail Merchants Assoc., *Checklist on Customer Service* (New York: National Retail Merchants Assoc. 1977), p. 2.

Set up performance standards and let your salespersons know what they are. Include nonselling activities if they are also expected. You cannot measure performance and take action where needed if you have not set standards. Hold periodic reviews with your salespeople. Also, make sure your salespersons have the tools they need and current information about the product they are selling. Make sure your people know how their performance will be measured. Performance may be judged on such bases as level of total sales, sales of selected items, number of returned items, or a similar standard.

Finally, decide on how you will reward employees who exceed the standards you have set. You may decide to give them an extra holiday with pay, hold a recognition dinner for outstanding persons, provide an extra merchandise discount for a set period of time, or provide a similar incentive. Let your employees know the recognition they will receive for a job well done. Many of the details of managing retail sales personnel were covered in Chapter 9 on staffing problems.

HOW WILL YOU PAY YOUR RETAIL SALESPEOPLE?

We covered the question of how to pay sales personnel in Chapter 9. However, it probably is good to briefly look at this topic once again since it is such an important part of a successful sales program. A commission in addition to a basic salary is usually paid to salespersons. The commission is an incentive for them to make higher levels of sales. Many retailers use a combination of a commission and a basic salary in order to keep retail salespersons from becoming too "pushy," which might happen if they were totally on commission. Also, a 100 percent commission plan can lead salespersons to ignore customers who they think are simply browsing or who are not likely to make large purchases.

In addition to salary, salespersons often receive a variety of indirect means of pay which are tax free. Often salespersons, for example, will receive a large discount on merchandise they purchase in the store, especially clothes. Clothing discounts are offered to encourage salespersons to dress appropriately for the store by which they are employed.

One final issue on the subject of pay needs to be brought up. Management works hard to motivate salespersons to perform at high levels of competence. Too often they fail to think about the persons at the checkout counter or in customer services, for example. They are an important part of the selling process. Too often all other elements in the store become slow, annoying, and time consuming to say the least. Personnel at the checkout counter, for example, need to be adequately paid so that they are as friendly, courteous, and efficient as the sales personnel in the store.

SUMMARY

The trend in retailing is toward more self-service by customers. Improved signing, displays, packaging, and store layouts all make self-service possible. But you still may need salespersons to answer customer questions about technical products, reassure customers about items of fashion apparel, and to help customers fit items such as shoes.

The quality of retail selling is often poor. Training or retraining of employees is not good. The training which does occur too often focuses on the store and its policies and not on how to sell. A little more time spent in training salespersons would result in almost pure profit since you could get more from the same person.

The problem of salespersons is nonending. You can't expect high performance if you pay low wages to untrained persons. Yet, you can't pay higher rates unless higher sales occur. Other problems in hiring good retail employees include problems of long hours and evening hours. Retailers are turning more and more to part-time people including students, persons wanting a second job, and persons who only want to work a few hours each week. These kinds of persons help keep wage rates low and fringe benefits to a minimum. But they are largely untrained, change jobs often, and have little loyalty to the company. It's no wonder that retailers are increasingly moving to self-service.

What can we offer as guides to you? A move to more self-service by informative signs, displays, and item arrangements is possible if customer shopping habits allow it. If salespersons are needed, look at training as a way to increase sales, not simply as a higher expense item. Help your employees to increase their sales levels so that you can increase the wage rates paid to them. A good sales team gives you a strong edge on competition.

NOTES

1. Don L. James, Bruce J. Walker, and Michael J. Etzel, *Retailing Today* (New York: Harcourt, Brace, Jovanovich, 1975), p. 352.
2. Kenneth H. Mills and Judith E. Paul, *Successful Retail Sales* (Englewood Cliffs, N.J.: Prentice-Hall, Inc., 1979), p. 44.
3. Robert Spohn and Robert W. Allen, *Retailing* (Reston, Va.: Reston Publishing Company, 1977), p. 246.
4. Gerald Pintel and Jay Diamond, *Retailing* (Englewood Cliffs, N.J.: Prentice-Hall, Inc., 1977), pp. 298–99.
5. Steven Cron, "Control of Retail Selling Costs," *Retail Control* (August 1976), p. 60.
6. This material is based on Edwin W. Crooks, Jr., "Improved Department Store Selling," *Journal of Retailing* (Summer 1962), pp. 34–40.

DISCUSSION QUESTIONS

1. What are the various types of retail selling? How do the skills required vary by type of selling?
2. Why is training and retraining of salespersons so important?
3. What are the major ways of increasing sales force productivity?
4. Why is self-service and self-selection becoming more common in retailing?
5. What are some of the things which can be done to make self-service more attractive to customers?
6. Review the basic techniques of retail selling.
7. What should be the content of a good retail sales training program?
8. What are the problems in using part-time persons in selling?
9. What could be done to make retail selling more attractive as a career?

PROJECTS

1. Visit with the personnel manager of the leading department store in your community and discuss briefly their training programs for salespeople. Find out what fringe benefits are available to the salespersons and their major problems with sales personnel. Do the same thing with the manager of a fast-food franchise. Be prepared to discuss the differences you find.

2. Interview 10–15 of your student friends and find out their overall impression of salespersons in your community. Are they satisfied? If yes, why? If not, why not? Get their thoughts on what can be done to improve the quality of service in retail outlets. Now, talk to several of your friends who have worked for or are working as part-time salespersons. Prepare a report based on their experiences. Get them to talk

about their reaction to most customers in the stores where they work, their likes and dislikes about their jobs, and what could be done to make their jobs easier.

3. Visit three of the new car dealers in your community and act as a serious buyer. Develop a list of questions ahead of time about such things as miles per gallon of the auto, service requirements, warranty, and safety features. Compare and contrast the results you get in talking to the different salespersons about each of these points. Find out if they have what you consider the needed knowledge for selling the product. Do they conduct themselves in the way you would expect from persons who are selling items valued at $5,000–15,000? If not, make suggestions for improving their quality of service to customers.

Minicase 15-1

Al Linear recently told the following story to Sam McGee, his long-time friend and part-owner of A&T sporting goods. "I was in your store last week to purchase a tennis racket. Several other people whom I know were also in the store. Suddenly Mary (the store manager) yelled across the store and said, 'Al, when are you going to pay your bill here? It's overdue you know.' What else could I say but 'Don't worry, Mary, I'll take care of it soon.' Sam, I am so mad I probably will not go back to that store again. Mary really overstepped her bounds and embarrassed me in front of a couple of friends and one of my customers. Besides, the bill was only two days overdue."

Mary and Al had been acquaintances since their high school days. Mary was recently appointed as store manager and supervised the other two salespersons.

What did Mary do wrong? What had Mr. McGee failed to do? How would you make sure that such a situation did not develop again?

Minicase 15-2

Patsy Brown recently went into the local bank at noon to deposit several small checks totaling $250. She requested $50 back in cash. The teller correctly made out the deposit slip for $200 but gave Patsy $200 in cash and kept the $50. Patsy knows that the error is not traceable since she has a deposit slip stating that she deposited $200. She left the bank with the money and told her husband, who is an officer of the bank at another branch, about it. She asked him to take care of the situation. "Besides," she said, "banks ought to pay more attention to the training they give their personnel. After all, bank tellers are just like salespersons in a department store. You should have your best people up front. Mistakes like this should not happen. To make matters worse, the teller was sitting down looking at a Tupperware catalog while the other teller was trying to wait on two customers. I had to ask her to wait on me."

Mr. Brown brought up the case at the next meeting of the Management Committee. What steps would you take to make sure this kind of thing doesn't happen again?

16

WHAT ARE THE KEYS TO SUCCESSFUL PROMOTION?

The purposes of this chapter are to help you understand:

- The requirements for good promotion plans.
- How to establish advertising budgets.
- Media options available to you.
- How to determine the effectiveness of media.
- How to measure the results of advertising.
- Whether to use an ad agency.
- The essentials of a good advertisement.
- Special promotional events.
- Principles of display.
- The meaning of the following terms:

Co-op advertising
Percent-of-sales method of budget
    allocation
The task method of budget allocation
The media mix
Advertising supplements
Retail advertising rates

General advertising rates
Column inch rate
Cost per thousand
Reach
Frequency

Promotion means communication from the retailer to the consumer in order to achieve a profitable sales level. Some persons define promotion to include advertising, personal selling, and displaying of merchandise. Personal selling was covered in detail in Chapter 15 and store display and layout in Chapter 6. We define promotion in this chapter as communicating with consumers. Promotion includes advertising of all types, publicity, coupons, trading stamps and premium offers. We also highlight the principles of merchandise display.

Promotion is a key factor in the merchandising mix. Your promotion should fit in with pricing and other elements of the mix. Otherwise, a poor image will result. Begin with the goals of the firm. Decide on (1) who you want to reach, (2) what you want to sell them, (3) the message you want to get across, and (4) when and how often the message should reach the audience.

As we saw in Chapter 2, you cannot be all things to all people. You have to segment your messages, your markets, and your merchandise. Above all, understand your customer.

WHAT ARE YOUR GOALS?

Promotion plans begin with what you want to do. Your plans can include any or all of the tasks shown in Table 16–1. But even the best ads cannot change an image overnight, or make a store better than its location. Promotions really have two goals: (1) build store traffic, and (2) build a strong image. But image is based on all parts of the retail mix, not just advertising.

WHAT MAKES FOR GOOD PROMOTION PLANS?

The key to good promotions is planning. Define your goals, decide how to meet them, and on the funds needed. Develop the right media mix.

If we agree that the basic goals of advertising are:

1. To communicate the total character of the store.
2. To get consumer acceptance for individual groups of merchandise.
3. To have a strong flow of traffic.
4. To sell goods directly.

By combining these goals with merchandising and store image objectives, the following framework can be a useful guide[1]:

What to advertise .... merchandise
When to advertise .... timing
Where to say it .... media
How to say it .... technique
Whom to reach .... audience
How to provide balance .... planning

HOW DO YOU SET BUDGETS?

Begin with a good budget. A budget is the amount of money set aside for each department or each promotion.

Why have a budget? A budget forces you to plan. This step alone can go a long way toward better ads. Why? (1) You are forced to make decisions

TABLE 16-1
Some tasks for retail promotions

1. Increase the variety and volume of merchandise and services sold to present customers.

2. Step up traffic in dull periods.

3. Clear leftover merchandise at the end of a selling season.

4. Develop weak departments into strong ones, and create ad awareness of new departments (or services that may not have been offered in the past).

5. Turn special opportunities like manufacturers' cooperative advertising offers or townwide promotional events into sources of sales for the store.

6. Attract new customers from among newcomers to the community, those dissatisfied with other stores, and those interested in new products, new fashions, and bargains.

7. Penetrate or create new markets for the store's goods and services.

8. Hold on to present customers when competitors make overtures to them, and win over other stores' customers.

9. Build up the store's reputation.

10. Introduce a new product.

11. Increase the sales of a product by suggesting new uses for it.

12. Build goodwill by providing a public service.

13. Directly support the store's personal selling program.

14. Reach customers who seldom or never come in person to the store.

15. Acquire a list of prospects for salespersons to call on.

16. Increase shopper traffic (and hence sales) in the district or shopping center as a whole.

17. Encourage more people to become charge account customers of the store or use bank credit cards.

18. Make people more aware of conveniences offered by the store, including free or inexpensive parkings, delivery service, and evening, weekend, or holiday shopping hours.

19. Build consumer confidence by explaining how to select, use, and care for certain types of merchandise.

20. Identify the store with specific nationally advertised brands.

21. Produce telephone and mail orders.

22. Contribute to the store's overall public relations effort.

23. Explain store policies, including "negative" ones that will have less adverse effect on the public if they are fully understood.

24. Reach the public quickly with messages of an emergency nature.

Source: William Haight, *Retail Advertising: Management and Technique* (Morristown, N.J.: Silver Burdette Co., 1976), pp. 139-40. Copyright 1976, Silver Burdett Company. Reprinted by permission.

among the choices open. (2) Budgets are more likely to result in well-planned ads. (3) A budget forces you to set goals so you can measure the success of your plans.

What should be in the budget? Most people can't agree on just what should be in the budget. Still, Table 16-2 shows the items usually included. They are the cost of media space and time, supplies, salaries, and artwork.

What should you spend for advertising? The amount to spend is hard to answer. However, you can choose among several methods.

The most common method is percent of sales. Advertising is budgeted as a percent of last year's sales or as a percent of projected sales. The percent of sales average by store type spent on advertising is shown in Table 16-3. Normally 2-3 percent of sales is spent.

TABLE 16–2
Master budget planning chart

		Salaries	Newspapers	Periodicals & programs	Shows & exhibits	Supplies	Cuts, art, & mats	Miscellaneous	Radio & TV	Direct mail	Display supplies	Display payroll	Reserve	Total publicity expense	Sales
JAN	1979														
	%														
	1980														
	%														
FEB	1979														
	%														
	1980														
	%														
MARCH	1979														
	%														
	1980														
	%														
APRIL	1979														
	%														
	1980														
	%														
MAY	1979														
	%														
	1980														
	%														
JUNE	1979														
	%														
	1980														
	%														
First 6 months	1979														
	%														
	1980														
	%														

Source: National Retail Merchants Association, *1979 Merchandising Planbook & Sales Promotion Calendar* (New York: National Retail Merchants Association, 1978).

TABLE 16–3
Advertising budget guide

Commodity or class of business	Percent of sales average	Commodity or class of business	Percent of sales average
Appliance, radio, TV dealers	2.3%	Home centers	1.3
Auto accessory and parts stores	0.9	Hotels	7.0
Auto dealers (new car/franchised)	0.8	Insurance agents, brokers	1.8
Auto parking and repair service	0.9	Jewelry stores	4.4
Bakeries	0.7	Laundromats	1.2
Banks (commercial)	1.3	Liquor stores	0.9
Beauty shops	2.0	Lumber and building	
Book stores	1.7	Material dealers	0.9
Camera stores	0.8	Menswear stores	2.8
Children's and infant's wear stores	1.4	Motion-picture theaters	5.5
Credit agencies (personal)	2.4	Music stores	1.8
Department stores	2.8	Office supplies dealers	0.7
$1,000,000–$2,000,000	2.5	Paint, glass, and wallpaper stores	2.4
$2,000,000–$5,000,000	2.9	Photographic studios and	
$5,000,000–$20,000,000	2.8	supply shops	2.4
$20,000,000–$50,000,000	2.7	Real estate (subdividers, developers,	
$50,000,000 and over	2.4	operative builders, and combina-	
Discount stores	2.4	tions of real estates, insurance,	
Drugstores		loan, and law offices)	3.6
Chain drugstores	1.7	Restaurants	0.8
Independent drugstores	1.3	Savings banks (mutual)	1.5
Dry cleaning shops	1.7	Savings and loan associations	1.5
Florists	2.1	Shoe stores	1.9
Food chains	1.1	Specialty stores	3.0
Furniture stores	5.0	Sporting goods stores	3.5
Gasoline service stations	0.8	Tire dealers	2.2
Gift and novelty stores	1.4	Travel agents	5.0
Hardware stores	1.6	Variety stores	1.5

Source: William L. McGee, *A Marketing Approach to Building Store Traffic with Broadcast Advertising* (San Francisco: Broadcast Marketing Company, 1978), p. 168.

The advantage of the percent of sales method is that the amount to be spent on advertising is *easy* to calculate. However, sales determines the amount of money to be spent on advertising when using this approach. Logically, advertising should help determine the level of sales, not the other way around. Still, many retailers use this approach because they are unable to determine the relationship between sales and promotion.

A second method is the *task method*. Here you set the goals of the firm for the next year. For example you may want to increase the sales of a certain item by 10 percent. Budgets are then set to reach this goal. This is a better way than percent of sales.

Advertising can be budgeted by week, month, quarter, or semiannually by department. These budgets are then totaled to set the overall budget.

Too many managers do a bad job of budgeting. For example, some do what they did last year without looking to see if things have changed. The budget should be looked at each year for improvement.

Above all, don't simply copy the budget of your competition. Who knows? Maybe their plan is a dog and they may be overspending to support the dog!

Also, consider co-op ads to stretch your budget. Co-oping means the cost of advertising is split by two or more persons. Often a supplier will pay part of the cost. You can increase your ad budget this way.

No magic formula exists for setting budgets. You need to consider (1) competition, (2) the goals of the firm (3) the prices of ads, (4) the need to reach certain market segments, and (5) the market coverage of various media.

Study Aid 16–1 shows the ten steps of the National Retail Merchants Association for planning budgets. Begin by dividing the budget into expense groups. Next, make plans for storewide and departmental promotions by the month. Then, plan weekly budgets. An example of a six-month budget chart was shown in Table 16–2. Such charts should be keyed to major selling themes as shown in Table 16–4.

Dividing your budget by line of goods is not easy. One way is by department or merchandise line sales as a percentage of total sales. But sales can vary by month. Thus your allocations should also vary.

Monthly percentages of annual sales by store type are shown in Table 16–5. But the best selling times vary by region. Also economic conditions can cause you to change your budget plans. Other ways for allocating funds are the traffic drawing power of some items, or the growth potential of key lines.

Cooperative advertising is one way to extend ad dollars. Cooperative advertising occurs when the manufacturer pays part of the cost for advertising at the retail level. Often such allowances are based on the amount of goods purchased. Such ads now account for 25 percent of all retail advertising. Often the co-op ads are part of an overall campaign being run nationally by the supplier.

Retailers often obtain a lower per unit ad rate from the media for co-op advertising. Such advertising also provides small retailers with professional ads developed by ad agencies. This process brings more professionalism than management could develop on its own and can greatly help the image of the store. Co-op ads are sometimes tied to window displays and other types of sales promotion activities. In spite of their popularity, however, more than $1 billion budgeted for co-op ads by manufacturers each year go un-spent. These funds are a gold mine for the smart retailer.

WHAT ARE YOUR MEDIA OPTIONS?

Radio is becoming more popular, as is TV. Newspapers are becoming less popular but are by far the number one medium. But no longer is a good feel for newspaper promotions enough.

STUDY AID 16-1

TAKE THESE TEN STEPS TO BETTER SALES PROMOTION PLANNING

A. Enter last year's figures

On the Master Budget Planning Chart (Table 16–2) enter your store's sales promotion and publicity expenses and actual sales by month for 1979.

B. Enter your 1980 planned sales goals

On the Master Budget Planning Chart (Table 16–2) enter your store's six-month sales goals for 1980.

Next, distribute your store's total planned volume by months, recognizing that the pattern of sales tends to repeat itself year after year. Table 16–5 shows how store sales are distributed by month.

C. Decide how much and what kind of promotion is needed

When your store sales goals are set, determine how much promotional effort the store needs to reach these goals. The type of store, location, nature of competition, media rates and coverage, and business conditions will play a part in making this decision.

D. Assign expenditures to each publicity classification

When your total sales promotion budget is decided, break this down into the various publicity expense classifications on the Master Budget Planning Chart (Table 16–2). Many stores divide these appropriations into two six-month periods.

See what various stores spent percentagewise on advertising in Table 16–3.

E. Determine total store monthly budget

Break your six-month total store budget down into individual months. In general, it is wise to promote in proportion to volume expected. Closely parallel your advertising to your sales curve.

F. Set aside a budget reserve

To avoid overspending, designate an amount of the total budget for institutional advertising and as a reserve for special promotions such as new items, special purchases, community drives, and so on. Many stores reserve 10 percent; some withhold as high as 20 percent.

G. Allocate six-month appropriations by departments

The next step is to distribute advertising dollars to each department. Allocate money in proportion to sales volume. Capitalize on your strengths.

H. Plan your major promotions

Advance planning is the key to better sales promotion. Good stores plan their major promotions six months ahead. They hold periodic reviews of these plans as the target dates approach. Consider the following opportunities for department stores:

1. Fashion shows.
   a. Fashion shows.

b. Spring and fall fashion campaigns.

c. Campaign on store's own brands.

2. Departmental promotions.

a. February sales of furniture.

b. March sales of housewares.

c. Home sewing week.

d. Women's coat event.

e. Graduation campaign.

f. Travel week, baby week.

g. Fur storage campaign, August fur sale.

3. Usual storewide or multiple department events

a. Anniversary sales.

b. Spring or May sales.

c. Mother's Day, Father's Day, Easter.

d. White sales.

e. Month-end sales.

f. Clearances

g. Special storewide sales, such as Thrift Day, Opportunity Day, Dollar Day, Remnant Day, and so on.

4. Storewide or departmental import fairs and promotions.

5. Institutional campaigns and special events.

I. Make the monthly sales promotion plan

About six to eight weeks prior to any given month, collate all scheduled advertisements into a master plan. The master plan is comparatively simple. You list the size of the advertisement or broadcast schedule, the newspaper(s) or broadcast station(s), the date, the promotion, the prices, the store's planned sale of the day, and so on.

Simultaneously, of course, all the other advertising media must be planned . . . direct mail, radio, TV, and so on. Scheduling of window space is also done at this time.

J. Prepare daily advertising

Day-to-day advertising roughs are made from these plans with a minimum of checking. There should be room within this framework for special purchases or repeats of a sellout or clearances which could not be anticipated or planned. That is the reason for the suggested 10 percent to 20 percent reserve.

Source: National Retail Merchants Association, *1979 Merchandising Planbook and Sales Promotion Calendar,* (New York: National Retail Merchants Association, 1978).

As shown below, the cost of advertising climbed rapidly between 1970 and 1977[2]:

	Percent
Newspaper rates increased	79
Spot radio rates increased	83
Spot television rates increased	30
Magazine rates increased	40
Outdoor advertising rates increased	42

TABLE 16-4
Merchandising-promotional opportunities

Flower of the month—Snowdrop or carnation
Birthstone of the month—Garnet

January

Accessories sales	Foundation and lingerie sales
Art needlework	Fur sales
Baby needs sales	Luggage sales
Bedding, furniture, floor covering and home furnishings sales	Men's and women's apparel sales
	Notions, yarn and fabric sales
Blankets, comforters, spreads	Pre-inventory sales
Bridal show	Resort wear (both north and south)
Commercial stationery sales	Storewide clearances
Diamond sales	TV and radio sales
Domestics	White sales
Dryers, irons, water heaters	Women's, misses' coats, suits sales
Drug and cosmetic sales	

Tie-in events

Tuesday	January	1	First Rose Bowl Game (1902) Orange Bowl (1933) Sugar Bowl (1935), and Cotton Bowl (1937)
			Emancipation Proclamation, 1863
			New Year's Day (United States, and Canada)
Wednesday	January	2	Georgia entered union as fourth state, 1788
Thursday	January	3	Alaskan statehood, 1959
Friday	January	4	Utah entered Union as 45th state, 1896
Sunday	January	6	Old Christmas Day (Epiphany)
Monday	January	7	Millard Fillmore born, 1800
			First national election, 1789
Tuesday	January	8	Battle of New Orleans, 1815
Thursday	January	10	First session of UN General Assembly, London, 1946
Sunday	January	13	First Sunday School in United States started by Philadelphia Quakers, 1791
Monday	January	14	First written Constitution adopted at Hartford, 1639
Tuesday	January	15	Dr. Martin Luther King born, 1929
Thursday	January	17	Benjamin Franklin born, 1709
Saturday	January	19	Robert E. Lee born, 1807
Sunday	January	20	First basketball game, 1892
Monday	January	21	Stonewall Jackson born, 1824
Saturday	January	26	Gen. Douglas MacArthur Day, Memorial Day in Arkansas Michigan entered Union as 26th state, 1837
Tuesday	January	29	William McKinley born, 1843
Wednesday	January	30	Franklin D. Roosevelt born, 1882, Legal holiday in Kentucky

Other important local dates

Source: *1979 Merchandising Planning and Sales Promotion Calendar* (New York: National Retail Merchants Association, 1979), p. 58.

Few retail ad budgets grew as fast. Thus, fewer *real* dollars exist for promotions. Yet promotion is more important than ever to reach target audiences, draw store traffic, and sell goods. Good media choice is a key. A media mix should be planned for each promotion.

Each medium has its strengths and weaknesses. Use a *media mix* to give

TABLE 16-5

Average monthly percentages of annual sales—For 46 U.S. retail business categories (percent)

Kind of business	Jan.	Feb.	Mar.	Apr.	May
All retail stores:	7.4	7.0	7.9	8.1	8.6
Appliance stores	8.2	7.1	7.4	7.7	7.8
Auto dealers:					
New cars	7.5	7.4	8.6	8.6	9.2
Used cars	7.8	7.9	8.9	9.0	9.9
Foreign cars	6.6	6.0	8.1	8.1	8.5
Auto loans	7.1	7.3	8.4	9.1	9.1
Bakeries	7.9	7.8	8.3	8.1	8.4
Beauty shops	8.2	7.8	8.1	8.2	8.3
Bedding	7.6	7.6	8.6	8.0	7.9
Boating	2.3	3.9	11.8	14.3	14.2
Bookstores	6.3	9.2	7.0	5.8	7.0
Building supplies	5.9	6.3	7.3	8.2	8.7
Carpets	7.0	9.0	13.0	11.0	9.0
Department stores	6.3	5.7	7.3	7.6	8.0
Drugstores	7.9	7.7	8.9	7.7	8.2
Dry cleaners	6.5	7.2	8.8	10.5	12.6
Family clothing stores	6.3	5.7	7.8	7.6	8.1
Farm equipment	4.9	5.4	7.6	9.4	9.5
Florists	7.3	7.1	8.1	8.9	8.2
Food stores	8.1	7.5	8.1	7.9	8.7
Furniture stores	7.7	7.1	7.7	7.9	8.4
Garden supplies	3.9	2.8	10.0	16.1	17.1
Gasoline stations	7.8	7.2	8.0	8.2	8.7
Hardware stores	6.2	5.7	6.3	7.8	9.3
Heating and plumbing	8.2	7.9	8.7	8.3	7.9
Hotels/motels	7.3	7.4	7.9	7.7	8.2
Insurance	7.0	7.6	8.6	8.6	8.2
Investments	8.7	7.6	7.4	7.5	8.5
Jewelry stores	5.8	5.9	8.1	7.9	6.7
Loan companies	7.2	6.8	7.9	8.4	8.5
Menswear	7.4	5.9	7.0	7.7	8.0
Mobile homes	6.0	6.0	7.4	9.9	8.2
Motorcycles	7.7	8.8	7.1	6.9	9.6
Movies	9.3	7.5	7.6	8.4	8.1
Music stores	7.7	7.4	7.9	6.5	6.7
Office supplies	8.3	7.8	9.2	7.6	7.8
Paint	5.6	6.7	8.5	8.6	9.3
Photo dealers	7.0	6.0	6.0	7.0	7.0
Real estate (houses)	7.3	7.9	8.8	9.1	9.0
Restaurants	7.3	7.0	7.7	8.0	8.8
Savings and loans					
(savings)	12.0	8.0	8.6	9.6	6.1
Shoe stores	6.5	5.9	8.4	8.9	8.0
Sporting goods	4.0	3.0	4.0	10.0	11.0
Tire dealers	6.6	6.0	7.3	8.7	9.0
Trucks	7.1	6.1	7.6	9.2	9.2
Variety stores	5.9	6.8	7.5	7.2	8.3
Women's wear	6.8	6.3	7.7	8.0	8.2

Source: William McGee, *A Marketing Approach to Building Store Traffic with Broadcast Advertising* (San Francisco: Broadcast Marketing Company, 1978), p. 205

June	July	Aug.	Sept.	Oct.	Nov.	Dec.
8.6	8.5	8.3	8.2	8.7	8.3	10.3
8.4	8.6	8.2	8.0	8.6	8.3	11.7
9.3	8.5	7.8	7.8	9.1	8.4	7.7
9.2	8.5	8.4	7.6	8.0	7.6	7.2
9.6	9.1	8.9	8.4	9.1	8.1	9.4
9.4	9.4	8.4	7.8	8.9	7.5	7.5
8.4	7.9	8.1	8.2	8.9	8.9	9.0
8.3	8.3	8.3	8.4	8.4	8.5	9.3
8.9	9.1	9.4	9.6	8.6	7.4	8.0
20.7	11.9	8.9	4.1	3.0	2.2	2.7
5.8	5.3	4.9	10.7	8.2	11.0	18.8
9.4	9.5	9.6	9.3	9.5	8.3	7.8
8.0	5.0	4.0	12.0	9.0	7.0	6.0
7.9	7.6	8.0	8.1	8.7	9.6	15.4
8.2	8.2	8.4	8.1	8.5	8.1	11.1
8.0	6.3	4.6	7.5	11.4	9.5	7.1
7.7	7.5	8.2	7.6	8.8	9.1	15.5
9.8	9.3	8.6	9.9	10.7	7.4	7.5
8.2	8.3	8.2	8.3	8.3	7.9	11.4
8.3	8.5	8.7	8.1	8.7	8.4	9.0
8.6	8.3	8.5	8.2	8.7	8.9	10.0
12.5	8.1	8.6	5.6	3.7	4.0	7.6
8.8	9.1	8.6	8.1	8.5	8.3	8.6
9.8	9.4	8.7	8.3	8.9	8.4	11.2
7.9	8.1	8.3	8.5	8.7	9.0	8.5
9.0	10.5	10.8	8.4	8.6	7.2	6.9
8.8	8.3	7.9	7.9	8.6	8.6	10.1
8.8	8.3	6.5	9.3	10.0	7.1	10.3
6.7	7.1	7.5	7.5	8.2	8.4	20.3
9.2	9.1	8.6	8.2	8.3	7.9	9.8
8.3	7.2	7.6	7.6	8.2	9.4	15.7
8.9	9.3	9.6	10.3	10.2	7.6	6.7
13.9	9.0	10.0	7.3	6.8	7.0	5.9
8.6	10.1	9.6	8.8	7.7	7.7	7.5
7.1	6.0	6.5	9.0	8.8	9.1	14.5
8.1	7.6	8.6	8.6	8.3	8.3	9.8
10.6	10.0	9.8	9.4	8.0	7.0	6.3
9.0	9.0	9.0	8.0	7.0	10.0	16.0
9.0	8.9	9.5	8.4	8.1	7.3	6.8
8.9	9.1	9.4	8.7	8.8	8.1	8.3
8.6	10.0	6.0	7.7	7.9	6.0	9.5
8.1	7.3	9.1	9.0	8.6	8.7	11.6
14.0	11.0	7.0	7.0	7.0	8.0	14.0
9.3	9.2	8.6	8.1	8.9	8.7	9.6
8.5	9.0	8.1	7.9	9.2	7.8	9.8
7.8	7.6	8.0	7.9	8.4	8.9	16.7
7.8	7.4	8.0	8.2	8.9	9.1	13.6

you the strengths of each when combined with the other. Your media choices are radio, TV, daily and weekly newspapers, shoppers, magazines, direct mail, outdoor and transit. These media are compared in Table 16–6.

How do you evaluate radio?

Radio is popular with retailers because it is a local medium. Most programming is local except for news and weather.

Radio stations segment their programming to appeal to specific groups. For example, stations may play country music, popular music, be known for talk shows, or as black or Spanish market stations. Each of these programs has a different audience. With radio you can (1) choose stations with the audiences you want, and (2) schedule ads when your market will be listening.

Radio rates are based on the size of the audience at given times in a day. The price you pay depends on when you want your commercial to be broadcast. Retailers tend to buy 10-, 30-, or 60-second spots.

The strengths of radio. They are (1) the way to reach a large audience, (2) to limit your ads to target audiences, (3) the ability to reach people at home, in their cars, on the beach, and almost anywhere else, and (4) low cost.

Major *problems* are: (1) no pictures, (2) short messages, (3) the need to use several stations in large cities to reach a large target audience, (4) production problems since most programming is local, and (5) large wasted audiences for small local retailers.

How do you evaluate TV?

Many persons say that TV has the most overall strength of any medium. TV has the visual impact of print and the sound impact of radio plus color, motion, and emotion. People now spend as much time viewing TV as with radio, newspapers, and magazines combined.

Local TV stations carry the programs of one of the three networks, ABC, NBC, or CBS. These programs include the ads bought by national retailers such as Sears. The stations sell local ad time during station breaks. *You should plan to use daytime, newsprograms, and early evening times—the hours before TV prime time.*

TV ads are costly. The cost for a 30-second commercial in prime time (8 P.M.–11 P.M.) in a small local market may cost $50–$60 and go up to several thousand dollars for a local ad in a major market.

The strengths of TV for local retailers include: (1) the ability to reach target audiences, (2) color, (3) emotion, and (4) the chance to combine sight, color, music, motion, and emotion. *Problems* are (1) the high cost of time, (2) high production costs, (3) most people view TV at night after stores are closed, and (4) low summer viewing.

Cost per viewer is the lowest for a national audience. Few retail firms other than Penneys, Wards, Sears, and Kmart, however, have enough outlets to justify national TV ads. Use of local TV by large retailers is up. But no more than 4 percent of retail ad budgets go to TV today.

What about newspapers?

About 70 percent of all retail ad dollars go to newspapers. Most markets have some type of newspaper. Newspaper ad supplements are very popular. (*Supplements* are preprinted pages of ads which are inserted into the papers.) Sunday papers are usually full of them. Local department stores are heavy users.

Newspaper ad rates are quoted as weekly insertion rates for short-term advertisers, as monthly rates, and as yearly rates. Newspapers quote local retailers a *retail rate* which is below the *general rate* (charged to agencies for national advertisers).

Newspapers talk in terms of column inches at the retail level when quoting prices. A *column inch* is one column wide and one inch deep. Special rates are set for supplements. Also, color rates are higher than black and white rates.

The *strengths* of newspapers include: (1) broad market coverage, (2) short lead time for ads, (3) the large number of items you can advertise at once, (4) wide use by most persons needing shopping information, and (5) assistance in ad preparation (important for a small retailer). *Weaknesses* include: (1) problems in reaching the younger market and children, (2) the chance of many readers missing an ad, (3) fast rising rates, (4) little ability to segment readers, and (5) lower suburban coverage by big city papers.

The newspaper office can also be a great help in planning your copy and layout. Many small retailers have few skills in these areas and rely on the newspaper professionals to provide the needed services.

Should you use magazines?

Until recently the only retailers using magazines were national firms such as Penneys or Sears. However, local retailers can now place ads in regional editions of such magazines as *Time* and *TV Guide*.

Magazine *strengths* include: (1) well-defined audiences, (2) good color, (3) long ad life, and (4) low cost per thousand. The primary *problems* are (1) high cost, (2) long closing dates, (3) slower response, and (4) wasted circulation.

What about direct mail?

Direct mail is "the" most selective form of retail advertising. But cost per person reached is high. Direct mail is among the top three forms of retail advertising today.

Most retailers use some form of direct mail. The *strengths* include: (1) the high response rate by consumers, (2) ability to send material to a specific person, (3) not being bound by media format (you may use as much space as needed to tell the story of your product and use colors or other creative effects as your budget allows), and (4) your message does not have to compete with other editorial matter. The *weakness* is the high cost compared to other media. Mailing costs alone are 7.5 cents per letter or $75 per thousand for third-class mailing. This per thousand cost is many times higher than for other media.

TABLE 16–6
Strengths and weaknesses of various retail advertising media

Medium	Market coverage	Type of audience	Sample time/space costs

Radio	Definable market area surrounding the station's location, coverage area varies by strength of signal.	Selected audiences provided by stations with distinct programming formats.	Per 60-second morning drive time spot:
			Pop: 25,000 $ 7.50
			       250,000 25.00
			    1,000,000 76.00

Television	Definable market area surrounding the station's location. Extended by cable into outlying areas.	Varies with the time of day; tends toward younger age group, less print-oriented.	Per 30-second daytime spot. highest priority status:
			Pop: 100,000 $ 40.00
			     500,000 75.00
			  7,000,000 350.00

Daily newspaper	Single community or entire metro area; zoned editions sometimes available.	General. Tends more toward men, older age group, slightly higher income and education.	Per agate line, daily:
			Circ: 20,000 $0.36
			     50,000 0.58
			   250,000 1.34

Weekly newspaper	Single community usually; mostly nonmetro.	General; usually residents of a smaller community.	Per agate line, weekly:
			Circ: 5,000 $0.15
			    10,000 0.31
			    30,000 0.40

Shopper	Most households in a small community; chain shoppers can cover a metro area.	Consumer households.	Per agate line, shoppers:
			Circ: 10,000 $0.08
			    20,000 0.20
			    50,000 0.43

Magazines	Metro area/regional editions sometimes available; city-oriented magazines available in large metro areas.	Selected audiences by special interests.	Full page, black and white: Circ: 25,000 $ 875.00 60,000 1,958.00
Direct mail	Advertiser-controlled.	Controlled by the advertiser through use of demographic lists.	Postage costs only: 1st cl. $0.15/oz; 3d cl. $0.20/oz.; 3d cl. (bulk piece rate, 300 or more) $0.084/oz.

Outdoor	Entire metro area or single neighborhood.	General, especially auto drivers.	Per 12′ × 25′ poster; 100 GRP per month:
			Pop: 25,000 $ 400.00
			    100,000 2,100.00
			  1,000,000 10,946.00

Transit	Urban or metro community served by transit system; may be limited to a few transit routes.	Transit riders, especially wage earners and shoppers; pedestrians.	Per inside 11″ × 28″ card; full run; 25 buses: $108.00 90 buses: 180.00 230 buses: 400.00

Source: William McGee, *A Marketing Approach to Building Store Traffic with Broadcast Advertising* (San Francisco; Broadcast Marketing Company, 1978), pp. 232–33.

Particular suitability	Major Advantage	Major disadvantage
Business catering to identifiable groups: teens, commuters, housewives.	Market selectivity, reach and frequency. Highly flexible to meet changing needs.	No visual presentation of product
Sellers of products or services with wide appeal.	Dramatic impact, wide market coverage, audience selectivity by program type.	Relatively high cost of time and production
All general retailers.	Flexibility; ease of ad production.	Nonselective audience.
Retailers who service a strictly local market.	Targets local audience.	Limited coverage.
Neighborhood retailers and service businesses.	Consumer orientation.	Lack of entertainment or news; not always read.
Chain stores.	Delivery of a loyal, special interest audience.	Wide coverage area; must be preplanned months ahead.
New and expanding businesses; those using catalogs.	Personalized approach to an audience of good prospects.	High cost per thousand; number of variables that can thwart success of a mailing. Difficulty in obtaining prospect customer list.
Amusements, tourist businesses, brand-name retailers.	Dominant size, frequency of exposure.	Cost; limited exposure time; lack of flexibility; short copy only.
Businesses along transit routes, especially those appealing to wage earners.	Repetition and length of exposure.	Limited audience; lack of creative flexibility.

Think for a moment and you will see how popular direct mail really is. Think about bill stuffers (which are about 70 percent of direct mail), catalogs, flyers for store openings, sales letters, and all the stuff we call "junk mail."

HOW CAN YOU LOOK AT THE EFFECTIVENESS OF MEDIA?

Media effectiveness is usually measured in terms of (1) cost per thousand and (2) reach and frequency.

The most common method is the cost of reaching 1,000 persons in the desired audience (CPM). Measure the cost by dividing the cost of an ad by the number of households or persons reached. The formula is:

$$CPM = \frac{Cost \qquad (1,000)}{Audience\ or\ circulation}$$

For example, radio station A provides 100,000 impressions weekly (the target audience reached by each spot in your schedule) and costs $500. Your cost per 1,000 impressions is thus $5.00.

$$\frac{\$500}{100} = \$5.00$$

Broadcast schedules are often planned in terms of reach and frequency. *Reach* is the number of different persons exposed at least once to your message during your ad campaign. Reach is often expressed as a percentage of the total audience. *Frequency* is the average number of times a person who is exposed will see or hear your message during the period.

Remember, (1) CPM for *cost,* plus (2) reach and frequency for *audience* are the most common "quantitative" measures of ad effectiveness. But you need to relate your measures to media strengths and weaknesses as discussed above. They are the "qualitative" dimensions. For example, radio may have a lower CPM and higher reach and frequency than newspaper. But you may need to present your product visually. This cannot be done by radio.

HOW DO YOU MEASURE THE RESULTS OF ADVERTISING?

Sales response ads can be checked daily during the period of the ad. The effects of image ads are harder to measure. You cannot always tie a purchase to image advertising. But your message may stay in the minds of people who have heard it. Sooner or later it may help trigger a purchase. But research like that touched on in the store image section of chapter 2 is needed to measure the success of image ads.

What are the tests for sales response?

Coupons may result in sales for a product or requests for information. By using coupons, properly dated, you can find out the returns for your ad dollar.

Requests by telephone or letter which refer to your ad can also be used. An offer in the middle of an ad is one way to see if your ads are being read.

Customer interviews are also useful. Your salesclerks can ask customers when they check out how they knew of the sale.

The U.S. Small Business Administration has suggested the following way to judge the effectiveness of your promotional advertising:[3] Compare gross margin on sales of specific goods advertised with ad costs plus other direct promotion expenses. For example, let's say you have an ad in Wednesday's paper, and by Friday's closing you have made sales of $500 on goods costing $300—giving you a $200 margin. Say the ad itself cost $100 and other handling and related costs totaled $40. Then the ad has contributed $60 to joint expenses and profits, or 12 percent of sales of the advertised goods. You can judge that it has been moderately successful provided traffic in your store has also materially increased.

Whatever your situation, it's up to you to set the appropriate dividing point between a successful and an unsuccessful result. When an ad is unsuccessful, you should try to determine the probable reasons for its failure: Was your selection of merchandise poor or untimely? Did you use the wrong medium? Was the copy, illustration, or layout dull? Did the ad appear inappropriate in either size or position? When you discover a mistake, make a record of it so that in future ad planning you will recall it and not repeat it.

Many times, merchandise ads are run more to develop store traffic than to sell the particular articles advertised. In a small store, you may find it best to judge the results of your advertising by the overall sales increase in the entire store rather than by sales and margin of the items you have advertised.

Tally the sales of the store or department during the two to five days following the appearance of the ad because this is the period when you'll expect the most results. Apply to the sales the gross margin percentage normally realized during the month or season. This will give you the approximate margin above cost for the period. Next, estimate your expenses for the period as follows (assuming a three-day response): If the month has 27 selling days, you have 1/9 (3 ÷ 27) of the month's fixed expenses. Calculate the normal variable expense ratio to sales, exclusive of advertising, and apply it to the three-day sales figure. Next take your overhead costs and variable expenses for the three days, add them to the cost of the advertisement, and compare this figure with the sales margin for the three days. If the two figures are the same, your promotion has merely broken even and would not be considered satisfactory.

The greater the difference between the margin and the cost, the more successful the promotion. For example, suppose you run a 25-inch ad which costs you $5 an inch, or $175. Store sales during the three days following the ad may total $4,500. At a gross margin rate of 35 percent, your dollar margin is $1,575. If your fixed expenses for the month are $9,000, fixed expenses for the 3 days are $1,000 (1/9 of monthly fixed expenses in a month with 27 selling days). Variable expenses are normally 10 percent, or $450 for three days. Total expenses for the three days are $175 (ad cost), $1,000 (overhead), $450 (variable expenses), $1,625. With a dollar margin of $1,575,

TABLE 16–7
Break-even ratios:
Sales to advertising costs

Ad cost, $5 per inch; three-day overhead, $500; variable expenses, 10 percent of sales; and gross margin, 35 percent.

Advertising		Overhead plus cost (fixed expenses)	Sales break-even point*	Break-even ratio (sales to ad cost)
Size of ad (inches)	Cost			
18	$ 90	$590	$2,360	26
24	120	620	2,480	21
30	150	650	2,600	17
42	210	710	2,840	14
60	300	800	3,200	11

* Margin on sales equals fixed expenses plus variable expenses (expressed as a percentage of sales). Because gross margin, predetermined at 35 percent, includes fixed expenses, the break-even point will be four times the fixed expenses—determined as follows, using the 18-inch ad as the example:

$$\text{Let } x = \text{sales}$$
$$0.35x = \$590 + 0.10x$$
$$0.25x = \$590$$
$$x = \$2,360$$
$$\frac{x}{4} = \$590$$

Source: U.S. Small Business Administration, *Small Store Planning for Growth*, Small Business Management Series No. 33, 2d ed. (Washington, D.C.: U.S. Government Printing Office, 1977, p. 71.

you have not broken even. (A convenient way to check results, is given in Table 16–7. Lineage cost is the same for each ad.)

GUIDES TO MEDIA PLANNING

Here are a few guidelines to help in media planning[4].

Guidelines across store types:
1. Radio exposure declines over the day with highest exposure during the morning drive.
2. Highest TV exposure occurs during prime viewing hours for heavy users as well as all TV viewers.
3. Television and Sunday newspapers are good media for reaching target segments. The local newspaper is the most used source of shopping news for consumers.
4. Readership of specific newspaper sections appears to be somewhat consistent across patronage segments of all store types. However, those newspaper sections with national, state, and local news are the most heavily read for all consumer types.
5. Specific firms planning newspaper ads should still consider specialized sections if their patrons are heavy readers of that section (e.g., sporting goods stores should still consider advertising in the Sports Section even though it might not be the most read part of the paper).

Now consider the following guidelines for specific store types:
1. Grocery and discount store managers should rely most heavily on day and prime-time scheduling when doing TV advertising.

2. Convenience, department, and fast-food retail managers should place their messages in prime and late fringe viewing hours when employing television in their media plan.

3. Convenience and fast-food heavy patrons listen to radio more heavily during afternoon drive time than do other consumers and hence may be reached better by radio messages aired at this time.

ESSENTIALS OF A GOOD ADVERTISEMENT
Select a strategy

You first need to decide on a strategy for an ad before focusing on the creative dimensions. Numerous goals can be achieved by your ads. Clearly, the ultimate of all advertising is to increase sales and profitability. Still, other purposes exist. For example, you may want to feature an ad which will help the image of the store. If so, you may want to feature a high fashion item even though it is not your best seller. You might in this way attract people who are interested in higher fashion merchandise.

Other goals might include: (1) correcting wrong impressions about a store, (2) making people aware that you are open at night, (3) that you feature repair services, or (4) that you have particular brands of merchandise.

Small retailers especially have a problem because many people are not aware that their store even exists. Thus advertising can serve as a reminder of the store's existence and of the product lines which it features.

Developing the copy

Copy can either be rational or emotional. The rational approach focuses essentially on the product itself and various facts about the product. The emotional appeal addresses the benefits which one can obtain from using the product. Normally a combination of the two possibilities is very effective.[5] Your headlines in the ads can focus on benefits, promises, or even news.

The text of the advertisement can do many things, including "(1) stating reasons for doing something (buying the product, patronizing the store), (2) making promises or giving testimonials, (3) publicizing the results of performance tests, (4) telling a story, (5) reporting a real or imaginary dialogue, (6) solving a predicament, or (7) amusing the audience."[6]

The bulk of all advertising by small retailers is in the newspaper. Thus, we have chosen to highlight the keys to successful newspaper ads. Certain elements are very important in achieving a successful advertisement (see Table 16–8). Give special attention to the merchandise you choose, the headline, the information you include in the ad, point of view, believability, call to action, and store identity. Neglect of these elements greatly increases your probability of failure.

SHOULD YOU USE AN AGENCY?

Ad agencies often handle small retail accounts. An agency gives you the *advantages* of (1) an outside point of view, (2) use of skilled personnel, and (3) help in planning how to get the most out of your ad dollars.

Most retailers can handle their print ads if they are price oriented such as

**TABLE 16–8
Checklist for promotional
advertising (newspaper)**

* Merchandise . . . . Does the ad offer merchandise having wide appeal, special features, price appeal, and timeliness?

Medium . . . . Is a newspaper the best medium for the ad, or would another—direct mail, radio, television, or other—be more appropriate?

Location . . . . Is the ad situated in the best spot (in both section and page location)?

Size . . . . Is the ad large enough to do the job expected of it? Does it omit important details, or is it overcrowded with nonessential information?

* Headline . . . . Does the headline express the single major idea about the merchandise advertised? The headline should usually be an informative statement and not simply a label. For example, "Sturdy shoes for active boys, specially priced at $6.95," is certainly better than "Boys' Shoes, $6.95."

Illustration . . . . Does the illustration (if one is used) express the idea the headline conveys?

* Merchandise information . . . . . . Does the copy give the basic facts about the goods, or does it leave out information that would be important to the reader? ("The more you tell, the more you sell.")

Layout . . . . Does the arrangement of the parts of the ad and the use of white space make the ad easy to read? Does it stimulate the reader to look at all the contents of the ad?

Human interest . . . . Does the ad—through illustration, headline, and copy—appeal to customers' wants and wishes?

* "You" attitude . . . . Is the ad written and presented from the customer's point of view (with the customer's interests clearly in mind), or from the store's?

* Believability . . . . To the objective, nonpartisan reader, does the ad ring true, or does it perhaps sound exaggerated or somewhat phony?

Type face . . . . Does the ad use a distinctive typeface—different from those of competitors?

* Spur to action . . . . Does the ad stimulate prompt action through devices such as use of a coupon, statement of limited quantities, announcement of a specific time period for the promotion or impending event?

* Sponsor identification . . . . Does the ad use a specially prepared signature cut that is always associated with the store and that identifies it at a glance? Also, does it always include the following institutional details: store location, hours open, telephone number, location of advertised goods, and whether phone and mail orders are accepted?

* The seven items starred are of chief importance to the smaller store.
Source: U.S. Small Business Administration, *Small Store Planning for Growth*, Small Business Management Series No. 33, 2d ed. (Washington, D.C.: U.S. Government Printing Office, 1977, p. 69.

grocery ads. Radio and TV ads present problems which can best be handled by an agency. Most agencies charge a fee of 15 percent of media billings.

Too much retail advertising today looks alike and is often "lost" among all the other look alike advertising. Focus on your own strengths and how to get your message across. A creative agency may be the answer for anything other than price ads.

SPECIAL PROMOTIONAL EVENTS

Although customers usually favor stores carrying regular assortments that are always available, they also respond to special events[7]. They are interested in "doings" that make a show, especially ones in which they can participate.

Special sales

A good way to attract bargain seekers is through special sales—if you don't overdo them and if you offer genuine values. You'll want to consider special offprice promotions as well as special sales of regular merchandise from stock. But carefully check the results on regular stock of any temporary reductions you make. Often volume will drop both before and after a promotion; and this, coupled with the extra cost of the promotion, may make it actually unprofitable.

Other special events

In addition to your merchandise sales, you should attempt to conduct some dramatic event. It might be a contest, an exhibition, a celebrity visit, a parade, a giveaway, an auction, or a fashion show. In some fields, particularly foods, manufacturers continually run contests, make premium offers, conduct offprice sales, and distribute samples. They are anxious to get their dealers' cooperation in these activities. As in the case of cooperative advertising, if you think you have something to gain by cooperating with a manufacturer's promotional events, do so. But hold off taking part in those events that clutter up your store, take the time of your staff, and show you no increase in total volume. A promotion that merely switches demand from one product to another is of little value to you.

Trading stamps, coupons, tickets

The use of trading stamps as a sales promotion device reached a peak in the mid-1960s and then declined. Trading stamps did increase sales for many merchants, but they cost money as well. Any merchant contemplating their use (or discontinuing it) should carefully weigh their cost against promotional gain. Another plan, probably less expensive than trading stamps, is the distribution of coupons that give specific discounts on certain items (but not on all purchases).

Another promotional tool that often works well is the redeemable ticket. Customers are given tickets that are punched when they make purchases. After perhaps 12 articles of a kind (such as hosiery) have been bought, or a total of $10 has been spent in the store, the ticket is redeemable for another

Macy's Parade—An image-creating promotional event

here comes the parade

Macy's traditional holiday treat for children of all ages.

Don't miss a moment of it! The balloons! The bands! The floats! The clowns! The celebrities! And, of course, the arrival of Santa himself, marking the official start of the Christmas season in New York. It all starts at 9 a.m. sharp at Central Park West and 77th Street and marches down Broadway (and into the hearts of millions) to Macy's Herald Square at 34th Street. Come share it with us.

MACY★S 53RD ANNUAL
THANKSGIVING DAY PARADE
See it live or on NBC-TV

Courtesy Macy's

article or for an allowance on future purchases. Where markon is substantial, using such tickets can bring return customers at a reasonable cost.

Publicity

As your business expands, you will be seeking opportunities for publicity in the press or over the air. If you can carry out an event having some news value, you have a good chance of getting mentioned on a local news program or in a write-up in the news columns. In fact, it's a good idea to prepare a news release whenever you have a special sale or special event in view. If you are presenting a fashion show, a set of model rooms, or some new line of merchandise, you can invite radio-TV, press, and community leaders to a preview. It's not necessary to be big to do this, so long as your presentation is out of the ordinary and truly newsworthy. As a matter of habit, you should always be in touch with the communications media in your community.

ESSENTIALS OF DISPLAY

Display differs from advertising in that it is a device to present the merchandise itself, not simply to supply information about it. Display, however, can be a major part of the total promotional effort.

Displays are a part of the so-called silent language of communications which affect consumer-purchasing behavior. As observed: "retail space, i.e., the environment that surrounds the retail shopper, is never neutral. The retail store is a funnel of news, messages and suggestions which communicate to shoppers. Retail store designers, planners and merchandisers shape space, and that space in turn affects and shapes customer behavior. The retail store . . . creates moods, activates intentions and generally affects customer reactions."[8]

Thus, the effective use of displays can modify customer demand, buying habits and store patronage. Too often we think only of costs in discussing merchandise displays. Costs are important, but look beyond such measures as cost per square foot. Remember that planning for space is an extension of overall merchandising strategy.

HOW DISPLAYS AFFECT BEHAVIOR

The following principles can serve to guide you in understanding the role of display in promotion and overall image development for the firm[9].

1. There is a relationship between status and space. Higher status people have more and better space as well as greater freedom to move about. They will thus be attracted by spacious displays in uncrowded surroundings.

2. Creative use of space creates expectations through stimulation. "Displays in retail outlets have the primary purpose of providing cues toward which energy can be expended . . . what is expended is energy and what is purchased is reward, pleasure, satisfaction, and excitement."

3. Customer behavior can often be affected by changing or modifying attitudes and images through design. "Through design features, attitudes and images are created, that is, store personalities are created and shaped, and these personalities—friendly, aloof, high quality, etc.—are meant to affect customer attitudes and image and hence buying behavior.''

One of the best known writers in marketing is Philip Kotler. He suggests that the following questions should be asked before developing any retail display:

1. Who is the target audience?
2. What is the target audience seeking from the buying experience?
3. What atmospheric variables (color, movement, sound, smell, and so on) can fortify the beliefs and emotional reactions that buyers are seeking?
4. Will the resulting atmosphere compete effectively with competitors' atmospheres?[10]

Look for a moment at Figure 16-1, an image building display for Macy's. How would you answer the above four questions in the context of this display?

Displays when properly used can help accomplish a variety of goals for the firm. *Most important,* the purpose of display is to sell goods. The merchandise must be visible in order to sell. *Second,* as indicated above, display is a key to creating an overall atmosphere for the store. Think for a moment about the different types of displays you have come to expect in discount stores, supermarkets, and boutiques. The displays contribute to your overall image of the store. *Third,* displays can help to speed up transactions, especially where

FIGURE 16-1
Macy's, New York—Image creation and maintenance

Courtesy Macy's

self-service selections are used. *Fourth,* display can serve to protect merchandise either for reasons of security or to keep it from getting soiled by customer handling.

THE PRINCIPLES OF DISPLAY

Everyone is a "pro" when it comes to display. Have you ever noticed that customers in a retail store stop at various displays, move quickly past some, and smile at still others. They are professional display watchers and *know* what they like. Of course, they don't see the displays with a concrete checklist in mind. But they react either positively or negatively, and you can be sure that the mental computer is "checking off" the good and bad. Customers are not consciously judging the displays either. Your job as a retail manager is to "prejudge" for the customer. Be clever and creative enough to affect behavior as *you* desire the behavior to be. We give you sound, proved principles of display, but we must be honest with you. We believe that you cannot *teach* effective display. Just as we believe that it is impossible to *teach* creative merchandising.

The excitement, stimulation, and pure beauty of a good display must be *experienced.* It may be trite, but one picture is worth 1,000 words—especially in a subject such as display. The pictures in this chapter assist you in experiencing the highest level of good display (a personal appraisal always!). We encourage you, after studying this material and looking at these pictures, to become conscious of displays in stores.

Learn the principles and objectives of good display—but more important "feel" the display and start your creative juices flowing. You may never be able to paint a picture of a beautiful flower, but you know when you see one. The point? You may never be a display specialist, but a manager of a retail operation must know what the customer wants to see and assist the specialist in selecting merchandise, space, and fixtures to accomplish the merchandising objectives. You can almost feel the excitement of entering The Arcade at Macy's, a world renown example of creative display in action. Farsighted and creative merchants turned a drab upstairs area into the collection of shops shown in Figure 16–2.

In spite of the basically artistic and creative flair needed for display, some tried and true principles do exist. The basic principles developed over the years are as follows:[11]

1. Build displays around fast-moving, hot items.
2. Goods purchased largely on impulse should be given ample amounts of display space.
3. Keep your displays simple. Do not try to cram them with too many items.
4. Displays should be timely. Feature seasonal goods (see Figure 16–3).
5. Not only does color attract attention, but it sets the right tone, and affects the very essense of the display.

FIGURE 16-2
The entrance to the Arcade at Macy's (note the effective use of lighting as a means of lowering the ceiling height.)

Courtesy Macy's

FIGURE 16-3
Seasonal display—Macy's Arcade

Courtesy Macy's

6. Use motion. It attracts attention.
7. Most good displays have a theme or a story to tell.
8. Show goods in use.
9. Proper lighting and props are essential to an effective display.
10. Guide the shopper's eye where you want it.
11. Masculine-feminine symbolism should be observed.

TYPES OF DISPLAYS

Displays can be grouped into two primary categories; namely, window and interior displays. We will offer a brief overview of some of the many possibilities for variations in display. Entire courses are devoted to the technical aspects of display.

Window display

Window displays have become less popular in recent years. They often add to the energy bill of the firm because they are a prime source of energy loss. *Second,* they are expensive to maintain and keep clean and must be changed on a regular basis, probably at least every two weeks. *Third,* window displays often make inefficient use of good retail space. Many firms today are thus relying less on large window displays and are making more creative use of the space with good interior display.

Still, until small stores expand their trading area, window displays are their chief tool for creating traffic. They can continue to be important as a business expands. Show windows must take on a more professional look with better lighting and more use of settings to help dramatize the goods. And usually, you'll want to tie in the windows with your advertising to increase the impact of your message. But remember always to leave a certain amount of window space free to use for advertised specials.

Plan window displays with the same care you devote to advertising. Check your windows just as you check your ads (see Table 16–9).

You'll find it harder to evaluate the results of display than of advertising, but try to determine: (1) the number of people passing the window in a certain period (one hour in the late morning and one in the afternoon perhaps), (2) the number of passersby that glance at the window, (3) the number that stop, and (4) the number that enter the store after looking at the window.

If you see any mistakes in the display, you can correct them in your next one. Studying your own windows, you can learn the difference between right and wrong, good and bad, the common and the unusual. And through a trial-and-error method, you will develop a keener sense of what a display needs to bring customers into your store.

Interior displays

Interior displays can take a wide variety of forms, depending on the type of merchandise carried and the image to be projected by the firm. The essence of all retail stores really is a wide variety of assortment displays highlighting the

**TABLE 16–9
Checklist for
window display**

I. Merchandise selected
1. Is the merchandise timely?
2. Is it representative of the stock assortment?
3. Are the articles harmonious—in type, color, texture, and use?
4. Are the price lines of the merchandise suited to the interests of passersby?
5. Is the quantity on display suitable (that is, neither overcrowded nor sparse)?
II. Setting
1. Are glass, floor, props, and merchandise clean?
2. Is the lighting adequate (so that reflection from the street is avoided)?
3. Are spotlights used to highlight certain parts of the display?
4. Is every piece of merchandise carefully draped, pinned, or arranged?
5. Is the background suitable, enhancing the merchandise?
6. Are the props well suited to the merchandise?
7. Are window cards used, and are they neat and well placed?
8. Is the entire composition balanced?
9. Does the composition suggest rhythm and movement?
III. Selling power
1. Does the window present a readily recognized central theme?
2. Does the window exhibit have power to stop passersby through the dramatic use of light, color, size, motion, composition, and/or item selection?
3. Does the window arouse a desire to buy (as measured by shoppers entering the store)?

Source: U.S. Small Business Administration, *Small Store Planning for Growth,* Small Business Management Series No. 33, 2d ed. (Washington, D.C.: U.S. Government Printing Office, 1977), p. 77.

items carried. We have all come to expect the tasteful, but traditional displays of shoes, for example, shown in Figures 16–4 and 16–5. On the other hand, consider the new concept of assortment dominance as reflected in the B. Dalton shop shown in Figure 16–6. A B. Dalton book outlet features a tre-

**FIGURE 16–4
Jarman—Traditional assortment display for men's shoes**

Courtesy Aronov Realty, Montgomery, Alabama

FIGURE 16–5
Miss Capezio—Traditional assortment display for women's shoes

Courtesy Aronov Realty, Montgomery, Alabama

FIGURE 16–6
B. Dalton Bookseller—Assortment dominance in action

Courtesy Aronov Realty, Montgomery, Alabama

mendous variety and depth of books. Even here, however, books are arranged into basic categories to facilitate browsing by shoppers. Note, for example, the sign directing the shopper to the children's books section.

The essence of many interior displays today is to facilitate self-service. Here are some generally recognized ideas developed by the U.S. Small Business Administration that will help you plan attractive, efficient self-service layouts for many types of merchandise:

1. Put impulse goods near the front of your store, and intersperse them with demand products, so that as many people as possible will see them.
2. Place shopping goods, that the customer would have in mind before entering the store, in sections with less traffic that are reached after passing impulse and convenience lines.
3. Frequently change "ends," special displays set at the end of counters that are readily observable from many points in the store.
4. Locate and arrange your stock so that customers are drawn toward the side of the store and then toward the rear. (You'll be wanting to create a circular traffic pattern that exposes customers to at least a third of the entire assortment before they leave the store.)
5. Place larger sizes and heavy, bulky goods near the floor.
6. If you carry competing brands in various sizes, give relatively little horizontal space to each item, and make use of vertical space for the different sizes and colors. This exposes customers to a greater variety of products as they move through the store.
7. Avoid locating impulse goods directly across the aisle from demand items that most customers are looking for. The impulse item may not be seen at all.
8. Make use of vertical space through tiers and step ups, but be careful to avoid displays much above eye level or at the floor. The area of vertical vision is limited. (See appendix for a detailed checklist on interior displays and arrangement.)

Floor displays. Floor displays serve a variety of purposes. When outlets such as supermarkets construct a large floor display they frequently generate significant levels of "plus" sales. Other forms of floor displays are permanent and can be a major image builder for an outlet. Figure 16–7 shows the tasteful use of a floor display for crystal, ceramics, silver, and other expensive items. Note also the special use of lighting and contrasting floor designs and color in highlighting the displays. How many different ways are lighting used in the outlet, for example?

Counter displays. These are very common in all types of outlets. You have to decide on the specific type of display for yourself, however. The most effective display will vary with merchandise. Figures 16–8, 16–9, and 16–10 illustrate various types of counter displays available to you. Each type of display varies widely yet is highly effective in its own setting.

FIGURE 16-7
Tasteful use of floor displays for china, crystal, and ceramics

Courtesy Macy's

FIGURE 16-8
Graphic wraps—Macy's Arcade

This outlet specializes in the sale of sweaters. Effective use of various display techniques, including counters, floor displays, and use of wall and ceiling space.

Courtesy Macy's

FIGURE 16-9
David's Chocolates—Macy's Arcade

Effective use of small corner space and a minimum of fixtures. Note the use of David's Chocolates bags and boxes as the highlights of the displays.

Courtesy Macy's

FIGURE 16-10
Fancy This—Macy's Arcade
(inexpensive, movable fixtures in an easygoing, informal setting)

Courtesy Macy's

SUMMARY

Good promotion plans take time. Try to both sell goods and to create a strong image for the store with your ads. But, promotion is no magic cure-all for bad products, a poor location, or other problems. You also have to consider the media available, supplier willingness to pay for part of your ad costs, the competition, and even the state of the economy.

The choice of the best medium is not easy. Newspapers have always been popular with retailers. But a mix of media is the way to go.

Try to make your ads hard hitting and different. Give useful information and strive to be believed. You can't always be having a "going out of business sale"! or getting rid of excess inventory. Consumers don't believe these kinds of stories.

NOTES

1. Marvin J. Rothenberg, "Retail Research Strategies for the 1970s," in Ed Mazze, ed., *1975 Combined Proceedings* (Chicago: American Marketing Association, 1975), p. 409.

2. William McGee, *Building Store Traffic with Broadcast Advertising* (San Francisco: Broadcast Marketing Company, 1978), p. 220.

3. U.S. Small Business Administration, *Small Store Planning for Growth,* Small Business Management Series, No. 33, 2d ed. (Washington, D.C.: U.S. Government Printing Office, 1977), pp. 68–71.

4. William O. Bearden, Jesse E. Teel, Jr., and Richard M. Durand, "Guidelines for Advertising Media Management," *Journal of Small Business Management,* vol. 16 (January 1978), p. 40.

5. Laurence W. Jacobs, *Advertising and Promotion for Retailing: Text and Cases* (Glenview, Ill.: Scott, Foresman and Co., 1972), pp. 152–53.

6. William Haight, *Retail Advertising: Management and Technique* (New Jersey: General Learning Press, 1976), p. 357.

7. This material is taken from U.S. Small Business Administration, *Small Store Planning,* pp. 74–76.

8. Rom J. Markin, Charles M. Lillis, and Chem L. Narayana, "Social-Psychological Significance of Store Space," *Journal of Retailing,* vol. 52 (Spring 1976), p. 43.

9. Markin, Lillis, and Narayana.

10. Phillip Kotler, "Atmospherics as a Marketing Tool," *Journal of Retailing,* vol. 49 (Winter 1973–74), p. 48.

11. Richard H. Buskirk, and Bruce D. Buskirk, *Retailing* (New York: McGraw-Hill, Book Co., 1979), pp. 332–38.

DISCUSSION QUESTIONS

1. Is it possible to increase advertising expenses as a percentage of sales and yet also increase the profitability of the firm?

2. Why is it important to plan advertising well in advance of the time at which it is actually to reach the public?

3. What is the role of institutional advertising for the retailer?

4. What are the various factors to be considered in deciding how much of the promotion budget is to be allocated to the various departments within a retail outlet?

5. Why should a retailer consider the use of co-op advertising funds?

6. What are the strengths of the following media: newspaper, radio, television, direct mail, and preprinted inserts?

7. What is the CPM formula? What is its usefulness?

8. Why do you believe that local retailers continue to use more newspaper advertising than any other type of media?

9. What are the reasons that a retail outlet should consider a multimedia mix?

10. Briefly discuss the ways of measuring the effectiveness of retail advertising.

11. How may a retailer judge the effectiveness of promotional advertising?

12. Comment on the following statement: The only possible goal of advertising is to increase sales and profitability.

13. How is merchandise display different from advertising? Is the only purpose of merchandise display to display goods? Explain your answer.

14. What are the basic principles retailers should consider in developing merchandise displays?

15. Why are many retail firms today relying less on large window displays?

16. What are some of the guidelines retailers should consider in setting up interior store displays of merchandise?

PROJECTS

1. Imagine you work for the promotion division of a department store and have been told that you are to prepare a campaign for a new product. Select your own "new product." Plan the campaign, select the media, and prepare the message.

2. Choose any currently popular product. Determine how many different ways it is advertised. What are the differences and similarities among the methods?

3. Make contacts with dealers in a specific product line (e.g., automobiles) which have definite differences in product image, price, quality, and so on. Through interviews with the dealership managers, attempt to determine the allocation of the advertising (promotional) budget among the various media. Compare and contrast among the group. If actual dollars of

promotional expenditures are not available, then utilize percentage allocations. Additionally collect national and local ads for the same dealerships/brands and evaluate the differences and similarities noted.

4. Select several local automobile dealerships who seem to you to project differing public images. Interview management of each to determine their particular image perceptions of themselves and perhaps of their competition. Prepare a portfolio of ads of each dealership and also of the national ads of that same dealership's make of auto. Compare the images which seem to be projected by the local versus the national promotions. Attempt to reach certain strategy conclusions from your investigation.

Minicase 16-1   Charles Brady, Sr., operated a neighborhood grocery store during and after World War II serving an old central city market. During and after the war, goods, especially gift items, were in short supply. Charles, Sr., realized this and decided to package fruit and sell it as gifts. His suppliers provided him with good fruit and he hired high school students to package and wrap it. Then he added cheeses to his gift packages. He began finding himself less and less in the grocery business and more and more in the gift business. He started carrying fine china, crystal, and imported objects of art, still within a grocery store atmosphere. Presently he has no groceries and Brady's advertising budget is devoted to national magazine advertising. The rest of the ad budget is spent on spot radio ads, resorting to the newspaper only at Christmas.

Did Charles Brady, Sr., communicate with his customers? How was his image established?

Minicase 16-2   Ezell's is a strong regional department store group which has recently opened an outlet in Metro city. This is their first outlet in the state and Ezell's does not have a strong image in the market. After two years' operations, management has decided to start an advertising campaign to strengthen its image. The Management Committee is split on two possible ways to go. One group supports an image campaign which focuses on the quality of the merchandise offered, the length of time the firm has been in business and its desire to be a part of mainstream community life. Other members of the committee argue that the best way to go is to feature a cross-section of store employees in a media mix plan. The argument was that the employees could be used as centers of influence among their friends in building a strong image for the firm.

What are the advantages and disadvantages of these two approaches. Which one would you recommend? Why?

Minicase 16-3   Bob Smith recently opened a high-quality stereo shop in a city of 70,000 persons. The shop is the only one in town limited to stereo hi-fi equipment and accessories. Bob sells only the best name brands. He is convinced that the low end of his equipment is priced competitively with popular mass merchandise of much lower quality. Also, his equipment, priced up to $4,000 can meet the needs of the serious hi-fi hobbyist.

Bob has been in business for a year now in a downtown location. Business was great during December, the month of his opening. Since then, he has been struggling to break even. He has personally been in a few television spots to indicate to his friends that he is now in business. Also, he has used flyers which are given out at local rock concerts. He also has one billboard in the vicinity of his business.

Bob is concerned over his low volume of sales. He has budgeted $7,000 in promotion this year but is uncertain how he wants to spend the money. He feels that he has some equipment which will appeal to most market segments.

The market is served by a daily newspaper, one television station, and a dozen radio stations. The various stations appeal to such listening habits as country and western, rock, middle of the road, and rhythm and blues.

Outline the goals you think Bob should accomplish in his advertising. Suggest a media mix for him. Think about an annual media schedule for his shop.

APPENDIX	Checklist for Interior Arrangement and Display*

I. Layout
1. Are your fixtures low enough and signs so placed that the customer can get a bird's-eye view of the store and tell in what direction to go for wanted goods?
2. Do your aisle and counter arrangements tend to stimulate a circular traffic flow through the store?
3. Do your fixtures (and their arrangement), signs, lettering, and colors all create a coordinated and unified effect?
4. Before any supplier's fixtures are accepted, do you make sure they conform in color and design to what you already have?
5. Do you limit the use of hanging signs to special sale events?
6. Are your counters and aisle tables *not* overcrowded with merchandise?
7. Are your ledges and cashier/wrapping stations kept free of boxes, unneeded wrapping materials, personal effects, and odds and ends?
8. Do you keep trash bins out of sight?

II. Merchandise emphasis
1. Do your signs referring to specific goods tell the customer something significant about them, rather than simply naming the products and their prices?
2. For your advertised goods, do you have prominent signs, including tear sheets at the entrances, to inform and guide customers to their exact location in the store?
3. Do you prominently display both advertised and nonadvertised specials at the ends of counters as well as at the point of sale?
4. Are both your national and private brands highlighted in your arrangement and window display?
5. Wherever feasible, do you give the more colorful merchandise in your stock preference in display?
6. In the case of apparel and home furnishings, do the items that reflect your store's fashion sense or fashion leadership get special display attention at all times?
7. In locating merchandise in your store, do you always consider the productivity of space—vertical as well as horizontal?
8. Is your self-service merchandise arranged so as to attract the customer and assist in selection by the means indicated below:
   a. Is each category grouped under a separate sign?
   b. Is the merchandise in each category arranged according to its most significant characteristic—whether color, style, size, or price?
   c. In apparel categories, is the merchandise arranged by price lines or zones to assist the customer to make a selection quickly?

---

* Source: U.S. Small Business Administration, *Small Store Planning for Growth,* Small Business Management Series No. 33, 2d ed. (Washington, D.C.: U.S. Government Printing Office, 1977), pp. 101–2.

d.   Is horizontal space usually devoted to different items and styles within a category (vertical space being used for different sizes—smallest at the top largest at the bottom)?

e.   Are impulse items interspersed with demand items and *not* placed across the aisle from them, where many customers will not see them?

9.   Do you plan your windows and displays in advance?

10.   Do you meet with your sales force after windows are trimmed to discuss the items displayed?

11.   Do you use seasonal, monthly, and weekly plans for interior and window displays, determining the fixtures to be used and merchandise to be displayed?

12.   Do your displays reflect the image of your store?

13.   Do you budget the dollars you will set aside for fixtures and props to be used in your displays, as well as the expense of setting them up and maintaining them?

14.   Do you keep your fixtures and windows clean and dust free?

15.   Do you replace burned out light bulbs immediately?

16.   Do you take safety precautions in setting up your fixtures?

17.   Do garments fit properly on mannequins and fixtures?

17

WHAT REMAINS? SALES SUPPORT

The purposes of this chapter are to:

- Discuss the various types of retail credit you can offer.
- Acquaint you with the various types of credit cards available to you.
- Point out the laws affecting sales support services.
- Help you to think about such sales support activities as shopper services, educational programs, delivery, and extended shopping hours.
- Help you understand the various ways of handling customer complaints.
- Help you to evaluate the services you should and should not offer.
- Help you understand the meaning of the following terms:

Installment credit	Umbrella shopping card
Open charge credit	Credit scoring
Revolving credit	Equal Credit Opportunity Act
Deferred billing credit	Fair Debt Collection Practices Act
Layaway plan	Magnuson-Moss Warranty Act
Third-party credit	Blue laws
Private label credit card	

Services offer you the opportunity to make your store different from competition. But services cost a lot of money and many retailers do not agree on what services should be offered. As a result, many are cutting down on the number of services they offer.

Think for a moment and you will realize how many customers now bag their own groceries, price mark goods at warehouse outlets, serve themselves in restaurants, handle their own delivery, and pump their own gas. All of these are efforts by retailers to lower their costs and increase profit margins by shifting the work to consumers. Some firms offer many different services but charge a price for each. In this way a customer can pick and choose among the services wanted.

You probably cannot get rid of some services if you want to stay in business. Among these are credit, repair on warranty service, and others depending upon the goods sold.

The number of services which you can offer is very high. Table 17–1, for example, shows 40 frequently used sales support services by retailers. Table 17–2 shows many of the same services regrouped into three categories: (1) prepurchase services, (2) postpurchase services, and (3) ancillary services. Seldom are all of these services offered by any one retailer.

A high-class store appealing to the upper income trade will usually offer more services than a discount store. Also, two different stores may offer wide

TABLE 17–1
Forty frequently used sales support services

Free (or reduced rate) parking	Public rest rooms
Free (or reduced rate) bus service	Birthday (anniversary) reminders
Product delivery	Extended product warranties
Telephone shopping	Use of *Consumer Reports* or other
Mail-order (catalog) shopping	consumer journals
Layaway	Special orders for items not stocked
COD payment	Free coffee (or champagne) while shopping
Bridal registry	Information desks
Fashion shows	Party counseling
Gift wrapping	Baby strollers
Alterations	Gift certificates
Liberal returned goods policies	Trade-ins
Check cashing	Children's playrooms
On-site product usage (such as pools	Product locator (checking with other stores
for testing fly casting equipment)	on product availability)
Demonstration models (for at-home use)	Product repair
Parcel pickup service	In-store banking
Baggage/parcel lockers	Free telephone calls
After-hours shopping (for preferred	Personal shopping
customers)	Lost and found
Stag nights (male shopping only)	Bill payment (in-store)
Shopping consultants	
Home economists	

Source: Albert D. Bates, *Retailing and its environment* (New York: D. Van Nostrand Company, 1979). © 1979 by Litton Educational Publishing, Inc. Reprinted by permission of D. Van Nostrand Company, p. 290.

TABLE 17-2
Typical retail services

Prepurchase services	Postpurchase services	Ancillary services
1. Accepting telephone orders	1. Delivery	1. Check cashing
2. Accepting mail orders (or purchases)	2. Regular wrapping or bagging	2. General information
3. Advertising	3. Gift wrapping	3. Free parking
4. Window display	4. Adjustments	4. Restaurants
5. Interior display	5. Returns	5. Repairs
6. Fitting rooms	6. Alterations	6. Interior decorating
7. Shopping hours	7. Tailoring	7. Credit
8. Fashion shows	8. Installations	8. Rest rooms
9. Trade-ins	9. Engraving	9. Baby attendant service
	10. COD delivery	

Source: Carl M. Larson, John S. Wright, and Robert E. Weigand, *Basic Retailing* (Englewood Cliffs, N.J.: Prentice-Hall, Inc., 1976), p. 364.

variations in the same service. For example, a discount store may accept a bank credit card as the only means of paying other than cash for goods. But a department store may accept a bank credit card, the store's own credit card, or may have a customer charge plan. Also, department stores may deliver large items like furniture free of charge. A warehouse furniture store may also deliver but charge extra for it.

Let's look at a few of the services.

WHAT ABOUT RETAIL CREDIT?

The average American credit user now has more than five cards for credit or check cashing.[1] More than 80 percent of all people in the United States now have some type of credit card, while more than 50 percent have a Wards, Sears, or Penneys card.[2] But you might as well face the fact that even though you may want to offer credit (unless you are a supermarket) you are going to lose money on your internal credit programs.

Advantages and disadvantages of credit

You need to be familiar with the advantages and disadvantages of credit in general before deciding on whether to grant it. If you decide to grant credit, many different options are available to you, as discussed below.

Credit is expensive. Still, many retailers believe that granting credit is necessary. Consumers apparently feel the same way since they often shop only in those stores where various credit cards are honored. Retailers as a rule believe that they can also increase the demand for their products and services with good credit programs. However, poor credit policy is a major reason for business failures among retail firms. Collection problems can also lead to difficulties for the firm.

Some of the major advantages of credit are:

1. Credit customers are more store loyal than noncredit customers.
2. Retail outlets often have a more personal relationship with customers with whom they have granted credit.

3. The use of credit can lead to "plus" sales which can help your return on investment since these extra sales can be made with little or no addition to your cost structure.
4. Credit account records can provide you with a mailing list for announcing special sales and other promotional efforts.

You need to think about some of the disadvantages. Major disadvantages include the following:

1. High overhead costs are necessary for handling the opening of new accounts, mailing out statements, collections, and similar problems.
2. You tie up your working capital in merchandise bought on credit by your customers.
3. You are going to have some problems with bad debts.
4. Some customers are more likely to abuse your return goods privileges and take goods out on approval when they have store credit accounts.

You need to do a benefit-cost analysis for all of your services, not just credit, before deciding whether to offer them. Don't be myopic in doing the evaluation. All services should be viewed as an expense of sales and you need to be convinced that offering a particular service is money well spent. The above advantages and disadvantages can help you develop a cost benefit framework for that service. Think also in the same context about the advantages and disadvantages of the various other services discussed in this chapter.

What types of credit can you offer?

You have five choices available to you in offering credit: (1) installment payments, (2) open charge credit, (3) revolving credit, (4) deferred billing payment, and (5) layaway.

Installment credit (a monthly payment account) occurs when a customer pays for a product in equal monthly installments, including interest. Automobiles and major appliances are often paid for this way.

Open charge credit means that the customer must pay the bill in full when it is due. Credit limits are set which the customer cannot exceed. Also, part payments on the account are not allowed.

Revolving credit occurs when a customer charges items during a month and is billed at the end of the month on the basis of the outstanding balance. Here the consumer can purchase several items without having a separate contract for each purchase.

You may also operate with *deferred billing credit*. Deferred billing occurs when you allow customers to buy goods and not pay for them for several months with no interest charge. Most of you have seen advertisements on television during the Christmas season that will say "no down payment and first payment not due for 90 days." The store is talking about deferred billing credit.

A *layaway plan* is similar to credit. In this situation you allow a customer to make a small deposit, perhaps $2 or $3, to hold the item. You keep the item until the customer completes paying for it. The advantage to the customer is not having to worry about whether the item will be in stock when they need it.

Clearly you have a wide choice of credit plans. Your job is to choose the one(s) which fits your customer needs and the image that you are trying to project for your store.

What about a charge card?

Most retailers today honor some type of credit card which allows customers to have a revolving credit account. You have two basic choices with credit cards. You can (1) have your own card or (2) use third-party credit programs. *Third-party credit* can consist of *(a)* a bank card such as Visa or Master Charge (Master Card), *(b)* your own *private label credit card* which is issued by a third party such as a bank, or *(c)* an *umbrella shopping card* which is good at several different stores under common ownership, or which perhaps can be used at all stores in a shopping center, *(d) travel and entertainment cards* such as American Express or Diners Club.

A customer transacts business with the credit department

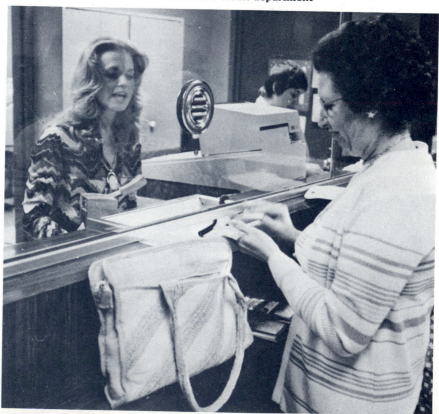

Courtesy NCR

Why have your own card? Several advantages exist in having your own card : (1) you avoid having to pay the 3–6 percent of sales which banks charge for allowing you to honor their credit cards; (2) you can build better customer loyalty among those customers with your cards because they cannot use the card to make purchases at another store; (3) you can promote by direct mail to your charge customers.

But *disadvantages* exist. Specifically (1) maintaining your own credit card costs a lot of money in overhead; (2) you have the hassle of collecting unpaid bills and of getting money from slow payers; (3) you have to run credit checks and put up with a lot of other unpleasant chores; (4) you may lose sales of consumers who have a bank card but not your store card.

Today department stores are about the only stores which run their own credit operations. They believe they get a strong marketing advantage from in-house credit. Still, many have added bank credit card plans to their own programs, particularly to take advantage of out-of-town business. But in-house credit probably is on its way out, even in department stores.

What about third-party credit? Bank credit cards or travel and entertainment cards such as Diners Club are not controlled by the merchant. Rather, the bank or the entertainment company receives applications and issues cards. They are responsible for customer billing and collection. As noted above, they simply charge merchants accepting the card a flat percentage of all sales made. You as a retailer (1) lose the advantage of having your own list of customers to whom you can direct mail promotion, (2) do not build any store loyalty as you would if you had your own card, (3) have no chance for special promotions such as deferred billings at Christmas.

The more recent version of the third-party card is the "private label card." One example is the General Electric Credit Corporation (GECC) custom credit program now used by over 350 retail firms. GECC works with each merchant to tailor a package to the store's needs. Sometimes the GECC employees are actually in the store to handle credit processing and collection. Often customers are not aware that they are dealing with an outside agency.

As part of a third-party program, the banks may (1) purchase all of your accounts from you, (2) handle credit applications, credit processing and authorization, (3) customer inquiries, (4) promotion, (5) issue each customer a card with the name of your store on it. Recently Visa has gone this route and will place your store name on the face of their card. The advantage here is that you get more loyal customers plus the wide acceptability of Visa.

Another version of third-party credit is the *umbrella shopping center card.* A bank normally handles all of the details. The program operates the same way as any regular bank credit card plan. But the card is honored only by the participating merchants in the shopping center.

In summary, more and more retailers are dropping in-house credit as a service. Many are (1) going to a private label, third-party system, (2) honoring bank cards such as Visa, (3) honoring travel and entertainment cards, or (4) structuring a program to encourage the use of checks and cash. A few retailers, for example, are giving discounts of 3–5 percent on cash purchases. This is the same discount which they pay banks for the right to allow customers to make purchases with the bank's credit card.

MANAGING INTERNAL CREDIT?

Almost any firm issuing credit uses an application form. Figure 17–1 is an example of such a form. The application calls for information which allows you to decide whether the person should be granted credit. Your forms may ask for such information as the size of savings and checking account balances,

FIGURE 17–1

Charge Application

homeownership, extent of debts, and various other personal information. Often the application is sent to a credit bureau for further study.

Use credit scoring

Some firms use *credit scoring*. This method gives points to various types of personal information about the applicant. Points are determined through a study of information obtained from former accounts which were both good and bad. An example of a credit-scoring system for screening accounts is shown in Table 17–3. Depending upon the number of points received a person may be given a credit limit or may be rejected. Table 17–4 shows how the result of an application might look based on the information contained in

TABLE 17–3
Sample credit-scoring system

Applicant characteristics	Allotted points
Home phone	
Yes	36
No	0
Own or rent	
Own	34
Rent	0
Other finance company	
Yes	−12
No	0
Bank credit card	
Yes	29
No	0
Applicant occupation	
Professional and official	27
Technical and manager	5
Proprietor	−3
Clerical and sales	12
Craftsman and nonfarm-laborer	0
Foreman and operative	26
Service worker	14
Farm worker	3
Checking or savings account	
Neither	0
Either	13
Both	19
Applicant age	
30 or less	6
30+ to 40	11
40+ to 50	8
Over 50	16
Years on job	
5 or less	0
5+ to 15	6
Over 15	18

Source : Gilbert Churchill, et al., "The Role of Credit Scoring in the Loan Decision," *The Credit World,* March 1977, p. 7. Reprinted with permission of *The Credit World,* official publication of the International Consumer Credit Association, St. Louis, Missouri.

TABLE 17-4
Hypothetical sample applicant and the associated credit score

Applicant characteristics	Allotted points
Home phone	36
Rents	0
No other finance company debt	0
Bank credit card	29
Farm worker	3
Both checking and savings accounts	19
Age 48	8
Same job for 18 years	18
	113

Source : Gilbert Churchill, et al., "The Role of Credit Scoring in the Loan Decision," *The Credit World,* March 1977, p. 8. Reprinted with permission of *The Credit World,* official publication of the International Consumer Credit Association, St. Louis, Mo.

Table 17-3. Experience can help you decide on the minimum number of points necessary to approve an application.

Don't violate the Equal Credit Opportunity Act

Many retailers are going to credit scoring because of the federal Equal Credit Opportunity Act (1977). The act states that a person who is denied credit can demand a written statement of reasons for denial. You now have a lot of pressure to operate with objective and consistent credit approval policies. A credit-scoring system provides such a way of evaluating applications. Scoring also gives you the following advantages : (1) better management control over credit, (2) benefits in training new personnel, (3) lower cost of processing loan applications, (4) a more legally defensible way of granting or denying credit.[3]

Study Aid 17-1 gives more specifics on practices that are illegal under the Equal Credit Opportunity Act.

Remember the Fair Debt Collection Practice Act

You need to study the requirements of the federal Fair Debt Collection Practices Act. As of March 20, 1978 federal law prohibited abusive, deceptive, and unfair debt collection practices by debt collectors. What does this mean to the consumer? What is the law designed to do? Its purpose is to see that people are treated fairly by debt collectors. The law will not permit debt collectors to use unjust means while attempting to collect debt. But the law does not cancel genuine debts which consumers owe. Further details are shown in Study Aid 17-2. Figure 17-2 shows a typical sequence of collection letters which are often used by management to collect on overdue accounts.

You also need to decide on how credit is to be verified whenever a purchase is made. Some firms still have *manual credit verification.* A clerk calls the credit department whenever a sale is made and gives the account number and the size of the sale.

STUDY AID 17-1

EQUAL CREDIT OPPORTUNITY ACT

The ECO Act, which was enacted by Congress to give consumers important rights when applying for and using credit, went into effect in two stages. First, discrimination in giving credit because of sex or marital status was prohibited in October 1975, and then discrimination because of race, national origin, religion, age (with certain exceptions) and receipt of public assistance payments was prohibited in March 1977. A major provision of the new law gives married women the right to establish their own credit records based on jointly held accounts.

Other important provisions state that in evaluating an applicant's creditworthiness a creditor must not:

1. Consider sex, marital status, race, national origin, religion, or age (with limited exceptions).
2. Refuse to consider reliable public assistance income (such as social security or Aid to Families with Dependent Children).
3. Discount or refuse to consider income derived from part-time employment or from a pension, annuity, or retirement benefit program.
4. Discount income because of sex or marital status, or assume that a woman of childbearing age will stop work to raise children.
5. Refuse to consider consistently received alimony, child support, or separate maintenance payments in the same manner as other income, if the applicant wants this income considered.

The act does not guarantee that an applicant will get credit. Creditors may still determine creditworthiness by considering economic factors such as income, expenses, debts, and previous billpaying habits.

For further information, write the Director, Office of Bank Customer Affairs, Federal Deposit Insurance Corporation, Washington, D.C. 20629 and ask for their publications entitled ''Equal Credit Opportunity for Women,'' and ''Equal Credit Opportunity and Age.''

Some stores set a limit, say $20, above which all credit charges must be approved. All sales less than the amount are approved on the floor. The approval limit is often raised in the busy seasons of the year to handle more customers.

Credit authorization is now sometimes done electronically. The clerk enters the account number and the amount of the sale at the cash register. The system then automatically checks the accounts receivable information stored in the computer and indicates whether a credit charge should be approved.

Next, now let's look at some of the other sales supporting services which can be offered.

STUDY AID 17-2

FAIR DEBT COLLECTION PRACTICES ACT

What types of debt collection practices are prohibited?

A debt collector may not *harass, oppress,* or *abuse* any person. For example, *a debt collector cannot:*

1. Use threats of violence to harm anyone or anyone's property or reputation.
2. Publish a list of consumers which says you refuse to pay your debts (except to a credit bureau).
3. Use obscene or profane language.
4. Repeatedly use the telephone to annoy anyone.
5. Telephone any person without identifying the caller.
6. Advertise your debt.

A debt collector may *not* use any *false* statements when collecting any debt. For example, *the debt collector cannot:*

1. Falsely imply that the debt collector represents the U.S. government or any state government.
2. Falsely imply that the debt collector is an attorney.
3. Falsely imply that *you* committed any crime.
4. Falsely represent that the debt collector operates or works for a credit bureau.
5. Misrepresent the amount of the debt.
6. Represent that papers being sent are legal forms, such as a summons, when they are not.
7. Represent that papers being sent are *not* legal forms when they *are.*

Also, a debt collector may not say:

1. That you will be arrested or imprisoned if you do not pay your debt.
2. That he will *seize, garnish, attach wages,* or *sell your property, unless* the debt collector or the creditor intends to do so and it is legal.
3. That any *action* will be taken against you which *cannot legally* be taken.

A debt collector may not:

1. Give false *credit information* about you to anyone.
2. Send you anything that looks like an *official* document which might be sent by any *court* or *agency* of the *United States* or any *state* or *local* government.
3. Use any false name.

A debt collector must *not* be *unfair* in attempting to collect any debt. For example, *the debt collector cannot:*

1. Collect *any amount* greater than the amount of your debt, unless allowed by law.

2. Deposit any postdated check before the date on that check.
3. Make you accept collect calls or pay for telegrams.
4. Take or threaten to take your property unless there is a present right to do so.
5. Contact you by post card.
6. Put anything on an envelope other than the debt collector's address and name. Even the name cannot be used if it shows that the communication is about the collection of a debt.

What control do you have over specific debts?

If you owe several debts, any payment you make must be applied as you choose. And, a debt collector cannot apply a payment to any debt you feel you do not owe.

What can you do if the debt collector breaks the law?

You have the right to sue a debt collector in a state or federal court within one year from the date the law was violated. You may recover money for the damage you suffered. Court costs and attorney's fees can also be recovered.

A group of persons may sue a debt collector and recover money for damages up to $500,000.

Who can you tell if the debt collector breaks the law?

You should contact the proper federal government enforcement agency. The agencies use complaints to decide which companies to investigate.

Many states also have debt collection laws of their own. Check with your state attorney general's office to determine your rights under state law.

Where should you send complaints and questions?

Unless your complaint is about collection practices by banks and other financial institutions, write to: Federal Trade Commission, Debt Collection Practices, Washington, D.C. 20580.

To find out more.

If you have any general questions about the Fair Debt Collection Practices Act or you wish to complain about collection practices by creditors, write to the Federal Trade Commission, Debt Collection Practices, Washington, D.C. 20580 or to one of its regional offices.

WHAT ABOUT SHOPPING SERVICES?

More and more smart retailers are making it possible for customers to buy goods without having to shop in the store. Shopping services are making a comeback these days. The most common shopper services are (1) telephone shopping, (2) in-home shopping, and (3) personal shopping.

Telephone shopping is being pushed by retailers because of the shortages of fuel and less time available to many people for shopping. Usually the store will issue a catalog to the consumer. After looking at the catalog, the customer

FIGURE 17-2
**Sample collection
letter sequence**

AT THE TIME . . .

your account was reviewed recently, your statement showed an overdue balance.

Of course, you may have sent us this payment since the date the account was reviewed. If you have, please disregard our notice and accept our thanks.

If you haven't already mailed us your check, we are sure you will appreciate this reminder.

Cordially,

PAST DUE NOTICE . . .

Several days have elapsed since we notified you relative to the payment which is past due on your account; however we are still without remittance from you. Your future credit with us will be determined by your present payment record. It is essential that this matter be taken care of without further delay.

Cordially,

TIME FLIES . . .

and another month has almost slipped by without a payment on your account.

When you miss a payment, or pay less than our minimum terms, the overdue payment grows larger and reflects on your credit standing with us.

We are sure that you are concerned about your past due account and will send us a check by return mail.

Cordially,

WE ARE WILLING TO MAKE ALLOWANCES . . .

for any emergency which may have arisen that made it impossible for you to meet our credit terms, but, for a lack of a reply, we must assume that you do not intend to pay.

UNLESS YOUR PAYMENT HAS ALREADY BEEN SENT, WE MUST HEAR FROM YOU IN THE NEXT 5 DAYS, SO WE WILL NOT HAVE TO SEND THIS ACCOUNT TO OUR COLLECTION DEPT.

Credit Department

IF . . .

you realized that your continued disregard of the many notices we have sent you has made your account 90 days or more overdue, we are sure your check would have been sent to us before the date we reviewed your account.

We cannot continue to hold this account in our hands without positive action on your part to make your account current.

Your credit is a valuable asset—we are sure you realize this and will send your check today before it is too late. If it has been mailed in the last few days, please accept our thanks.

Collection Department

WE HAVE HAD NO RESPONSE

to our recent notices to you about the overdue amount on your charge account.

Silence is golden except where your failure to reply is certain to affect your credit record with us.

If a check hasn't already been sent, enclose it in the attached envelope, and mail it to us today . . . before you forget again.

Collection Dept.

FIGURE 17-2 *(continued)*

RELUCTANTLY . . .

WE ARE CLOSING YOUR ACCOUNT TO ALL FURTHER PURCHASES. THIS MEANS THAT YOUR ACCOUNT CANNOT BE USED AGAIN WITHOUT THE SPECIFIC PERMISSION OF THIS OFFICE.

TO PROTECT YOUR CREDIT RECORD, we are giving you the consideration of a 10-day period to pay your delinquent balance before turning this account over to an outside collection agency.

Very truly yours,

YOUR CONTINUED PURCHASES . . . . .

ON YOUR SERIOUSLY OVERDUE ACCOUNT FORCE US TO RELUCTANTLY CLOSE YOUR ACCOUNT AT ONCE, AND TO NOTIFY OUR STORES TO DISCONTINUE ANY FURTHER CREDIT TO YOU.

WE ARE STILL WILLING TO DISCUSS ARRANGEMENTS ON YOUR ACCOUNT WITH YOU, BUT ANY FURTHER ATTEMPT TO PURCHASE WILL RESULT IN STRINGENT COLLECTION ACTION.

TO AVOID THE EMBARRASSMENT OF HAVING OUR COLLECTION AGENT CALL IN PERSON TO PICK UP YOUR CHARGE PLATE, YOUR PLATE MUST BE RETURNED TO OUR OFFICE WITHIN 4 DAYS FROM THE POSTMARK OF THIS LETTER.

COLLECTION DEPT.

calls the store and pays for the goods by credit card. The goods are then delivered to the shopper's home.

In-home shopping is becoming popular with such firms as home decorators who bring samples of draperies, carpeting, and wallpaper to a customer's house. The customer can then see how the materials look in the house under normal lighting conditions. They also don't have to waste time in "dressing up" and driving to the store.

Personal shopping is one of the fastest growing services. Individuals can call the store and tell a clerk the type of product they want and the price range they want to pay. The consultant then makes the purchase and has it wrapped and delivered.

Some boutiques are also now specializing in assembling wardrobes for working women. The female executive goes to the store and provides a list of needed measurements and preferences about styles and colors. After that, she simply calls the store and indicates the type of item she wants. The store personnel then assemble several choices and have them ready for the person to examine when she enters the store. We are likely to see this type of service expand in the future.

SERVICES THAT MAKE MONEY FOR YOU

Most services are designed to help sell merchandise and are offered at no cost. But you can offer some services for which you charge and get that which will help you to sell more. One of the most common is *extended warranties* or service contracts. Here, you simply agree to extend a manufacturer's warranty for a period of time, commonly a year or so, for a set price. Then, the customer does not have to pay a repair bill regardless of how much the repair service costs. Extended warranties are common on major household appliances and television sets. Other services such as carpet and drapery cleaning and appliance repair can also add to the money earned by your outlet.

But be aware of truth in warranty legislation. Satisfaction guaranteed is a phrase often heard. But today such a statement is more of a contract than a courtesy. You have to be aware of the provisions of the Magnuson-Moss Warranty Act, Federal Trade Commission rules, and state and county laws which may affect warranties you make as a service to customers.

Many state laws also determine where and how store refund policies must be displayed so that they can be easily read by the public. Many catalogs now tell consumers that warranty information is available by mail from the store before purchasing. Some retailers include a special section in the store which has information about product warranties. The key is to try to balance store interest with consumer satisfaction. But having to keep an up-to-date warranty file on every item sold in the store is a tough thing to do.

The specifics of warranty policies are still left up to you as a retailer. You need to make decisions on (1) the length of the exchange period, (2) how to handle charge, cash, and check refunds, (3) how to handle complaints against unwarranted goods, and (4) how to handle returned "gift" merchandise.

HOW ABOUT EDUCATIONAL PROGRAMS?

Some retailers have had great success in offering sewing lessons, cooking lessons, and sessions on interior decorating, such as how to hang wallpaper. Cooking sessions to help sell microwave ovens have been very popular in recent years.

You can turn these programs into money-makers or at the very least make them break even. How? Limit the classes to those who have purchased the products you are promoting. Spreading the classes over several different time periods and days can keep customers coming back to the store. This increases the chances of making additional sales to these persons.

WILL YOU DELIVER?

Delivery will be a high expense item for you if you deliver "big ticket" items such as furniture and household appliances. You are often pressured not to charge extra for such delivery service, but think carefully about it.

The cost of delivery has increased rapidly because of unionization, increasing fuel costs, and labor costs. Also, deliveries to outlying areas are very expensive. Delivery systems can be (1) store owned, (2) independently owned, or (3) can involve the use of parcel post.

You may, as a small retailer, operate your own delivery service. Most of us are familiar with deliveries from the corner drugstore by a person in a worn-out compact car who delivers at odd hours of the day. Typically, you can either lease a car for such purposes or pay an employee a mileage allowance to use a personal car for delivery.

You can help your image as a full-service retailer by having your own fleet of trucks for delivery. Also, your deliveries can then be more flexible. But the cost of having your own trucks is high. You may want to use independent services such as United Parcel.

A third way to use parcel post and service express. You may want to use these services in addition to independent delivery services. Parcel post is a good way to deliver small packages to customers who may live a sizable distance from the store. Mail-order retailers often deliver in this way.

WILL YOU OFFER EXTENDED SHOPPING HOURS?

More and more retailers are offering consumers longer shopping hours—either late night or Sunday shopping. Sunday and evening hours are more likely to be found in areas other than the central business district.

Some retailers are happy about late night or 24-hour shopping. They have high fixed costs in buildings and equipment and utilities are about the same since the equipment runs all the time anyway. The extra sales volume spreads the fixed costs over more units of sales. You may pick up some loyal customers who can only shop at night because of ther jobs, college students, and people who simply like to shop late at night. You may do very well since only a few stores are usually open 24 hours a day. But study it carefully before you make a decision. You will have to pay overtime to employees, the chance of being robbed is greater, and your energy bills will go up somewhat.

Sunday openings are another way of giving customers more opportunity to shop with you. You will probably get some add-on store volume. But remember that the "blue laws" (laws against opening on Sunday) are a hot issue in some areas. Such laws are particularly a sore spot in the East and Southeast. Enforcement is spotty but you may find yourself in jail if a pressure group forces the police to enforce the law against opening. Blue laws are likely to be a thing of the past in the next few years, however. Most consumers want Sunday shopping.

HOW WILL YOU HANDLE COMPLAINTS?

You also need a policy in dealing with customer complaints. Customers are allowed to return items in most stores. You may feel that the customer should be satisfied at any price. Almost all retailers, while not guaranteeing satisfaction, do try to be fair to the consumer. You may face many complaints, including complaints about products, poor installation, problems with delivery, damaged goods, errors in billing, and so forth.

Complaints can be handled in either of two ways: (1) on a centralized or (2) decentralized basis. Stores with a *centralized complaint policy* deal with all complaints at a central level in the store. In this way they can be sure that a standardized policy is followed for all departments. In a *decentralized approach,* complaints are handled on the sales floor by the person who sold the item to the consumer. The customer gets greater personal attention in this way.

You probably will prefer not to give a cash refund. Rather, most retailers try to get the customer exchanging an item to accept a slip (a "due bill") which allows them to purchase an item at the same price in the future. These policies are designed to keep the customer coming back to the store. You may feel, however, that the consumer should be given cash because you believe they are more likely to be satisfied if they are given a refund.

You have to make a decision on whether the emphasis in handling complaints and returned merchandise will be on the customer or on the store. Here again a cost-benefit analysis is called for. Providing an elaborate system for handling complaints and returns is quite costly, especially when the consumer wants money instead of merchandise when returning an item. Still, you may be better off by viewing returns primarily from the viewpoint of the consumer. You may be able to generate goodwill among customers by going out of your way to have a liberal returned goods policy.

You will have many problems even under the best of circumstances. For example, what will be the store policy on merchandise returned after Christmas? The merchandise probably was purchased at full price when it was bought. The customer probably will bring the merchandise back to the store after Christmas when you are running the after-Christmas markdown sale. Should the customer, assuming the person wants cash, receive the regular price of the merchandise or should they receive the sale price at the time the merchandise is returned? Other problems come to mind. Will you, for example, allow consumers to return such items as formal wear or perhaps swimsuits after they have been worn a time or two? Customers have been known to buy formal wear for a special occasion and then return the items the next day for a full refund. The merchandise may be smudged or perhaps stained. Many stores exclude made-to-order goods, swimwear, mattresses, bedding, pierced earrings, millinery, and foundations from their return policy for health reasons. Finally, will you require proof of purchase before accepting returned merchandise?

ARE YOUR SERVICES COST EFFECTIVE?

All services you offer will cost money. You may need more employees to offer certain services. You must balance the cost against planned revenue or the loss of goodwill if you do not offer the services.

You cannot precisely determine the effect of each service on sales. Also, if certain services are offered by competition, you may also have to offer them to remain competitive.

Table 17–5 depicts the cost of four of the more common department store services which are offered. The costs range from a low of 0.25 percent of sales for customer services to 1.42 percent for credit and collection.

Many factors must be considered in deciding to either offer or discontinue

TABLE 17–5
Typical cost of selected services for a department store with sales of over $50 million (percent of total company sales)

Service	Typical figure	Middle range
Credit and collection	1.42	1.05–1.91
Customer services.................	0.25	0.16–0.36
Wrapping and packing	0.54	0.46–0.65
Delivery	0.66	0.49–0.82

Source : Jay Scher, *Financial and Operating Ratios of Department and Specialty Stores* (New York : National Retail Merchants Association, 1975), p. 53.

a service. The same is true when the retailer is trying to decide to charge for a service such as a merchandise return which is not the fault of the retailer.

Review your service offering

You should review your services from time to time and decide whether to continue all of them. Customer attitudes may change and you may improve your profit margins by having customers bag their own groceries, for example, or carry their own trays in a cafeteria.

SUMMARY

Many features of your store will affect how consumers view the store and whether they will shop with you. The kind and quality of services is a key factor in this regard.

You face a variety of decisions in deciding whether to offer credit, for example. You can offer in-store credit or have credit handled by an outside agency such as a bank issuing a Visa card to your customers. You may issue a store credit card of your own, or have a card with your name on it but which is actually handled by a bank. The pressure for bank credit cards is increasing and most stores will have them within a few years. Most types of credit are offered by the retailer at a loss. However, credit is necessary to keep up with competitors.

You can also offer a variety of other services as part of your retailing mix. These include extended hours and Sunday openings, delivery, services such as baby sitting, interior design counseling, nonstore shopping opportunities, appliance installation, and an almost endless variety of other services. However, always try to balance likely revenue against the cost of the services. Also, watch out for the legal issues involved in many of the services you may offer.

NOTES

1. "Over 586 Million Credit Cards in Circulation in the United States," *Journal of Consumer Credit Management* (Spring 1978), p. 123.

2. Douglas Hawes, Roger Blackwell, and Wayne Talarzyk, "Consumers Use of Credit : Result of a Nationwide Study," paper presented at the Southwestern Marketing Association Annual Meeting, San Antonia, Texas, March 18, 1976, p. 4.

3. Gilbert A. Churchill et al., "The Role of Credit Scoring in the Loan Decision," *The Credit World* (March 1977), p. 9.

DISCUSSION QUESTIONS

1. Explain the differences among: prepurchase services, postpurchase services, and ancillary services. Give several specific examples of each type.

2. What might be the major reason for a retailer offering services? Why are many retailers cutting down on the number of services they offer?

3. Briefly explain the choices of credit a retailer may offer customers.

4. Briefly describe the differences among the third-party credit card programs.

5. Why should a retailer have his or her own card for credit? What problems or disadvantages exist with having your own card? What seems to be the status of "in-house" credit today?

6. Evaluate the third-party card as a credit card program from the retailer's point of view.

7. What is the role of the bank in the *private label card?*

8. What are some retailers doing to encourage customers to pay cash for purchases?

9. What kinds of information will the typical credit application form include?

10. Explain *credit scoring*. How does it relate to the Equal Credit Opportunity Act? What are some of the important provisions of this act?

11. Briefly describe the importance of the Fair Debt Collection Practices Act.

12. Explain the most common shopper (shopping) services available to customers.

13. Discuss briefly the significance of *Extended warranties*.

14. "The specifics of warranty policies are still left up to you as a retailer." What must you make decisions on relating to this statement?

15. Discuss the issues relating to educational programs in retailing.

16. Why has the cost of delivery to customers increased rapidly recently? What kinds of delivery systems exist and what are the advantages of each? Disadvantages?

17. Discuss the implications of extended shopping hours for the retailer.

18. Discuss possible policies relative to check cashing by retailers.

19. Discuss the problems and issues concerning handling complaints.

PROJECTS

1. Talk to the credit manager at a couple of the local department stores in your community and to the loan officer at a couple of banks to determine how they evaluate customer applications for credit. Try to get a copy of the forms they use, if possible. Find out if they use credit scoring. If not, what do they do in order to be objective in their evaluations? Find out if they are reasonably current on the regulations about granting credit to women.

2. Visit several different types of stores in your community including supermarkets, department stores, and specialty stores. Find out the nature of their check

cashing policies. Specifically, what sorts of identification are required? Check cashing policies are likely to vary by type of store. Think about the reasons why the policies are different and be prepared to discuss them.

3. Ask for an interview with the credit manager of a large department-type store in your community. Attempt to get an interview and find out the types of credit offered in the store; how the decision is made whether or not to extend credit; and see if you can get the credit application form used.

4. Interview a group of students at random and select a

department store, a supermarket, a discount store (e.g., Kmart), and a national chain like Sears; have a list of services which they might offer (from the text listing, e.g.); then have each student check the services which they perceive are offered by each type of store chosen. Write up a report on your findings and suggest what they mean to you in terms of the material included in the chapter.

5. Make a list of the key services noted in the chapter. Make an appointment with managers of the types of

stores noted in (2) above. Get the impressions of each manager as to the importance to the operation of each service and summarize your findings in a brief report. Can you see any trends in the information collected?

6. Discuss with several friends complaints which they may have had against a store or stores. Describe how each was handled by (1) the customer, and (2) the store. Evaluate the process which you discover in this project.

Minicase 17–1   The Fashion Store is a college-oriented, trendy boutique which has been just "off campus" for some ten years. Mrs. Curtis and her two daughters have run a "cozy" store for young women in a very profitable and imaginative way. A major problem that Roxy Curtis, the daughter with the "figure sense," had been worrying about was the cash flow problem. The in-house charge accounts were just not being paid quickly and it was putting a lot of pressure on Fashion's financial position. Because of the very "personalized" atmosphere of Fashion, Pete Curtis (mother) did not want any kind of installment or revolving credit. She just knew that her "friends" (never customers—too impersonal!) would resent service charges—that would make her operation look just like "a chain" and that would destroy the image the Curtises had worked so hard to develop over the years. But Roxy told her mother that they had real "money problems" and something had to be done. Their average account was outstanding over three months without a payment—and since it was a college town, some of the accounts were never paid! Graduation came, and students went—without settling obligations. It was not worth the cost or effort to collect the Curtises agreed some years ago. What can be done to keep the image and yet help Roxy in her cash flow problem. Try to be creative here.

Minicase 17–2   Super Shoes, a family shoe store in the CBD area of a city of over 120,000 trade area population, was the most successful shoe store in town. Their children's department was a real "draw" as Mr. Right was a pro at fitting youngsters. A regular customer, Ms. Sage, came into the store on a fairly slow Wednesday with her 12-year-old son, Butch. As Mr. Right noted in the past, Butch was a pain; whatever he wanted didn't fit and whatever was a good fit, he didn't want. He also had some orthopedic problems and shoes he purchased had to be equipped with steel arches which meant a rather time-consuming activity which Mr. Right did without charge for the labor but just for the raw materials used in adjusting the shoes. On this particular Wednesday, even though it was slow, Butch was his usual obnoxious self. He and mom got into it several times, but finally Butch insisted on a pair of shoes which Right felt was a good choice and everyone appeared quite happy. Mrs. Sage told Right to do his "usual good arch job" and they'd pick the shoes up in a day or so as she worked downtown and it would be no problem. Butch said he wanted the shoes as soon as possible, but mother said that wasn't really necessary since he needn't be in such a hurry. With that event, the Sages departed and Right felt he would have the shoe repair department do the arches right away. He also thought he could do a real nice thing and drop the shoes off at the Sages on his way home—it wasn't too far out of his way, and it would be a good customer-relations gesture. Time passes, and Right was proud of his consumer orientation as he drove up to the Sages with the newly adjusted shoes for Butch. He rang the door bell; Ms. Sage answered it and Mr. Right was shocked when Ms. Sage said, "Oh, I wish you had called—Butch has decided he doesn't like the shoes after all. I'm sure you can sell them to someone else!" Mr. Right stood there in shock and mounting concern that he was going to be angry! Advise Mr. Right quickly.

Minicase 17–3   Frank Walker, the store controller, has just walked into your office and said that the external auditor had found some problems with the way that interest charges were calculated when the store financed consumer purchases for major durables such as appliances. The overcharges were normally less than $1 per account but the overcharges were on approximately 600 purchases, some of which had already been paid off. Now you as store manager face a dilemma. Should you arrange a refund for each of the persons who was overcharged or should you simply say nothing? You are understandably concerned about (1) gaining a bad image in the minds of your customers for making the error in the first place and (2) you are also concerned that perhaps one of the customers will discover the overcharge and bring a class action suit on behalf of all consumers in a similar situation.

Discuss the merits of (1) informing the customers of the error, and (2) simply doing nothing.

APPENDIXES TO PART III

A.   Business plan for retailers*

by Staff Members, Education Division

SUMMARY

A business plan can provide the owner-manager or prospective owner-manager of a small retail firm with a pathway to profit. This Aid is designed to help an owner-manager in drawing up his business plan.

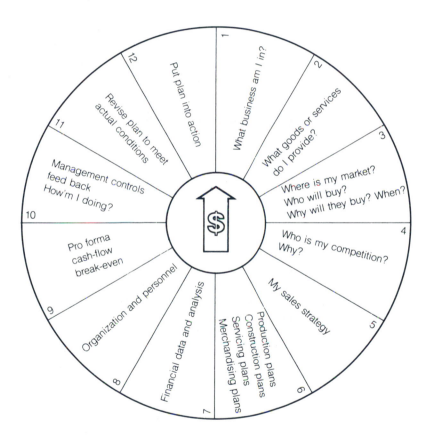

In building a pathway to profit you need to consider the following questions: What business am I in? What goods do I sell? Where is my market? Who will buy? Who is my competition? What is my sales strategy? What merchandising methods will I use? How

_____

* Small Business Administration, *Business Plans for Retailers,* by Staff members, Education Division, Office of Management Assistance, Small Marketers Aid No. 150 (Washington, D.C.: U.S. Government Printing Office, September 1972).

361

much money is needed to operate my store? How will I get the work done? What management controls are needed? How can they be carried out? When should I revise my plan? Where can I go for help?

No one can answer such questions for you. As the owner-manager you have to answer them and draw up your business plan. The pages of this Aid are a combination of text and work spaces so you can write in the information you gather in developing your business plan—a logical progression from a commonsense starting point to a commonsense ending point.

A NOTE ON USING THIS AID

It takes time and energy and patience to draw up a satisfactory business plan. Use this Aid to get your ideas and the supporting facts down on paper. And, above all, make changes in your plan on these pages as that plan unfolds and you see the need for changes.

Bear in mind that anything you leave out of the picture will create an additional cost, or drain on your money, when it unexpectedly crops up later on. If you leave out or ignore enough items, your business is headed for disaster.

Keep in mind, too, that your final goal is to put your plan into action. More will be said about this step near the end of this Aid.

WHAT'S IN THIS FOR ME?

You may be thinking: Why should I spend my time drawing up a business plan? What's in it for me? If you've never drawn up a plan, you are right in wanting to hear about the possible benefits *before* you do your work.

A business plan offers at least four benefits. You may find others as you make and use such a plan. The four are:

1. The first, and most important, benefit is that a plan gives you a path to follow. A plan makes the future what you want it to be. A plan with goals and action steps allows you to guide your business through turbulent economic seas and into harbors of your choice. The alternative is drifting into "any old port in a storm."

2. A plan makes it easy to let your banker in on the action. By reading, or hearing, the details of your plan he will have a real insight into your situation if he is to lend you money.

3. A plan can be a communications tool when you need to orient sales personnel, suppliers, and others about your operations and goals.

4. A plan can help you to develop as a manager. It can give you practice in thinking about competitive conditions, promotional opportunities and situations that seem to be advantageous to your business. Such practice over a period of time can help increase an owner-manager's ability to make judgments.

WHAT BUSINESS AM I IN?

In making your business plan, the first question to consider is: What business am I really in? At the first reading, this question may seem silly. "If there is one thing I know," you say to yourself, "it is what business I'm in." But hold on. Some owner-managers go broke and others waste their savings because they are confused about the business they are in.

Look at an example. Mr. OPQ on the East Coat maintained a dock and sold and rented boats. He thought he was in the marina business. But when he got into trouble and asked for outside help, he learned that he was not necessarily in the marina business. He was in several businesses. He was in the restaurant business with a dockside cafe—serving when a boating party wanted a meal. He was in the real estate business—buying and selling lots up and down the coast. He was in the boat repair business—buying parts and calling in a mechanic as the demand arose.

The fact was that Mr. OPQ was trying to be "All things to all people." With this approach he was fragmenting his slim resources.

Before he could make a profit on his sales and a return on his investment, Mr. OPQ had to decide what business he really was in and concentrate on it. After much study, he realized that his business really was "a recreation shopping center."

Decide what business you are in and write your answer in the following spaces. To help you decide, think of the answers to questions such as: What do you buy? What do you sell? Which of your lines of goods yields the greatest profit? What do people ask for that you don't have?

What is it that you are trying to do better or more of or differently from your competitors?

_____

_____

_____

_____

_____

_____

MARKETING

When you have decided what business you are in, you are ready to consider another important part of your business plan. Marketing. Successful marketing starts with the owner-manager. He has to know the merchandise lines he sells and the wants and desires of the customers he needs to reach. The objective is to move the stock off the shelves and display racks at the right price and bring in sales dollars.

The narrative and work blocks that follow are designed to help you work out a marketing plan for your store. The blocks are divided into three sections:

Section One—Determining the sales potential.

Section Two—Attracting customers.

Section Three—Selling to customers.

SECTION ONE—DETERMINING THE SALES POTENTIAL

In retail business, your sales potential depends on location. Like a tree, a store has to draw its nourishment from the area around it. The following questions should help you to work through the problem of selecting a profitable location.

In what part of the city or town will you locate?

In the downtown business section?

In the area right next to the downtown business area?

In a residential section of the town?

On the highway outside of town?

In the suburbs?

In a suburban shopping center?

List the reasons for your choice here:

I plan to locate in _____ because

_____

_____

_____

_____

What is the competition in the area you have picked?

The number of stores there that handle my lines of merchandise is _____

How many of these stores look prosperous? _____

How many look as though they are barely getting by? _____

How many similar stores went out of business in this area last year? _____

How many new stores opened up in the last year? _____

What price line does competition carry? _____

Which store or stores in the area will be your biggest competition? _____

_____

List the reason for your opinion here: _____

_____

Is the area in which you plan to locate supported by a strong economic base? For example, are nearby industries working full time? Only part time? Did any industries go out of business in the past several months? Are new industries scheduled to open in the next several months?

Write your opinion of the area's economic base and your reason for that opinion here. _____

_____ _____

_____

_____

When you find a store building that seems to be what you need, answer the following questions:

Is the neighborhood starting to run down? _____

Is the neighborhood new and on the way up?[1] _____

Are any super highways or throughways planned for the neighborhood? _____

Is street traffic fairly heavy all day?_____

Do the pedestrians who pass the building look as though they would be prospects for your store? _____

How close is the building to the bus line or other public transportation? _____

Are there adequate parking facilities convenient to the building? _____

Are the sidewalks in good repair? _____

Is the street lighting good? _____

Is the parking lot well-lighted if you are open at night? _____

What is the occupancy history of this store building? Does the store have a reputation for failures? (that is, stores opening and closing after a short time?) _____

If the store has housed several failures in recent years, can you find out why they failed? _____

Was it the location, excessive rent, or some other factor? _____

What rent will you have to pay each month? _____

What is the physical condition of the store? _____

What services, if any, does the landlord provide? _____

_____

What are the terms of the lease? _____

_____

I expect to do $_____ in annual sales in this location.

Finally, when you think you have solved the site-location of your new business, ask your banker to recommend the three people who in his opinion know the most about

---

[1] The local Chamber of Commerce may have information on the population of the area or be able to refer you to other local sources. Census Tracts on Population, published by the Bureau of Census, may also be useful. Other sources of such marketing statistics are trade associations and directories.

locations in your line of business. Contact these people and listen to their advice, weigh what they say, then decide.

SECTION TWO—ATTRACTING CUSTOMERS

When you have a location in mind, you should work through another aspect of marketing. How will you attract customers to your store? How will you pull business away from your competition?

It is in working with this aspect of marketing that many small retailers find competitive advantages. The ideas which they develop are as good, and often, better than those which large companies develop with hired brains. The work blocks that follow are designed to help you think about image, pricing, customer service policies, and advertising.

Image

A store has an image whether or not the owner is aware of it. For example, throw some merchandise onto shelves and onto display tables in a dirty, dimly lit store and you've got an image. Shoppers think of it as a dirty, junky store and avoid coming into it. Your image should be concrete enough to promote in your advertising and other promotional activities. For example, "home-cooked" food might be the image of a small restaurant.

Write out what image you want shoppers and customers to have of your store.

_____

_____

_____

_____

_____

Pricing

Value received is the key to pricing. The only way a store can have low prices is to sell low-priced merchandise. Thus, what you do about the prices you charge depends on the lines of merchandise you buy and sell. It also depends on what your competition charges for these lines of merchandise. Your answers to the following questions should help you to decide what to do about pricing.

In what price ranges are your lines of merchandise sold?

Quality? _____ Medium? _____ Low? _____

Which range will you stock? _____ Will you sell only for cash? _____

What services will you offer to justify your prices if they are higher than the prices of your competitors? _____

If you offer credit, will your price have to be higher than if all sales are for cash? _____

The credit costs have to come from somewhere. Plan for them.

If you use a credit card system, what will it cost you? Will you have to add to your prices to absorb this cost? _____

Customer service policies

The services you provide your customers may be free to them, but not to you. For example, if you provide parking, you pay for your own parking lot or pick up your part of the cost of a lot which you and other retailers use.

List the services that your competitors provide customers:

Services	*Your estimate of the cost of this service*
_____	_____
_____	_____
_____	_____
_____	_____

How many of these services will you have to provide just to meet competition?

_____

Are there services which would attract customers, but which competitors are not offering? _____

_____

If so, what are your estimates of the cost of such services?

Service	*Estimated cost*
_____	$ _____
_____	$ _____
_____	$ _____
_____	$ _____

Now list the services you plan to offer:

Service	*Estimated cost*
_____	$ _____
_____	$ _____
_____	$ _____
_____	$ _____
Total	$ _____

Advertising

In this section on attracting customers, advertising was saved until the last because you have to have something to say before advertising can be effective. When you have an image, price range, and customer services you are ready to *tell* prospective customers why they should shop in your store.

When the money you can spend for advertising is limited, it is vital that your advertising be on target. Before you think about how much money you can afford for advertising, take time to determine what jobs you want advertising to do for your store. The work blanks that follow should be helpful to your thinking.

The strong points of my store are _____

_____

My store is different from my competition in the following ways _____

_____

My advertising should tell shoppers and prospective customers the following facts about my store and its merchandise _____

_____

When you have these facts in hand, you are ready to think about the form your advertising should take and its cost. Ask the local media (newspapers, radio and television, and printers of direct mail pieces) for information about the services and the results they offer for your money.

How you spend advertising money is your decision, but don't fall into the trap that snares many businessmen. As one consultant describes this pitfall: It is amazing the way many businessmen consider themselves experts on advertising copy and media selection without any experience in these areas.

The following blanks should be useful in determining what advertising is needed to *sell* your strong points to prospective customers.

Form of advertising	Size of audience	Frequency of use		Cost of a single ad		Estimated cost
_____	_____	_____	× $	_____	= $	_____
_____	_____	_____	×	_____	=	_____
_____	_____	_____	×	_____	=	_____
_____	_____	_____	×	_____	=	_____
				Total	$	_____

When you have a figure on what your advertising for the next 12 months will cost, check it against what similar stores spend. Advertising expense is one of the operating ratios (expenses as a percentage of sales) which trade associations and other organizations gather. If your estimated cost for advertising is substantially higher than this average for your line of merchandise, take a second look. No single expense item should be allowed to get way out of line if you want to make a profit. Your task in determining how much to spend for advertising comes down to: How much can I afford to spend and still do the job that needs to be done?

SECTION THREE—SELLING TO CUSTOMERS

To complete your work on marketing, you need to think about what you want to happen *after* prospects get inside your store. Your goal is to *move stock off your shelves and displays—at a profit*—satisfy customers, and put money into your cash register. You also have to replenish the stock. To do this you have to encourage shoppers to become customers. Moreover, one-time customers can't do the job. You need repeat customers to build a profitable annual sales volume.

At this point, if you have decided to sell only for cash, take a second look at your decision. Don't overlook the fact that Americans like to buy on credit. Often a credit card, or other system of credit and collections, is needed to attract and hold customers.

The work blocks that follow are designed to help you think about in-store sales promotion, buying, stock control, and stock turn.

In-store sales promotion

In encouraging people to buy, self-service stores rely on layout, attractive displays, signs, and clearly marked prices on the items offered for sale. Other stores combine these techniques with personal selling. The work blocks that follow are designed to help you decide what to do and to estimate the cost of your actions.

If your store is to be self-service, list the display counters, racks, special equipment (such as frozen food display bins), and other fixtures:

Fixture	Number needed	×	Unit cost	×	Cost
_____	_____		$ _____		$ _____
_____	_____		_____		_____
_____	_____		_____		_____
_____	_____		_____		_____
_____	_____		_____		_____
_____	_____		_____		_____
_____	_____		_____		_____
_____	_____		_____		_____

Your plan for buying

I plan to buy merchandise from:

Name of Item	Name of supplier	Address of supplier	Discount offered	Delivery time*	Freight costs†	Fill-in policy‡
___	___	___	___	___	___	___
___	___	___	___	___	___	___
___	___	___	___	___	___	___
___	___	___	___	___	___	___
___	___	___	___	___	___	___
___	___	___	___	___	___	___
___	___	___	___	___	___	___
___	___	___	___	___	___	___
___	___	___	___	___	___	___

* How many days or weeks does it take the supplier to deliver the merchandise to your store?

† Who pays? You, the buyer? The supplier? (This cost can be a big expense item.)

‡ What is the supplier's policy on fill-in orders? That is, do you have to buy a gross, a dozen, or will he ship only 2 or 3 items? How long does it take him to deliver to your store?

If you are starting a new store and your line of merchandise calls for "back room" equipment, such as a meat slicing machine or food grinder, list such equipment:

Type of equipment	Number needed	×	Unit cost	=	Cost
_____	_____		$ _____		$ _____
_____	_____		_____		_____
_____	_____		_____		_____
_____	_____		_____		_____

How will you place your fixtures and displays to encourage people to buy? Draw up layouts on scratch paper. When you have a layout that suits you, attach it to this work sheet.

Will you make your display signs or buy them from a sign painter? Either way, determine how many signs you will need for a 12 months' operation and their cost.

I will need _____ signs at a cost of $_____ per sign. In 12 months, $_____ will be spent for display signs.

If your store is a combination of self-service and personal selling, how many sales-persons will you need?

I will need _____ salespersons at $_____ per week. (Include payroll taxes and insurance in this cost.) In 12 months, $_____ will be spent for sales people.

Personal attention to customers is one strong point which a small store can use as a competitive tool. What training will you provide for your retail salespeople in the following techniques?

How to greet customers _____

How to show merchandise _____

How to do suggestion selling _____

How to handle customer complaints _____

Buying

In buying merchandise, you need to answer questions such as:

> Who sells the line to retailers? It is sold directly by the manufacturer? Through job-bers? Through wholesalers?
>
> What delivery dates can you get?
>
> How quickly can the vendor deliver fill-in orders?
>
> What are his terms of sale?
>
> Can you establish terms of credit with him?
>
> If you plan to carry more than one line of merchandise, you should establish a source of supply on acceptable terms for each line before you open for business.

Stock control

In this plan, stock control is included under "Marketing" because "walkouts" can be a problem in a small store. Often shoppers leave without buying because the store did not have the items in the colors they wanted or the sizes they needed. Stock control, combined with suppliers whose policies on fill-in orders are favorable to you, provides a way to reduce "walkouts."

The types of system you use to keep informed about your stock depends on your line of merchandise and the delivery dates provided by your suppliers.

Your stock control system should enable you to determine what needs to be ordered on the basis of: (1) what is on hand, (2) what is on order, and (3) what has been sold. (Some trade associations and suppliers provide systems to members and customers.)

When you have determined the system you will use to control stock, estimate its cost. My system for stock control will cost me $_____ for the first year.

Stock turn

When an owner-manager does his buying job reasonably well, he can expect to turn his stock over several times a year. For example, the stock in a small retail camera shop should turn over four to four-and-one-half times a year. Fill in the blanks that follow:

The average stockturn for my line of merchandise is _____ times per year.

I expect to turnover my stock _____ times per year. List the reasons for your answer.

Behind-the-scenes work

In a retail store, behind-the-scenes work consists of the receiving of merchandise, preparing it for display, maintaining display counters and shelves, and keeping the store clean and attractive to customers. The work blocks which follow are designed to help you determine what to do and the cost of those actions.

List the equipment, for example, a marking machine, you will need for: (1) receiving merchandise into your back room, (2) preparing merchandise for display, (3) maintaining display counters and shelves, and (4) keeping the store clean and attractive to customers.

Name of equipment	Number needed	×	Unit cost	=	Cost
_____	_____		$ _____		$ _____
_____	_____		_____		_____
_____	_____		_____		_____
_____	_____		_____		_____
_____	_____		_____		_____
_____	_____		_____		_____
_____	_____		_____		_____

List the supplies you will need for 12 months for doing the four jobs listed above. For example, brooms, mops, price tags, and staples.

Kinds of supplies		
_____	$ _____	$ _____
_____	_____	_____
_____	_____	_____
_____	_____	_____
_____	_____	_____
_____	_____	_____

Who will do the back room work and the cleaning that is needed to make a smooth operation in the store? If you do it yourself, how many hours a week will it take? Will you do these chores after closing? If you use employees, what will they cost? Use the space below to describe how you plan to handle these tasks. For example: "Back room work will be done by one employee during the slack sales times of the day. I estimate that he will spend _____ hours per week on these tasks and will cost me $_____ (number of hours times his hourly pay) per week and $_____ per year.

I will need _____ square feet of space for the back room operation. This space will cost $_____ per square foot or a total of $_____ per month.

Overhead.   List the overhead items which will be needed. Examples are: utilities, office help, insurance, telephone, postage, accountant, payroll taxes, and licenses or other local taxes. If you plan to hire others to help you manage, their salaries should be listed as overhead.

_____

_____

_____

_____

_____

_____

_____

_____

_____

Getting the work done

Organization is needed if your store is to produce what you expect it to produce; namely, profitable sales dollars.

Organization is essential because you as the owner-manager cannot do all the work. You have to *delegate work, responsibility,* and *authority.* A helpful tool in getting this done is the organization chart. It shows at a glance who is responsible for the major activities of a business. Examples are given here to help you in preparing an organization chart for your business.

An organization chart for a small retail store will reflect the fact that the owner-manager does most of the managing work himself. For example, if your store is run by yourself and two salespersons, the chart should show what you expect each of them to do. It could look like this:

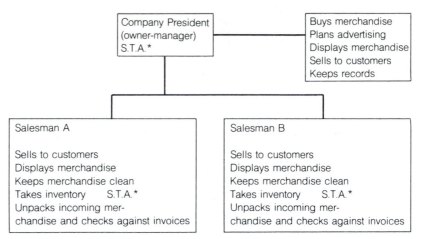

* A small store exists to serve customers. They want to be served promptly and don't like to be ignored even by the stock boy. A device to insure that they are recognized is S.T.A.—special team assignment. When all the salespeople are tied up, the available employee moves into special team assignment.

As the business grows, the owner-manager might set up the job of assistant manager. The organization chart should look like this:

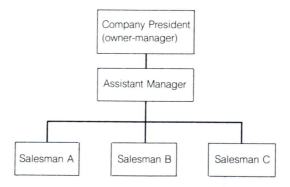

In training employees, you may want to emphasize that in a small business everyone has to pitch in and get the job done. Customers are not interested in job descriptions, but they are interested in being served promptly. Nothing is more frustrating to a customer than to be ignored by an employee.

In the space below, draw up an organization chart for your business.

Put your plan into dollars

At this point, take some time to think about what your business plan means in terms of dollars. This section is designed to help you put your plan into dollars.

The first question concerns the source of dollars. After your initial capital investments, in a small retail store, the principal source of money is sales. What sales volume do you expect to do in the next 12 months? Write your answer here $_____$.

Start-up costs. If you are starting a new store, list the following estimated start-up costs:

Fixtures and equipment*	$_____
Starting inventory	$_____
Decorating and remodeling	$_____
Installation of equipment	$_____
Deposits for utilities	$_____
Legal and professional fees	$_____
Licenses and permits	$_____
Advertising for the opening	$_____
Accounts receivable	$_____
Operating cash	$_____
Total	$_____

*If you listed the cost of these items, transfer your figures.

Whether you have the funds (savings) or borrow them, your new business will have to pay back these start-up costs. Keep this fact in mind as you work on the next section. "Expenses," and on other financial aspects of your plan.

Expenses.   In connection with annual sales volume you need to think about expenses. If, for example, you plan to do sales amounting to $100,000, what will it cost you to do this amount of business? And even more important, what will be left over as profit at the end of the year? Never lose sight of the fact that profit is *your* pay. Even if you pay yourself a salary for living expenses, your business must make a profit if it is to continue year after year and pay back the money you invested in it.

The following formula is designed to help you make a quick estimate of your expenses. To use this formula you need to get only one figure—the cost of goods sold figure for your line of merchandise. If you don't have this operating ratio for your firm, check with your trade association or with other sources.

	Expressed in	Percentage	Expressed in dollars	Your percentage	Your dollars
1.	Sales	100	$100,000	100	$_____
2.	Cost of goods sold	−66*	−66,000		−$_____
3.	Gross margin	34*	$ 34,000		
				_____	$_____

* These figures are intended only as a sample. The percentages (cost of goods sold, advertising, and so on) vary from one line of business to another.

Break down your expenses.   Your quick estimate of expenses provides a starting point. The next step is to break down your expenses so they can be handled over the 12 months. Use the "Expenses Work Sheet" form to make up an expense budget.

Matching money and expenses.   A budget helps you to see the dollar amount of your expenses each month. Then from month to month the question is: Will sales bring in enough money to pay the store's bills on time? the answer is "maybe not" or, "I hope so" unless the owner-manager prepares for the "peaks and valleys" that are in many retail operations.

A cash forecast is a management tool which can eliminate much of the anxiety that can plague you if your sales go through lean months. Use the work sheet. "Estimated Cash Forecast," or ask your accountant to use it, to estimate the amounts of cash that you expect to flow through your business during the next 12 months.

Is additional money needed?   Suppose at this point, you have determined that your business plan needs more money than can be generated by sales. What do you do?

What you do depends on the situation. For example, the need may be for bank credit to tide the store over during lean sales months. The loan can be repaid during the fat sales months when expenses are far less than sales. Adequate working capital is necessary for success and survival.

Whether an owner-manager seeks to borrow money for only a month or so or on a long-term basis, the lender needs to know whether the store's financial position is strong or weak. He will ask to see a current balance sheet.

Estimated cash forecast

	Jan.	Feb.	Mar.	April	May	June	July	Aug.	Sept.	Oct.	Nov.	Dec.
1. Cash in bank (start of month)												
2. Petty cash (start of month)												
3. Total cash—add (1) and (2)												
4. Expected cash sales												
5. Expected collections												
6. Other money expected												
7. Total receipts—add (4), (5), and (6)												
8. Total cash and receipts—add (3) and (7)												
9. All disbursements (for month)												
10. Cash balance at end of month in bank account and petty cash—subtract (9) from (8)*												

* This balance is your starting cash balance for the next month.

Expense worksheet: Sample figures for hardware stores

	Percent of sales	Percent of your sales	Your annual sales dollars	Your dollars Jan.	Your dollars Feb.	Your dollars Mar.
Net sales	100.00	_____	_____	_____	_____	_____
Cost of goods sold	66.05	_____	_____	_____	_____	_____
Margin	33.95%	_____	_____	_____	_____	_____
Salary expense:						
Owners and managers	7.15					
Salespeople, office, and other	9.60	_____	_____	_____	_____	_____
Total salaries	16.75	_____	_____	_____	_____	_____
Other expense:						
Office supplies and postage	0.40	_____	_____	_____	_____	_____
Advertising	1.55	_____	_____	_____	_____	_____
Donations	0.05	_____	_____	_____	_____	_____
Telephone and telegraph	0.30	_____	_____	_____	_____	_____
Losses on notes and accounts receivable	0.15	_____	_____	_____	_____	_____
Delivery expense (exclusive of wages)	0.50	_____	_____	_____	_____	_____
Depreciation of delivery equipment	0.25	_____	_____	_____	_____	_____
Depreciation of furniture, fixtures, and tools	0.35	_____	_____	_____	_____	_____
Rent	2.70	_____	_____	_____	_____	_____
Repairs to building	0.10	_____	_____	_____	_____	_____
Heat, light, water, and power	0.80	_____	_____	_____	_____	_____
Insurance	0.80	_____	_____	_____	_____	_____
Taxes (not including federal income tax)	1.10	_____	_____	_____	_____	_____
Interest on borrowed money	0.05*	_____	_____	_____	_____	_____
Unclassified (including store supplies)	1.20	_____	_____	_____	_____	_____
Total expense (not including interest on investment)	27.05	_____	_____	_____	_____	_____
Net profit	6.90	_____	_____	_____	_____	_____

* The interest on funds for start-up costs if yours is a new store.

Your dollars Apr.	*Your dollars May*	*Your dollars June*	*Your dollars July*	*Your dollars Aug.*	*Your dollars Sept.*	*Your dollars Oct.*	*Your dollars Nov.*	*Your dollars Dec.*

A blank current balance sheet is included below. Even if you don't need to borrow, use it, or have your accountant use it, to draw the "picture" of your firm's financial condition. Moreover, if you don't need to borrow money, you may want to show your plan to the bank that handles your store's checking account. It is never too early to build good relations with your banker, to let him know that you are a manager who knows where he wants to go rather than a store owner who *hopes* to make a success.

Current balance sheet
for

_____

(name of your firm)

As of _____

(date)

Assets

Current assets :
  Cash :
    Cash in bank . . . . $_____
    Petty cash . . . . _____ $_____
  Accounts receivable . . . . $_____
    Less allowance for doubtful
    accounts . . . . _____   _____
  Merchandise inventories . . . . _____
       Total Current assets . . . . $_____
Fixed assets :
  Land . . . . $_____
  Buildings . . . . _____
  Delivery equipment . . . . _____
  Furniture and fixtures . . . . _____ $_____
    Less allowance for depreciation . . . . $_____   _____
  Leasehold improvements, less
    amortization . . . . _____
       Total Fixed assets . . . .   _____
Total Assets . . . . $_____

Liabilities and Capital

Current liabilities :
  Accounts payable . . . . $_____
  Notes payable, due within 1 year . . . . _____
  Payroll taxes and withheld taxes . . . . _____
  Sales taxes . . . . _____
       Total Current Liabilities . . . . $_____
Long-term liabilities :
  Notes payable, due after 1 year . . . . _____
Total Liabilities . . . . $_____
Capital :
  Proprietor's capital, beginning of
    period . . . . $_____
  Net profit for the period . . . . $_____
  Less proprietor's drawings . . . . _____
  Increase in capital . . . . _____
    Capital, end of period . . . . $_____
Total Liabilities and Capital . . . . $_____

Control and feedback

To make your plan work you will need feedback. For example, the year-end profit and loss statement shows whether your business made a profit or loss for the past 12 months.

But you can't wait 12 months for the score. To keep your plan on target you need readings at frequent intervals. A profit and loss statement at the end of each month or at the end of each quarter is one type of frequent feedback. However, the income statement or profit and loss statement (P and L) may be more of a *loss* than a profit statement if you rely only on it. You must set up management controls which will help you to insure that the right things are being done from day to day and from week to week. In a new business, the record-keeping system should be set up *before* the store opens. After you're in business is too late. For one thing, you may be too busy to give a record-keeping system the proper attention.

The control system which you set up should give you information about : stock, sales, and disbursements. The simpler the system, the better. Its purpose is to give you current information. You are after facts with emphasis on trouble spots. Outside advisers, such as an accountant, can be helpful.

Stock control. The purpose of controlling stock is to provide maximum service to your customers. Your aim should be to achieve a high turnover on your inventory. The fewer dollars you tie up in stock, the better.

In a small store, stock control helps the owner-manager to offer his customers a balanced assortment. The control system should enable him to determine what needs to be ordered on the basis of: (1) what is on hand, (2) what is on order, and (3) what has been sold.

In setting up inventory controls, keep in mind that the cost of the stock is not your only cost. There are inventory costs, such as the cost of purchasing, the cost of keeping stock control records, and the cost of receiving and storing stock.

Sales. In a small store, sales slips and cash register tapes give the owner-manager feedback at the end of each day. To keep on top of sales, you will need answers to questions, such as: How many sales were made? What was the dollar amount? What were the best selling products? At what price? What credit terms were given to customers?

Disbursements. Your management controls should also give you information about the dollars your company pays out. In checking on your bills, you do not want to be "penny wise and pound foolish." You need to know what major items, such as paying bills on time to get the supplier's discount, are being handled according to your policies. Your review system should also give you the opportunity to make judgments on the use of funds. In this manner, you can be on top of emergencies as well as routine situations. Your system should also keep you aware that tax moneys, such as payroll income tax deductions, are set aside and paid out at the proper time.

Break even. Break-even analysis is a management control device because the break-even point shows about how much you must sell under given conditions in order to just cover your costs with *no* profit and *no* loss.

Profit depends on sales volume, selling price, and costs. Break-even analysis helps you to estimate what a change in one or more of these factors will do to your profits. To figure a break-even point, fixed costs, such as rent, must be separated from variable costs, such as the cost of goods sold.

The formula is :

Break-even point (in sales dollars) =

$$\text{Total fixed costs divided by } 1 - \frac{\text{Total variable costs}}{\text{Corresponding sales volume}}$$

An example of the formula is : Bill Mason plans to open a store and estimate his fixed expenses at about $9,000, the first year. He estimates his variable expenses at about $700 for every $1,000 of sales.

$$\text{BE Point} = \frac{\$9,000}{1-\dfrac{700}{1,000}} = \frac{\$9,000}{1 - 0.07} = \frac{\$9,000}{0.30} = \$30,000$$

Is your plan workable?

Stop when you have worked out your break-even point. Whether the break-even point looks realistic or way off base, it is time to make sure that your plan is workable.

Take time to reexamine your plan *before* you back it with money. If the plan is not workable, better to learn it now than to realize six months down the road that you are pouring money into a losing venture.

In reviewing your plan, look at the cost figures you drew up when you broke down your expenses for one year. If any of your cost items are too high or too low, change them. You can write your changes in the white spaces above or below your original entries on that work sheet. When you finish making your adjustments, you will have a *revised* projected statement of sales and expenses for 12 months.

With your revised figures work out a revised break-even point. Whether the new break-even point looks good or bad, take one more precaution. Show your plan to someone who has not been involved in working out the details.

Your banker, contact man at SBA, or other adviser outside of your business may see weaknesses that failed to appear as you pored over the details of your plan. And he may put his finger on strong points which your plan should emphasize and convert your strong points in the profit.

Put your plan into action

When your plan is as near on target as possible, you are ready to put it into action. Keep in mind that action is the difference between a plan and a dream. If a plan is not acted upon, it is of no more value than a pleasant dream that evaporates over the breakfast coffee.

A successful owner-manager does not stop after he has gathered information and drawn up a plan, as you have done in working through this Aid. He begins to use his plan.

At this point, look back over your plan. Look for things that must be done to put your plan into action.

What needs to be done will depend on your situation. For example, if your business plan calls for an increase in sales, one action to be done will be providing funds for this expansion.

Have you more money to put into this business?

Do you borrow from friends and relatives? From your bank? From your suppliers by arranging liberal commercial credit terms?

If you are starting a new business, one action step may be to get a loan for fixtures, stock employee salaries, and other expenses. Another action step will be to find and hire capable employees.

In the spaces that follow, list things that must be done to put your plan into action. Give each item a date so that it can be done at the appropriate time. To put my plan into action, I must do the following:

Action	*Completion date*
_____	_____
_____	_____
_____	_____
_____	_____
_____	_____

Keeping your plan up to date

Once you put your plan into action, look out for changes. They can cripple the best made business plan if the owner-manager lets them.

Stay on top of changing conditions and adjust your business plan accordingly.

Sometimes the change is within your company. For example, several of your salespersons quit their jobs. Sometimes the change is with customers; for example, their desires and tastes shift. Sometimes the change is technological as when new raw materials are put on the market and new products are created.

In order to adjust his plan to account for such changes, an owner-manager must:

1. Be alert to the changes that come about in his line of business, in his market, and in his customers.
2. Check his plan against these changes.
3. Determine what revisions, if any, are needed in his plan.

The method you use to keep your plan current so that your business can weather the forces of the market place is up to you. Read the trade papers and magazines for your line of business. Another suggestion concerns your time. Set some time—two hours, three hours, whatever is necessary—to review your plan periodically. Once each month, or every other month, go over your plan to see whether it needs adjusting. If revisions are needed, make them and put them into action.

B. Marketing checklist for small retailers*

by George Kress and R. Ted Will

If your retail firm is to be successful over the long run, it must satisfy the needs and desires of its present and/or potential *customers.* Sound *buying* means knowing where to buy, what to buy, how much to buy, and how to place an order. This requires familiarity with old and new products, adequate amounts of the right stock on hand, and selecting and working with suppliers in ways that benefit the store. In *pricing,* you need to understand the market forces affecting your business, plan the price policies that you will follow, and know whether your pricing policies meet state and federal regulations.

You need to be familiar with various types of *promotion* and when, where, and how to use them. In addition, a credit program or other special customer services can be attractions.

Under the heading of *management* goes the establishment both at long- and short-range goals. How you set up your organization and how you communicate with your employees are crucial factors in the accomplishment of your objectives. Of equal importance to good management is the ability to keep and make use of accurate *financial records.* It also pays to examine your *insurance* coverage in various areas.

In answering the following questions, you will be reminded of what you may still need to do to round out all marketing aspects of your business.

CUSTOMER ANALYSIS

Who are your target customers and what are they seeking from you?

	Yes	No
Have you estimated the total market you share with competition?	☐	☐
Should you try to appeal to this entire market rather than a segment(s)?	☐	☐
If you concentrate on a segment, is it large enough to be profitable?	☐	☐
Have you looked into possible changes taking place among your target customers which could significantly affect your business?	☐	☐
Can you foresee changes in the makeup of your store's neighborhood?	☐	☐
Are incomes in the community apt to be stable?	☐	☐
Is the community's population subject to fluctuation or seasonal?	☐	☐
Do you stress a special area of appeal such as lower prices, better quality, wider selection, convenient location, or convenient hours?	☐	☐
Do you ask your customers for suggestions on ways to improve your operation?	☐	☐
Do you use "want slips"?	☐	☐
Do you belong to your trade association?	☐	☐
Do you subscribe to important trade publications?	☐	☐
Have you considered using a consumer jury or consumer questionnaire to aid you in determining customer needs?	☐	☐
Do you visit market shows and conventions to help anticipate customer wants?	☐	☐

---

* George Kress and R. Ted Will, *Marketing Checklist for Small Retailers,* Small Business Administration, Small Marketers Aid No. 156 (Washington, D.C.: U.S. Government Printing Office, November 1978).

	Yes	No
Do most of your customers buy on weekends?	☐	☐
Do sales increase in the evening?	☐	☐
Does the majority of your customers prefer buying on credit?	☐	☐

BUYING

Have you a merchandise budget (planned purchases) for each season?

	Yes	No
Does it take into consideration planned sales for the season?	☐	☐
Does it achieve a planned stock turnover?	☐	☐
Have you broken it down by departments and/or merchandise classifications?	☐	☐
Have you a formal plan for deciding what to buy and from whom?	☐	☐
Have you a system for reviewing new items coming onto the market?	☐	☐
Have you considered using a basic stock list and/or a model stock plan in your buying?	☐	☐
Are you using some sort of unit control system?	☐	☐
Do you keep track of the success of your buying decisions in previous years to aid you in next year's buying?	☐	☐
Do you attempt to consolidate your purchases with two or three principal suppliers?	☐	☐
Have you a useful supplier evaluation system for determining their performance?	☐	☐
Have you established a planned gross margin for your firm's operations and are you buying so as to achieve it?	☐	☐

PRICING

Have you established a set of pricing policies?

	Yes	No
Have you determined whether to price below, at, or above the market?	☐	☐
Do you set specific markups for each product?	☐	☐
Do you set markups for product categories?	☐	☐
Do you use a one-price policy rather than bargain with customers?	☐	☐
Do you offer discounts for quantity purchases, or to special groups?	☐	☐
Do you set prices so as to cover full costs on every sale?	☐	☐
Have you developed policy regarding when you will take markdowns and how large?	☐	☐
Do the prices you have established earn planned gross margin?	☐	☐
Do you clearly understand the market forces affecting your pricing methods?	☐	☐
Do you know which products are slow movers and which are fast?	☐	☐
Do you take this into consideration when pricing?	☐	☐
Do you know which products are price sensitive to your customers; that is, when a slight increase in price will lead to a big dropoff in demand?	☐	☐
Do you know which of your products draw people when put on sale?	☐	☐
Do you know the maximum price customers will pay for certain products?	☐	☐
If the prices on some products are dropped too low, do buyers hesitate?	☐	☐
Is there a specific time of year when your competitors have sales?	☐	☐

	Yes	No
Do your customers expect sales at certain times?	☐	☐
Have you determined whether a series of sales is better than one annual clearance sale?	☐	☐
Do you know what role you want price to play in your overall retailing strategy?	☐	☐
Are you influenced by competitors' price changes?	☐	☐

Are there restrictions regarding prices you can charge?

	Yes	No
Do any of your suppliers "fair trade" their product by setting a minimum standard at which it can be sold?	☐	☐
Does your state have fair trade practice acts which require you to mark up your merchandise by a minimum percentage?	☐	☐
Are there any state regulations on how long "closeout" sales can be advertised?	☐	☐
Are you sure you know all the regulations affecting your business, such as two-for-one sales and the like?	☐	☐
Do you issue "rain checks" to customers when sale items are sold out so they can purchase later at sale price?	☐	☐

PROMOTION

Are you familiar with the strengths and weaknesses of various promotional methods?

	Yes	No
Have you considered how each type might be used for your firm?	☐	☐
Do you know which of your items can be successfully advertised?	☐	☐
Do you know which can best be sold through personal selling?	☐	☐
Do you know which can best be sold by demonstrations?	☐	☐
Do you know when it is profitable to use institutional advertising?	☐	☐
Do you know when product advertising is better?	☐	☐
Do you know which of the media (radio, television, newspapers, yellow pages, handbills) can most effectively reach your target group?	☐	☐
Do you know what can and cannot be said in your ads (Truth in Advertising requirements)?	☐	☐
Can you make use of direct mail?	☐	☐
Is a good mailing list available?	☐	☐
Are your promotional efforts fairly regular?	☐	☐
Do you concentrate them on certain seasons?	☐	☐
Are certain periods of the week better than others?	☐	☐

Is there available financial or technical assistance which you can use to enhance your promotional efforts?

	Yes	No
Can you get help from local newspapers, radio, or television?	☐	☐
Are cooperative advertising funds available from suppliers?	☐	☐
Do you tie your local efforts to your suppliers' national program?	☐	☐
Do you join with other merchants in areawide programs?	☐	☐
Have you looked for guidelines or ratios to estimate what comparable firms are spending on promotion?	☐	☐
Do you study the advertising of other successful retail firms, as well as of your competitors?	☐	☐
Have you some way of measuring the success of the various promotional programs you are using?	☐	☐

Are your products displayed to maximize their appeal within the store?   Yes   No

Do you know which of your items have unusual eye appeal and can be effective in displays?   ☐   ☐

Have you figured out the best locations in the store for displays?   ☐   ☐

Are you making use of window displays to attract customers?   ☐   ☐

If you use multitiered display stands or gondolas, do you know which shelves are the best sellers?   ☐   ☐

Have you a schedule for changing various displays?   ☐   ☐

Do you display attention-getting items where they will call attention to other products as well?   ☐   ☐

Do you know which items are bought on "impulse" and therefore should be placed in high traffic areas?   ☐   ☐

Where price is important, do you make sure the price cards are easy to read?   ☐   ☐

Do your suppliers offer financing of accounts receivable, floor planning, and so forth?   ☐   ☐

Do you know what type of credit program (if any) you should offer?   Yes   No

Does the nature of your operation require some type of credit for your customers?   ☐   ☐

Have you discussed credit operations with your local credit bureau?   ☐   ☐

Would a credit program be a good sales tool?   ☐   ☐

Is a credit program of your own desirable?   ☐   ☐

Have you looked into other programs or credit cards?   ☐   ☐

If you set up your own credit program, do you know what standards you should use in determining which customers can receive credit, for what time periods, and in what amounts?   ☐   ☐

Do you know all of the costs involved?   ☐   ☐

Will the interest you charge pay for these costs?   ☐   ☐

Do you know about the Fair Credit Reporting Act?   ☐   ☐

Are you familiar with the Truth-in-Lending legislation?   ☐   ☐

Have you determined a safe percentage of your business to have on credit that won't jeopardize paying your own bills?   ☐   ☐

Have you discussed your credit program with your accountant and attorney?   ☐   ☐

Do you offer some special customer services?   Yes   No

If you offer delivery service, do you own your vehicles?   ☐   ☐

Have you considered leasing them instead?   ☐   ☐

Have you thought about using commercial delivery service?   ☐   ☐

Do you charge for delivery?   ☐   ☐

If not, do you know how to work the delivery expenses into the selling price of your products?   ☐   ☐

Have you a policy for handling merchandise returned by customers?   ☐   ☐

Have you considered certain obligations to your community, in terms of charitable contributions, donations for school functions, ads in school yearbooks?   ☐   ☐

Do you participate in activities of your chamber of commerce, merchants' association, Better Business Bureau, or other civic organizations? ☐ ☐

MANAGEMENT

Have you developed a set of plans for the year's operations?   Yes   No

Do your plans provide methods to deal with competition? ☐ ☐
Do they contain creative approaches to solving problems? ☐ ☐
Are they realistic? ☐ ☐
Are they stated in such a way that you know when they have been achieved? ☐ ☐
Have you a formal plan for setting aside money to meet any quarterly tax payments? ☐ ☐

Are you organized effectively?   Yes   No

Are job descriptions and authority for responsibilities clearly stated? ☐ ☐
Does your organizational structure minimize duplication of effort and maximize the use of each employee's skills? ☐ ☐
Do employees understand how they will be rated for promotion and salary increases? ☐ ☐
Does your wage schedule meet the local rate for similar work and retain competent employees? ☐ ☐
Would you or some of your employees profit by taking business education courses offered at local schools? ☐ ☐
Will training help your employees achieve better results? ☐ ☐
Do your experienced employees help train new and part-time employees? ☐ ☐
Have you provided for good working conditions? ☐ ☐
Do you use positive personal leadership techniques like being impartial, giving words of encouragement and congratulations, and listening to complaints? ☐ ☐
Are you familiar with the Fair Labor Standards Act as it applies to minimum wages, overtime payments, and child labor? ☐ ☐
Do you avoid all forms of discrimination in your employment practices? ☐ ☐
Do you have a formal program for motivating employees? ☐ ☐
Have you taken steps to minimize shoplifting and internal theft? ☐ ☐

Have you an effective system for communicating with employees?   Yes   No

Are they informed on those plans and results that affect their work? ☐ ☐
Do you hold regular meetings that include all personnel? ☐ ☐
Do your employees have their own bulletin board for both material you need to post and items they wish to post? ☐ ☐
Have the "rules and regulations" been explained to each employee? ☐ ☐
Does each employee have a written copy? ☐ ☐
Is each employee familiar with other positions and departments? ☐ ☐
Do you have an "open door" policy in your office? ☐ ☐

FINANCIAL ANALYSIS AND CONTROL

Have you established a useful accounting system?	**Yes**	**No**
Do you know the minimum amount of records you need for good control?	☐	☐
Do you know all the records you should keep to aid you in meeting your tax obligations on time?	☐	☐

Do your "sales" records give you the key information you need to make sound decisions?	**Yes**	**No**
Can you separate cash sales from charge sales?	☐	☐
Can sales be broken down by department?	☐	☐
Can they be broken down by merchandise classification?	☐	☐
Do they provide a way to assess each salesperson's performance?	☐	☐

Do your "inventory" records give you the key information you need to make sound decisions?	**Yes**	**No**
Do they show how much you have invested in merchandise without the necessity of a physical inventory?	☐	☐
Do you know the difference between inventory valuation at cost and at market?	☐	☐
Can you tell which one shows a loss in the period earned?	☐	☐
Can you tell which one conserves cash?	☐	☐
Do you understand the pros and cons of the cost method of inventory accounting versus the retail method?	☐	☐
Have you found an accounting method that shows the amount of inventory shortages in a year?	☐	☐

Do your "expense" records give you the key information you need to make sound decisions?	**Yes**	**No**
Do you know which expense items you have the greatest control over?	☐	☐
Are the records sufficiently detailed to identify where the money goes?	☐	☐
Can you detect those expenses not necessary to the successful operation of your business?	☐	☐

Do you effectively use the information on your profit and loss statement and balance sheet?	**Yes**	**No**
Do you analyze monthly financial statements?	☐	☐
Can you interpret your financial statements in terms of how you did last year and whether you met this year's goals?	☐	☐
Do your financial statements compare favorably with other similar businesses in terms of sales, cost of sales, and expenses?	☐	☐
Are you undercapitalized?	☐	☐
Have you borrowed more than you can easily pay back out of profits?	☐	☐
Can you see ways to improve your profit position by improving your gross margin?	☐	☐
Do you use the information contained in your financial statements to prepare a cash budget?	☐	☐

INSURANCE

Have you adequate insurance coverage?

	Yes	No
Do you have up-to-date fire coverage on both your building equipment and inventory?	☐	☐
Does your liability insurance cover bodily injuries as well as such problems as libel and slander suits?	☐	☐
Are you familiar with your obligations to employees under both common law and workmen's compensation?	☐	☐
Do you spread your insurance coverage among a number of agents and take the risk of overlapping coverage or gaps which may raise questions as to which firm is responsible?	☐	☐
Has your insurance agent shown you how you can cut premiums in areas like fleet automobile coverage, proper classification of employees under workmen's compensation, cutting back on seasonal inventory insurance?	☐	☐
Have you looked into other insurance coverage, such as business interruption insurance or criminal insurance?	☐	☐
Do you have some fringe benefit insurance for your employees (group life, group health, or retirement insurance)?	☐	☐

PART IV

Have you done a good job? You must measure results . . .

You are very fortunate that in retailing certain things exist to help you answer the critical question raised above. "Have you done a good job?" Everyone wants to know that. Your grades in courses give you a measure of how well you've done. You "aim" for an A and receive a B. Have you done well? We suggest you did not meet your "budget."

So in this part you will learn how to set up a control system and an accounting system. These activities help you measure your results. We stress at first that your *plan* (look back at Part III) is essential.

Let's move on to . . . developing a control system and developing an accounting system.

18

HOW DO YOU DEVELOP
A CONTROL SYSTEM?

This chapter helps you understand:

- The relationship between planning and control.
- How to set up a dollar control system and an open-to-buy system to control your dollar merchandise investment.
- How to set up a unit control system to control your width (breadth) and support (depth) of merchandise inventory.
- What is meant by expense control.
- The meaning of the following terms:

Dollar control   Unit control
Book (perpetual) inventory   Expense control
Open-to-buy

You are coming down the home stretch! If you will look again at "The Student's Guide to Retailing" (Figure I-1) you'll see how close you are.

You are now going to see how to tell if you have done a good job. You've already planned for profitable operations. How effective have you been?

THE RELATIONSHIP BETWEEN PLANNING AND CONTROL

You learned how to plan for profits in Chapter 11. You might refer back to Figure 11-1 and review the process. Remember, you were involved in planning the following assortment aspects: (1) dollars, (2) width, and (3) support. We came up with a merchandise budget in dollars. We also developed a model stock. We planned "dollars to spend" and "what to spend the dollars *for.*"

Figure 18-1 carries the planning process forward to control. This will be your road map for much of this chapter. Figure 18-2 also shows how control relates to planning but in a slightly different way. We shall refer to this diagram too.

As you can see by the two figures, planning comes before control. You can't have control without a plan. And you can only control if you have a plan.

Thus the relationship is *essential, direct,* and two way. (See the two-way arrows, Figure 18-1, between "purchase plan" and "dollar control" and between "model stock" and "unit control.") You can't plan without information from control records. Remember "last year's sales figures" from Chapter 11? Each time we planned a factor in the budget, we started with "last year's figures."

Those "last year's figures" come from the firm's control records. So what is the two-way relationship? You need control records to plan and you need them to see if your plan is working.

You can look at it this way:

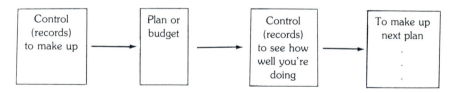

In summary, without control, planning is wasted effort.

DOLLAR CONTROL

Dollar control is a way of controlling dollar investment in inventory (see Figure 18-1). You get the information to set up dollar control from your accounting records.

Dollar control is of most concern to top management, especially in large firms. It is to regulate inventory values of merchandise departments or units of a chain.

In a small organization, no real difference exists between top management

FIGURE 18-1
From planning to control

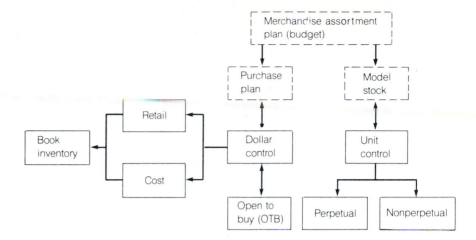

and operating management (e.g., buyers and store managers). So, dollar control is really a part of the total stock control activities. (Figure 18–2 shows that the two types of control—dollar and unit—work together). For example:

Book (perpetual) inventory

To control dollar inventory investments, you must know the following:

1. What dollar inventory you started with.
2. What has been added to stock.
3. How much inventory has moved out of stock.
4. How much inventory is on hand now.

The following illustration shows the basic things you must know to control your dollar inventory investment:

	1.	Inventory at the beginning of the period	$10,000
+	2.	Purchases added to stock	2,000
=		Available for sale during the period	$12,000
−	3.	Sales	2,500
=	4.	Inventory at the end of the period	$ 9,500

FIGURE 18-2
Diagram of merchandise planning and control

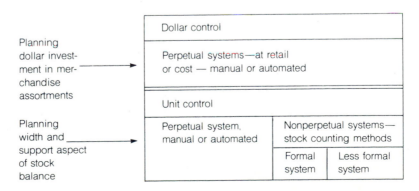

In the following discussion of retail dollar control, a more complex statement appears. The illustration above simply sets the stage for what follows. If you see these simple additions and subtractions from your beginning inventory, the more complicated example (only complicated because of the additional things which affect the dollars you have invested in inventory) is quite easy to follow.

You can get the answer to (4) by *(a)* taking a physical inventory or *(b)* setting up a book or perpetual inventory. It is impractical to take a *physical inventory* (actually count all of your inventory) every time you want to know what you have on hand. So set up a *book inventory system* which lets you know what you have in stock without actually counting it.

This means that to have dollar control, you must have some kind of book inventory. The information you need must be collected continually. The inventory can be collected in *retail* dollars or in *cost* dollars.

Retail dollar control. Figure 18–3 includes the typical items in a dollar control system. The system is a perpetual one in retail dollars. You can find out at any time with this system answers to the following questions:

1. What dollar inventory did you start with? The BOM inventory, 3/1 gives the answer to that question. This March BOM inventory figure is the EOM February figure.

2. What has been added to stock? The "additions to stock": purchases, transfers, and additional markups add dollars to the beginning inventory.

3. How much inventory has moved out of stock? The "deductions from stock": sales, markdowns, and employee discounts reduce the total dollars available for sale.

4. How much inventory is on hand now? The "EOM Inventory, 3/31" is the difference in what was available and what moved out of stock. This is the book inventory figure.

We have made an effort to make the book inventory statement complete. Don't confuse this with an accounting statement (see following chapter). Even though the information here comes from the accounting data, it is for control only.

It is important to understand the items that affect your book inventory. The explanations in Figure 18–3 should be carefully studied. It will make the next chapter easier for you. You will have much information which you'll need "under your belt."

Open-to-buy. One of the most valuable outputs of a retail dollar control system is open-to-buy (OTB) (Figure 18–1). Dollar control gives you the essential things needed to set up an OTB system. These essentials are the BOM and EOM inventories.

OTB is the control system which tells you how much your merchandise budget will allow you to buy. (See Chapter 11, section on planned purchases.)

If we assume the following, we can illustrate OTB as of February 15:

Planned purchases = $25,000 (EOM February or BOM March at retail)
+   2,500 (Planned sales—February)
+   600 (Planned reductions—February)
= $28,100 (Dollars needed)
− 24,000 (BOM February at retail)
= $ 4,100 (Planned purchases)

Commitments against planned purchases during the month of February:

On order to be delivered in February: $1,000

Merchandise received as of February 15: 1,500

OTB as of February 15

  −2,500 (Commitments against planned purchases)

= $ 1,600 (Note: The $1,600 figure is in retail dollars and must be converted to cost to use as a buying guide in the market.)

What does OTB tell you? First, it deducts from your planned purchases commitments you make. The two commitments made above are: (1) merchandise on order which has not been delivered and (2) merchandise which has been delivered. Remember, planned purchases relate to one particular month (in the case above to February). So, OTB relates to only one month. You could order merchandise in January to be delivered in March. That amount would not be a February commitment and would not affect the OTB for February.

The $1,600 OTB as of February 15 says that you have $1,600 left to spend to be delivered in February.

At the beginning of any month with no commitments, planned purchases and OTB are equal.

If you use up all of your OTB you are "overbought." That means that you have used your budgeted amount. Your control figure "kept you in line."

FIGURE 18-3
Illustration of retail dollar book (perpetual) inventory—tie classification—for month of March

Items affecting dollar value of inventory during month			Necessary explanations of certain items	Where do you get the information
BOM inventory. 3 1		$10,000		EOM February inventory
Additions to stock:				
Purchases	$2,000			Purchase records or invoices
Less—Vendor returns . . .	(100)		Goods go back to resource	Vendor return records
Net purchases		$1,900		
Transfers in	$ 200		In multistore firm goods transfer from one store to another	Interstore transfer forms in multistore firm
Less—Transfers out	(100)			
Net transfers in		100		
Additional markups		300	Price increase after goods in stock	Price change forms
Total additions		2,300		
Total available for sale		$12,300		
Deductions from stock:				
Gross sales	$2,500			Daily sales report
Less—Customer returns	(100)			Return forms
Net sales		$2,400		
Gross markdowns	$ 500		Reduction from original price	Price change forms at start of a sale
Less—Markdown cancellations	(100)			Price change cancellation at end of sale to bring prices back to regular
Net markdowns		400		
Employee discounts		200	Employee pays less than merchandise price	
Total deductions from stock		$ 3,000		Form completed at sale
EOM inventory. 3 31 (including shortages)		$ 9,300	A book inventory figure so actual amount is somewhat different (Physical inventory necessary for actual)	Derived figure from additions and deductions from BOM inventory

It is important to understand, however, that OTB must be used *only* as a guide. The system must not be used to dictate what you should do. You must always be ready to adjust OTB when necessary. (Of course, any budget must be flexible and adjusted when necessary.)

Look at Figure 18–4 and you will see a sample open-to-buy report form. Understand that this form would vary by company based on what management felt it needed to know for decision making. Note also that the "actual" last year and for this year to date can assist you in making adjustments during the month to your open-to-buy. At any time during the month, your OTB could be derived by:

Column 11 + Column 7 + Column 14 − Column 5 = Planned purchases − Column 17 = OTB (column 18).

FIGURE 18-4
Example of an open-to-buy report

Open-to-Buy Report				Department _____				Date prepared _____									
Last month ( )					This month ( )												
Sales			Stock		Sales				Stock			Markdowns					
(1)	(2)	(3)	(4)	(5)	(6)	(7)	(8)	(9)	(10)	(11)	(12)	(13)	(14)	(15)	(16)	(17)	(18)
Actual last year	Adjusted plan this year	Actual this year	Adjusted Plan EOM this year	Actual EOM this year	Actual last year	Adjusted plan this year	Month to date this year	Balance of month this year	Actual EOM last year	Adjusted plan EOM this year	Actual as of this report	Actual last year	Adjusted plan this year	Actual as of this report	Balance of month this year	On order to be received and received to date	Open-to-buy

You always want to have OTB to be able to take advantage of good market buys. For example, a special purchase of an item is offered. You want enough OTB to be able to buy it.

If you need more open-to-buy, you must be convinced that a budget adjustment is called for. Ways of increasing planned purchases, thus OTB are: (1) a contemplated purchase is good enough to increase planned sales; (2) increasing planned reductions or taking more markdowns than budgeted; or (3) increasing EOM inventory.

Cost dollar control. (Figure 18–1). You are less likely to use cost dollar control in retailing. The major problem in using cost (versus retail) control is "costing" each sale.

Because of the "costing" problem, you find control of inventories when: (1) merchandise is of an unusually high-unit value, and (2) there are relatively few transactions. With furniture or automobiles cost dollar control is practical. Figure 18–5 shows the kind of information needed for perpetual cost inventory.

Our tie illustration is ideal for retail dollar control. It would be unmanageable to use cost dollar control in this classification. The costing of sales would be too difficult.

UNIT CONTROL

If you refer again to Figures 18–1 and 18–2 you can see where we are. We have completed dollar control. We are now ready to discuss unit control. Unit control is simpler than dollar control. There are fewer factors which affect units than dollars invested. *The major difference is that price changes do not affect the units carried.* As Figures 18–1 and 18–2 indicate the two types of unit control are *perpetual* and *nonperpetual* (or stock counting).

Perpetual unit control

You can see from Figure 18–6 that perpetual unit control is a book inventory. Figure 18–3 (retail dollar control example) gives you the basic framework for unit control.

Note that in both Figures 18–3 and 18–6 there is a notation at the end, "including shortages." It needs explanation. Since these are "book" figures, there is chance for error. You can tell how accurate the book figure is only by taking a *physical inventory*.

To illustrate, let's compare a physical inventory to the book figure of 1,014 units in Figure 18–6. Assume the physical inventory is 1,000. This tells you

FIGURE 18–5
Perpetual cost dollar control

Date	BOM inventory	Cost of items received	Cost of items sold	Net change
March 1	$15,000	$1,500	$1,000	+ $ 500 ($1,500 − $1,000)
March 2	15,500	—	2,000	− 2,000
March 3	13,000	400	1,200	− 800 (+$400 − $1,200)
March 4	12,700			

FIGURE 18-6
Illustration of
perpetual unit control—
Tie classification for
month of March

BOM inventory			1,000
Additions to stock:			
Purchases	250		
Less—vendor returns	(40)		
Net purchases		210	
Transfers in	41		
Less—transfers out	(20)		
Transfers in		21	
Total additions			231
Total available for sale			1,231
Deductions from stock:			
Gross sales	225		
Less—customer returns	(8)		
Net sales		217	
Total deductions from stock			217
EOM inventory, 3/31 (including shortages)			1,014

that you have a shortage (or shrinkage) of *14* units. *If* the physical inventory had been 1,020, you would have an overage of 6 units.

How information on sales is collected. In a manual, perpetual system, sales information can be recorded by:

1. Writing on a sales check and having the information recorded in the back office.
2. Detaching a part of a sales ticket and counted later.
3. Deducting items sold from a floor sample.

Nonperpetual unit control

As you can see in Figure 18-2, nonperpetual unit control systems are also called stock counting methods. These methods include *formal* and *less formal* systems. You will find that perpetual systems are more expensive and often the cost cannot be justified.

Also, stock counting systems are *not* book inventory methods. So you will not be able to determine shortages or overages. You can see that if there is no book inventory against which to compare a physical inventory, no shortage can be determined.

Formal systems. The requirements of *formal, nonperpetual systems* are:

1. A planned model stock.
2. A periodic counting schedule.
3. Definite, assigned responsibility for counting.

You can think of our tie classification. Every tie-in stock might be counted once a month. You might select the first Tuesday of each month for your count schedule. Based on the stock on hand, the stock on order, and the stock sold, you will place a reorder. Figure 18-7 is an example of a type of count sheet that you might use.

FIGURE 18-7
Formal unit control sheet

Department: *Men's Furnishings* Classification: *Ties* Stock Number: *1320*

Item Description: *Regimental Stripe* Fabric: *Silk Rep* Style: *Four-in-hand*

Design: *Diagonal* *Stripes* Cost: *$10.00* Retail: *$20.00* Vendor Number: ____
_____

Miscellaneous: _____

Date of Count_____ On Hand_____ On Order_____ Received_____
Sold_____

You must realize that this nonperpetual system for unit control is really a compromise. Perpetual control is better and you get more and better information. But sometimes the benefits just do not justify the cost. Under certain conditions, however, the formal system which is nonperpetual can work quite successfully. The rate of sale of the items being controlled must be predictable. If it is a seasonal item such as beach towels, you must be able to predict the sales behavior. The formal system does account for items on order (which the less formal system does not). The items controlled by this system also should not be of such a fast-moving fashion nature that you should know the status of your stock more often than the periodic count schedule will permit. Of course let's admit that the alert merchant will "spot-check" between count dates to catch any "out of stocks" which can occur between the times you count.

A less formal system. You will find that some kinds of merchandise can be controlled with a less formal system. Characteristics to consider are:

1. Immediate delivery of goods is possible.
2. Thus no need to account for "on order amounts."

You still must, however:

1. Have a planned model stock.
2. A specific time for visually inspecting the stock.

You will probably set a minimum stock level (e.g., shelf level or number of cases in stockroom) that your stock must not go below. When your stock reaches that level, you place an order.

In the canned goods department in a supermarket, you might use this system quite effectively.

Summary

The dollar and unit control systems are essential in making sure your merchandise budget is working. You have important techniques to use in your merchandising efforts.

This material provides a natural springboard for the next chapter. Our accounting systems complete our measurement of our profit planning success.

EXPENSE CONTROL

The final objective of this chapter is to introduce you to expense control.

You must set up an expense budget just as a merchandise budget. As in merchandise plans, you must look at your expense plans on a routine basis. The review of expense budgets is to see how actual commitments compare to plan. If you find differences, action can be taken. An expense report is similar to an open-to-buy report in merchandising. The expense report is actually an "open-to-spend" report. You can see an example of how you might set up an expense control form in Figure 18–8.

SUMMARY

Planning preceded control and the relationship is essential, direct, and two way. You need control records to plan and you need these same records to see how well your plan is working.

This chapter explains dollar and unit control of inventory. You now know how to set up perpetual inventory control systems for both dollars of inventory and actual units. Dollar control can be maintained at retail or cost. Open-to-buy is one of the real valuable advantages of setting up a dollar control system at retail. Certain types of merchandise adapt neatly to cost dollar control. Understanding this is important and can save you money and time.

You also can now appreciate the fact that if book systems are too costly, and if the situation is acceptable, you can control your units by something less than a perpetual book system. The nonperpetual systems may be a good compromise under certain conditions which must be understood.

Finally, the importance of expense control was reviewed.

We are now ready to move to the next chapter which assists you in measuring your results.

FIGURE 18–8
Illustration of open-to-spend report based on expense budget for_____ season for_____ classification*

Expenses†		January	February . . . Total
	Plan	1,000	
	Committed	400	
	Open-to-spend	600	
	Actual at end of month	‡	

* As of January _____
† Other expenses handled similarly.
‡ Actually put in at end of month.

DISCUSSION QUESTIONS

1. Explain the relationship between *planning* and *control*.

2. Diagram the process which takes place from planning to control.

3. What is dollar control? What is its value to management?

4. What must you know to control your investment in dollars in your inventory?

5. What is the relationship between dollar control and book inventory?

6. How does dollar control relate to open to buy

(OTB)? Exactly what does OTB tell you? How is it determined?

7. What is the major problem faced in "cost" dollar control (versus retail)? When is a retailer likely to use cost dollar control?

8. Compare the mechanics of maintaining a dollar versus a unit control system.

9. How are shortages determined in a retail store?

10. Compare the formal and the less formal systems of unit control, nonperpetually maintained. Can you determine shortages in a nonperpetual unit control system? Explain.

PROBLEMS

1. Assume that planned sales for August are $8,000, that planned reduction is $500, that planned BOM stock is $24,000, and that planned EOM stock is $18,000. Calculate the planned purchase figure for the month in question.

2. Given the following data for a certain department as of March 12, calculate the planned purchases and OTB for March 12.

Planned sales for the month $11,000
BOM inventory 23,000
Planned reductions for the month 900
Merchandise received to date 7,000
On order, March delivery 2,000
Planned EOM stock 25,000

3. With the following figures, find open-to-buy for January:

Stock on hand—January 1 .... $365,000
Planned stock on hand—February 1 342,000
On order for delivery in January 73,500
Planned sales for January 109,000

4. Find open-to-buy for August, given the following figures:

Stock on hand, July 31 .... $10,000
Merchandise purchased for delivery in August .. 8,000
Planned sales for August 5,000
Planned stock on hand, August 31 15,000

5. In a certain department the following figures have been planned for the month of October: sales, $70,000; markdowns and other retail reductions, $6,000; BOM retail stock, $280,000; EOM retail stock, $300,000; planned initial markup, 35 percent of retail. Calculate planned purchases at retail and at cost.

6. The following data represent conditions in a certain department as of February 12.

Planned sales for the month $14,000
BOM inventory 25,000
Planned reductions for the month 1,000
Merchandise received to date 7,500
On order, February delivery 2,500
Planned EOM stock 27,000

Compute the OTB as of February 12.

PROJECTS

1. If you have a friend who is a retailer, make an appointment with that person and ask to see: (a) the types of controls which are used in the store; (b) what they are used for. Report your findings to the class.

2. Visit a local grocery store. See if they have "scanning" equipment at the checkout. If they do, ask to see the manager and tell that person that you are a student and want to ask him a few questions. Design

your questions so that you can find out if information which is gotten from the new equipment is being used for control. If not, what is it being used for?

3. If you can, find a person who sells *to* retailers. Ask that person what he or she knows about retailer's "open-to-buy." Report your findings to your class.

4. Make an appointment with a merchandising executive at a department store or rather large specialty store in your community. Ask to be allowed to see the forms used to prepare the dollar control, open-to-buy, perpetual inventory, and unit control figures. If possible ask the executive to let you have a "real" report for a season past and trace through all the procedures discussed in this chapter. The forms may differ a bit, but the information obtained will be quite similar. It is difficult to arrange such a project; if you know someone to make the contact, it is advisable. The retailer will share if you make it clear it is for learning purposes. Remember, a person always likes to talk about his or her business!

Minicase 18–1

Mr. and Mrs. Catton own a small grocery store in a middle-income neighborhood in the central city of a southwestern city of 100,000. Mr. Catton started the business many years ago and has run it as his "baby" ever since. Mrs. Catton, his ostensible "right hand," has in reality been the checker, bagger, and general greeter. She has not been involved in the "back office" procedures of the store, including buying merchandise.

Some months ago Mr. Catton had a slight, but frightening, heart attack. Mrs. Catton insisted that he "take it a bit easier," and since she too was not feeling completely fit, she begged her husband to hire a young man to come in and help with the business. The business had been very profitable for the Cattons, and he did not like the idea of bringing someone else in, but he finally agreed with his wife (and his doctor) that this was essential.

Jim Smith, a local young man and a recent graduate of the state university, was hired. Jim had a degree from the College of Business and specialized in Marketing/Retailing. He was looking for a small retail opportunity rather than a large, multiunit organization, and the Catton job appealed to him. His family was well respected in the neighborhood of the Catton store; he had good connections with the present customers; and his new bride was a neighborhood girl who wanted to "come back home." It all looked perfect, especially when Mr. Catton said that he was willing to work out a purchase plan for Jim since there were no Catton children to come into the business.

Jim's first challenge came during the first week. Mr. Catton could not come in at all, and the salesman for the wholesaler who was the major supplier came in for the wholesaler's regular order. Mrs. Catton knew nothing about how the order was placed and told Jim, "Let's see what you learned at that fine school of yours." She also implied that the salesman from the wholesale establishment was new and said that she had heard her husband complain that he was a "little high pressure for me." Jim gathered from that statement that the salesman overstocked the Cattons upon occasion. Mr. Catton kept no records except purchase invoices which were merely filed by date and supplier. He also had a daily sales record. His accountant kept the tax information. So Jim was "high and dry" as far as merchandise records were concerned.

Jim probably has no option now but to work with the salesman on the basis of past history in filling the orders. However, since the salesman comes by every two weeks, some type of plan is necessary. Suggest an outline of a control system that might work for Jim, at least in the short run, and that he could manage himself without hiring additional help.

Minicase 18-2   Joe Williams has recently been hired as assistant buyer for menswear in Oak Department Store. Oak's is actually a limited-line junior department store which is located in a new community mall in a medium-sized southern city. The downtown store was recently closed, and plans for a new branch in another planned mall are on the drawing boards.

Williams had worked for the past three years as assistant store manager of Becks, a small, family-owned men's store in the deteriorating downtown area. He had also had previous, similar experience at another men's store in the downtown area. However, virtually all of the stores in the CBD have either branched to shopping centers or closed their downtown sites and moved to a center, making the mall store, in effect, the "main" store.

Joe's move to Oak Department Store as assistant buyer was actually a somewhat "lower status" job at essentially the same salary. Also, he had been in management in his past jobs, and this job was the first which could be considered merchandising specifically. Of course, he was knowledgeable about men's fashions, prices, display, and so on, but he had never had real buying authority or market contact.

Ransom Reese, the buyer of Oak's men's department, is an "old-timer" and has run the store's profitable men's area for over 30 years. Reese, as he admitted himself, "ran the whole show out of his hip pocket," and one could not argue with success. But with future plans for expansion and the fact that Reese wasn't getting any younger, management insisted that an assistant be hired in the large department, which included furnishings, clothing, and sportswear. Ran had never been interested in classification merchandising; he did not have any real controls, either dollar or unit. The controller of Oak's was making noises about putting in some system, but rumor had it that he feared the reactions of oldsters like Reese.

For the three months that Joe has been with Oak's he has followed Ran around, observed his working methods, and learned a lot about the customer market served. Most of the customers want special attention from Reese even though there are three good young salespersons in the department on a full-time basis and a part-time salesperson in furnishings who comes in during the evening hours. Reese told Joe that it was time for the old-timers to admit that fashions were moving rapidly and that his hip pocket was getting stuffed with too much information. Consequently, Joe's first assignment was to pre-pare the department for classifications or dissections and to make a report within a month as to what would be needed to set up a unit control system for each classification established. Reese didn't know much about dollar con-trol—he had no open-to-buy even though some departments were experi-menting with the system. Ran asked Joe to make a recommendation about that too, since Joe was working on all the merchandise.

Joe was somewhat shocked and frightened. He had been good at per-sonnel relations in his prior jobs and he kept a neat, clean store! But this—he was beside himself and really didn't know where to start.

Advise Joe carefully, and make his job easy. Prepare the report and re-commend what should be done about dollar control.

19

DEVELOPING AN ACCOUNTING SYSTEM

The purpose of this chapter is to explain:

- The meaning of accounting systems in retailing.
- The importance of such systems to you as a retailer.
- The simplest form of financial statements.
- How to develop an appreciation for the importance of and the difficulty in determining the value of the ending inventory.
- Alternatives for inventory evaluation, especially the "retail method."
- The meaning of the following terms:

Accounting system	Gross margin
Balance sheet	Cost or market whichever is lower
Income statement	Retail method of accounting
Current and fixed assets	Lifo
Current and fixed liabilities	Fifo
Net worth	

If you have had a basic course in accounting, this chapter will be a snap. If not, don't let it frighten you. We will give you the ideas necessary to accomplish the purposes of the chapter.

WHAT IS AN ACCOUNTING SYSTEM?

An *accounting system* provides people (or computers) with ways to: (1) record, classify, and accumulate data such as sales and (2) present and interpret such information so that operations (past, present, and future) can be evaluated.

An accounting system assists you in determining how well you've done as a manager. The system shows you how much profit you've made—your measure of success.

You may remember that several times in the previous chapter we mentioned that "the information came from accounting data." In other words, you must get the data from your accounting system for use in planning and control.

All of your key information comes from accounting systems. The amount and types of data vary by firm size. The farther you as a manager are from day-to-day contacts with customers and operations, the more important the accounting system becomes.

KEY FINANCIAL STATEMENTS

The two statements which you will work with here are : (1) the *balance sheet* and (2) the *income statement*. Think of the balance sheet as a snapshot—a picture of the condition of your business at one point in time. The income statement, on the other hand, is more like a moving picture. It shows how well you have done (profitwise) during a particular period of time.

"I'm here to take on a computer."
Reprinted by permission The Wall Street Journal

The balance sheet

What balances? Look at Figure 19–1.

As you can see from this figure, *Total assets = Total liabilities + Net worth.* The total assets include everything a business *owns.* Everything a business *owes* is called total liabilities. Net worth, in the simplest form, is the owner's capital (or investment).

Assets. Assets are either *current* or *fixed.* The basic difference between these two types of assets is "time." *Current assets* are expected to be converted into cash during a year's operations. As you see in Figure 19–1, cash, accounts receivable, and inventory are examples.

Fixed assets are *not* to be converted into cash in an operating period. In fact they are not owned to be sold. They are used in operating the business. The furniture, fixtures, equipment, building, and land are typical examples.

Liabilities. Liabilities may be broken down into debts that will come due within a year *(current)* and those that will mature within a longer period *(fixed).* You can see typical examples in Figure 19–1.

Net worth. When you look at the balance sheet, you see that *net worth* is really the difference between total assets and total liabilities. As an owner, it is your capital. It represents your initial investment in the business. It also reflects any *additions* of income earned or *deductions* of losses suffered.

The balance sheet is important: (1) it tells you what your financial position is at any time; (2) if you compare balance sheets for previous operating periods, you can see how your financial position has changed; (3) you can tell from the balance sheet how your assets are distributed; and (4) the balance sheet, in summary, tells you if your firm is overcommitted or undercommitted in assets or is too far in debt.

The income statement

Let's look at a sample income statement so that we can see what goes into finding out "how you've done" in an operating period.

The *income statement* tells you how successful you have been in carrying out your retail management functions. The time period covered can be a

FIGURE 19–1
Example of a simple balance sheet

Current Assets :			Current Liabilities :		
Cash	$ 5,000		Accounts payable	$ 25,000	
Accounts receivable	25,000		Salaries payable	25,000	
Merchandise inventory	125,000		Accrued taxes	5,000	
Fixed Assets :			Fixed Liabilities :		
Furniture, fixtures, and equipment	50,000		Notes payable	100,000	
Property (building and land)	100,000				
			Net Worth	150,000	
Total Assets	$305,000		Total Liabilities and Net Worth	$305,000	

month, a season, or a year. You can see that the statement tells you (1) how much net profit was made ($2,500); (2) how much was spent on total expenses ($12,500); and (3) how much gross margin was made ($15,000). Clearly, the *gross margin* is the difference between net sales and cost of goods sold. Cost of goods sold is computed as follows (Figure 19–2):

 1.   What did I start with? (beginning inventory)
+2.   What did I add to this beginning inventory (purchases)?
=3.   What did I have available for sale?
−4.   What did I have left at the end of the period (ending inventory)?
=5.   The cost value of the merchandise which moved out of stock (cost of goods sold).

Notice that the key elements of the statement are also in percentages. (e.g., Gross margin percent = Gross margin dollars ÷ Net sales dollars or $35,000 ÷ $50,000 = 70%). Percentages help you compare your performance with (1) prior years or with (2) similar stores.

Information in the income statement assists you in making adjustments where you feel they are necessary. If your expenses are higher than in the past and higher than similar stores, then you may want to take some action. The income statement is a valuable tool in your job of measuring the results of your operations.

Summary

The balance sheet and the income statement provide you the basis for evaluating the financial condition of your store. You can tell: (1) Can I pay my bills on time? (2) Am I making a profit? (3) Do I have a healthy balance between debt and ownership funds?

FIGURE 19–2
Income statement

			Percent of net sales
Gross sales	$55,000		
− Sales returns and allowances	5,000		
= Net sales		$50,000	100%
Cost of goods sold			
Beginning inventory	$25,000		
+ Purchases	50,000		
= Total merchandise available for sale	$75,000		
− Ending inventory	40,000		
= Cost of goods sold		35,000	70
= Gross margin		$15,000	30%
− Operating expenses			
Payroll	7,500		
Rent	2,500		
Miscellaneous	2,500		
Total expenses		12,500	25
Net profit		$ 2,500	5%

ENDING INVENTORY

If you look at Figures 19–1 and 19–2 you can begin to see why the remainder of this chapter is concerned with ending inventory.

Why is ending inventory important?

Ending inventory is usually the most important asset item. In Figure 19–1 you see an example of this.

Ending inventory appears not only on the balance sheet, but it is also an item on the income statement (Figure 19–2).

Finally, ending inventory valuation has great impact on the gross margin (and thus net profit) of the firm. To illustrate, let's use the income statement in Figure 19–3 and just look at cost of goods sold and gross margin. Assume the $50,000 sales in each case.

FIGURE 19–3

If Ending Inventory is $40,000 then:	If Ending Inventory is $30,000 then:	If Ending Inventory is $50,000 then:
Cost of goods sold = $35,000	Cost of goods sold = $45,000	Cost of goods sold = $25,000
and	and	and
Gross Margin = $15,000	Gross Margin = $5,000	Gross Margin = $25,000

Why is placing a valuation on inventory difficult?

"*Taking* a physical inventory" means simply that each item in your stock is counted. You know that even though you may have a book inventory (Chapter 11), you must take a physical inventory. That is the only way you know *exactly* what you have on hand.

Of course taking a physical inventory is time consuming and tedious for sales personnel and management. Not only are items counted, but you must place a "price" (or "value") on each one. The total dollar value of the ending inventory can be determined only when this is done.

Listing the price (either cost or retail) is mechanical. The salesperson who is listing merely indicates the value. But for management the valuation process is more difficult. Why?

Let's compare inventory valuation with two other asset items. When management places a value on *accounts receivable,* the process is routine. Based on how long an account has been owed by a customer, experience tells you the worth of the account. For example, if an account has been "on the books" 90 days or less, it will be valued at 100 percent of the amount owed. The longer the time the account has been owed to the store, the less the chance of collection. Thus the percentage valuation is smaller. The process we're describing is "aging" the accounts. After they are aged, a valuation can be placed on them with confidence.

Shift now to fixed assets. Furniture is valued at a cost price less "depreciation." *Depreciation* is an amount deducted each year from the value of a fixed asset. This method of valuation of fixed assets is simple. It is legal.

Inventory presents different problems. What is the inventory worth? Unlike accounts receivable, you can't "age" inventory and get a value. Market value (what customers will pay for the merchandise) is not necessarily related to age.

Market value not determined by depreciation.   You are not going to sell fixed assets, so market value has no real meaning. Your inventory *is* for sale so what it's worth in the market is critical.

What are the methods of inventory valuation?

We have shown why ending inventory is important in retailing. We have also explained why valuation is difficult in a retail organization. The next logical question is, "So how do we place a value on this important asset?" Answering this question is the final objective of this chapter.

You know that inventories may be valued at either cost or retail. The cost method of valuing inventories is most widely used in retailing because the great majority of retailers believe it is an easier method. This is the opinion of the small retailer—and the vast majority of retail organizations are small. The more complex nature of the retail method and the additional records which are needed convince small operators that the cost method is satisfactory.

Most large store managements value inventory in retail terms. (This is especially true of large department and specialty stores.)

Original cost.   Some stores find the original cost method very satisfactory. Where turnover is fast and retail prices change often (e.g., grocery items) it can be the simplest method to use.

One of the problems you will face in using the original cost method is how to determine the original cost.

One way is to "cost code" on the price ticket. In taking inventory, when the item is listed, you also list the quantity and "decode" the cost and enter the total. An example of a cost code is:

1	2	3	4	5	6	7	8	9	0
y	o	u	n	g	b	l	a	d	e

If the cost is $14,25, the code would read *y n o g*. No letter may repeat itself.

Cost-or-market-whichever-is-lower method.   Accountants consider this method conservative. If you use this method in valuing your inventory, you must record your merchandise at both original cost and market value. Then you must use the lower figure when you "take" the inventory. The reason accountants tell us to value at the lower of cost or market is based on the fact that profits are not made until merchandise is sold. Under this method profits are stated at a minimum. There are tax advantages in this method.

You must work out some way to determine the market value of merchandise. It is a difficult process, but if market prices have gone down, they must be known. Vendor catalogs is one source of current value.

Retail method.   If merchandise is listed at retail, it is unnecessary to search for original cost or current market values. The method is only possible

FIGURE 19-4
Statement of retail method of inventory costing method

Calculations	Step	Items
	1	Beginning inventory
		Gross purchases
		Less: Returns to vendor
		Transfers in
		Less: Transfers out
		Transportation charges
		Additional markups
		Less: Cancellations of additional markup
		Total merchandise handled
($270,000 ÷ $435,000)	2	Cost percent/Cumulative markon
	3	Sales, gross
		Less: Customer returns
		Gross markdowns
		Less: Cancellations
		Employee discounts
		Total retail deductions
($435,000 – $312,000)	4	Closing book inventory at retail
		Closing physical inventory at retail
($123,000 – $120,750)		Shortages
($120,750 × 0.62069)		Closing physical inventory at cost
($270,000 – $74,949)	5	Gross cost of goods sold
($300,000 – $195,051)	6	Maintained markup
		Less: Alteration costs
		Plus: Cash discounts
($104,949 + $3,000)		Gross margin
		Less: Operating expenses
		Net profit

Cost	Retail	Cost	Retail	Percent
		$ 60,000	$105,000	
$216,000	$345,000			
(9,000)	(14,000)	207,000	330,900	
3,000	4,800			
(4,500)	(7,200)	(1,500)	(2,400)	
		4,500		
	2,100			
	(600)		1,500	
		270,000	435,000	
				62.069/37.931
	309,000			
	(9,000)		300,000	
	12,000			
	(1,500)		10,500	
			1,500	
			312,000	
			123,000	
			120,750	
			2,250	0.75
		74,949		
		195,051		
		104,949		34.9
		(3,000)		
		6,000		
		107,949		35.9
		75,000		25.0
		32,949		10.9

when the merchandise grouping being considered is homogeneous. This is the reason, as noted earlier, why large stores have chosen this method. They subdivide large quantities of merchandise into "like" groupings. The reason for "homogeneous" (turnover and margin) requirements will be clarified when the steps of the book inventory for the retail method are presented. The system makes it possible to determine "cost" by a "programmed" step-by-step process.

Fifo and Lifo valuation methods. If you are either a *cost* or a *retail* valuation method, you may also use either Fifo (first in, first out) or Lifo (last in, first out) in determining the inventory figure for your financial statements.

The methods we have already discussed (original cost or retail) use Fifo. You normally would assume that goods would flow into and out of a store in that manner. It is logical.

During our high inflation (especially in the late 1970s) firms began considering Lifo. Lifo does not have anything to do with physical flow of merchandise. Fifo does. Lifo offers tax advantages in times of inflation. The reason is complex and such an analysis is not appropriate here.

Book inventory with retail method. You will remember when we discussed book (perpetual) inventories in Chapter 18, in the "Control" section, we stressed that book inventories at retail were more common than at cost. You will also remember that we noted that *the retail method of inventory accounting* is an extension of the perpetual book inventory figure.

If you use the retail method of inventory valuation, you will prepare an income statement (a book inventory extension) periodically. The usual period is a month. With this retail method (based on a book inventory computation) you can determine your estimated profitability monthly. You do not have to wait for a physical inventory. (Of course, you can only determine your shortages, or overages, with a physical inventory.)

The following illustrates the steps of the retail method of inventory accounting (an income statement for retailers using the retail method of valuation). In addition, Figure 19–4 illustrates a simplified income statement using the retail method. Please refer to Figure 18–3 for an explanation of the various items in the book inventory for dollar control. We said that this illustration was important because the retail income statement uses the same items. It is wise for you to refer to that figure if you need the review. The following steps are not discussed in detail—the income statement (Figure 19–4) shows the process and is adequate for our purposes here.

Steps of the retail method of inventory accounting

1. Determine the total dollars of merchandise handled at cost and retail.
2. Calculate the cost multiplier.
3. Compute the retail deductions from stock.

4. Calculate the closing book inventory at cost and retail.
5. Determine the gross cost of goods sold.
6. Determine maintained markup, gross margin, and net profit.

SUMMARY

This chapter has introduced you to accounting systems which assist you in determining how well you've done as a manager—how much profit you've made. Profit is your measure of success.

You can now read simple balance sheets and income statements and know what they mean to management. These key statements tell you if you can pay your bills on time; if you're making a profit; and if you have a good balance between your ownership funds and your debt.

The importance of and problems in placing a valuation on ending inventory were clarified. The key concern of this chapter was in fact valuation of inventory. You saw that cost and retail methods of valuation methods are available to you as a retailer. The technical nature of accounting forced a rather surface treatment of the subject. But you have at your fingertips a good guide to the issues facing retailers as they attempt to develop a system to assist in measuring results of operations.

We urge you to keep the appendix to this chapter handy. As we have indicated previously, the various Small Marketers Aids have great value. You will find the *Checklist for Profit Watching* a good way to check out the elements we have discussed in this part of the text. Use it well!

DISCUSSION QUESTIONS

1. Discuss the meaning and purposes of accounting systems.
2. Point out the major differences between the balance sheet and the income statement.
3. What balances in the balance sheet? Be specific.
4. Explain the various components of the balance sheet.
5. Draw up a simple income statement without the figures to illustrate "what goes into it."
6. Explain why the "ending inventory" is important in retailing information systems. Why is placing a valuation on this inventory difficult?
7. Discuss the problems and possible solutions to utilizing the original costs method to value inventory.
8. What do accountants mean by "conservative" valuation of inventory? Explain.
9. What are the steps in the "retail method of inventory accounting?

PROBLEMS

Use the retail method of accounting. Prepare well-organized statements and determine for each of the following sets of figures:

a. Cumulative mark-on percentage.
b. Ending inventory at retail and cost.
c. Maintained markup in dollars and percent.
d. Gross margin of profit in dollars and percent.
e. Net profit in dollars and percent.

	Item	Cost	Retail
1.	Gross sales		$ 25,800
	Inventory, June 1	$11,000	16,000
	Customer returns and allowances		350
	Gross markdowns		2,000
	Gross additional markups		620
	Transportation charges inward	550	
	Merchandise returned to vendors	800	1,300
	Discounts to employees		350
	Gross purchases	16,400	26,310
	Markdown cancellations		300
	Operating expenses	7,200	
	Cash discounts earned on purchases	410	
	Additional markups canceled		150
	Alteration and workroom net costs	325	
	Estimated shortages, 0.5% of net sales		
2.	Beginning inventory	20,000	35,000
	Gross purchases	72,000	115,000
	Purchase returns and allowances	3,000	4,700
	Transfers in	1,000	1,600
	Transfers out	1,500	2,400
	Freight in	1,500	
	Additional markups		700
	Additional markup cancellations (revision of retail downward)		200
	Gross sales		110,000
	Customer returns and allowances		10,000
	Gross markdowns		4,500
	Markdown cancellations		1,000
	Employee discounts		500
	Ending physical inventory		40,250
	Cash discounts on purchases		2,000
	Workroom costs	1,000	
	Operating costs (expenses)	30,000	
3.	Additional markup cancellation		150
	Estimated shortages		0.75% of net sales
	Gross markdowns		2,150
	Workroom expenses	510	
	Sales returns and allowances		385
	Transportation charges	580	
	Beginning inventory	14,300	20,100
	Vendor returns	830	1,650
	Markdown cancellations		300
	Gross purchases	17,200	27,520
	Gross additional markups		650
	Gross sales		27,200
	Employee discounts		500
	Cash discounts		505
	Operating expenses	7,700	

PROJECT

1. Interview several small retailers and perhaps one large. (e.g., several dress shops, men's stores, and a department store). Ask if you might speak with the person in charge of the accounting records. Find out if any of them is using the "retail method of ac-counting." If not, find out how they operate the cost method. How do they determine shortages? Try to "strike up" a conversation about the subject of the chapter; report back your findings.

Minicase 19-1   Janet Roling was annoyed with her accountant. She had just returned from a good seminar put on by the State Retail Association on the subject of accounting for nonaccounting executives of small retail stores. She had found it very interesting but really she was somewhat confused about why they had insisted that the retail method was best for her junior boutique. She had five departments and enjoyed good business and a nice profit. But she wondered if she really was showing the proper profit using the cost method. She called Frank Miller, the young man who had conducted the seminar and who had asked the participants to call him at any time. She called him in frustration. "Frank, could I arrange a meeting with my accountant and you for next week? He simply does not want to be bothered with the retail method and says I'm doing fine and just relax. Frank, I'm really 'up' since the seminar and I want to be progressive. He tells me as long as I watch expenses I'm OK. I know that's not right." Assume you are Frank. Prepare a statement to convince Janet's accountant that there is more to accounting for retailing than "cutting expenses."

| **APPENDIX** | A Checklist for Profit Watching* |

ARE YOU MAKING A PROFIT?

Analysis of revenues and expenses

Since profit is revenues less expenses, to determine what your profit is you must first identify all revenues and expenses for the period under study.

1. Have you chosen an appropriate period for profit deter-   Yes   No
mination?   ☐   ☐

For accounting purposes firms generally use a 12-month period, such as January 1 to December 31 or July 1 to June 30. The accounting year you select doesn't have to be a calendar year (January to December); a seasonal business, for example, might

---

* Narendra C. Bhandari, *A Checklist for Profit Watching,* Small Business Administration, Small Marketers Aids No. 165 (Washington, D.C.: U.S. Government Printing Office, May 1978).

close its year after the end of the season. The selection depends upon the nature of your business, your personal preference, or possibly tax considerations.

2. Have you determined your total revenues for the ac-   **Yes   No**
counting period?   ☐   ☐

In order to answer this question, consider the following questions:

What is the amount of gross revenue from sales of your goods or service? **(Gross sales)**

What is the amount of goods returned by your customers and credited? **(Returns and rejects)**

What is the amount of discounts given to your customers and employees? **(Discounts)**

What is the amount of net sales from goods and services? **(Net sales = Gross sales − [Returns and rejects + Discounts])**

What is the amount of income from other sources, such as interest on bank deposits, dividends from other sources, such as interest on bank deposits, dividends from securities, rent on property leased to others? **(Nonoperating income)**

What is the amount of total revenue? **(Total revenue = Net sales + Nonoperating income)**

                                                                                     Yes   No
3. Do you know what your total expenses are?   ☐   ☐

Expenses are the cost of goods sold and services used in the process of selling goods or services. Some common expenses for all businesses are?

Cost of goods sold (Cost of goods sold = Beginning inventory + Purchases − Ending inventory)

Wages and salaries (Don't forget to include your own—at the actual rate you'd have to pay someone else to do your job.)

Rent

Utilities (electricity, gas, telephone, water, etc.)

Supplies (office, cleaning, and the like)

Delivery expenses

Insurance

Advertising and promotional costs

Maintenance and upkeep

Depreciation (Here you need to make sure your depreciation policies are realistic and that all depreciable items are included.)

Taxes and licenses

Interest

Bad debts

Professional assistance (accountant, attorney, etc.)

There are, of course, many other types of expenses, but the point is that *every* expense must be recorded and deducted from your revenues before you know what your profit is. Understanding your expenses is the first step toward *controlling them* and *increasing* your *profit*.

Financial ratios

A *financial ratio* is an expression of the relationship between two items selected from the income statement or the balance sheet. Ratio analysis helps you evaluate the weak and strong points in your financial and managerial performance.

         Yes No

4. Do you know your current ratio?   ☐   ☐

The *current ratio* (current assets divided by current debts) is a measure of the cash or near cash position (liquidity) of the firm. It tells you if you have enough cash to pay your firm's current creditors. The higher the ratio, the more liquid the firm's position is and, hence, the higher the credibility of the firm. Cash, receivables, marketable securities, and inventory are current assets. Naturally, you need to be realistic in valuing receivables and inventory for a true picture of your liquidity, since some debts may be uncollectable and some stock obsolete. Current liabilities are those which must be paid in one year.

         Yes No

5. Do you know your quick ratio?   ☐   ☐

Quick assets are current assets minus inventory. The *quick ratio* (or acid-test ratio) is found by dividing quick assets by current liabilities. The purpose, again, is to test the firm's ability to meet its current obligations. This test doesn't include inventory to make it a stiffer test of the company's liquidity. It tells you if the business could meet its current obligations with quickly convertible assets should sales revenues suddenly cease.

         Yes No

6. Do you know your total debt to net worth ratio?   ☐   ☐

This ratio (the result of total debt divided by net worth then multiplied by 100) is a measure of how the company can meet its total obligations from equity. The lower the ratio, the higher the proportion of equity relative to debt and the better the firm's credit rating will be.

         Yes No

7. Do you know your average collection period?   ☐   ☐

You find this ratio by dividing accounts receivable by daily sales. (Daily sales = Annual sales divided by 360). This ratio tells you the length of time it takes the firm to get its cash after making a sale on credit. The shorter this period the quicker the cash inflow is. A longer than normal[1] period may mean overdue and uncollectible bills. If you extend credit for a specific period (say, 30 days), this ratio should be very close to the same number of days. If it's much longer than the established period, you may need to alter your credit policies. It's wise to develop an aging schedule to guage the trend of collections and identify slow payers. Slow collections (without adequate financing charges) hurt your profit, since you could be doing something much more useful with your money such as taking advantage of discounts on your own payables.

---

[1] See Question 15 for where to go to get information on "normal" or "average" ratios.

8. Do you know your ratio of net sales to total assets?

Yes No

☐ ☐

This ratio (net sales divided by total assets) measures the efficiency with which you are using your assets. A higher than normal ratio indicates that the firm is able to generate sales from its assets faster (and better) than the average concern.

9. Do you know your operating profit to net sales ratio?

Yes No

☐ ☐

This ratio (the result of dividing operating profit by net sales and multiplying by 100) is most often used to determine the profit position relative to sales. A higher than normal ratio indicates that your sales are good, that your expenses are low, or both. Interest income and interest expense should not be included in calculating this ratio.

10. Do you know your net profit to total assets ratio?

Yes No

☐ ☐

This ratio (found by multiplying by 100 the result of dividing net profit by total assets) is often called return on investment or ROI. It focuses on the profitability of the overall operation of the firm. Thus, it allows management to measure the effects of its policies on the firm's profitability. The ROI is the single most important measure of the firm's financial position. You might say it's the bottom line for the bottom line.

11. Do you know your net profit to net worth ratio?

Yes No

☐ ☐

This ratio is found by dividing net profit by net worth and multiplying the result by 100. It provides information on the productivity of the resources the owners have committed to the firm's operations.

All ratios measuring profitability can be computed either before or after taxes, depending on the purpose of the computations. Ratios have limitations. Since the information used to derive ratios is itself based on accounting rules and personal judgments as well as facts, the ratios cannot be considered absolute indicators of a firm's financial position. Ratios are only one means of assessing the performance of the firm and must be considered in perspective with many other measures. They should be used as a point of departure for further analysis and not as an end in themselves.

SUFFICIENCY OF PROFIT

The following questions are designed to help you measure the adequacy of the profit your firm is making. Making a profit is only the first step: making enough profit to survive and *grow* is really what business is all about.

12. Have you compared your profit with your profit goals?

Yes No

☐ ☐

13. Is it possible your goals are too high or too low?

Yes No

☐ ☐

14. Have you compared your present profits (absolute and ratios) with the profits made in the last one to three years?

Yes No

☐ ☐

**15.   Have you compared your profits (absolute and ratios)   Yes   No
with profits made by similar firms in your line?**   ☐   ☐

A number of organizations publish financial ratios for various businesses, among them Dun & Bradstreet, Robert Morris Associates, the Accounting Corporation of America, the National Cash Register Company, and the Bank of America. Your own trade association may also publish such studies. Remember, these published ratios are only averages. You probably want to be better than average.

TREND OF PROFIT

**16.   Have you analyzed the direction your profits have been   Yes   No
taking?**   ☐   ☐

The preceding analyses, with all their merits, report on a firm only at a single time in the past. It is not possible to use these isolated moments to indicate the trend of your firm's performance. To do a trend analysis, performance indicators (absolute amounts or ratios) should be computed for several time periods (yearly for several years, for example) and the results laid out in columns side by side for easy comparison. You can then evaluate your performance, see the direction it's taking, and make initial forecasts of where it will go.

MIX OF PROFIT

**17.   Does your firm sell more than one major product line   Yes   No
or provice several distinct services?**   ☐   ☐

If it does, a separate profit and ratio analysis of each should be made:

a.   To show the relative contribution by each product line or service.
b.   To show the relative burden of expenses by each product or service.
c.   To show which items are most profitable, which are less so, and which are losing money.
d.   To show which are slow and fast moving.

The profit and ratio analysis of each major item help you find out the strong and weak areas of your operations. They can help you to make profit-increasing decisions to drop a product line or service or to place particular emphasis behind one or another.

RECORDS

Good records are essential. Without them a firm doesn't know where it's been, where it is, or where it's heading. Keeping records that are accurate, up-to-date, and easy to use is one of the most important functions of the owner-manager, his or her staff, and his or her outside counselors (lawyer, accountant, banker).

Basic records

**18.   Do you have a general journal and/or special journals,   Yes   No
such as one for cash receipts and disbursements?**   ☐   ☐

A general journal is the basic record of the firm. Every monetary event in the life of the firm is entered in the general journal or in one of the special journals.

	Yes	No
19. Do you prepare a sales report or analysis?	☐	☐
a. **Do you have sales goals by product, department, and accounting period (month, quarter, year)?**	☐	☐
b. **Are your goals reasonable?**	☐	☐
c. **Are you meeting your goals?**	☐	☐

If you aren't meeting your goals, try to list the likely reasons on a sheet of paper. Such a study might include areas such as general business climate, competition, pricing, advertising, sales promotion, credit policies, and the like. Once you've identified the apparent causes you can take steps to increase sales (and profits).

Buying and inventory system

	Yes	No
20. Do you have a buying and inventory system?	☐	☐

The buying and inventory systems are two critical areas of a firm's operation that can affect profitability.

	Yes	No
21. Do you keep records on the quality, service, price, and promptness of delivery of your sources of supply?	☐	☐

	Yes	No
22. Have you analyzed the advantages and disadvantages of:		
a. **Buying from several suppliers,**	☐	☐
b. **Buying from a minimum number of suppliers?**	☐	☐

	Yes	No
23. Have you analyzed the advantages and disadvantages of buying through cooperatives or other such systems?	☐	☐

	Yes	No
24. Do you know:		
a. **How long it usually takes to receive each order?**	☐	☐
b. **How much inventory cushion (usually called safety stock) to have so you can maintain normal sales while you wait for the order to arrive?**	☐	☐

	Yes	No
25. Have you ever suffered because you were out of stock?	☐	☐

	Yes	No
26. Do you know the optimum order quantity for each item you need?	☐	☐

	Yes	No
27. Do you (or can you) take advantage of quantity discounts for large size single purchases?	☐	☐

	Yes	No
28. Do you know your costs of ordering inventory and carrying inventory?	☐	☐

The more frequently you buy (smaller quantities per order), the higher your average ordering costs (clerical costs, postage, telephone costs, etc.) will be, and the lower the average carrying costs (storage, loss through pilferage, obsolescence, etc.) will be. On the other hand, the larger the quantity per order, the lower the average ordering cost and the higher the carrying costs. A balance should be struck so that the minimum cost overall for ordering and carrying inventory can be achieved.

Yes   No

29.   Do you keep records of inventory for each item?   ☐   ☐

These records should be kept current by making entries whenever items are added to or removed from inventory. Simple records on 3×5 or 5×7 cards can be used with each item being listed on a separate card. Proper records will show for each item: quantity in stock, quantity on order, date of order, slow or fast seller, and valuations (which are important for taxes and your own analyses).

Other financial records

Yes   No

30.   Do you have an accounts payable ledger?   ☐   ☐

This ledger will show what, whom, and why you owe. Such records should help you make your payments on schedule. Any expense not paid on time could adversely affect your credit, but even more importantly such records should help you take advantage of discounts which can help boost your profits.

Yes   No

31.   Do you have an accounts receivable ledger?   ☐   ☐

This ledger will show who owes money to your firm. It shows how much is owed, how long it has been outstanding and why the money is owed. Overdue accounts could indicate that your credit granting policy needs to be reviewed and that you may not be getting the cash into the firm quickly enough to pay your own bills at the optimum time.

Yes   No

32.   Do you have a cash receipts journal?   ☐   ☐

This journal records the cash received by source, day, and amount.

Yes   No

33.   Do you have a cash payments journal?   ☐   ☐

This journal will be similar to the cash receipts journal but will show cash paid out instead of cash received. The two cash journals can be combined, if convenient.

**34.   Do you prepare an income (profit and loss or P&L)   Yes   No
statement and a balance sheet?**   ☐   ☐

These are statements about the condition of your firm at a specific time and show the income, expenses, assets, and liabilities of the firm. They are absolutely essential.

Yes   No

35.   Do you prepare a budget?   ☐   ☐

You could think of a budget as a "record in advance," projecting "future" inflows and outflows for your business. A budget is usually prepared for a single year, generally to correspond with the accounting year. It is then, however, broken down into quarterly and monthly projections.

There are different kinds of budgets: cash, . . . sales, etc. A cash budget, for example, will show the estimate of sales and expenses for a particular period of time. The cash budget forces the firm to think ahead by estimating its income and expenses. Once reasonable projections are made for every important product line or department, the owner-manager has set targets for employees to meet for sales and expenses. You must plan to assure a profit. And you must prepare a budget to plan.

PART V

Now—is retailing for you. . . ?

It's not a "cop-out" but no one can answer that question but you. We have attempted to take you through all the basics you need to help you answer that important career question.

The final answer is, of course, up to you. What we've left for this last part will put on the finishing touches and lead you into a frame of mind to face up to some important lifetime decisions. Whether you're thinking of going into the field, or are perhaps already working in it, we believe two more things must be addressed. What are they?

What about a Career in Retailing?

What about the Future?

At the conclusion of the next two chapters you just may be able to face the question raised in this final part of "The Student's Guide to Retailing" (see Figure I-1).

As the song from *Oklahoma* goes, ". . . we've gone about as far as we can go!" The rest is up to you.

20

WHAT ABOUT A CAREER IN RETAILING?

The purposes of this chapter are to:

- Show you what a career in retailing is like.
- Highlight the contents of retail training programs.
- Help you decide if retailing is the right career for you.
- Show you how to prepare for a career in retailing.
- Offer some do's and don'ts for the job interview.

Career planning is more than training for a job. Sure, you need job skills. But you also need to develop *all* of your skills. Thus, we want to help you grow as a person. Also, this chapter gives a way for thinking about a career in retailing.

Retailing offers you more job choices than almost any other career. You can choose a store ranging from the most swinging ''with it'' firm to a very conservative one. Think about the contrasts between Kmart and Saks, for example. If you are turned on by money, the chance for fast advancement, or a good environment, retailing may be for you.

More than 15 million people work in retailing. Retail firms are located all the way from the smallest rural town to the largest urban area. You can fulfill almost every kind of ambition or desire in retailing. Further, the chances for jobs in retailing are good during the 1980s. Let's look at some of the elements of this exciting career path.

WHAT ARE THE FEATURES OF A CAREER IN RETAILING?

What about security?   To many persons, job security is important. Retailing offers good job security. Even during bad times, retailing has less layoffs than other types of jobs. Why? People still buy goods even during hard times. Items sold at decent prices will always be in demand. Thus, a steady job is likely at all times.

Where are the jobs?   Jobs in retailing are everywhere. All persons must buy goods to survive. Thus, jobs in retailing exist even if you do not want to move far from home. Surely you can find a good job in the 2 million or more retail stores in the United States. If you want to move on a regular basis, jobs are available, and you may move from New York to California.

What are the types of retail firms?   The U.S. government lists more than 80 types of retail firms. These firms range from drugstores to cheese shops. You can also work in nonstore retailing. Each of these jobs needs different skills and abilities. The largest number of jobs are in eating and drinking places, followed by stores like Sears. Other large employers are food stores and car dealers.

What are the chances to move up?   Many management jobs exist because of the large number of retail firms. Retailing is still expanding. Thus, jobs in management will keep opening up.

What are the chances for women?   Retailing offers good careers for women. Almost half of all retail employees are women. The use of women in retailing is greater than for any other part of the economy.

Good chances to move up also exist.[1] Many stores prefer women as buyers for some items. Women are also holding more management jobs today. However, jobs above the position of buyer are still too few for women.

What about the pay?   Beginning pay is lower than for many other types of jobs. However, within five to ten years your pay will be at least as high as what you could earn in other types of firms. Your beginning pay likely will increase over three times by the end of ten years.

What are other rewards?   Your skills will be quickly visible. The job of store manager, for example, is a tough one and is for persons who can organize and direct others. In retailing you come in contact with customers every day and must take care of special requests and complaints.

You can set your own sales and profit goals, control expenses, pay employees, and perform other needed functions. In effect, you can manage your own business but use someone else's money. Retailing also offers you the chance to seek creative ways of increasing sales and profits.

What job skills are needed?   Many people think only of selling or working as a cashier when retailing is mentioned. Yet, these jobs are only a few of the ones available. Don't think only of the persons you see when you buy something. Rather, think about the "behind the scenes" jobs. Figure 20-1 shows some of the many jobs in a large retail firm.

What are the working conditions?   Job conditions are about the same as in other types of industry. The work week is 40 hours, but you may need to put in some overtime. Work in the evenings and on weekends is common.

You have the same fringe benefits as in other types of jobs. The benefits

FIGURE 20-1

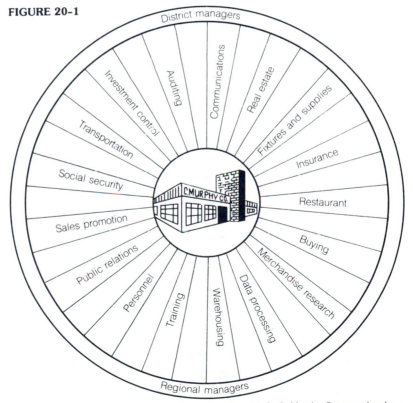

Source: G. C. Murphy Company brochure.

Creative display—Room setting—Calls for creative people

Courtesy Macy's

include vacations, sick leave, and insurance programs. You also get discounts on goods you buy. Also many have good retirement plants. Sears has a good program as does JCPenney.

Types of jobs available

Five areas are common to most retail firms. Let's look at each of these job types.

Merchandising. Merchandising involves buying and selling goods. As such, merchandising is one of the most important jobs. Trainees often start out in this area because it is the heart of the store. Buyers work with suppliers in buying goods. They also work in advertising and display and may travel worldwide for the latest fashions. The next job up from buyer is merchandise manager. This job includes overseeing several buyers.

Operations. Operations means sales support. The jobs include store management, warehousing, receiving, delivery, security, and customer service.

Sales promotion. Sales promotion is closely related to merchandising. Sales promotion involves advertising, display, and public relations. You need creativity in these jobs. For example, writing and artwork skills are needed. Jobs include copywriter, decorator, and art director.

Control. Persons working in control manage the company's assets. You need skills in statistics, accounting, or data processing for these jobs. Credit, accounts payables and receivables, auditing, and data processing are some of the jobs.

Totally open store calls for good store planners

Courtesy Aronov Realty, Montgomery, Alabama

Personnel. Jobs in personnel involve recruiting, selecting, and training of employees. You also work with employee benefits programs and may handle union problems.

WHAT ABOUT TRAINING PROGRAMS IN RETAILING?

No two training programs are exactly alike. However, let's look briefly at the program of Rich's.

The history of Rich's is closely tied to the history of Atlanta and the Southeast. A dozen or more Rich's stores are located in the Southeast. Rich's also operates the Rich Way chain of discount stores, Rich's Bake Shops, and Rich's II boutiques. Rich's has over 200 different selling departments and almost 400 nonselling positions, ranging from advertising to data processing. Sales are over $300 million a year. The firm employs over 12,000 men and women.

As noted in Figure 20-2, the management climb with Rich's often begins with the head of sales position. From this position, you can follow the sales manager route to the position of store manager. You may also go the merchandising route and go from assistant buyer, to buyer, and then to divisional merchandise manager. As noted you will likely move between the two areas.

Overview. Training programs in most stores involve rotating among the departments until you are familiar with all store operations. In smaller stores, your upward movement depends on the openings which are available. Your movement may be slow and limited.

In a multi-store organization, the longest you are likely to remain in one

FIGURE 20-2

MERCHANDISING STORE MANAGEMENT

Rich's executives are characterized by their talent, ability, drive, and zest for the fast-paced competitive atmosphere of retailing. The attributes are more important at Rich's than specific degree requirements because the scope of opportunity here covers so many fields of interest.

It is important to understand that, while retail operations are basically categorized either as merchandising or sales management, Rich's executives are not limited to emphasis in one category or the other. On the contrary, Rich's believes executive potential is maximized by liberal experience in both areas, the pace and sequence of progress being frequently evaluated on an individual basis.

Rich's places management candidates in responsible positions at competitive salaries immediately and complements this invaluable experience with advanced classroom seminars.

The sequence of positions illustrated may be generally described as follows:

Head of sales

Retailing at its primary level including supervising department salespeople, implementing buyers merchandising directives, and maintaining the department's inviting attractive appearance.

Sales manager

Works with department buyer and store management to effect the best flow of merchandise, supervises heads of sales.

Assistant store manager

Works closely with the store manager in all phases of store operations.

Store manager

Charged with full responsibility for the smooth and profitable operation of a Rich's store, from the actual location of each department, its appearance and staff, to storewide events, and customer relations.

Assistant buyer

The understudy, practicing the challenging mercurial craft of acquiring merchandise customers will want, and seeing that it sells. Under a buyer's guidance, assistants learn the processes of planning, selection and purchase, sales promotion and branch distribution, and develop the insight and sense of timing that make a good buyer.

Buyer

The pivotal position in retailing, dominated by astute, perceptive, quick-thinking individuals. At this level the retail process achieves critical focus as each buyer assumes full control over a department.

Divisional merchandise manager

All buyers within a division report to a divisional merchandise manager who supervises overall divisional planning and operation, including financial and budgetary considerations.

Source: Company brochure.

store is two to three years. Movement after the training program may involve a transfer to a smaller branch store.

Your movement also depends on how the firm is organized. More management jobs are in the corporate offices of a centralized firm. In a decentralized firm, more openings may exist in the branch stores.

Chain store training. Chain training programs are like those of most department stores. However, the chains may have more jobs available because of the larger number of outlets in the chain.

Creative merchandise presentation calls for smart visual merchandisers

Courtesy Aronov Realty, Montgomery, Alabama

"Having rejected the older generation's money values, you should
love the salary on *this* job."

Reprinted by permission The Wall Street Journal

HOW DO YOU KNOW IF RETAILING IS FOR YOU?

Even after reading the material thus far in the chapter, you still may not be sure retailing is for you. But don't pass up a good career opportunity without looking further. Study the career planning workbook which follows (Figure 20–3). The workbook was prepared by the Macy Co. to help students decide whether to go into retailing. The workbook requires a lot of thought, but it may help you decide if retailing is for you. The workbook is not a test—it is a tool to help you make your own decision about a career.

HOW CAN YOU PREPARE FOR A CAREER IN RETAILING

Assuming you are still interested in retailing at this point, how do you prepare yourself for the career? Answers to the question can best come from retailers themselves.

Let's listen to Joseph L. Hudson, Jr., chairman of the board of the J. L. Hudson Co. in Detroit, Michigan:

When we recruit management trainees (entry-level position in Hudson management) the three criteria we consider are *education, experience,* and *personal qualities* that have consistently proved to be present in individuals who have experienced success in our business. We look for individuals who can handle pressure and can meet deadlines, individuals who have a sense of urgency and can assign priorities to their work. We select people who are highly motivated, have goals and a strong desire to succeed; people who are not afraid, who enjoy making decisions. We have to make decisions all day long. Each day is different. . . .

College curricula that emphasize mathematics, accounting, business and management skills have generally proved to be the ones that best prepare people for our business, regardless of whether the program is called retailing, fashion merchandising or general business.

Our experience shows that the single biggest performance deficiency of retail management can be traced to poor mathematical aptitude or insufficient mathematics education. Modern retailing is heavily oriented to "managing the numbers." College programs should address this critical aspect of the job. Basic mathematics, accounting, and retailing applications should be the backbone of programs to prepare students for a career in retailing.

Written and oral communication skills are also critical to the success of retailing executives. The demands for people who can clearly, precisely and persuasively present their ideas is great. And these skills become increasingly more important the higher the individual goes in the organization. Students should be provided with opportunities to identify their deficiencies in this area and develop their skills throughout their academic programs.

The broader subject of marketing, not simply retailing, should be studied as one of the important foundations of our capitalistic system. In this same vein, the new professionalism of the marketing executive and his arsenal of tools should be explored. Management information systems in retailing are growing more sophisticated every day. Such advents as the electronic point-of-sale terminals and on-line merchandise and financial data mean timely accessible information upon which better business decisions can be based. The uses and benefits of such systems and how to use the data effectively should be part of the curriculum. Exposure to both merchandising and store management should also be addressed in college programs.[2]

FIGURE 20-3

Your career planning workbook.*

Source: R. H. Macy Co. Inc., publisher Brecker and Merryman.

FIGURE 20–3 (continued)

1. Enjoy yourself.

1. Your fantasies.

Pretend you have one year to do anything you'd like. You have no financial or family constraints. What would you do with this year?

_____

_____

_____

_____

_____

_____

_____

Why have you selected what you did? (For example, you'd like to travel to Europe because you enjoy meeting people and learning first-hand about different ways of life; or perhaps you would like to train for the Olympics because you enjoy vigorous activity and want the personal achievement and recognition a gold medal would bring.)

Activity	Reasons
_____	_____
_____	_____
_____	_____
_____	_____
_____	_____
_____	_____

FIGURE 20–3 *(continued)*

2. *Your peak experiences.*

What five activities or events in your life do you remember with particular satisfaction?

1. _____
2. _____
3. _____
4. _____
5. _____

As with your fantasies, try to characterize what it was that made the five activities or events you listed above so enjoyable.

Activity	Reasons
1. _____	_____
	_____
2. _____	_____
	_____
3. _____	_____
	_____
4. _____	_____
	_____
5. _____	_____
	_____

FIGURE 20–3 *(continued)*

3. Can work be fun?

Look back at your reasons for selecting the activities and events you listed in exercises 1 and 2. What five reasons appear most often?

1. _____

2. _____

3. _____

4. _____

5. _____

How can these reasons be related to your career? What types of work activities do they indicate you would enjoy? (For example, your enjoyment in meeting new people may indicate that you would enjoy a job with public contact.)

Reason	Work implications
1. _____	_____
	_____
2. _____	_____
	_____
3. _____	_____
	_____
4. _____	_____
	_____
5. _____	_____
	_____

FIGURE 20–3 *(continued)*

2. Avoid it!

1. What turns you off?

What do you particularly dislike doing? What activities or situations do you consciously try to avoid? Please list three in each of the categories listed on the right.

A. Extracurricular (hobbies, travel, social, etc.)

1. _____   3. _____

2. _____

B. Work-related (paid or unpaid)

1. _____   3. _____

2. _____

C. Academic

1. _____   3. _____

2. _____

Why do you try to avoid each of these activities or situations? (For example, pressure, boredom, physical exertion, too much competition, etc.)

Activity/situation	*Reasons*
A1. _____	_____
2. _____	_____
3. _____	_____
B1. _____	_____
2. _____	_____
3. _____	_____
C1. _____	_____
2. _____	_____
3. _____	_____

FIGURE 20–3 *(continued)*

2. *What's the problem?*

What five reasons for dis-
liking certain activities or
situations were listed
most often in Exercise 1?

1. _____
2. _____
3. _____
4. _____
5. _____

Do these reasons indicate
that you should avoid certain situations on the job?
What other activities can
you think of which would
provide this situation?
(For example, if you par-
ticularly dislike 'bore-
dom,' what specific ac-
tivities do you consider to
be boring?)

Reason	Work implications (activities to avoid)
1. _____	_____
	_____
2. _____	_____
	_____
3. _____	_____
	_____
4. _____	_____
	_____
5. _____	_____
	_____

FIGURE 20-3 *(continued)*

3. Use what you've got.

1. Your accomplishments.

What have you done of which you were most proud? Think of two accomplishments in each of the categories listed on the right.

A. Extracurricular (hobbies, travel, social, etc.)

1. _____

2. _____

B. Work-related (paid or unpaid)

1. _____

2. _____

C. Academic

1. _____

2. _____

For each of these accomplishments, list those skills or abilities you feel you demonstrated in achieving them. (For example, writing, analyzing, working with people, creating, or the ability to work under pressure or handle a variety of things at once.)

Achievement	*Skills/abilities*
A1. _____	_____
2. _____	_____
B1. _____	_____
2. _____	_____
C1. _____	_____
2. _____	_____

FIGURE 20–3 *(continued)*

2. Learning experiences.

What other activities have you participated in that were learning experiences? (For example, a summer job as a secretary, although possibly not considered an accomplishment, would have taught you some things about the business world.)

A. Extracurricular (hobbies, travel, social, etc.)

1. _____

2. _____

B. Work-related (paid or unpaid)

1. _____

2. _____

C. Academic

1. _____

2. _____

What skills did you acquire or abilities did you demonstrate in each of the learning experiences described?

Experience	Skills/abilities
A1. _____	_____
2. _____	_____
	_____
B1. _____	_____
2. _____	_____
	_____
C1. _____	_____
2. _____	_____
	_____

FIGURE 20–3 *(continued)*

3. *Your skills inventory.*

List the five skills/abilities which appear most frequently in the two preceding exercises.

1. _____
2. _____
3. _____
4. _____
5. _____

How can these skills and/ or abilities be utilized on the job? (For example, if you excel in leading others, you probably would succeed in a supervising situation.)

Skill	Work implications
1. _____	_____
	_____
2. _____	_____
	_____
3. _____	_____
	_____
4. _____	_____
	_____
5. _____	_____
	_____

FIGURE 20–3 *(continued)*

4. Look to the future.

1. Your ideal career.

Think about what you enjoy doing and what your skills are. Describe your ideal career. Be as specific as possible.

_____
_____
_____
_____
_____
_____

Which five of the following characteristics or values best describe this ideal? What is your motivation to work? Please rank them in order.

Achievement
Being needed
Commitment to a goal
Discovering new things
Improving the world
Occupying your time
Opportunity to learn
Prestige
Protecting the status quo
Recognition
Respect
Rising up the social ladder
Salary
Security
Others (please list)

1. _____

2. _____

3. _____

4. _____

5. _____

FIGURE 20-3 (*continued*)

2. Your short term plans.

With your ideal career in mind, please describe what you hope you will be doing in five years.

_____
_____
_____
_____
_____
_____
_____

What skills and knowledge which you do not possess now will you need to acquire to attain your five-year goal?

_____
_____
_____
_____
_____
_____

How do you plan on attaining the skills and knowledge you'll need (on-the-job, company training, continuing education or on your own)?

Skill/knowledge	Attainment
_____	_____
_____	_____
_____	_____
_____	_____

FIGURE 20–3 *(continued)*

5. Your priorities.

1. Your first job.

Look back over your responses to the four previous sections– the things you enjoy, your skills, the activities you want to avoid and the skills you wish to acquire. With this in mind, what activities would you like to find on your first job?

___ Acquiring knowledge
___ Analyzing
___ Building things
___ Communicating
___ Computing
___ Coordinating
___ Creating
___ Dealing with the public
___ Developing new skills
___ Discovering
___ Evaluating situations
___ Evaluating work of others
___ Following orders
___ Implementing plans
___ Innovating
___ Making decisions

___ Making things
___ Managing
___ Organizing
___ Persuading
___ Planning
___ Predicting
___ Researching
___ Serving others
___ Solving problems
___ Training others
___ Traveling
___ Working with details
___ Working with technical data
___ Writing
___ Others (please indicate)

Of those activities you indicated, please rank the five most important.

1 _____

2. _____

3. _____

4. _____

5. _____

FIGURE 20–3 *(continued)*

2. *Your first job (continued).*

Think about your responses to the four previous sections again. This time think about the reasons you enjoy or avoid certain activities and what your values and goals are. Which of the following work situations would you like to find on your first job?

Of those situations you would like to find, please rank the five most important.

_____ Authority
_____ Autonomy of action
_____ Being told what to do
_____ Boss you respect
_____ Close supervision
_____ Competition
_____ Co-workers you respect
_____ Direct impact on the business
_____ Direct job assignment
_____ Freedom from worry
_____ High risk/high reward
_____ Independence

_____ Initiation of own action
_____ Interpersonal relations
_____ Job security
_____ Pressure
_____ Responsibility
_____ Results of job seen
_____ Reward for seniority
_____ Specialization
_____ Structured activities
_____ Training situation
_____ Variety of action
_____ Others (please list)

1. _____

2. _____

3. _____

4. _____

5. _____

FIGURE 20-3 *(continued)*

3. Your lifestyle.

The organization you choose will provide more than a job. It will directly influence your lifestyle, as well as your future. With your values and long-term goals in mind, which of the following job and non-job related factors are important to you in making your first job decision?

_____ Climate
_____ Cost of living
_____ Cultural activities
_____ Educational facilities
_____ Flexible hours
_____ Fringe benefits (vacations, insurance, tuition reimbursement, etc.)
_____ Growth-potential of company
_____ Hours worked per week
_____ Job location
_____ Living options
_____ Opportunity for advancement
_____ Prestige organization

_____ Proximity to friends
_____ Proximity to family
_____ Public schools
_____ Recreational activities
_____ Salary
_____ Size of company
_____ Spouse's desires
_____ The job itself
_____ Training programs
_____ Type of community (rural, urban, suburban)
_____ Type of industry
_____ Value of organization to society
_____ Others (please list)

Of those factors you indicated, please rank the five factors which are most important to you.

1. _____

2. _____

3. _____

4. _____

5. _____

FIGURE 20–3 *(concluded)*

6. *Putting it all together.*

The chart below is one method which might help you in making career decisions. Based on the priorities you determined to be most important to you, you can compare occupational options and job offers. Fill in the activities, situations and lifestyle factors you defined in Section 5 as being most important to you in the spaces indicated. With each occupation or job offer you are considering, find out which of these factors is offered. Indicate these with a checkmark in the appropriate column.

Which occupation or organization offers you the most of your top priorities? (By the way, this brochure should provide you with all the facts you need to complete a column for any Macy division.)

Career priorities (Section 5)	A Macy division	Organization A	Organization B	Organization C
Activities desired (Ex. 1)				
1.				
2.				
3.				
4.				
5.				
Work situation desired (Ex. 2)				
1.				
2.				
3.				
4.				
5.				
Lifestyle desired (Ex. 3)				
1.				
2.				
3.				
4.				
5.				
Totals				

Most retailers today look for on-the-job experience. They say that the best training for retailing happens on the job. As observed:

Entry-level jobs in retailing are simple and basic. And, more often than not, the individual is working below his potential and education until he learns the business. Therefore, students who participate in co-op programs or have part-time jobs in retailing while obtaining their college degrees receive early practical experience. This experience contributes to their ability to move faster into jobs with more prestige, greater challenges, and financial rewards. Those individuals whose practical experiences are weak or non-existent find themselves learning more about the retailing business on the job in a few months than they did in four years in the classroom.[3]

So above all, seek job experience, perhaps in a co-op program, an intern program, or part-time work. If you are unable to do any of these things, try to get your professor to (1) use case studies, (2) assign projects to study retail firms, (3) have on-site tours and seminars, (4) bring in guest lecturers from local stores, (5) have you read and discuss trade journal articles in class, and (6) help set up summer jobs in retailing for students. All of these things will help you see the practical side of retailing.[4]

WHAT ABOUT YOUR JOB INTERVIEW?

A little homework and time spent thinking about the interview will help you land the job you want. Too many students go into an interview without preparing for it. The result is a disaster. Here are a few items for you to think about:

1. *Know something about the company before going to the interview.* Read about them in the placement office, know the products they sell, and the location of their offices. Also, try to know a little about their annual report.
2. *Think about the way you dress.* Jeans, unruly hair, and overall sloppiness are out. Think about the retail salespersons with whom you come in contact. Show that you know what is expected of you.
3. *Think about how best to sell yourself.* Tell the interviewer why you are interested in the company and what talents and skills you have to offer. Give simple, honest answers. If you made poor grades for the first year or two, say so and explain why.
4. *Review all of your work experience and your on-campus activities.* These things show your drive and ambition.
5. *Don't ask about salary, hours of work, or retirement.* You are not in a position to bargain over salary at this point. If you are asked about salary, say you are more interested in the job than the salary. Besides, you can get salary ranges from your professor or the placement office.
6. *Have a good up-to-date résumé.* Check with the placement office for ideas. Above all make sure the résumé is neat, has no spelling errors, and point out your skills and work-related background. Focus on the jobs you have held and on your skills, talents, and interests. Figure 20–4

FIGURE 20-4

MILTON S. DELBRIDGE

Post Office Box 1234, Main City, State ZIP — (325) 555-5678

OBJECTIVE

Writing Editing — aiming for employment where a strong sense of responsibility, strong technical skills, and willingness to learn and grow are valued characteristics.

SKILLS, EXPERIENCE, AND ACCOMPLISHMENTS

Writing Editing — Staff writer for independent weekly newspaper, writer for college newspaper, editor of high school yearbook.

Reviews — Reviewer of concerts, movies, television (reviews for the newspaper, class assignments).

Public Relations — Publicity Chairman for fraternity; active in 1980 Presidential campaign.

Copywriting — Advertising copywriter for weekly newspaper, college newspaper.

Advertising Sales — Sold advertising space for weekly newspaper, college newspaper.

EDUCATION

B.A., West State University, May 1980.

    Major: Journalism and English   B average

ACTIVITIES HONORS

College: Communications Achievement Award; Men in Communications, Inc.; Alpha Omega Fraternity; Student Government Association.

High School: Valedictorial; Society of Outstanding American High School Students; Student Council Vice President; History Award (1976); French Award (1976); Beta Club; Youth Legislature.

EMPLOYMENT HISTORY

Summer, 1979: Staff writer and advertising space salesman for *The Maynard News*, Maynard, Texas.

Summer, 1978: Clerk for the U.S. Government Printing Office, Washington, D.C., under the Summer Intern Project.

Summer, 1977: Bookkeeper/Receptionist for the Robert Wayne Cattle Company, Maynard, Texas.

Summer, 1976: Traveled in Italy with Experiment in International Living (lived with an Italian family for five weeks).

REFERENCES

Will be furnished upon request.

Source: C. W. Wilkinson, Peter B. Clarke, and Dorothy C. M. Wilkinson, *Communicating through Letters and Reports* 7th ed. (Homewood, Ill.: Richard D. Irwin, 1980), p. 333. © 1980 Richard D. Irwin, Inc.

STUDY AID 20-1

RÉSUMÉ (OR DATA SHEET) CHECKLIST

1. Give your résumé an informative heading worded for the appropriate degree of "selling."
    a. Identify your name, the type of work desired, and (preferably) the company to which addressed.
    b. Be sure you apply for work, not a job title.
2. For appropriate emphasis, ease of reading, and space saving:
    a. Balance the material across the page in tabulated form.
    b. Use difference in type and placement to affect emphasis and show awareness of organization principles.
    c. Centered heads carry emphasis and help balance the page.
    d. Capitalize the main words in centered heads and underline the heads unless in solid caps.
    e. If you have to carry over an item, indent the second line.
    f. Remember to identify and number pages after the first.
3. Lead with whatever best prepares you for the particular job, but account for the chronology of your life since high school. (Gaps of more than three months may arouse suspicion.) When older and extensively experienced, such complete coverage is less necessary.
4. Education details should point up specific preparation.
    a. Show the status of your education early: degree, field, school, date.
    b. Highlight courses which distinctively qualify you for the job. Listing everything takes away emphasis from the significant and suggests inability to discriminate.
    c. In listing courses, give them titles or descriptions which show their real content or briefly give specific details of what you did.
    d. Give grade averages in an understandable form (letters, quartiles, or percentages; GPA systems vary too much).
    e. Avoid belittling expressions like "theoretical education."
5. Experience: for jobs listed,
    a. Give job title, duties, firm or organization name, full address, specific dates, *responsibilities*, and immediate superior's name.
    b. If experience is part time, identify it as such.
    c. Consider reverse chronology or other arrangement to emphasize the most relevant and important.
    d. Use noun phrases and employ action verbs that imply *responsibility*.
6. If you include a personal details section, it should present a clear, true picture. (Though law prevents employers from asking, no law prohibits you from volunteering information about race, religion, age, health, and marital status.)
    a. Tabulate, but try combining ideas to save words:

Born in East Lansing, Michigan, 1960	Married, no children
5'11", 185 lbs.	Member of (list appropriate organizations)
Good health, glasses for close work	Like fishing and reading

   b. Give your address(es)—and phone(s) if likely to be used—in minimum space where easily found but not emphasized.

7. List or offer to supply references. When you list references (to conclude your résumé or supply later on request):

   a. Give the names, titles, full addresses, and telephone numbers of references for all important jobs and fields of study listed.

   b. Unless obvious, make clear why each reference is listed.

8. Remember these points about style:

   a. A résumé is ordinarily a tabulation; avoid paragraphs and complete sentences.

   b. Noun phrases are the best choice of grammatical pattern.

   c. Items in any list should be in parallel form.

   d. Keep opinions out of résumés; just give the specific facts. Use impersonal presentation, avoiding first- and second-person pronouns.

Source: C. W. Wilkinson, Peter B. Clarke, and Dorothy C. M. Wilkinson, *Communicating through Letters and Reports* 7th ed. (Homewood, Ill.: Richard D. Irwin, 1980), p. 343. © 1980 Richard D. Irwin, Inc.

shows you the organization of a typical résumé for a person in college who is seeking employment. Study Aid 20–1 is a checklist for do's and don't in résumé preparation.

7. *Don't always try to please the interviewer.* Don't be a yes person. If you don't agree with a view as stated, say so in a pleasant way.

8. *Be pleasantly aggressive.* If you want the job, say so. Show ambition. You may get turned down for a few jobs you want but you may also get some good offers.

9. *Don't "hog" the interview.*

10. *Don't hesitate to tell an interviewer that you may not want the job* he/she has to offer if it really isn't for you. Then explain the kind of job you want. The interviewer may be able to help you find it.

11. *Remember the first five minutes of the interview are the most important.* Start with a firm handshake. Don't smoke unless the interviewer says you can do so. Above all, don't eat or drink while you are in the interview.

12. Try to help make the interviewer feel at ease.

13. Follow up with a short letter of thanks if a potential employer shows interest in you.

14. Figure out what kind of job you want before you go to the interview. Otherwise you will just waste your time and that of the person doing the interviewing.

15. Be prepared with answers for the kinds of questions you may be asked in the interview. Expect such questions as the following:[5]

What are your short-range objectives?

What are your long-range objectives?

What do you look for in a job?

What can you do for us that someone else cannot do?

Why should we hire you?

Can you work under pressure, deadlines, etc?

Do you prefer staff or line work? Why?

What business character references can you give us?

How long would it take you to make a contribution to our firm?

How long would you stay with us?

How do you feel about people from minority groups?

If you could start again, what would you do differently?

How do you rate yourself as a professional? As a future executive?

What new goals or objectives have you established recently?

What position do you expect to have in five years?

What is your feeling about women in business? . . . religion? . . . abortion?

Would you describe a few situations in which your work was criticized?

Would you object to working for a woman?

Do you generally speak to people before they speak to you?

How would you describe the essence of success?

What was the last book you read? Movie you saw? Sporting event you attended?

What interests you most about the position we have? The least?

Are you creative? Give an example?

Are you analytical? Give an example.

Are you a good manager? Give an example.

Are you a good leader? Give an example.

How would you describe your own personality?

Why do you want to work for us?

If you had your choice of jobs and companies, where would you go?

What other types of jobs are you considering? What companies?

Why do you feel you have top-management potential?

Tell us about yourself.

What kind of salary are you worth?

What are your five biggest accomplishments in your life so far?

Why didn't you do better in college?

What is your biggest strength? Weakness?

SUMMARY

Almost 2 million small businesses are in the United States. Most of these firms are small and have fewer than four employees. But such giants as Sears, Kroger, and Penneys offer super job opportunities.

Retailing offers more choices in jobs than any other career path. Too often we think only in terms of retail sales jobs. However, many other jobs are needed in such areas as real estate, accounting, data processing, and similar areas.

A retailing career offers good job security, the chance for jobs in large and small cities, and the chance to move up fast. Starting salaries are low but after a few years high salaries are likely.

Training programs are well developed in larger department stores and chain stores. Such programs may last from six months to three years and include on-the-job training.

NOTES

1. Kate Kelly, "Women in Retailing: The Search for Upward Mobility," *Stores*, August 1978, pp. 48–52.

2. Joseph L. Hudson, "What Should Be Emphasized in Retail Education?" *Journal of Retailing*, vol. 54 (fall 1978), pp. 67–68.

3. Hudson, "What Should Be Emphasized," pp. 69–70.

4. See also, Fred Lazarus III, "Can Academic Training of Retailers Be Improved?" *Journal of Retailing*, vol. 54 (Fall 1978); Stanley Marcus "Deficiencies in Retail Education," *Journal of Retailing*, vol. 54 (Fall 1978); Quinn McKay, "Different Perspectives on Retail Education," *Journal of Retailing*, vol. 54, (Fall 1978); G. Stockton Strawbridge, "Common Denominators among Successful Retailers," *Journal of Retailing*, vol. 54 (Fall 1978).

5. These points are made available through the courtesy of the Career Planning and Placement Service, The University of Alabama.

DISCUSSION QUESTIONS

1. Why do you think the job status of retailing appears to be low? What can be done to improve the situation?

2. What are the employment possibilities for women in retailing? What are the reasons why women should consider a career in retailing? Are the reasons different for men?

3. What is the typical advancement in a training program for a large department store?

4. What are the factors most likely to have an impact on retailing as a career for the next years?

5. If you are planning to own your own retail business in the next few years, what types of experience should you have first?

6. Why are starting salaries so low in retailing? Should salary be a major factor in choosing a career?

7. What are the major types of jobs in retailing? What are the skills which you need to work in each of these areas?

PROJECT

1. Write to several retail organizations and ask for any "career information" which they have. Then make up a summary chart contrasting and comparing the various "career components" which a potential trainee in retailing would want to evaluate. Try to get information on beginning salaries, promotional paths, career options, and so on.

2. Assume that you have been out of school for several years. You have been in a nonretailing position (assume anything you desire) and you want to change career patterns. You want to look at retailing as a career chance. Outline the steps you might go through to assist you. Then assume you decide on retailing as a career. What sources are available in your job search? Do an inventory of steps you will take and information you can develop. Then do a *marketing job* on yourself and prepare to offer yourself to the type of firm which you believe will offer you a good future.

3. Many companies do not recruit college graduates in the college placement office, if one exists. Thus, in your local community, find out the different choices which exist in the retail field for college graduates. Find out the entry level for college grads; kind and length of training program, if one exists; steps up the management ladder; and, if possible, beginning salaries and chances for promotion in each firm. Prepare a "career chart" for the city as a result of your findings.

21

WHAT ABOUT THE FUTURE?

This chapter is an effort to extend into the future the things which have been discussed in the earlier chapters. Specifically, the purposes of this chapter are to acquaint you with:

- The probable changes in household characteristics during the 1980s which will affect retail strategy planning.
- Changes in the operating environments which will affect the ways in which you do business.
- The meaning of the following concepts for you as a retailer:

Planning to manage change	Coping with energy shortages
Population age shift trends	Growth of remote retailing
Shifts in population growth areas	Quality of life issues
The need for increasing productivity in retailing	Changes in design layout

The environment in which you as a retailer will operate is changing at an ever faster rate. Thus far, we have tended to look at past developments which will affect your actions. But we also need to look to the future.

What is in store for retailing in the future? Managing change more than ever will be your key to success. Think for a moment about the past 20 years. The 1960s was an era of high growth in population, income, employment, and profits. Consumers thought in terms of "bigger and better." In contrast, the 1970s brought an energy crisis, inflation, high unemployment, a recession, and a loss of confidence in the future on the part of many people.

What will the 1980s bring to you as a retailer and to your consumers? Let's look at some components of change.

CHANGES IN HOUSEHOLD CHARACTERISTICS

What about population age trends? Table 21–1 shows actual and projected trends in U.S. population growth from 1960–2000. Growth is slowing but gains will be made through the year 2000. The two biggest segments of growth in the 1980s will be persons 35–44 and those 65 and over, especially persons 35–44 which is the core market for the 1980s.

But the 35–44-year-old market is not always a prime one for many retailers. For example, these people will already have most of the durables they need. They will spend heavily on services such as insurance, sending kids to college, and other expenses related to children.

The over-65 market is an easier one to serve since the people are more alike in their needs. They will also have larger incomes in the 1980s. But more of these persons will be elderly females living alone. The life expectancy of females is now 76 years compared to 68 years for men. The elderly as a market are surrounded by myths and half-truths about their background and lifestyles. But they can more accurately be portrayed as follows:

1. Are "younger older," not decrepit.
2. Amount to 10–12 percent of population in 1990.

TABLE 21–1
Population shifts in the United States, 1960–2000

	Population in millions					Percentage change			
	1960	*1970*	*1980*	*1990*	*2000*	*1960–1970*	*1970–1980*	*1980–1990*	*1990–2000*
Under 20	69	77	73	77	81	+11.1%	−5.2%	+5.7%	+4.3%
20–24	11	17	21	18	19	+54.3	+22.6	−15.4	+7.8
25–34	23	26	37	42	36	+10.4	+46.1	+13.1	−14.6
35–44	24	23	26	37	41	−4.5	+9.6	+45.5	+13.0
45–54	21	23	22	25	36	+13.3	−3.9	+9.9	+45.1
55–64	16	19	21	20	22	+19.4	+13.0	−3.4	+10.6
65 and over	17	20	24	28	29	+20.4	+19.8	+15.4	+3.9
	181	205	224	247	264	+13.4%	+ 9.4%	+10.0%	+ 7.2%

Note: Based on data from Bureau of the Census, *Current Population Reports*, Series P-25, using Series E for projection purposes.

Source: William Lazer, "The 1980s and Beyond: A Perspective, pp. 21–35. *MSU Business Topics*, Spring 1977. Reprinted by permission of the publisher, Division of Research, Graduate School of Business Administration, Michigan State University.

3. Have considerable resources—pensions.
4. Have more active and full retirement.
5. Political power will increase.
6. Are interested in maintenance of self.
7. Have more surviving children.
8. Family ties remain.
9. Live apart from children.
10. Higher proportion of women will be evident by 1990.
11. Are relatively free of work and want.
12. Are not disadvantaged, unskilled, uneducated, blue-collar.
13. Will become more visible.
14. Will live longer.[1]

The trends in all age-groups for the 1980s are shown in Table 21–2.

TABLE 21–2
Trends in age-groups in the 1980s

Age category		Age category	
0–4	Although they have been contracting since 1960, between 1980 and 1985 *they will grow almost four times as fast as* the average for the whole population.	45–54	The middle-age group is the one which enjoys the highest income and rate of savings. *It has been contracting* since 1970 and will continue to do so during the 1980s but will expand greatly in the 1990s.
5–15	They realized great growth during and since the 1950s and were one fourth of the population in 1970. *They will decline relatively* and account for less than 20 percent of the population in 1985.	55–64	The late middle-agers and younger senior citizens have high savings and buying power. They are empty nesters and *will grow at about the same rate as the general population* during the 1980s.
18–24	They are currently expanding and represent the age category of first marriage and first children for many Americans. *They will decline relatively* during the 1980s.	65 and over	The senior citizens present a growth market. Their incomes are lower than those of other adult population segments. The growth rate through 1985 is expected to *be twice that of the population rate*, and the proportion of women in this category is increasing.
25–34	The young marrieds *will continue to realize the greatest growth rate of all groups* through 1980. . . .		
35–44	The early middle-agers have high income, high home-ownership, and teenagers at home. *They will expand at a rate of four times that of the general population from 1980 to 1985.*		

Source: William Lazer, "The 1980s and Beyond: A Perspective," *MSU Business Topics*, Spring 1977, pp. 21–35. Reprinted by permission of the publisher, Division of Research, Graduate School of Business Administration, Michigan State University.

Regional shifts in population. Growth will vary widely by region between now and 1985. For example, the Southeast is forecast to experience the highest urban per capita income increase among all regions of the country and is also forecast to show the biggest spending jump. This is good news for retailers planning expansions into this part of the country. The Southwest and mountain regions are forecast to show the largest increases in population.

Trends in income

Inflation makes long-term projections of income difficult. Inflation in 1974 for the first time in recent U.S. history reached double-digit levels. Since then double-digit inflation has not been uncommon—hitting 14 percent in 1979, for example. These high levels of inflation are hard on all consumers, particularly persons on fixed income such as pensions or social security.

Still, increases in overall incomes of American families are occurring. Americans are expected to become a nation of upper middle-income families in the 1980s. This is at least partly because of the rapid increase in the number of households formed by persons 25–44 years of age. The markets for luxury goods and services will be high. These markets will be very good for families with incomes in excess of $25,000, based on 1975 dollars. Fifty four percent of all households are forecasted to be in this category by 1985. A reverse pyramid in income is forecasted to occur by 1985 as compared to a more nearly equal distribution of income in 1975 (see Table 21–3).

Decline in single-family housing. Single-family housing will probably decline because of rising costs. More older, and smaller houses will be

TABLE 21-3
Changing distribution of family income, 1975 dollars

Family income category	Percentage of all families in income categories	
	1975	1985
$35,000 and over	16	28
$25,000 to $35,000	16	26
$20,000 to $25,000	17	16
$15,000 to $20,000	21	14
$10,000 to $15,000	18	10
Under $10,000	12	6

Source: Fabian Linden, "Age and Income—1985," *Conference Board Record*, 13 (June 1976).

restored by young couples. Town houses and condominiums will be more popular.

What about trends in birthrate?

Birthrates vary by region of the country. They are forecasted to be the highest in the Southeast and Southwest over the next decade or so. Currently, the birthrate is 1.8–1.9 per woman of child-bearing age. This figure is below the zero population level of 2.1 (the number of births needed to replace a husband and wife). We are not likely to reach the zero population growth level for several decades.

Most couples still want to have children. But what we are seeing are (1) smaller families, (2) children born when the parents are somewhat older than in previous generations, (3) later marriages, and (4) two-career households which are hesitant to have children. In spite of all this, we are likely to see an average of about 4 million babies born per year through 1992. This is about the same number of babies born during the 1960s. The total population is considerably larger today, however, and this accounts for smaller families overall.

What about household size and makeup?

Expect the continuing growth of small, single-person households. These households will consist of young singles, empty nesters, senior citizens, and other individuals living alone. This group has made up more than 40 percent of all household growth since 1970. Such households have grown almost four times as fast as husband-wife households. Many of these persons are young professionals with rapidly increasing incomes. Their per household incomes are well above the average per capita income. But their merchandising needs will be different. Product sizes should be smaller. They are heavy users of services including such things as rental of furniture. They are also primary markets for luxury items. The trends in many of these household sizes are contained in Table 21–4.

Expect more working wives

Slightly more than half of all wives are expected to be working outside the home in the 1980s. The percentage of women in the labor force has grown very rapidly. Working women are found in large numbers at all household income levels. The women's rights movement and resulting legislation have helped the trend of women into the labor force. Many of these women work by choice in order to get out of the home, to have money for luxuries, and for self-fulfillment. Many of these persons now hold a full-time job plus tending to their family and household responsibilities. Overall, 70–80-hour workweeks are not uncommon for working women.

What does this mean for you as a retailer? As observed in Chapter 2, these persons increasingly value convenience, are more likely to purchase known national brands, have higher expectations as consumers, and pay more attention to their personal appearance. Also, their work schedules make them

TABLE 21–4
Distribution of households in the 1980s

Household category	Projected trends	Household category	Projected trends
Husband-wife households	They will continue to decline relative to singles' households. Most of their growth to 1980 will be in the under 35 age-group. From 1980 to 1990, it will be in the 35–44 age-group.	Primary female individuals	These households headed by single women, divorcees, and widows were made up largely of women over 35 in 1970. While the over 35 group comprised over 80 percent of such households, the under 35 group has doubled in numbers over the last five years and will continue to grow at a rapid rate through 1985. However, women over 35 living alone will still represent 12 percent of all households in 1980, more than four times as many as those under 35.
Female family heads	These households, headed by women where no husband is present, have realized a high rate of growth. They will continue to do so through 1985. Most of the growth is in the under 35 age-group, which is expanding at a rapid 7 percent growth rate.		
Male family heads	Families headed by men with no wife present comprise only about 2 percent of all households. They will continue to be a relatively small proportion.	Primary male individuals	Households with single and divorced men living alone have doubled since 1970. Much of the growth has occurred in the under 35 group. Whereas, in 1970, these households were mostly headed by men over 35, by 1980 the balance will start to move in the direction of men under 35.

Source: William Lazer, "The 1980s and Beyond: A Perspective," *MSU Business Topics*, Spring 1977, pp. 21–35. Reprinted by permission of the publisher, Division of Research, Graduate School of Business Administration, Michigan State University.

more interested in stores which offer late evening and Sunday shopping. They are interested in convenience foods and any products which will save them time.

LIKELY FUTURE ENVIRONMENTS

What are some of the specific changes in methods of operation likely to be?

Need to increase productivity

To offset rising costs you will need to invest a lot of money in equipment to reduce the costs of labor. A major way to battle inflation also is to increase productivity.

Productivity gains can come from (1) better use of employee time, (2) cooperative efforts of firms to buy in large volume, and (3) new technology.

Improvements in the use of labor will occur from better scheduling of employee hours and better training. Better use of existing space will likely occur to offset rising rents and construction costs. Fewer display windows and streamlined stockrooms are likely. Better inventory management will result in fewer markdowns, fewer returns, and faster turnover of goods.

We will also see more use of supermarket ideas (central checkout, self-

"I have thirty dollars to shop with so don't bother finding a place to park."

Reprinted by permission The Wall Street Journal

selection, and low gross margins) in types of retailing where they have not been used before. We already see toy supermarkets, home decorating centers, and self-service shoe stores. In this way retailers keep expenses low and prices competitive. More and more restaurants also have self-service salad bars and dessert bars. Many cafeterias are doing away with waiters so customers won't need to pay a 15 percent tip.

Coping with energy problems

A shortage of energy may not be as much a problem as the high cost of energy. High costs will bring about many changes. Management will seek the most efficient fuel. Roof insulation will be upgraded; the use of glass will be reduced, and exterior heat design will focus on reduced heat loss and solar gain. Also, we will see more studies of solar heat, recycling the heat of light and wastes, ideal lighting levels and sources, use of natural light through skylights, and measures to cope with brownouts and power shortages.

Burdened with government regulation

Government will continue to seek remedies for social ills. The consumer and the environmental movements of the 1970s brought about a variety of new tough agencies such as the Environmental Protection Agency (EPA), the Occupational Health and Safety Administration (OSHA), and the Consumer Product Safety Commission which sets standards for more than 10,000 different consumer goods. Other agencies such as the Equal Employment Opportunity Commission (EEOC) will continue to affect hiring practices. All of this adds to the cost of retailing without helping to increase productivity.

Watch for shortages of goods

The costs of many consumer products have skyrocketed with the rise in oil prices. Some products such as gasoline may be rationed. Delivery dates to retailers for many products are likely to be more uncertain in the future. Consumers will be more inclined to repair and continue to use old products. Deliveries of goods bought in foreign markets will be especially hard to predict.

Expect smaller stores

Stores of the 1980s will be smaller than in the 1960s and 1970s. Productivity is higher in smaller stores. Space for new large freestanding stores is also getting harder to find as is space for malls. Expansion will increasingly be into smaller secondary markets which can't support the huge stores built in large markets during 1950–75. The 1980s will also continue to be the era of specialty shops appealing to narrow market segments. Few stores will try to be all things to all people. You probably should think in terms of different sized stores depending on your market and existing competition. Also, consider the reuse of secondhand space to hold down costs.

Watch for growth in in-home shopping

Remote retailing will grow rapidly in the 1980s. Customers will be able to make some routine retail purchases without leaving their homes. Why?

1. Introduction of increasingly smaller, more powerful and less expensive computers, making their use as commonplace as today's pocket electronic calculators.
2. Expansion of cable television systems capable of two-way communication into a nationwide visual information transmission network.
3. Absorption of local store POS functions by an electronic funds transfer system that eventually will be nationwide.[2]

Cable TV offers good growth potential for such purposes since many channels are not now used for entertainment or information. By 1985, 5–7 million persons will be pay-cable subscribers while 20–26 million will use the basic cable service.[3] As noted, "retailers may purchase time to display and demonstrate selected products. Some retailers may choose to lease Cable TV channels for their exclusive use. With one-way service, subscribers can place their orders by telephone. As two-way service increases, subscribers can use their home terminals to transmit orders in digital form upstream for recording in the central data terminal."[4]

One such system is QUBE which started in Columbus, Ohio, and is now moving to other cities. QUBE is a two-way communication system. The system allows a consumer to push a button when they see a product they like. They can (1) request more information such as a brochure, (2) ask for a sales representative to call them, or (3) purchase items and charge them to their monthly cable TV bill.

Expect changes in store design and layout

What are some of the changes which we are likely to see? The move is away from a rigid plan in store layout to an open landscape which allows movement and change.

Standard four-foot, six-inch high fixtures will increasingly be replaced with those that are at least seven-feet high—the cube effect.

Weak departments will more readily be dropped. Such services as beauty salons, watch repair, travel agencies, and others may be dropped in the department store of the 1980s. Selling space will also be maximized by getting rid of as many nonselling functions and services as possible.

Permanent partitions are likely to go, as are partitions which reach to the ceiling. Changes in floor elevations will more often be used to separate merchandise. High-intensity discharge lighting, such as mercury vapor lighting, will be installed in most major specialty and department stores by the end of the 1980s.

Expect more store positioning

More and more retailers will be trying to appeal directly to various consumer lifestyles or demographic profiles. Their merchandise, personnel, store layout, design, and store policies seek to appeal to a specific lifestyle and thus set the store off from competition.

Retailers will be trying to use a combination of product offering and store image to create a unique "position" in the consumer's mind, especially in a market that is not well served. This approach, if successful, can bring strong customer loyalty and will help you avoid price competition.

What about quality of life issues?

Quality of life issues are likely to continue to face you in the 1980s. A few states such as Oregon have already passed bottle and can deposit legislation. These requirements can cost you a sizable amount of money in employee time and in inventory space. The recycling of other products such as motor oil is likely to be more common. Perhaps new types of businesses will emerge as a result.

Also, look for more legislation which is designed to improve quality of life. Guaranteed employment in industries with strong unions is likely to occur. Increasingly, wage demands by your employees will be tied to the rate of inflation. The rights of minorities, including handicapped, will continue to be a key issue. Rising energy costs and high inflation will push more groups of people, particularly white-collar employees, to unionize. Also, the consumerist movement will likely remain strong because of environmental problems.

Revitalizing downtown?

More and more cities will be trying to rebuild their downtown areas. Rising gasoline prices will help this trend. Many people work in the downtown areas and are a ready market for some retailers.

The cost of reworking old buildings is less than building new ones. Also, many urban planners are completely rebuilding parts of downtown to include high-rise apartments or condominiums, office space, shopping and entertainment outlets. Bringing all of these activities together in one convenient location appeals to higher income shoppers. A good example of rebuilding old downtown areas is Faneuil Hall marketplace in Boston. An example of new downtown construction in Renaissance Center in Detroit. Still, overall, the record of success in restoring downtown areas and attracting retail shoppers is modest at best.

Expect more international activity in retailing

Many retailers have long purchased products from foreign markets to sell in the United States. The primary reason is that the products are cheaper in these markets.[5] Also, as more and more U.S. markets become fully built with stores, smart thinking retailers are looking overseas. Firms such as McDonalds, Radio Shack, Sears, and others have retail outlets in many foreign nations. They plan to have more such outlets.

More foreign retail firms are also coming to the United States. They see the United States as a far larger and richer market than most other nations of the world. These foreign firms often bring a lot of capital with them and can be stiff competition. But they don't always build new outlets here in the states. Rather, like a German firm which bought controlling interest in A&P, they may purchase a major interest in a large chain which already has good market acceptance.

Fewer products offered

Customers in the future will have fewer choices in products. Product lines are being cutback by many firms and fewer are being offered. The push will be away from high-sales volume growth by manufacturers to a new stress on profit growth.[6] Such decisions may simplify your shelf stocking and inventory policies but will make it more important for you to make the right choices in deciding which products to stock.

Expect more services retailing

Services retailing will grow as a percentage of total retail sales. More and more products need professional service. Also, with higher incomes, consumers can afford such services. Firms offering furniture rental and auto repair specialists, for example, will grow very fast.

Research will be more important

Data on demographics, psychographics (measurement of attitudes), and lifestyles will increasingly be fed into retailers' computers so they can make decisions based on actual customer-spending patterns and estimate their inventory needs with less risk. Increasingly, as you seek to increase market share by taking business away from your competition you will need to know more about buying characteristics of the consumer groups you want to serve. Research will be the only viable basis for sales analysis, sales forecasting, traffic pattern studies, and advertising impact measurement.

What about the consumer?

Consumers will be more careful users of information in making choices involving products and services. They will know more about what they need to know in making wise product choices. Smart retailers will be able to take advantage of this by adjusting their offering to specific groups of consumers.

The right information presented in the right way more than ever will go a long way toward helping you to beat competition. You will need to focus on serving the *information* needs of the consumer whose *products* needs you want to satisfy.[7]

Expect more technology shifts

Technology changes will occur at an ever-increasing rate. Electronic funds transfer systems will be installed in many retail outlets during the 1980s. These systems will allow consumers to instantly transfer funds from their checking accounts to the accounts of the merchant. Universal vendor marking (UVM) in nonfood retailing will also make great progress. Once UVM reaches the 70 percent level in nonfood retailing, major increases in productivity will appear.

Scanning will also continue to make major inroads into such areas of retailing as drugs where in the past they have not been factors of importance. Conversion to the metric system also will accelerate. Major consumer education efforts will be necessary to help consumers overcome their fear of the new units of measurement.

WHAT ARE THE ENVIRONMENTAL UNCERTAINTIES?

What are some of the specific uncertainties which you will have to face in the 1980s? *First,* among these is economic uncertainty, as noted earlier. Estimates of the future inflation rate vary widely. This uncertainty means you will need to develop multiple strategies depending upon which economic forecast you believe. Flexibility will be the key to avoid being trapped with the wrong strategy.

Second, price awareness by consumers will continue to be a major issue. Shoppers increasingly will be price-oriented because of pressures on consumer incomes. Such retail innovations as warehouse retailing will continue to have a marketplace advantage with consumers for this reason. Still, consumers are not likely to be well informed about price levels at various retail outlets.[8]

Third, the level of investment in retailing will have to increase sharply. Land and building costs are up sharply, as are fixture and equipment costs. Actually, many retailers will face increasing financial problems because of the need to invest large sums of money in fixed assets. Some person suggests that the demand for additional capital will exceed new capital availability for $500–$700 billion during 1975–85. All firms can thus expect to pay more for capital and may be crowded out of many capital markets.[9]

DISCUSSION

Beyond question, you will be faced with more government regulation, higher energy costs, occasional materials shortages, and changes in consumer-spending patterns. We cannot say exactly what the store of the future will be like, other than to say it will be whatever the customer wants it to be.

As guidelines, stores will be smaller; more emphasis will be placed on higher productivity to maintain profit levels; multiuse shopping centers likely will emerge; and more self-service will occur to help reduce labor costs. You will have to be careful to avoid lowering the quality of your merchandise offerings as a result. The future probably also will include more telephone shopping and catalog shopping, more use of cable television for retailing purposes, various electronic advances, longer store hours, and more multipurpose shopping trips.

We have listed the retailers of the half-century below. All of the six retail industries listed were asked to cite the person who had done the most for their area of retailing since 1925. Use your imagination as to who may be awarded this honor at the end of the next 50 years. Perhaps their method of merchandising has not yet been introduced!

Man-of-the-Half-Century in the general merchandise/department store field: The late James Cash Penney. "... among his contributions are the first profit-sharing programs. He was a pioneer respondent to consumerism before it was recognized by that name; not only a believer in but an ardent practitioner of the Golden Rule."

Man-of-the-Half-Century in the food service field: Ray A. Kroc, chairman of the McDonald's Corp. "... for bringing to the restaurant industry the most advanced concepts of franchising and for the application of the most advanced marketing and operations techniques; ...."

Man-of-the-Half-Century in the supermarket field: Sidney R. Rabb, chairman of the Stop & Shop Co. "... reorganized the Super Market Institute into the kind of organization it is today. An industry leader in innovative merchandising and operations techniques; ...."

Man-of-the-Half-Century in the discount department store field: Harry B. Cunningham, honorary chairman of the S.S. Kresge Co. "... was the driving force behind the founding of Kmart, which not only revolutionized his own company but set a model for industry leadership."

Man-of-the-Half-Century in the chain drug field: the late Charles R. Walgreen, Sr. "... the pioneer who envisioned a chain drug industry when there was none, then built his chain into that industry's leading retailer."

Man-of-the-Half-Century in the home improvement center field: John A. Walker, executive vice president of Lowe's Companies, Inc. "... he introduced sophisticated marketing concepts to the lumberyard field, thereby creating a new retail apparatus, the modern home improvement center."[10]

We can only speculate about the "*People-of-the-Second-Half-Century in ...*" We suspect that among the names we will find women. Retailing provided middle-management positions for women long before it was fashionable. Top management is a reality for the female in the 1980s. Is it not reasonable to predict that by the end of the next 50 years the honor in some area will go to a woman?

Retailing more than ever needs bright people in meeting the many challenges of the 1980s which have been outlined throughout the text. You should consider sharing in the excitement of participation.

NOTES

1. William Lazer, "The 1980s and Beyond: A Perspective," *MSU Business Topics,* Spring 1977, pp. 21–35. Reprinted by permission of the publisher, Division of Research, Graduate School of Business Administration, Michigan State University.

2. Belden Menkus, "Remote Retailing: A Reality by 1985?" *Chain Store Age Executive,* September 1975, p. 42.

3. Jack M. Starling, "Cable Television: Prospects for Marketing Applications," *Akron Business and Economic Review,* Fall 1976, p. 31.

4. Retailers Test Two-Way Cable TV Ads," *Chain Store Age Executive,* May 1978, p. 13, "Two-Way Cable TV Makes Debut, Introduced by Warner Decision," *Direct Marketing,* 40 (December 1977), pp. 34–38.

5. William R. Clone, "Imports and Consumer Prices: A Survey Analysis," *Journal of Retailing,* vol. 55 (Spring 1979), pp. 3–24.

6. J. Barry Mason, Alan Resnik, and Peter Turney, "New Product Development Strategies for the 1980s," *1979 Proceedings Fall Educators Conference,* American Marketing Association.

7. Jack L. Engledow, Ronald B. Anderson, and Helmut Becker, "The Changing Information Seeker: A Study of Attitudes toward Product Test Reports—1970 and 1976," *Journal of Consumer Affairs,* vol. 13 (Summer 1979), p. 83.

8. Del. I. Hawkins and Gary McCain, "An Investigation of Returns to Different Market Strategies," *Journal of Consumer Affairs,* vol. 13 (Summer 1979).

9. Albert Bates, "The Superstores: Emerging Innovations in Food Retailing," in Robert Robicheaux, et. al., ed., *Marketing* (Boston: Houghton Mifflin Company, 1977), p. 207.

10. "The Man of the Half Century Awards," *Chain Store Age Executive,* September 1975, pp. 76–77.

DISCUSSION QUESTIONS

1. What are the major economic pressures which will impact retailing during the 1980s.

2. Why is so much emphasis being placed on increasing productivity in retailing? What are some of the ways in which productivity can be increased?

3. What are the major impacts you see on retailing with the trend toward electronic merchandising? For example, what will be the effects on labor costs, employment, and similar aspects of retail operations?

4. What are the impacts that smaller sized families, slowing levels of population growth, and more leisure time likely to have on retail merchandising?

5. Where are the greatest opportunities for expansion of retail sales likely to occur? Discuss this both in terms

of regional geography and in terms of community size and even areas within a community.

6. What will likely be the major effects of rising income levels and more uncommitted dollars in retailing in the 1980s.

7. Discuss the effects of more working wives in retail strategy decisions.

8. Why are world markets important to many retailers today?

9. Present arguments for and against the success of efforts to make retailing in the downtown areas more important in the future.

10. What are the major changes in strategy which you as a retailer can make to cope with the changes forecast for the 1980s?

PROJECTS

1. Look at the discussion in this chapter wherein we introduced the "Man-of-the-Half-Century" in six retail industries. In your local community use the listing suggested in the chapter and think of those retailers who you consider fit the person who best fits those categories. These would be local retailers who for one reason or another seems "special" to you. Give your reasons as a part of your discussion.

2. A major discussion in this chapter relates to "what are the likely future operating environments—what are some of the specific changes in methods of operations likely to be in the future?" List these changes. Then interview several retailers in your community and see if they agree or not. See if they believe other things are likely to be as important and why they feel that way. You might work with a classmate and work up a neat table showing your results and present your findings to the class. It will be a good learning experience.

3. Prepare a short questionnaire, one page or so, based on the various trends in the economic and social environments which will affect retailing in the 1980s. Interview a cross-section of retailers in your community to determine the strengths of their beliefs about the likelihood of these trends occurring or continuing in the near future. Prepare a short paper based on your findings.

4. Prepare a short questionnaire to be administered by telephone to a representative group of households in your community. Seek to find out (a) how they have adjusted to the effects of the energy shortages on their shopping behavior, (b) effects of working wives on the household, and (c) the continuing effects of inflation on the household budget.

5. Select a given type of retailing such as a specialty retail jeweler or a convenience food outlet. Assume you are preparing a report for management which will help shape their planning for the next several years. Highlight the trends which you think will most likely affect the type of retailing you selected. Additionally, make recommendations to management for ways of responding to the changes which you foresee.

Minicase 21-1   Sam Bush, a young engineer in his mid-30s, opened a firm called Nature's Own approximately 18 months ago. Sam specializes in the sale and installation of solar water heaters and heating units. He is convinced that these units will have a major market among consumers who are seeking to lower their energy costs. After 18 months, Sam's sales remain low and he is almost on the verge of bankruptcy. Few consumers have purchased the units. Likewise, few commercial or industrial firms have made purchases. Recently, Sam has had several inquiries from consumers about wood burning heaters, double-insulated panes for their windows, storm windows, and a variety of other less innovative but also less expensive ways for saving energy. But Sam is really dismayed. His heart was set on being the first in the community to sell solar heating units. What, if anything, is wrong with Sam's concept? Is his notion of a mass market for solar heating and cooling units in the near future too "blue sky"? If so, what can or should Sam do about it? Should he consider the addition of other energy conserving devices to his product line? Why or why not?

Minicase 21–2   Bill Adams has worked for the past ten years as general sales manager for three different new automobile dealerships. Bill feels he now has the experience to be a success as a new car dealer. He has lined up financial support and knows of a couple of dealerships which will be available in the near future. Now though Bill is puzzled and uncertain about whether he should purchase a dealership. He is bothered by the shortage and the high cost of energy. He is really worried about the future of transportation in the United States and whether an automobile dealership is really something he should go into now. Think about the trends for the future as we have outlined them in this chapter. Highlight the kinds of factors which you think should have a major bearing on Bill's decision. What kind of retailing mix—i.e., product, price, place, and promotion should he perhaps consider if he goes ahead with the dealership? But more fundamentally, would you view an automobile distributorship as a viable investment for the 1980s? Why or why not? Highlight the factors which you think Bill should consider before deciding whether to go ahead with the dealership.

Index

This book has been set VIP in 10 and 9 point Souvenir Light, leaded 3 points. Part title and chapter number are 36 point Souvenir Demibold; chapter title and part number are 18 and 20 point Souvenir Demibold. The size of the text page is 27 by 48× picas.